FORTUNE AND GLORY

A TRUE HOLLYWOOD COMIC BOOK STORY

BRIAN MICHAEL BENDIS

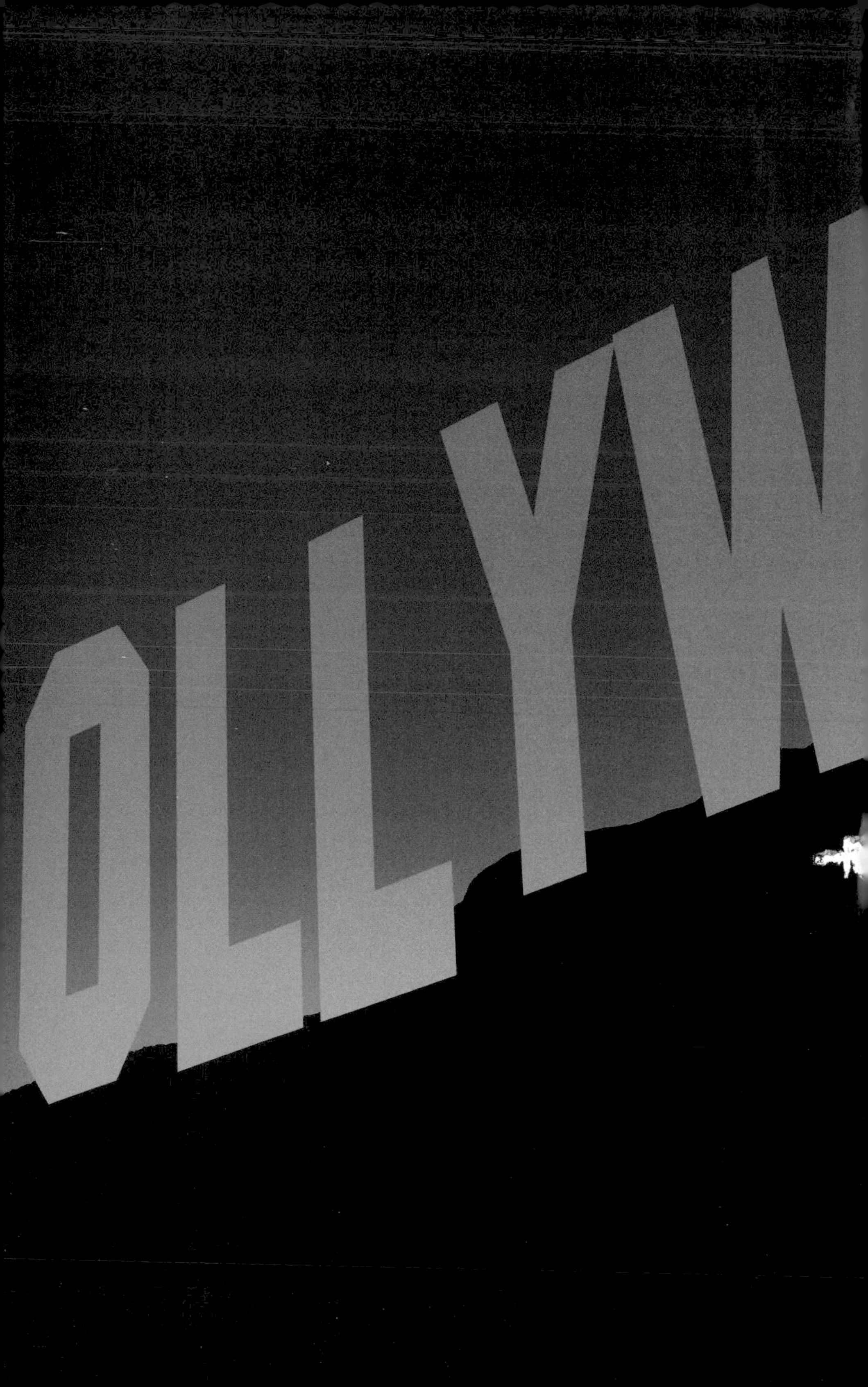
OLLYW

FORTUNE
AND
GLORY

A TRUE HOLLYWOOD COMIC BOOK STORY

Written & Drawn by
BRIAN MICHAEL BENDIS

Colorist: **MATTHEW WILSON**
Series Editors: **K.C. McCROY & JAMIE S. RICH**

Collection Editor: **JENNIFER GRÜNWALD**
Book Design: **PATRICK McGRATH**
Cover Design: **TIMOTHY DANIEL**
Business Affairs: **ALISA BENDIS**

FORTUNE AND GLORY: A TRUE HOLLYWOOD COMIC BOOK STORY DELUXE ANNIVERSARY EDITION. Contains material originally published in magazine form as FORTUNE AND GLORY #1-3. First printing 2010. ISBN# 978-0-7851-4309-3. Published by MARVEL WORLDWIDE, INC., a subsidiary of MARVEL ENTERTAINMENT, LLC. OFFICE OF PUBLICATION: 417 5th Avenue, New York, NY 10016. Copyright © 1999, 2000 and 2010 Jinxworld, Inc. All rights reserved. $19.99 per copy in the U.S. (GST #R127032852); Canadian Agreement #40668537. "Fortune and Glory" and all characters featured in or on this issue and the distinctive names and likenesses thereof, and all related indicia are trademarks of Jinxworld, Inc. ICON and its logos are TM & © Marvel Characters, Inc. No similarity between any of the names, characters, persons, and/or institutions in this magazine with those of any living or dead person or institution is intended, and any such similarity that may exist is purely coincidental. **Printed in the U.S.A.** Manufactured between 4/12/10 and 4/21/10 by R.R. Donnelley, INC. (CRAWFORD), CRAWFORDSVILLE, IN, USA.

10 9 8 7 6 5 4 3 2 1

introduction
by PAUL DINI

There's an old Looney Tune wherein Bugs Bunny, en route to Miami, mistakenly burrows up in the middle of a desert and encounters an enemy who spends the rest of the cartoon trying to destroy him. After finally vanquishing his foe, Bugs heads back to his hole only to see a gleeful Daffy Duck pop out and dash across the desert screaming, "Miami Beach at last!" Bugs tries to stop Daffy, but the duck is too enraptured with finally gaining the promised land to listen. Shrugging to the audience, Bugs says Daffy will have to figure it out for himself.

That's roughly the same feeling I had when I read *Fortune & Glory*, Brian Michael Bendis' funny, sobering, and ultimately brilliant account of his first foray into Hollywood. Having been through the Hollywood wringer once or twice, I can easily relate to the emotional odyssey Brain's cartoon alter ego endures. Hollywood has spent the last hundred years or so establishing itself (in our collective conscious, if nowhere else) as the creative person's Land of Oz. Beneath its glistening hilltop sign exists an Emerald City whose benevolent wizards labor tirelessly to turn our dreams into realities. No one can tell aspiring writers anything different and what's more, they want to believe it. But this is show *business*, and the frustrations, setbacks, and heartbreaks of that business walk hand in hand with our dreams like the school bully with the prom queen. Is it all bad? Of course not. But like Daffy Duck looking for the beach that isn't there, newcomers will have to figure out the lay of the land for themselves.

Fortunately, Bendis is a fast learner, and in *Fortune & Glory*, he's created a great primer for any show biz hopeful to follow. The book is an astute, painfully funny, and all too real account of the struggle and insanity that awaits 99.9% of the creative people when they first get involved with Hollywood. And if the other .01% don't get the treatment the first time, I promise you they will on the second.

Brian has perfectly captured the emotional highs and lows of a writer on the Hollywood see-saw. He also deftly skewers a number of the irritating nuances I've come to know and hate about LA. There's the hungry, desperate way the movers, shakers, and fakers that haunt trendy restaurants instantly scan your face and discard you as you enter, unless your last name is DiCaprio, of course. And let's not forget the strange paradox that while every agent, producer, and development person in town is a tremendous fan of the idea of your work as reported in a magazine or TV spot, none of them have actually sat down to read the work itself.

Riddle me that, huh?

Bendis' dry wit is perfectly matched by his clean, minimalist artwork. His round-headed caricature evokes both the innocent child and the shell-shocked war veteran. Another great visual touch I loved was the way Brian drew no development person or producer with their eyes open. I believe it was David Geffen who pioneered the sleepy-eyed, semi-conscious, semi-contemptuous air of casual disinterest which most power wannabes now adopt. In fact, I am reasonably sure they offer classes on mastering this attitude through the Hollywood Learning Annex.

In any event, congratulations to Brian on both the book and the well-deserved praise it has thus far received. I only hope the producers don't force him to write a happier ending for the movie version.

Paul Dini

Paul Dini has written a number of books, cartoons, comics and screenplays.

FOR
ALISA

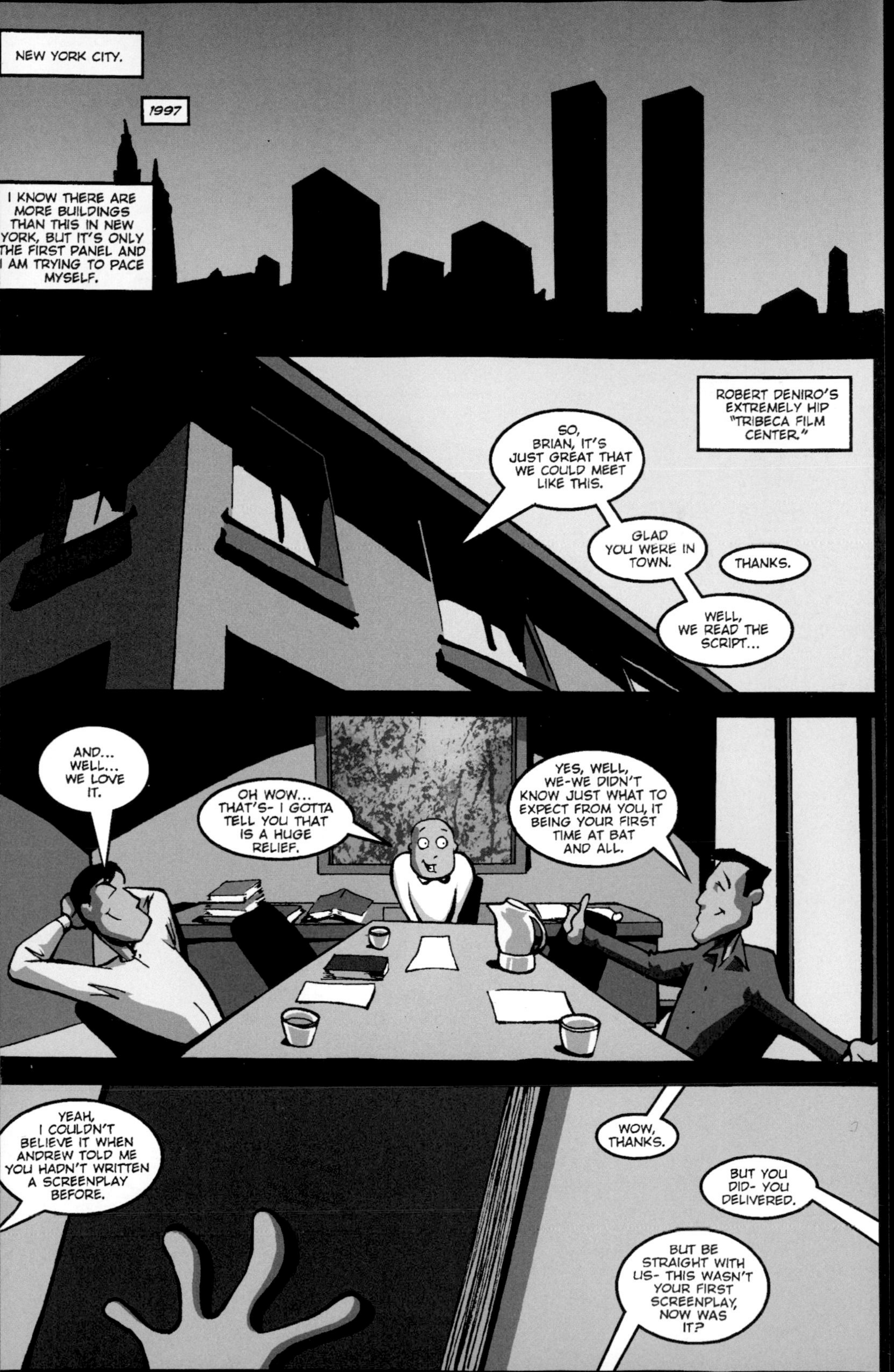

NEW YORK CITY.
1997
I KNOW THERE ARE MORE BUILDINGS THAN THIS IN NEW YORK, BUT IT'S ONLY THE FIRST PANEL AND I AM TRYING TO PACE MYSELF.
ROBERT DENIRO'S EXTREMELY HIP "TRIBECA FILM CENTER."
SO, BRIAN, IT'S JUST GREAT THAT WE COULD MEET LIKE THIS.
GLAD YOU WERE IN TOWN.
THANKS.
WELL, WE READ THE SCRIPT...
AND... WELL... WE LOVE IT.
OH WOW... THAT'S- I GOTTA TELL YOU THAT IS A HUGE RELIEF.
YES, WELL, WE-WE DIDN'T KNOW JUST WHAT TO EXPECT FROM YOU, IT BEING YOUR FIRST TIME AT BAT AND ALL.
YEAH, I COULDN'T BELIEVE IT WHEN ANDREW TOLD ME YOU HADN'T WRITTEN A SCREENPLAY BEFORE.
WOW, THANKS.
BUT YOU DID- YOU DELIVERED.
BUT BE STRAIGHT WITH US- THIS WASN'T YOUR FIRST SCREENPLAY, NOW WAS IT?

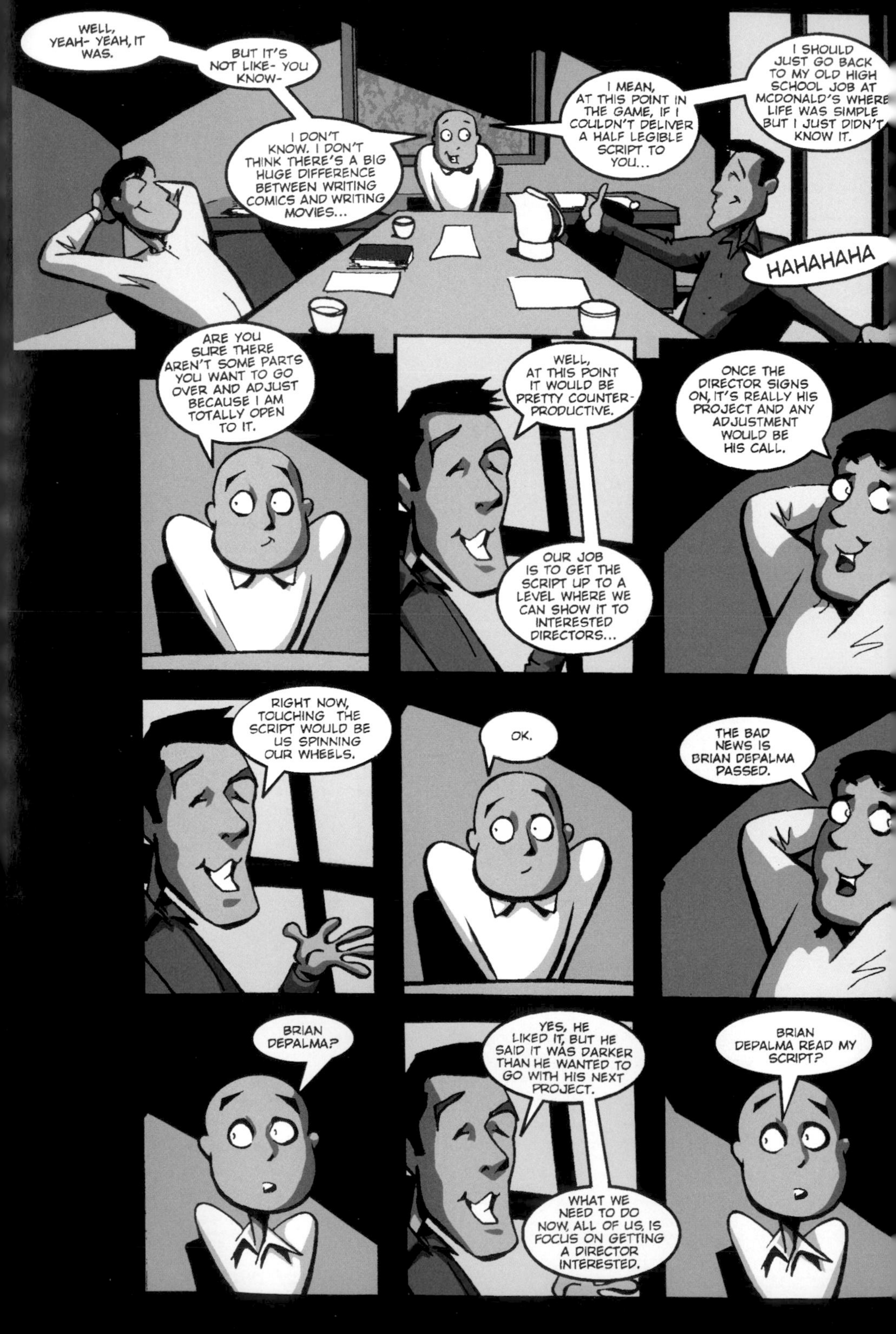

WELL, YEAH- YEAH, IT WAS.
BUT IT'S NOT LIKE- YOU KNOW-
I DON'T KNOW. I DON'T THINK THERE'S A BIG HUGE DIFFERENCE BETWEEN WRITING COMICS AND WRITING MOVIES...
I MEAN, AT THIS POINT IN THE GAME, IF I COULDN'T DELIVER A HALF LEGIBLE SCRIPT TO YOU...
I SHOULD JUST GO BACK TO MY OLD HIGH SCHOOL JOB AT MCDONALD'S WHERE LIFE WAS SIMPLE BUT I JUST DIDN'T KNOW IT.
HAHAHAHA
ARE YOU SURE THERE AREN'T SOME PARTS YOU WANT TO GO OVER AND ADJUST BECAUSE I AM TOTALLY OPEN TO IT.
WELL, AT THIS POINT IT WOULD BE PRETTY COUNTER-PRODUCTIVE.
OUR JOB IS TO GET THE SCRIPT UP TO A LEVEL WHERE WE CAN SHOW IT TO INTERESTED DIRECTORS...
ONCE THE DIRECTOR SIGNS ON, IT'S REALLY HIS PROJECT AND ANY ADJUSTMENT WOULD BE HIS CALL.
RIGHT NOW, TOUCHING THE SCRIPT WOULD BE US SPINNING OUR WHEELS.
OK.
THE BAD NEWS IS BRIAN DEPALMA PASSED.
BRIAN DEPALMA?
YES, HE LIKED IT, BUT HE SAID IT WAS DARKER THAN HE WANTED TO GO WITH HIS NEXT PROJECT.
WHAT WE NEED TO DO NOW, ALL OF US, IS FOCUS ON GETTING A DIRECTOR INTERESTED.
BRIAN DEPALMA READ MY SCRIPT?

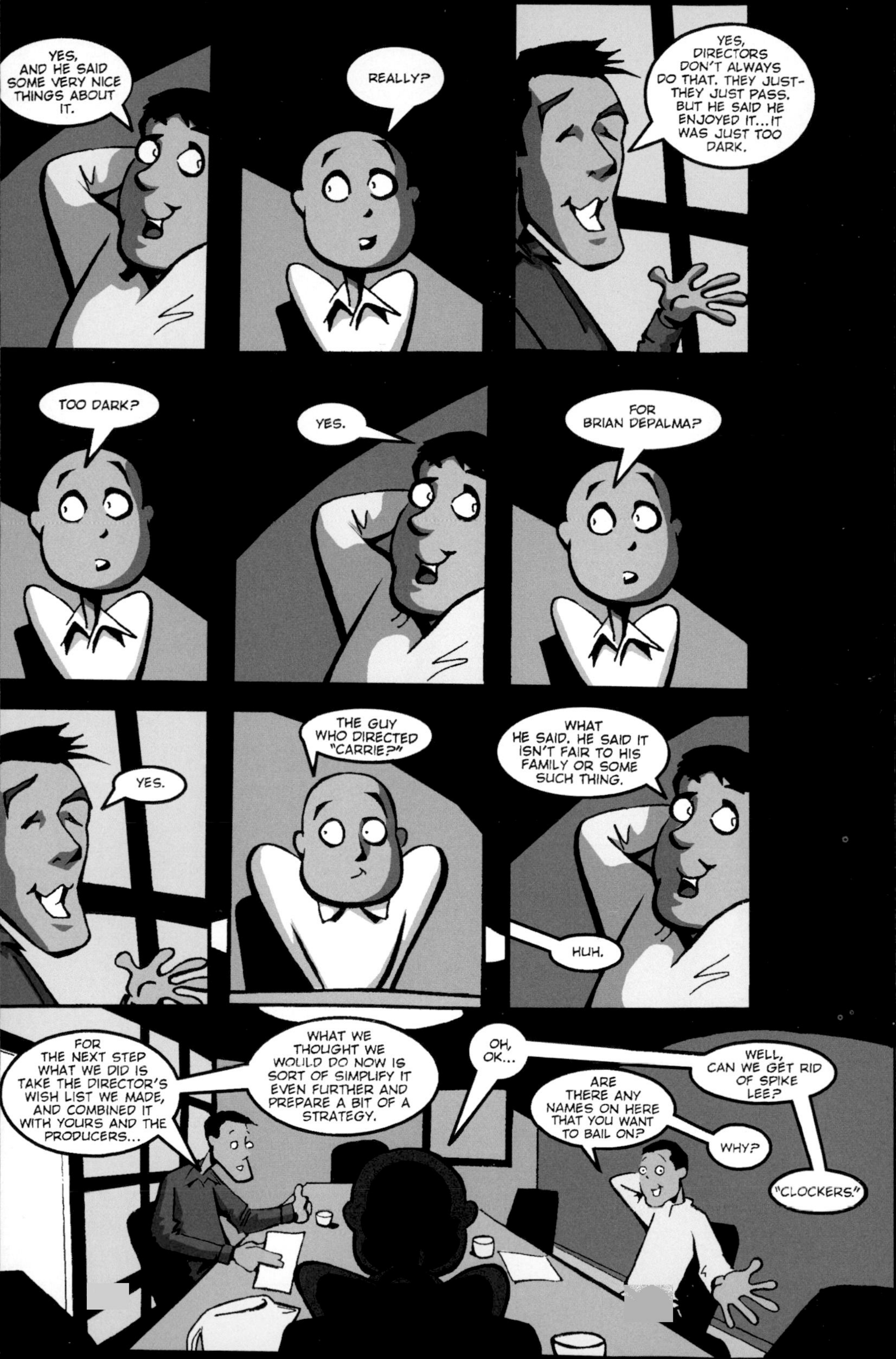
YES, AND HE SAID SOME VERY NICE THINGS ABOUT IT.
REALLY?
YES, DIRECTORS DON'T ALWAYS DO THAT. THEY JUST- THEY JUST PASS. BUT HE SAID HE ENJOYED IT... IT WAS JUST TOO DARK.
TOO DARK?
YES.
FOR BRIAN DEPALMA?
YES.
THE GUY WHO DIRECTED "CARRIE?"
WHAT HE SAID. HE SAID IT ISN'T FAIR TO HIS FAMILY OR SOME SUCH THING.
HUH.
FOR THE NEXT STEP WHAT WE DID IS TAKE THE DIRECTOR'S WISH LIST WE MADE, AND COMBINED IT WITH YOURS AND THE PRODUCERS...
WHAT WE THOUGHT WE WOULD DO NOW IS SORT OF SIMPLIFY IT EVEN FURTHER AND PREPARE A BIT OF A STRATEGY.
OH, OK...
ARE THERE ANY NAMES ON HERE THAT YOU WANT TO BAIL ON?
WELL, CAN WE GET RID OF SPIKE LEE?
WHY?
"CLOCKERS."

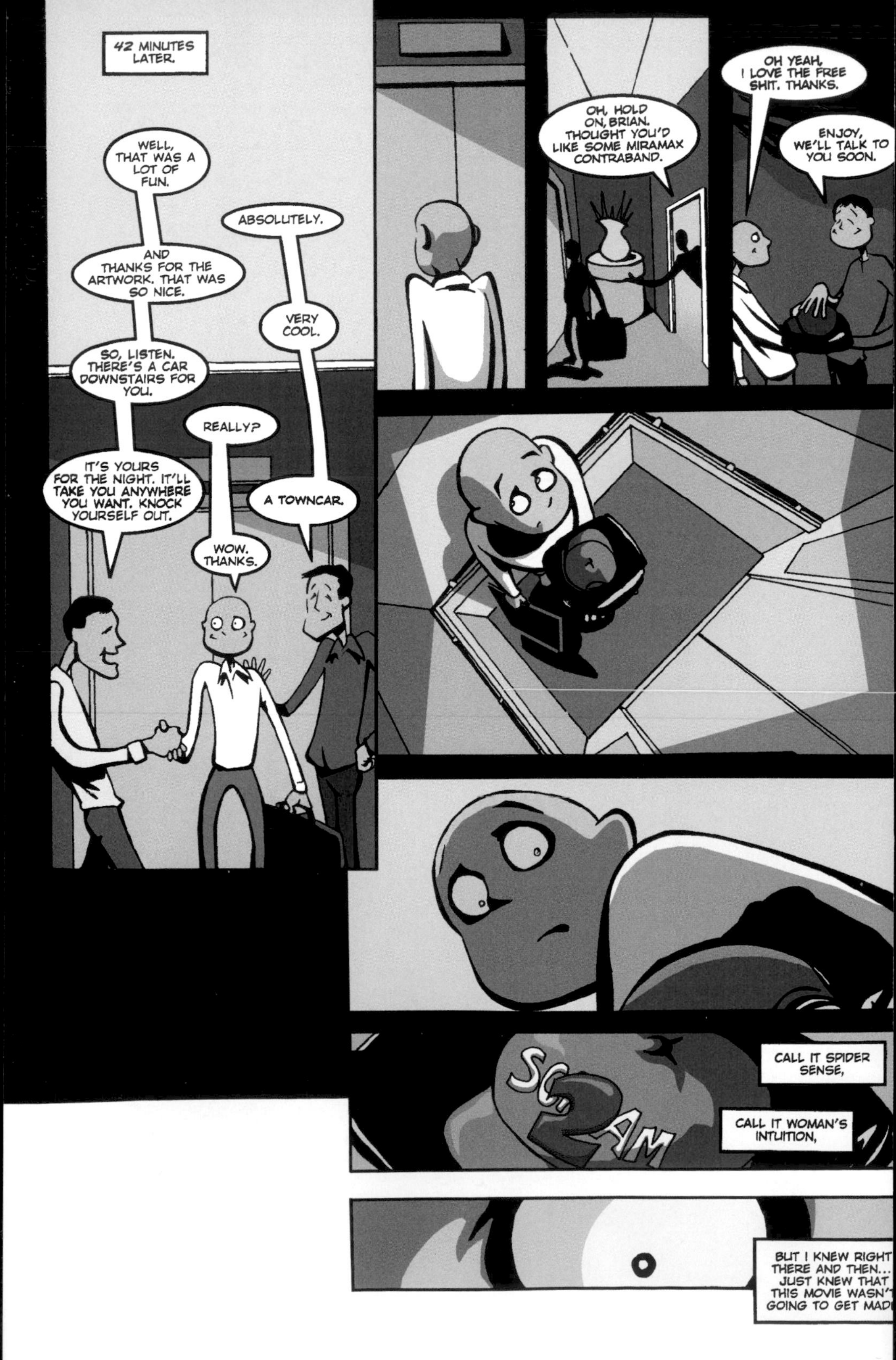
42 MINUTES LATER.
WELL, THAT WAS A LOT OF FUN.
AND THANKS FOR THE ARTWORK. THAT WAS SO NICE.
ABSOLUTELY.
VERY COOL.
SO, LISTEN. THERE'S A CAR DOWNSTAIRS FOR YOU.
REALLY?
A TOWNCAR.
IT'S YOURS FOR THE NIGHT. IT'LL TAKE YOU ANYWHERE YOU WANT. KNOCK YOURSELF OUT.
WOW. THANKS.
OH, HOLD ON, BRIAN. THOUGHT YOU'D LIKE SOME MIRAMAX CONTRABAND.
OH YEAH, I LOVE THE FREE SHIT. THANKS.
ENJOY, WE'LL TALK TO YOU SOON.
SCREAM
CALL IT SPIDER SENSE,
CALL IT WOMAN'S INTUITION,
BUT I KNEW RIGHT THERE AND THEN... JUST KNEW THAT THIS MOVIE WASN'T GOING TO GET MAD

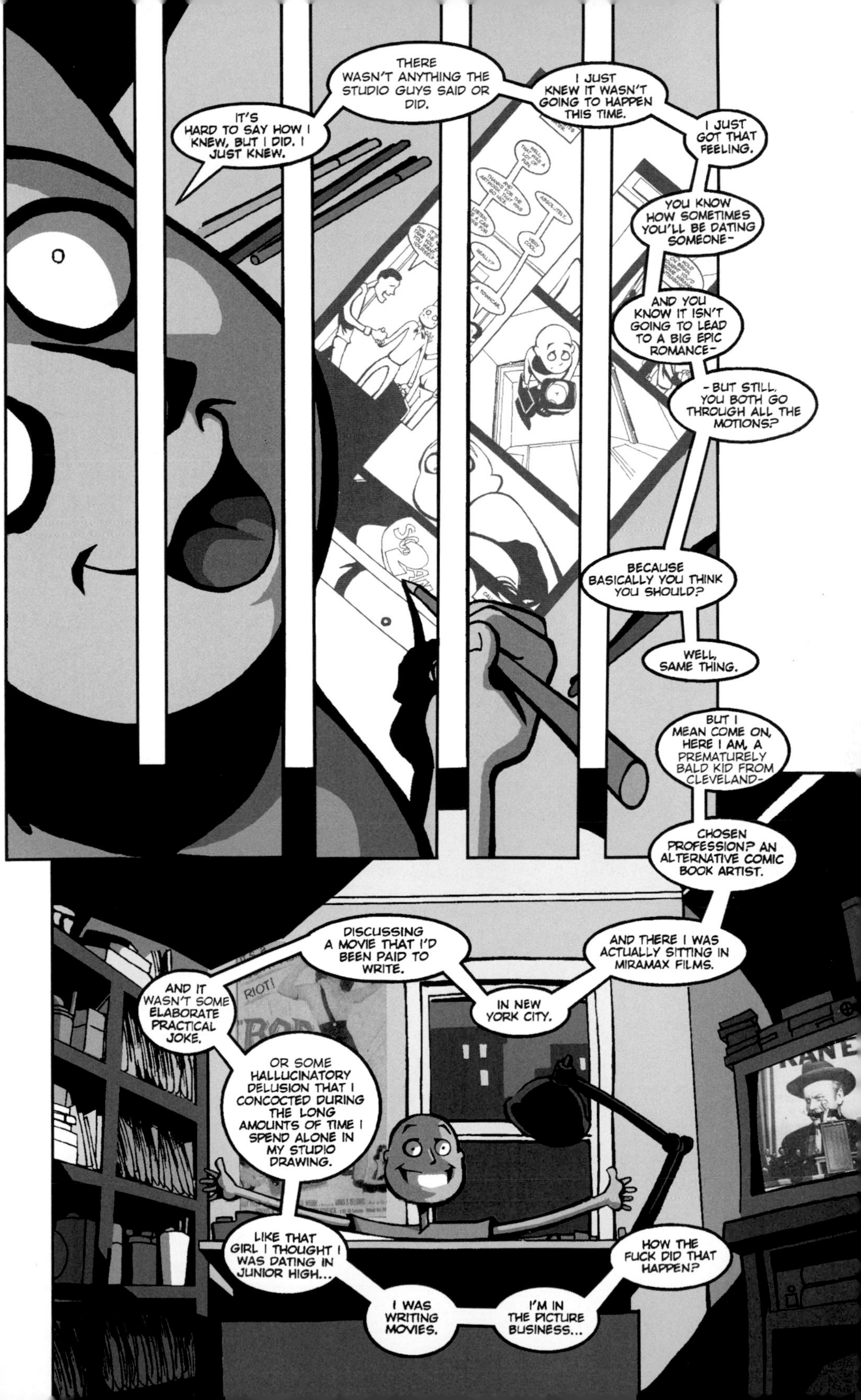
IT'S HARD TO SAY HOW I KNEW, BUT I DID. I JUST KNEW.
THERE WASN'T ANYTHING THE STUDIO GUYS SAID OR DID.
I JUST KNEW IT WASN'T GOING TO HAPPEN THIS TIME.
I JUST GOT THAT FEELING.
YOU KNOW HOW SOMETIMES YOU'LL BE DATING SOMEONE-
AND YOU KNOW IT ISN'T GOING TO LEAD TO A BIG EPIC ROMANCE-
-BUT STILL, YOU BOTH GO THROUGH ALL THE MOTIONS?
BECAUSE BASICALLY YOU THINK YOU SHOULD?
WELL, SAME THING.
BUT I MEAN COME ON, HERE I AM, A PREMATURELY BALD KID FROM CLEVELAND-
CHOSEN PROFESSION? AN ALTERNATIVE COMIC BOOK ARTIST.
AND THERE I WAS ACTUALLY SITTING IN MIRAMAX FILMS.
IN NEW YORK CITY.
DISCUSSING A MOVIE THAT I'D BEEN PAID TO WRITE.
AND IT WASN'T SOME ELABORATE PRACTICAL JOKE.
OR SOME HALLUCINATORY DELUSION THAT I CONCOCTED DURING THE LONG AMOUNTS OF TIME I SPEND ALONE IN MY STUDIO DRAWING.
LIKE THAT GIRL I THOUGHT I WAS DATING IN JUNIOR HIGH...
I WAS WRITING MOVIES.
I'M IN THE PICTURE BUSINESS...
HOW THE FUCK DID THAT HAPPEN?

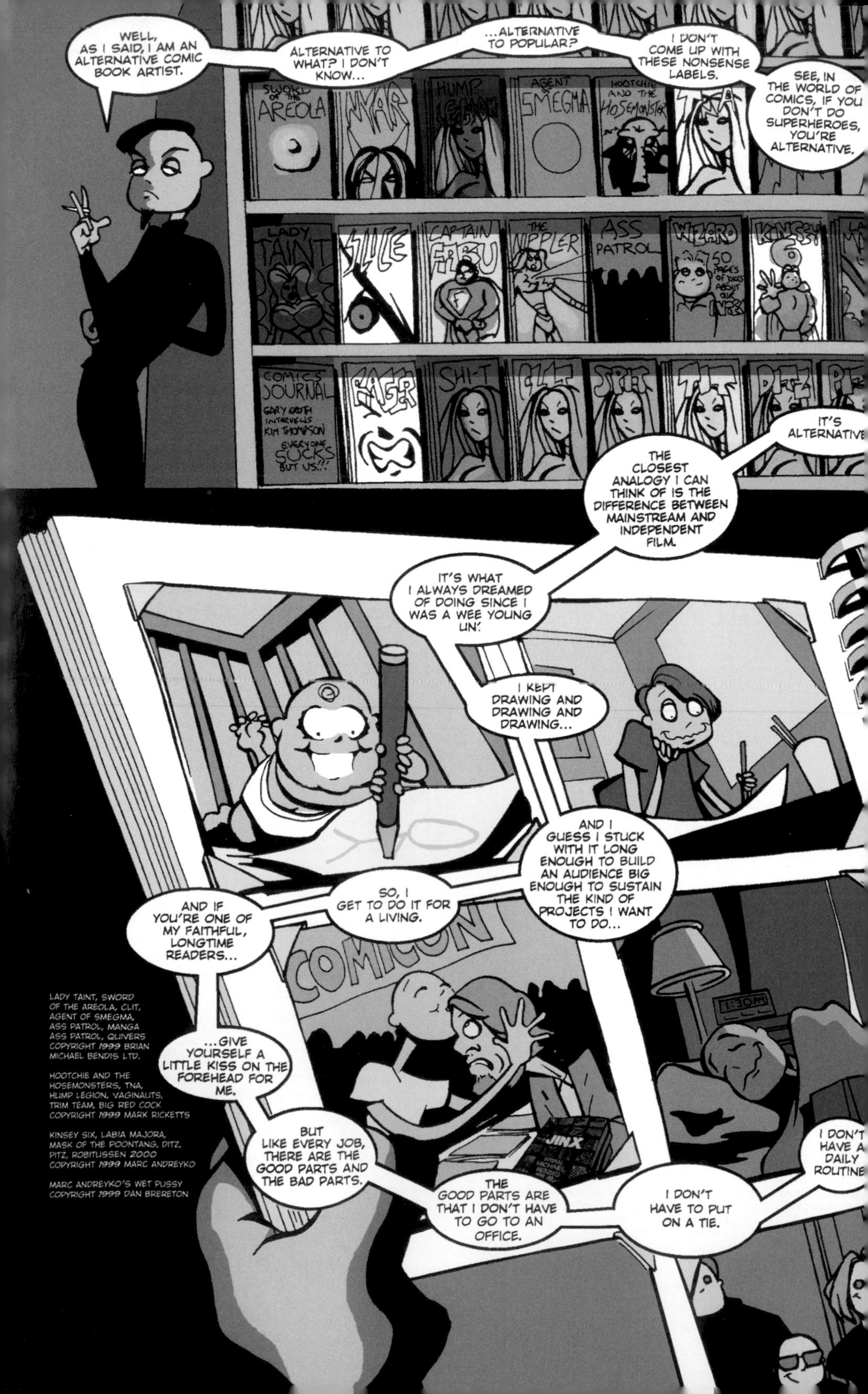
WELL, AS I SAID, I AM AN ALTERNATIVE COMIC BOOK ARTIST.
ALTERNATIVE TO WHAT? I DON'T KNOW...
...ALTERNATIVE TO POPULAR?
I DON'T COME UP WITH THESE NONSENSE LABELS.
SEE, IN THE WORLD OF COMICS, IF YOU DON'T DO SUPERHEROES, YOU'RE ALTERNATIVE.
COMICS JOURNAL
ASS PATROL
IT'S ALTERNATIVE
THE CLOSEST ANALOGY I CAN THINK OF IS THE DIFFERENCE BETWEEN MAINSTREAM AND INDEPENDENT FILM.
IT'S WHAT I ALWAYS DREAMED OF DOING SINCE I WAS A WEE YOUNG UN'.
I KEPT DRAWING AND DRAWING AND DRAWING...
AND I GUESS I STUCK WITH IT LONG ENOUGH TO BUILD AN AUDIENCE BIG ENOUGH TO SUSTAIN THE KIND OF PROJECTS I WANT TO DO...
SO, I GET TO DO IT FOR A LIVING.
AND IF YOU'RE ONE OF MY FAITHFUL, LONGTIME READERS...
...GIVE YOURSELF A LITTLE KISS ON THE FOREHEAD FOR ME.
COMICON
JINX
BUT LIKE EVERY JOB, THERE ARE THE GOOD PARTS AND THE BAD PARTS.
THE GOOD PARTS ARE THAT I DON'T HAVE TO GO TO AN OFFICE.
I DON'T HAVE TO PUT ON A TIE.
I DON'T HAVE A DAILY ROUTINE

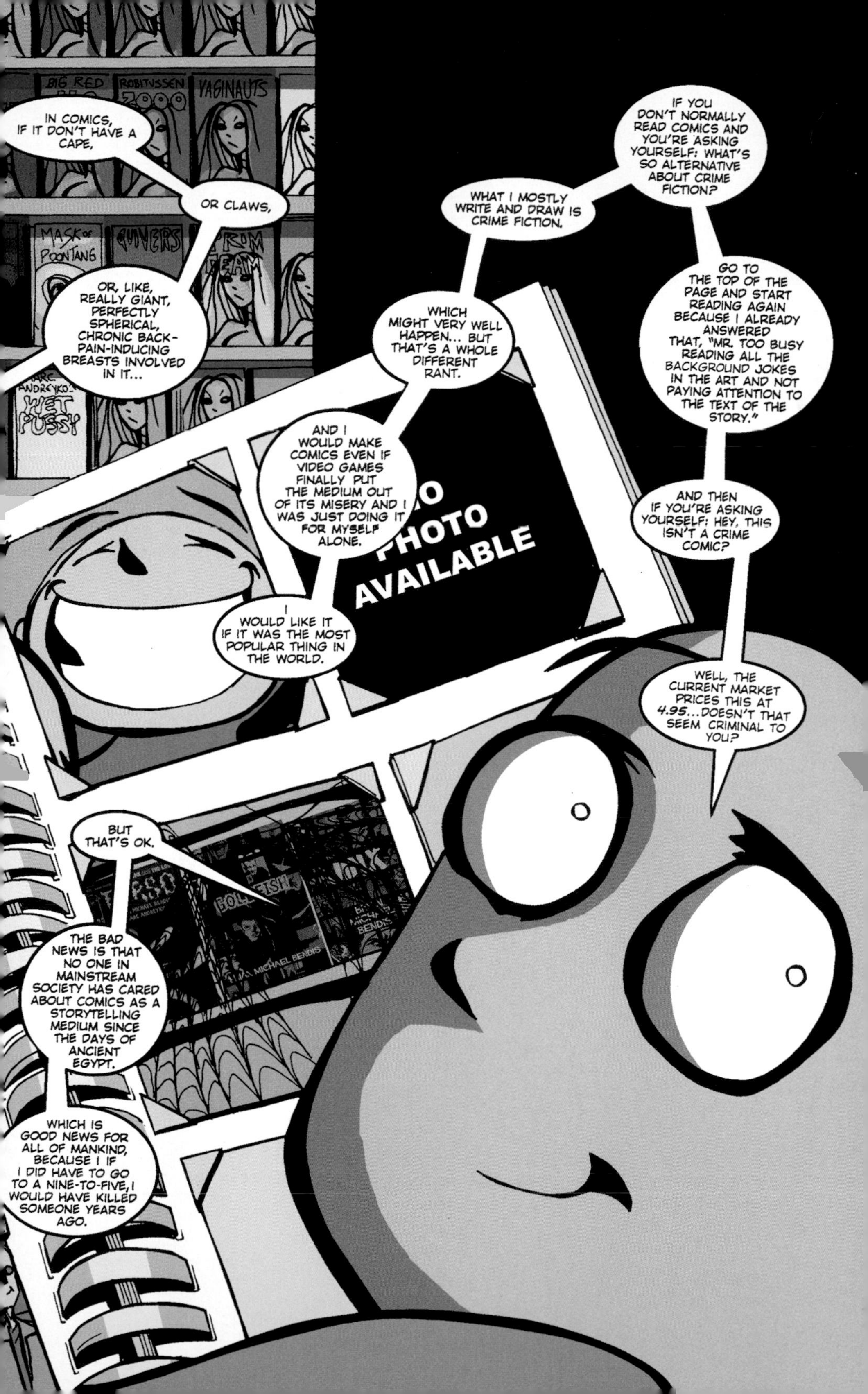
BIG RED
ROBITUSSEN ZOOO
VAGINAUTS
MASK OF POONTANG
QUIVERS
WET PUSSY
IN COMICS, IF IT DON'T HAVE A CAPE,
OR CLAWS,
OR, LIKE, REALLY GIANT, PERFECTLY SPHERICAL, CHRONIC BACK-PAIN-INDUCING BREASTS INVOLVED IN IT...
BUT THAT'S OK.
THE BAD NEWS IS THAT NO ONE IN MAINSTREAM SOCIETY HAS CARED ABOUT COMICS AS A STORYTELLING MEDIUM SINCE THE DAYS OF ANCIENT EGYPT.
WHICH IS GOOD NEWS FOR ALL OF MANKIND, BECAUSE I IF I DID HAVE TO GO TO A NINE-TO-FIVE, I WOULD HAVE KILLED SOMEONE YEARS AGO.
I WOULD LIKE IT IF IT WAS THE MOST POPULAR THING IN THE WORLD.
AND I WOULD MAKE COMICS EVEN IF VIDEO GAMES FINALLY PUT THE MEDIUM OUT OF ITS MISERY AND I WAS JUST DOING IT FOR MYSELF ALONE.
WHICH MIGHT VERY WELL HAPPEN... BUT THAT'S A WHOLE DIFFERENT RANT.
PHOTO AVAILABLE
WHAT I MOSTLY WRITE AND DRAW IS CRIME FICTION.
IF YOU DON'T NORMALLY READ COMICS AND YOU'RE ASKING YOURSELF: WHAT'S SO ALTERNATIVE ABOUT CRIME FICTION?
GO TO THE TOP OF THE PAGE AND START READING AGAIN BECAUSE I ALREADY ANSWERED THAT, "MR. TOO BUSY READING ALL THE BACKGROUND JOKES IN THE ART AND NOT PAYING ATTENTION TO THE TEXT OF THE STORY."
AND THEN IF YOU'RE ASKING YOURSELF: HEY, THIS ISN'T A CRIME COMIC?
WELL, THE CURRENT MARKET PRICES THIS AT 4.95...DOESN'T THAT SEEM CRIMINAL TO YOU?
BRIAN MICHAEL BENDIS

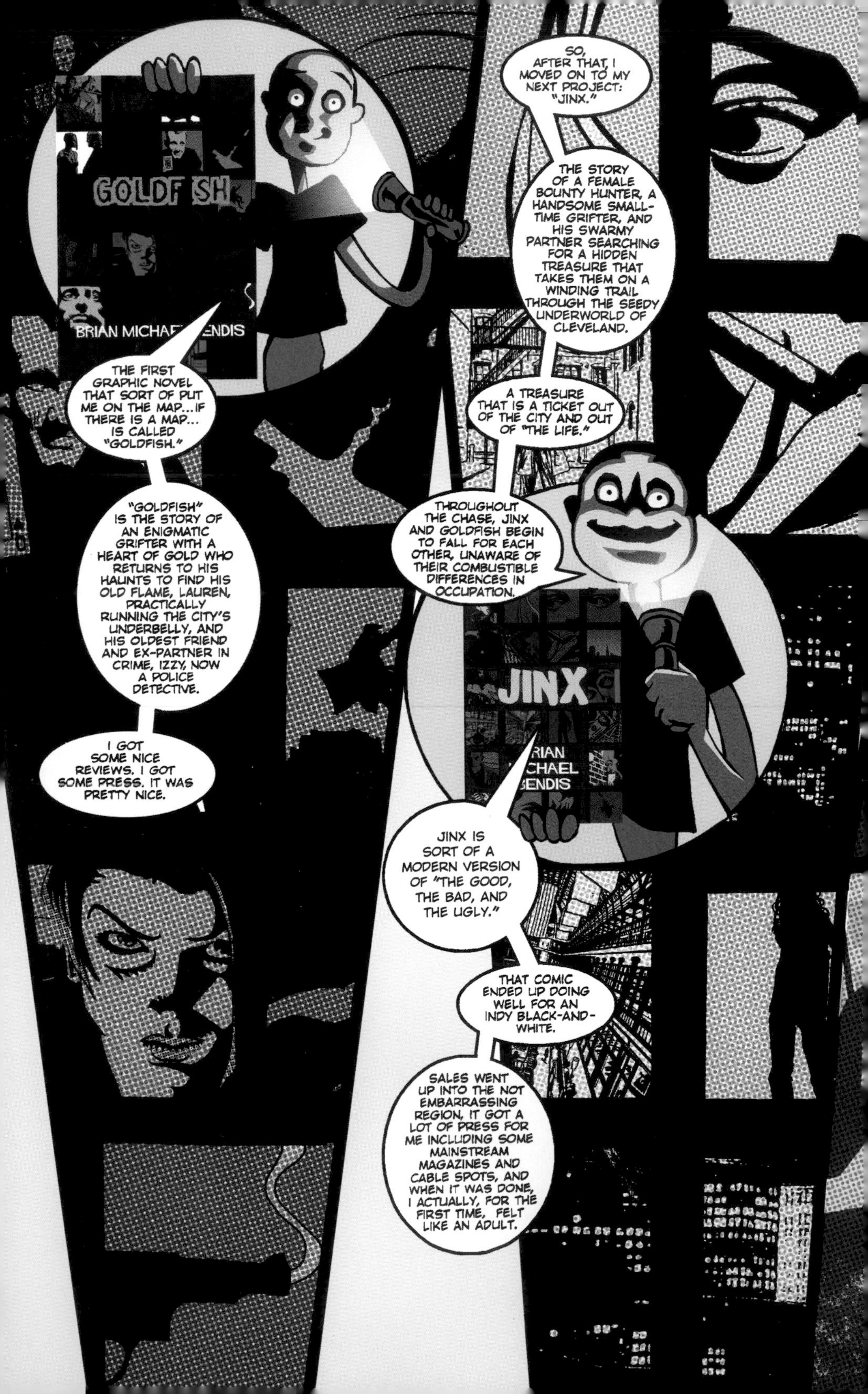
THE FIRST GRAPHIC NOVEL THAT SORT OF PUT ME ON THE MAP...IF THERE IS A MAP... IS CALLED "GOLDFISH."
"GOLDFISH" IS THE STORY OF AN ENIGMATIC GRIFTER WITH A HEART OF GOLD WHO RETURNS TO HIS HAUNTS TO FIND HIS OLD FLAME, LAUREN, PRACTICALLY RUNNING THE CITY'S UNDERBELLY, AND HIS OLDEST FRIEND AND EX-PARTNER IN CRIME, IZZY, NOW A POLICE DETECTIVE.
I GOT SOME NICE REVIEWS. I GOT SOME PRESS. IT WAS PRETTY NICE.
SO, AFTER THAT, I MOVED ON TO MY NEXT PROJECT: "JINX."
THE STORY OF A FEMALE BOUNTY HUNTER, A HANDSOME SMALL-TIME GRIFTER, AND HIS SWARMY PARTNER SEARCHING FOR A HIDDEN TREASURE THAT TAKES THEM ON A WINDING TRAIL THROUGH THE SEEDY UNDERWORLD OF CLEVELAND.
A TREASURE THAT IS A TICKET OUT OF THE CITY AND OUT OF "THE LIFE."
THROUGHOUT THE CHASE, JINX AND GOLDFISH BEGIN TO FALL FOR EACH OTHER, UNAWARE OF THEIR COMBUSTIBLE DIFFERENCES IN OCCUPATION.
JINX
JINX IS SORT OF A MODERN VERSION OF "THE GOOD, THE BAD, AND THE UGLY."
THAT COMIC ENDED UP DOING WELL FOR AN INDY BLACK-AND-WHITE.
SALES WENT UP INTO THE NOT EMBARRASSING REGION, IT GOT A LOT OF PRESS FOR ME INCLUDING SOME MAINSTREAM MAGAZINES AND CABLE SPOTS, AND WHEN IT WAS DONE, I ACTUALLY, FOR THE FIRST TIME, FELT LIKE AN ADULT.

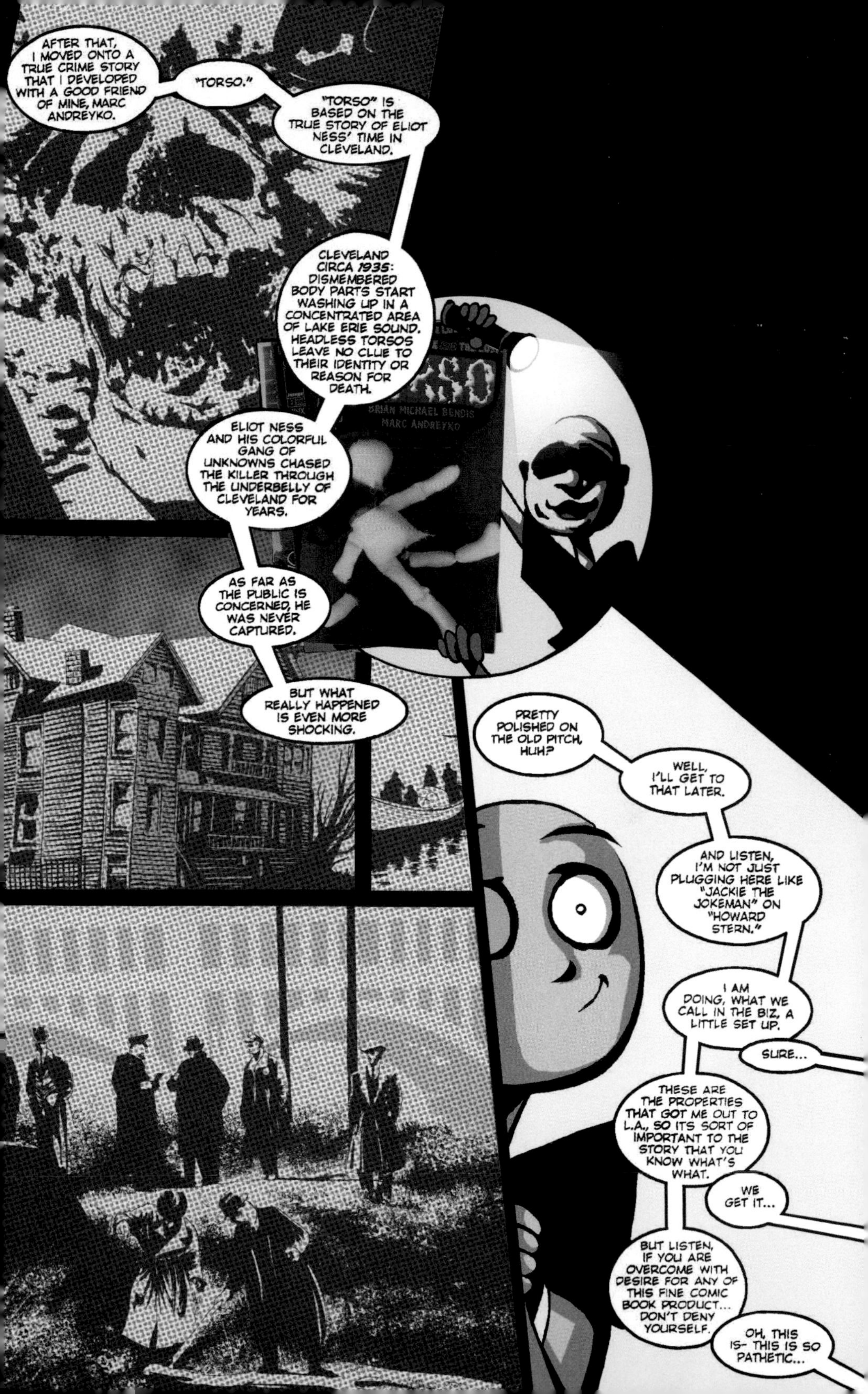
AFTER THAT, I MOVED ONTO A TRUE CRIME STORY THAT I DEVELOPED WITH A GOOD FRIEND OF MINE, MARC ANDREYKO.
"TORSO."
"TORSO" IS BASED ON THE TRUE STORY OF ELIOT NESS' TIME IN CLEVELAND.
CLEVELAND CIRCA 1935: DISMEMBERED BODY PARTS START WASHING UP IN A CONCENTRATED AREA OF LAKE ERIE SOUND. HEADLESS TORSOS LEAVE NO CLUE TO THEIR IDENTITY OR REASON FOR DEATH.
BRIAN MICHAEL BENDIS
MARC ANDREYKO
ELIOT NESS AND HIS COLORFUL GANG OF UNKNOWNS CHASED THE KILLER THROUGH THE UNDERBELLY OF CLEVELAND FOR YEARS.
AS FAR AS THE PUBLIC IS CONCERNED, HE WAS NEVER CAPTURED.
BUT WHAT REALLY HAPPENED IS EVEN MORE SHOCKING.
PRETTY POLISHED ON THE OLD PITCH, HUH?
WELL, I'LL GET TO THAT LATER.
AND LISTEN, I'M NOT JUST PLUGGING HERE LIKE "JACKIE THE JOKEMAN" ON "HOWARD STERN."
I AM DOING, WHAT WE CALL IN THE BIZ, A LITTLE SET UP.
SURE...
THESE ARE THE PROPERTIES THAT GOT ME OUT TO L.A., SO ITS SORT OF IMPORTANT TO THE STORY THAT YOU KNOW WHAT'S WHAT.
WE GET IT...
BUT LISTEN, IF YOU ARE OVERCOME WITH DESIRE FOR ANY OF THIS FINE COMIC BOOK PRODUCT... DON'T DENY YOURSELF.
OH, THIS IS- THIS IS SO PATHETIC...

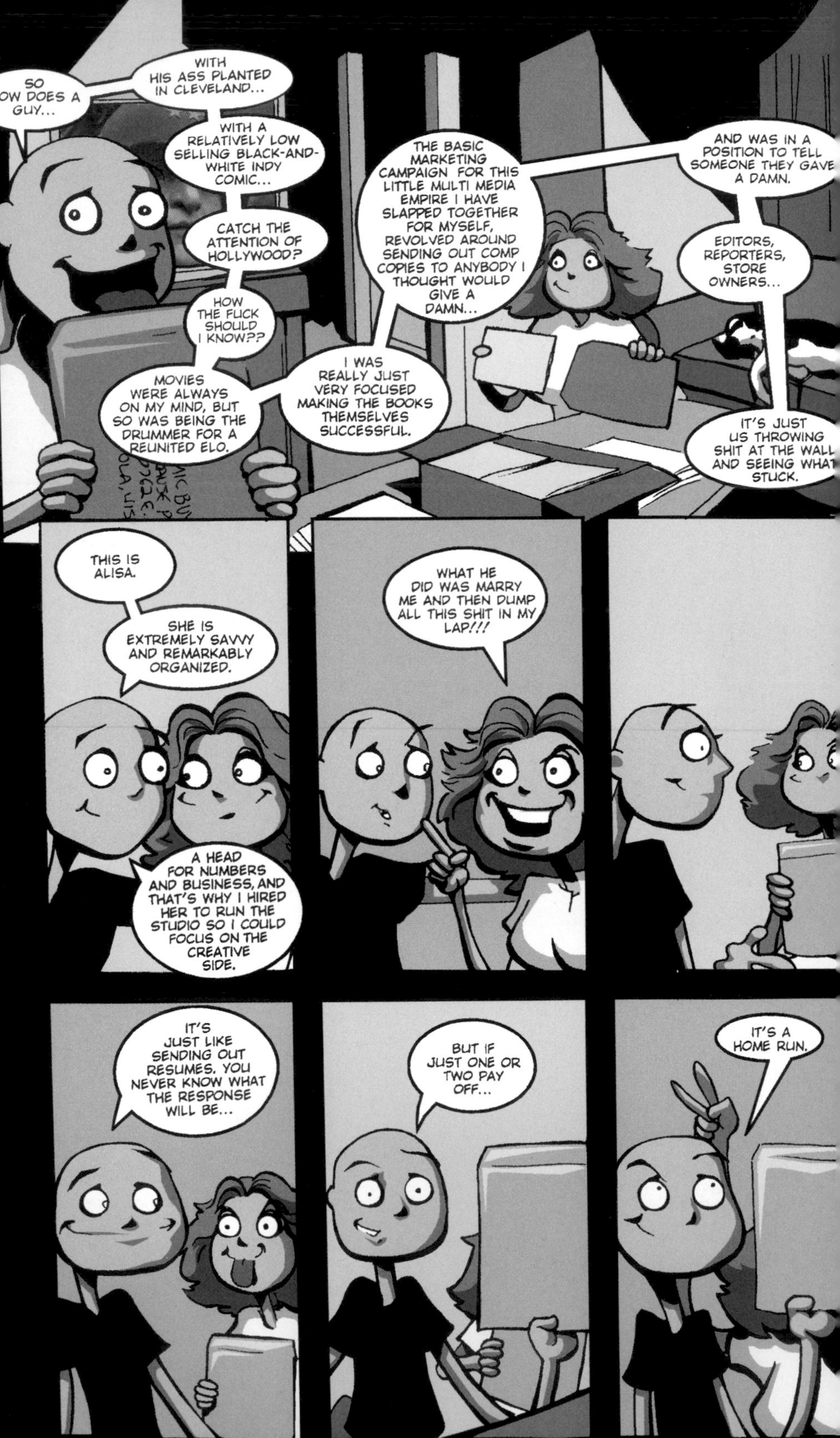
SO HOW DOES A GUY...
WITH HIS ASS PLANTED IN CLEVELAND...
WITH A RELATIVELY LOW SELLING BLACK-AND-WHITE INDY COMIC...
CATCH THE ATTENTION OF HOLLYWOOD?
HOW THE FUCK SHOULD I KNOW??
MOVIES WERE ALWAYS ON MY MIND, BUT SO WAS BEING THE DRUMMER FOR A REUNITED ELO.
I WAS REALLY JUST VERY FOCUSED MAKING THE BOOKS THEMSELVES SUCCESSFUL.
THE BASIC MARKETING CAMPAIGN FOR THIS LITTLE MULTI MEDIA EMPIRE I HAVE SLAPPED TOGETHER FOR MYSELF, REVOLVED AROUND SENDING OUT COMP COPIES TO ANYBODY I THOUGHT WOULD GIVE A DAMN...
AND WAS IN A POSITION TO TELL SOMEONE THEY GAVE A DAMN.
EDITORS, REPORTERS, STORE OWNERS...
IT'S JUST US THROWING SHIT AT THE WALL AND SEEING WHAT STUCK.
THIS IS ALISA.
SHE IS EXTREMELY SAVVY AND REMARKABLY ORGANIZED.
A HEAD FOR NUMBERS AND BUSINESS, AND THAT'S WHY I HIRED HER TO RUN THE STUDIO SO I COULD FOCUS ON THE CREATIVE SIDE.
WHAT HE DID WAS MARRY ME AND THEN DUMP ALL THIS SHIT IN MY LAP!!!
IT'S JUST LIKE SENDING OUT RESUMES. YOU NEVER KNOW WHAT THE RESPONSE WILL BE...
BUT IF JUST ONE OR TWO PAY OFF...
IT'S A HOME RUN.

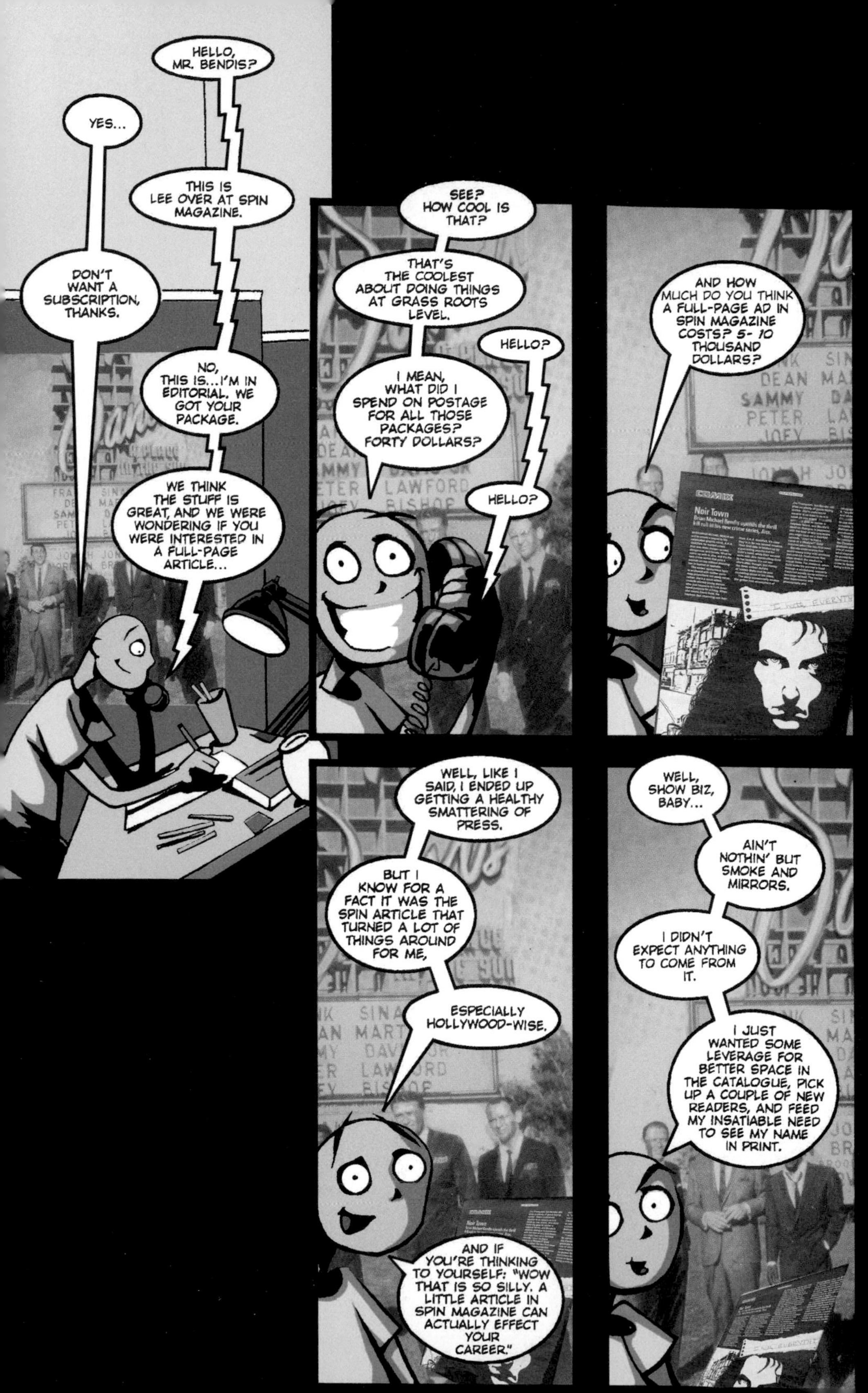
HELLO, MR. BENDIS?
YES...
THIS IS LEE OVER AT SPIN MAGAZINE.
DON'T WANT A SUBSCRIPTION, THANKS.
NO, THIS IS...I'M IN EDITORIAL. WE GOT YOUR PACKAGE.
WE THINK THE STUFF IS GREAT, AND WE WERE WONDERING IF YOU WERE INTERESTED IN A FULL-PAGE ARTICLE...
SEE? HOW COOL IS THAT?
THAT'S THE COOLEST ABOUT DOING THINGS AT GRASS ROOTS LEVEL.
I MEAN, WHAT DID I SPEND ON POSTAGE FOR ALL THOSE PACKAGES? FORTY DOLLARS?
HELLO?
HELLO?
AND HOW MUCH DO YOU THINK A FULL-PAGE AD IN SPIN MAGAZINE COSTS? 5- 10 THOUSAND DOLLARS?
WELL, LIKE I SAID, I ENDED UP GETTING A HEALTHY SMATTERING OF PRESS.
BUT I KNOW FOR A FACT IT WAS THE SPIN ARTICLE THAT TURNED A LOT OF THINGS AROUND FOR ME,
ESPECIALLY HOLLYWOOD-WISE.
AND IF YOU'RE THINKING TO YOURSELF: "WOW THAT IS SO SILLY. A LITTLE ARTICLE IN SPIN MAGAZINE CAN ACTUALLY EFFECT YOUR CAREER."
WELL, SHOW BIZ, BABY...
AIN'T NOTHIN' BUT SMOKE AND MIRRORS.
I DIDN'T EXPECT ANYTHING TO COME FROM IT.
I JUST WANTED SOME LEVERAGE FOR BETTER SPACE IN THE CATALOGUE, PICK UP A COUPLE OF NEW READERS, AND FEED MY INSATIABLE NEED TO SEE MY NAME IN PRINT.

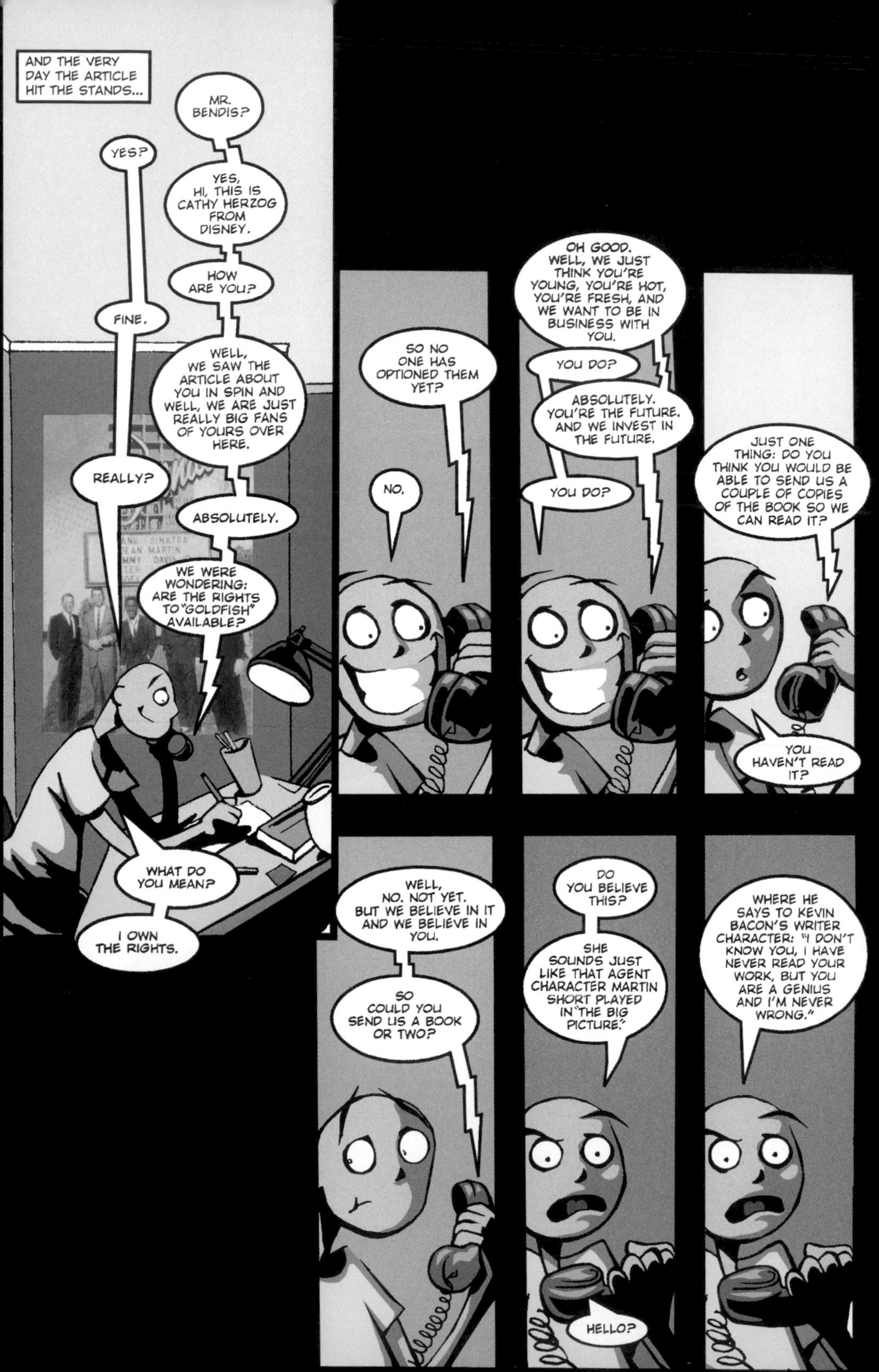

AND THE VERY DAY THE ARTICLE HIT THE STANDS...
MR. BENDIS?
YES?
YES, HI, THIS IS CATHY HERZOG FROM DISNEY.
HOW ARE YOU?
FINE.
WELL, WE SAW THE ARTICLE ABOUT YOU IN SPIN AND WELL, WE ARE JUST REALLY BIG FANS OF YOURS OVER HERE.
REALLY?
ABSOLUTELY.
WE WERE WONDERING: ARE THE RIGHTS TO "GOLDFISH" AVAILABLE?
WHAT DO YOU MEAN?
I OWN THE RIGHTS.
SO NO ONE HAS OPTIONED THEM YET?
NO.
OH GOOD. WELL, WE JUST THINK YOU'RE YOUNG, YOU'RE HOT, YOU'RE FRESH, AND WE WANT TO BE IN BUSINESS WITH YOU.
YOU DO?
ABSOLUTELY. YOU'RE THE FUTURE. AND WE INVEST IN THE FUTURE.
YOU DO?
JUST ONE THING: DO YOU THINK YOU WOULD BE ABLE TO SEND US A COUPLE OF COPIES OF THE BOOK SO WE CAN READ IT?
YOU HAVEN'T READ IT?
WELL, NO. NOT YET. BUT WE BELIEVE IN IT AND WE BELIEVE IN YOU.
SO COULD YOU SEND US A BOOK OR TWO?
DO YOU BELIEVE THIS?
SHE SOUNDS JUST LIKE THAT AGENT CHARACTER MARTIN SHORT PLAYED IN "THE BIG PICTURE."
HELLO?
WHERE HE SAYS TO KEVIN BACON'S WRITER CHARACTER: "I DON'T KNOW YOU, I HAVE NEVER READ YOUR WORK, BUT YOU ARE A GENIUS AND I'M NEVER WRONG."

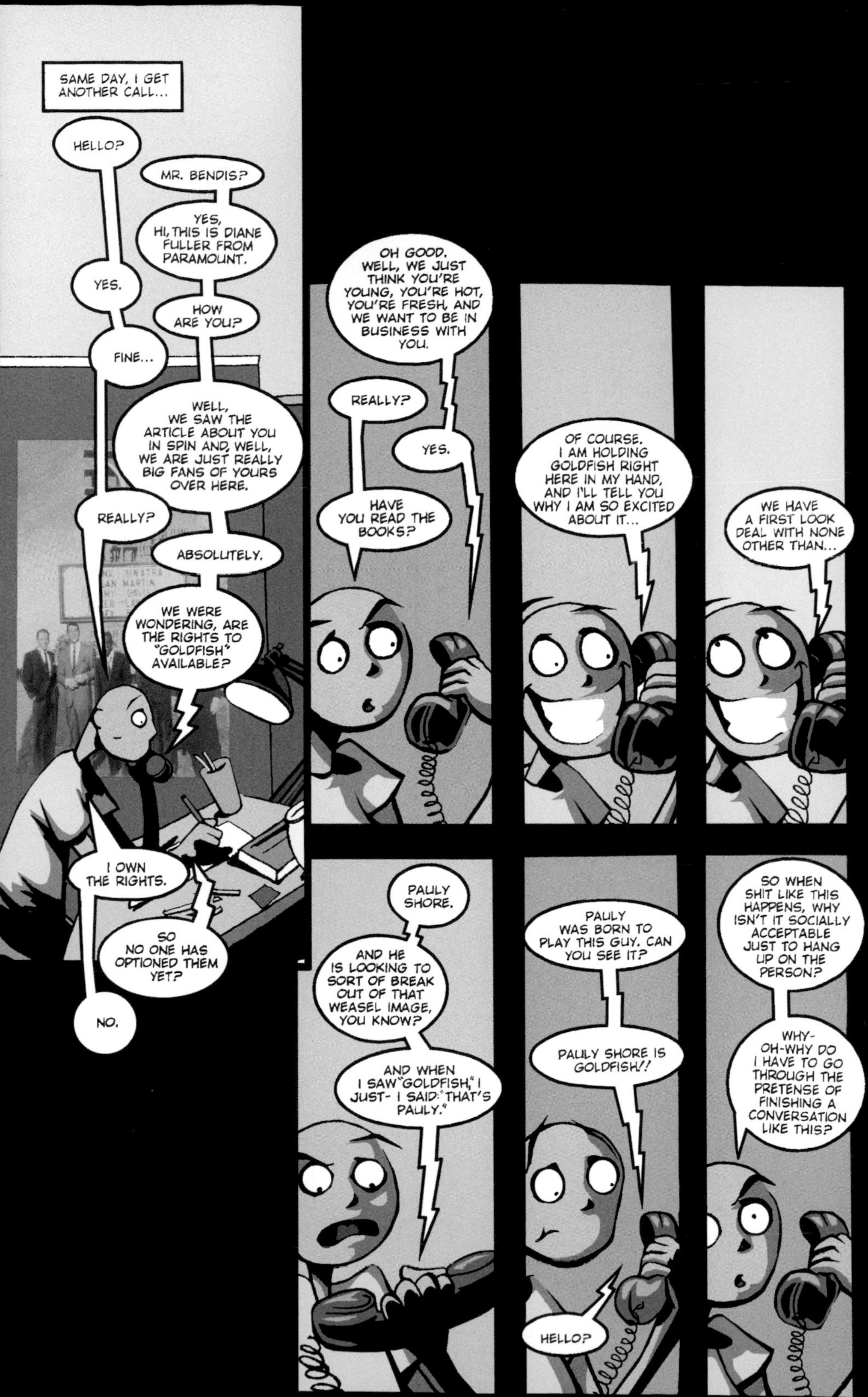
SAME DAY, I GET ANOTHER CALL...
HELLO?
MR. BENDIS?
YES.
YES, HI, THIS IS DIANE FULLER FROM PARAMOUNT.
HOW ARE YOU?
FINE...
WELL, WE SAW THE ARTICLE ABOUT YOU IN SPIN AND, WELL, WE ARE JUST REALLY BIG FANS OF YOURS OVER HERE.
REALLY?
ABSOLUTELY.
WE WERE WONDERING, ARE THE RIGHTS TO "GOLDFISH" AVAILABLE?
I OWN THE RIGHTS.
SO NO ONE HAS OPTIONED THEM YET?
NO.
OH GOOD. WELL, WE JUST THINK YOU'RE YOUNG, YOU'RE HOT, YOU'RE FRESH, AND WE WANT TO BE IN BUSINESS WITH YOU.
REALLY?
YES.
HAVE YOU READ THE BOOKS?
OF COURSE. I AM HOLDING GOLDFISH RIGHT HERE IN MY HAND, AND I'LL TELL YOU WHY I AM SO EXCITED ABOUT IT...
WE HAVE A FIRST LOOK DEAL WITH NONE OTHER THAN...
PAULY SHORE.
AND HE IS LOOKING TO SORT OF BREAK OUT OF THAT WEASEL IMAGE, YOU KNOW?
AND WHEN I SAW "GOLDFISH," I JUST- I SAID: "THAT'S PAULY."
PAULY WAS BORN TO PLAY THIS GUY. CAN YOU SEE IT?
PAULY SHORE IS GOLDFISH!!
HELLO?
SO WHEN SHIT LIKE THIS HAPPENS, WHY ISN'T IT SOCIALLY ACCEPTABLE JUST TO HANG UP ON THE PERSON?
WHY- OH-WHY DO I HAVE TO GO THROUGH THE PRETENSE OF FINISHING A CONVERSATION LIKE THIS?

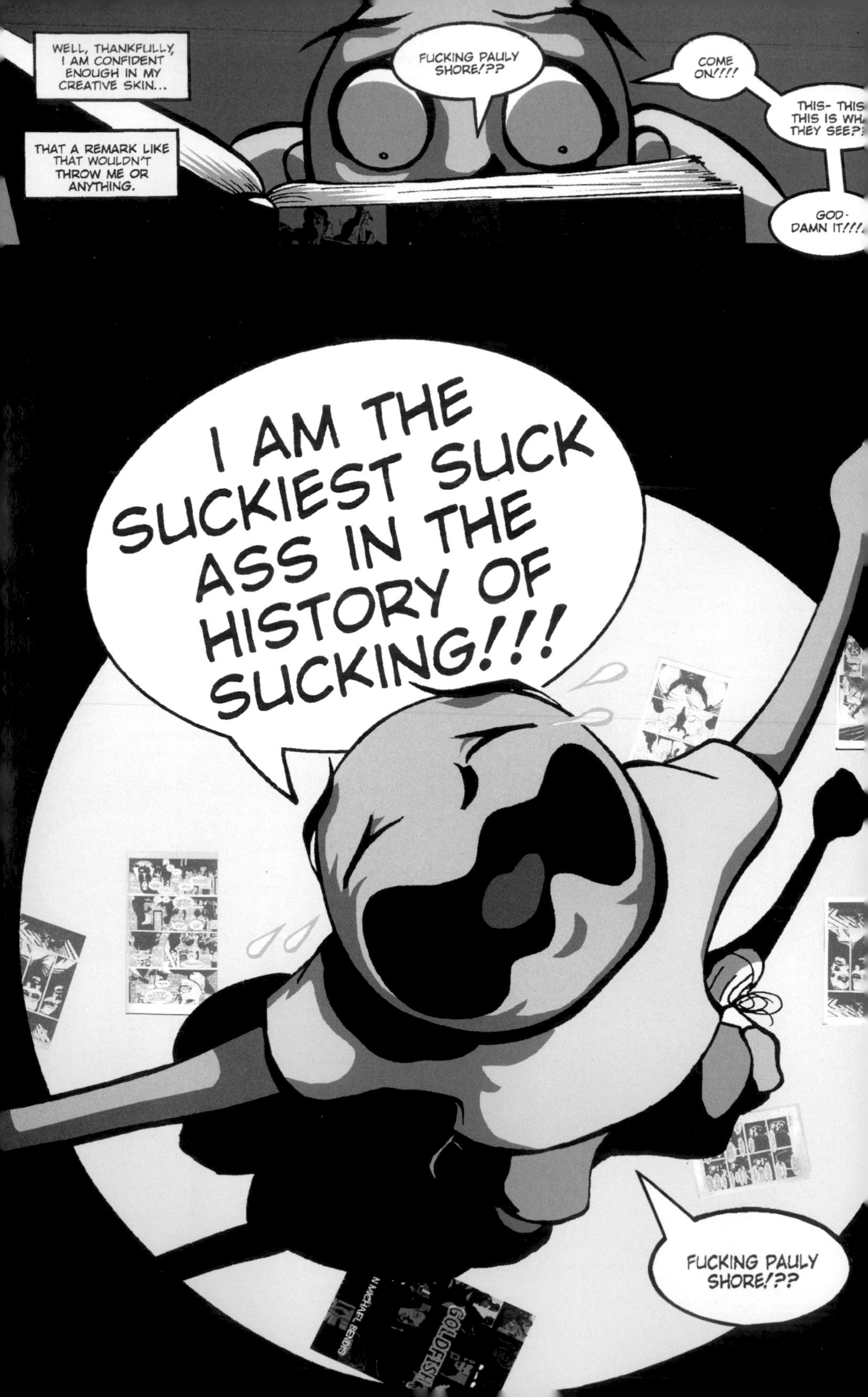
WELL, THANKFULLY, I AM CONFIDENT ENOUGH IN MY CREATIVE SKIN...
THAT A REMARK LIKE THAT WOULDN'T THROW ME OR ANYTHING.
FUCKING PAULY SHORE!??
COME ON!!!!
THIS- THIS THIS IS WH THEY SEE?
GOD-DAMN IT!!!
I AM THE SUCKIEST SUCK ASS IN THE HISTORY OF SUCKING!!!
FUCKING PAULY SHORE!??

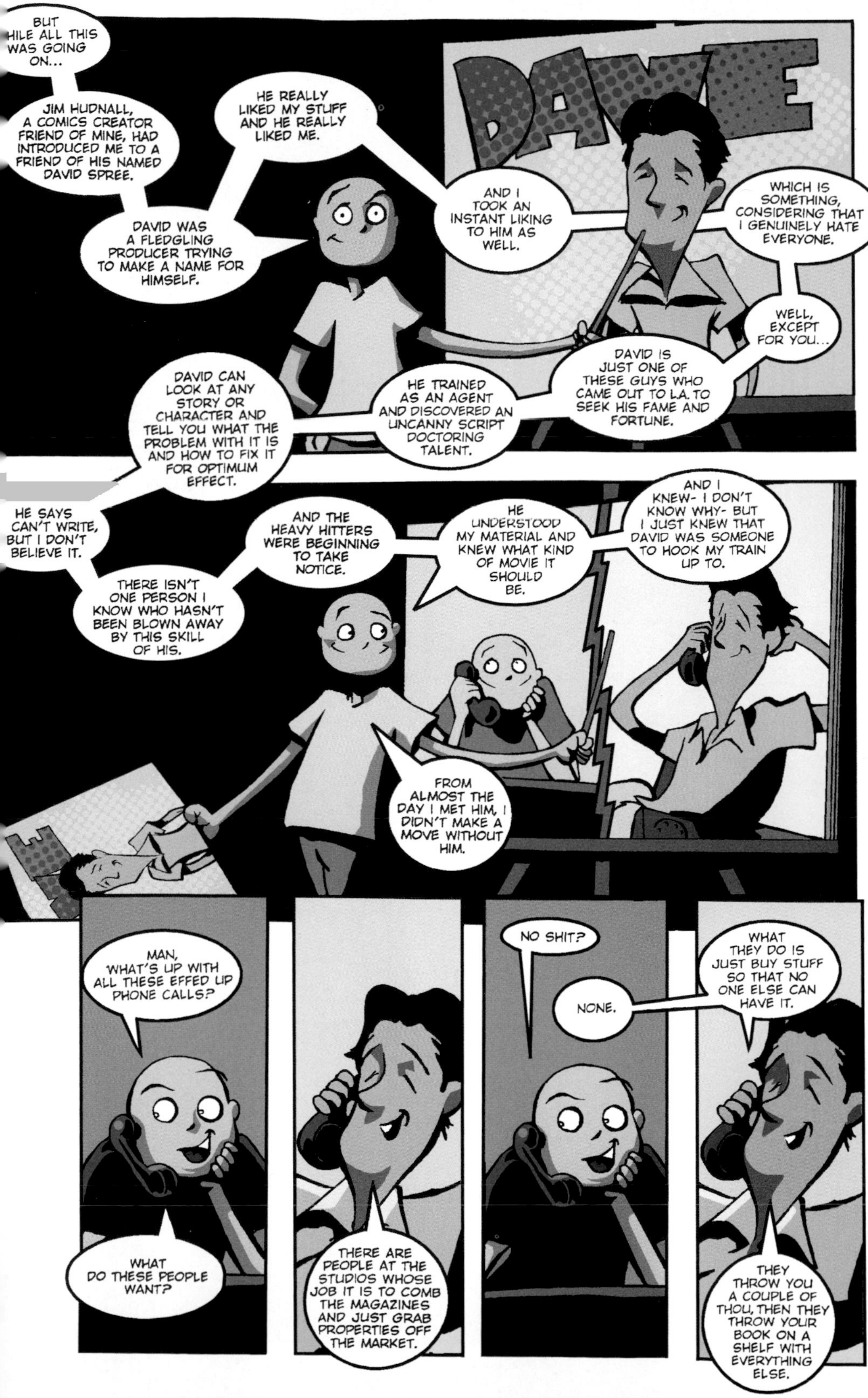
BUT HILE ALL THIS WAS GOING ON...
JIM HUDNALL, A COMICS CREATOR FRIEND OF MINE, HAD INTRODUCED ME TO A FRIEND OF HIS NAMED DAVID SPREE.
DAVID WAS A FLEDGLING PRODUCER TRYING TO MAKE A NAME FOR HIMSELF.
HE REALLY LIKED MY STUFF AND HE REALLY LIKED ME.
AND I TOOK AN INSTANT LIKING TO HIM AS WELL.
WHICH IS SOMETHING, CONSIDERING THAT I GENUINELY HATE EVERYONE.
WELL, EXCEPT FOR YOU...
DAVID IS JUST ONE OF THESE GUYS WHO CAME OUT TO L.A. TO SEEK HIS FAME AND FORTUNE.
HE TRAINED AS AN AGENT AND DISCOVERED AN UNCANNY SCRIPT DOCTORING TALENT.
DAVID CAN LOOK AT ANY STORY OR CHARACTER AND TELL YOU WHAT THE PROBLEM WITH IT IS AND HOW TO FIX IT FOR OPTIMUM EFFECT.
HE SAYS CAN'T WRITE, BUT I DON'T BELIEVE IT.
THERE ISN'T ONE PERSON I KNOW WHO HASN'T BEEN BLOWN AWAY BY THIS SKILL OF HIS.
AND THE HEAVY HITTERS WERE BEGINNING TO TAKE NOTICE.
HE UNDERSTOOD MY MATERIAL AND KNEW WHAT KIND OF MOVIE IT SHOULD BE.
AND I KNEW- I DON'T KNOW WHY- BUT I JUST KNEW THAT DAVID WAS SOMEONE TO HOOK MY TRAIN UP TO.
FROM ALMOST THE DAY I MET HIM, I DIDN'T MAKE A MOVE WITHOUT HIM.
MAN, WHAT'S UP WITH ALL THESE EFFED UP PHONE CALLS?
WHAT DO THESE PEOPLE WANT?
THERE ARE PEOPLE AT THE STUDIOS WHOSE JOB IT IS TO COMB THE MAGAZINES AND JUST GRAB PROPERTIES OFF THE MARKET.
NO SHIT?
NONE.
WHAT THEY DO IS JUST BUY STUFF SO THAT NO ONE ELSE CAN HAVE IT.
THEY THROW YOU A COUPLE OF THOU, THEN THEY THROW YOUR BOOK ON A SHELF WITH EVERYTHING ELSE.

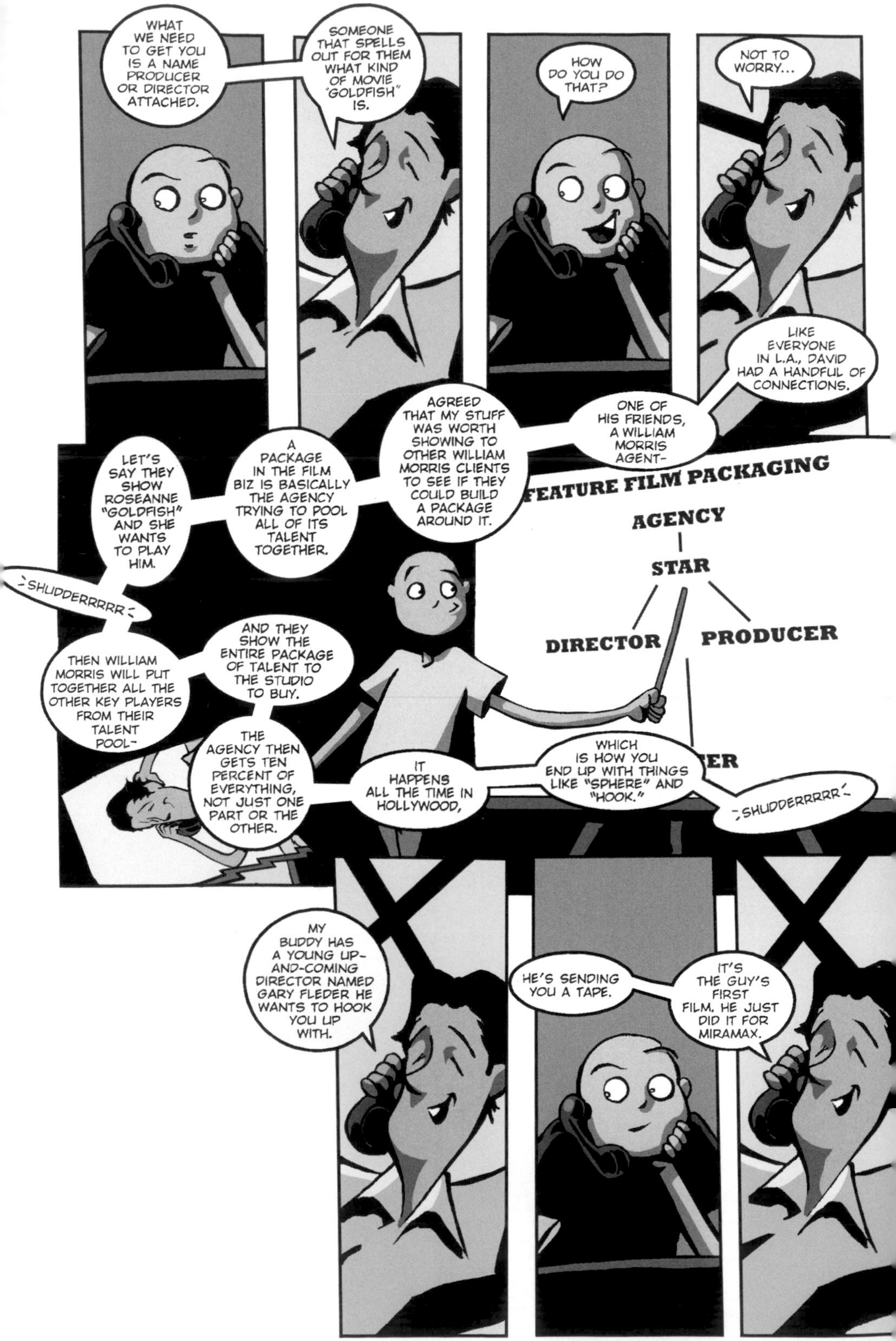
WHAT WE NEED TO GET YOU IS A NAME PRODUCER OR DIRECTOR ATTACHED.
SOMEONE THAT SPELLS OUT FOR THEM WHAT KIND OF MOVIE "GOLDFISH" IS.
HOW DO YOU DO THAT?
NOT TO WORRY...
LIKE EVERYONE IN L.A., DAVID HAD A HANDFUL OF CONNECTIONS.
ONE OF HIS FRIENDS, A WILLIAM MORRIS AGENT-
AGREED THAT MY STUFF WAS WORTH SHOWING TO OTHER WILLIAM MORRIS CLIENTS TO SEE IF THEY COULD BUILD A PACKAGE AROUND IT.
A PACKAGE IN THE FILM BIZ IS BASICALLY THE AGENCY TRYING TO POOL ALL OF ITS TALENT TOGETHER.
LET'S SAY THEY SHOW ROSEANNE "GOLDFISH" AND SHE WANTS TO PLAY HIM.
SHUDDERRRRR
THEN WILLIAM MORRIS WILL PUT TOGETHER ALL THE OTHER KEY PLAYERS FROM THEIR TALENT POOL-
AND THEY SHOW THE ENTIRE PACKAGE OF TALENT TO THE STUDIO TO BUY.
FEATURE FILM PACKAGING
AGENCY
STAR
DIRECTOR
PRODUCER
ER
THE AGENCY THEN GETS TEN PERCENT OF EVERYTHING, NOT JUST ONE PART OR THE OTHER.
IT HAPPENS ALL THE TIME IN HOLLYWOOD,
WHICH IS HOW YOU END UP WITH THINGS LIKE "SPHERE" AND "HOOK."
SHUDDERRRRR
MY BUDDY HAS A YOUNG UP-AND-COMING DIRECTOR NAMED GARY FLEDER HE WANTS TO HOOK YOU UP WITH.
HE'S SENDING YOU A TAPE.
IT'S THE GUY'S FIRST FILM. HE JUST DID IT FOR MIRAMAX.

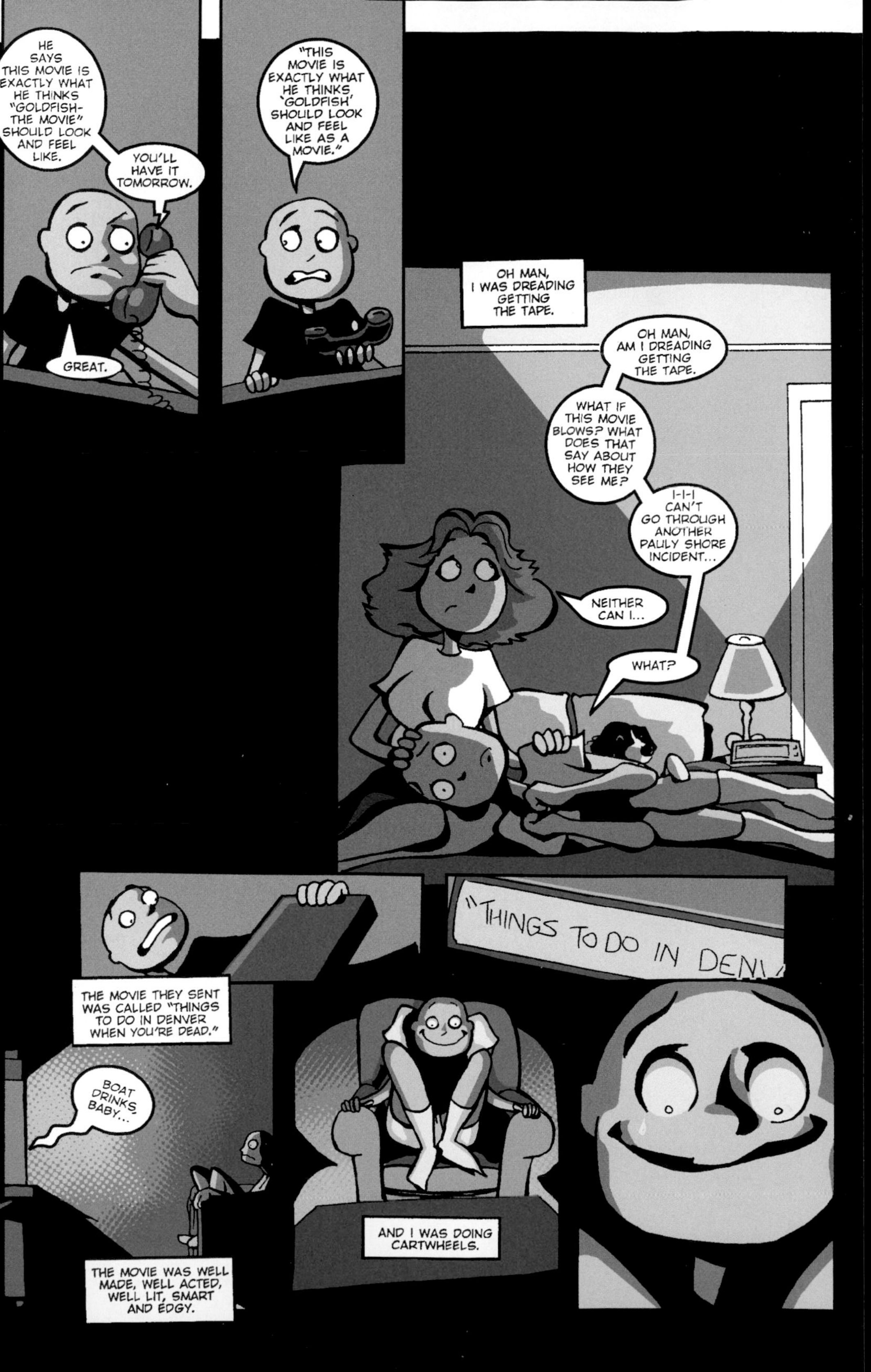
HE SAYS THIS MOVIE IS EXACTLY WHAT HE THINKS "GOLDFISH- THE MOVIE" SHOULD LOOK AND FEEL LIKE.
YOU'LL HAVE IT TOMORROW.
GREAT.
"THIS MOVIE IS EXACTLY WHAT HE THINKS, 'GOLDFISH' SHOULD LOOK AND FEEL LIKE AS A MOVIE."
OH MAN, I WAS DREADING GETTING THE TAPE.
OH MAN, AM I DREADING GETTING THE TAPE.
WHAT IF THIS MOVIE BLOWS? WHAT DOES THAT SAY ABOUT HOW THEY SEE ME?
I-I-I CAN'T GO THROUGH ANOTHER PAULY SHORE INCIDENT...
NEITHER CAN I...
WHAT?
"THINGS TO DO IN DEN
THE MOVIE THEY SENT WAS CALLED "THINGS TO DO IN DENVER WHEN YOU'RE DEAD."
BOAT DRINKS, BABY...
THE MOVIE WAS WELL MADE, WELL ACTED, WELL LIT, SMART AND EDGY.
AND I WAS DOING CARTWHEELS.

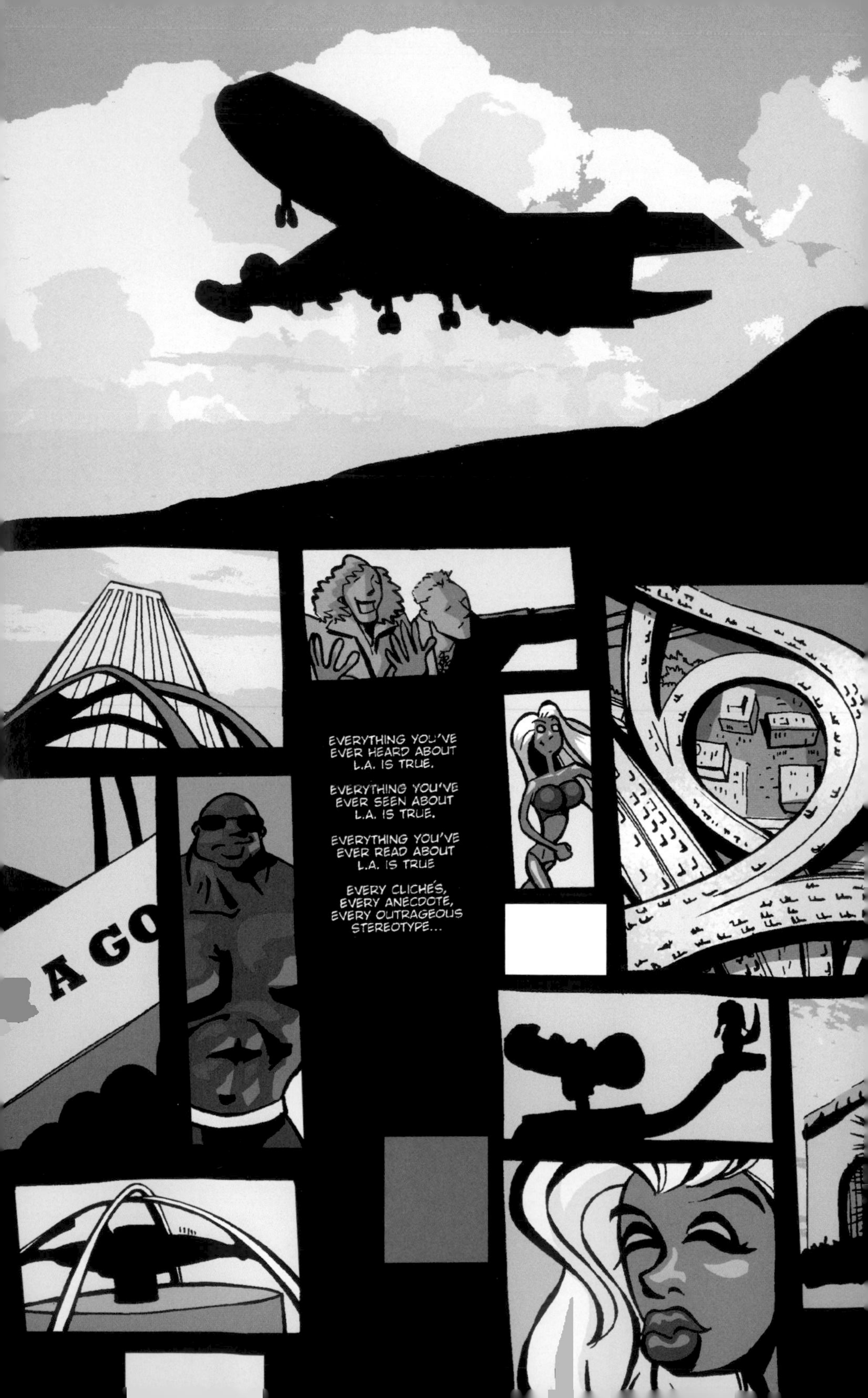
EVERYTHING YOU'VE EVER HEARD ABOUT L.A. IS TRUE.
EVERYTHING YOU'VE EVER SEEN ABOUT L.A. IS TRUE.
EVERYTHING YOU'VE EVER READ ABOUT L.A. IS TRUE
EVERY CLICHÉS, EVERY ANECDOTE, EVERY OUTRAGEOUS STEREOTYPE...
A GO

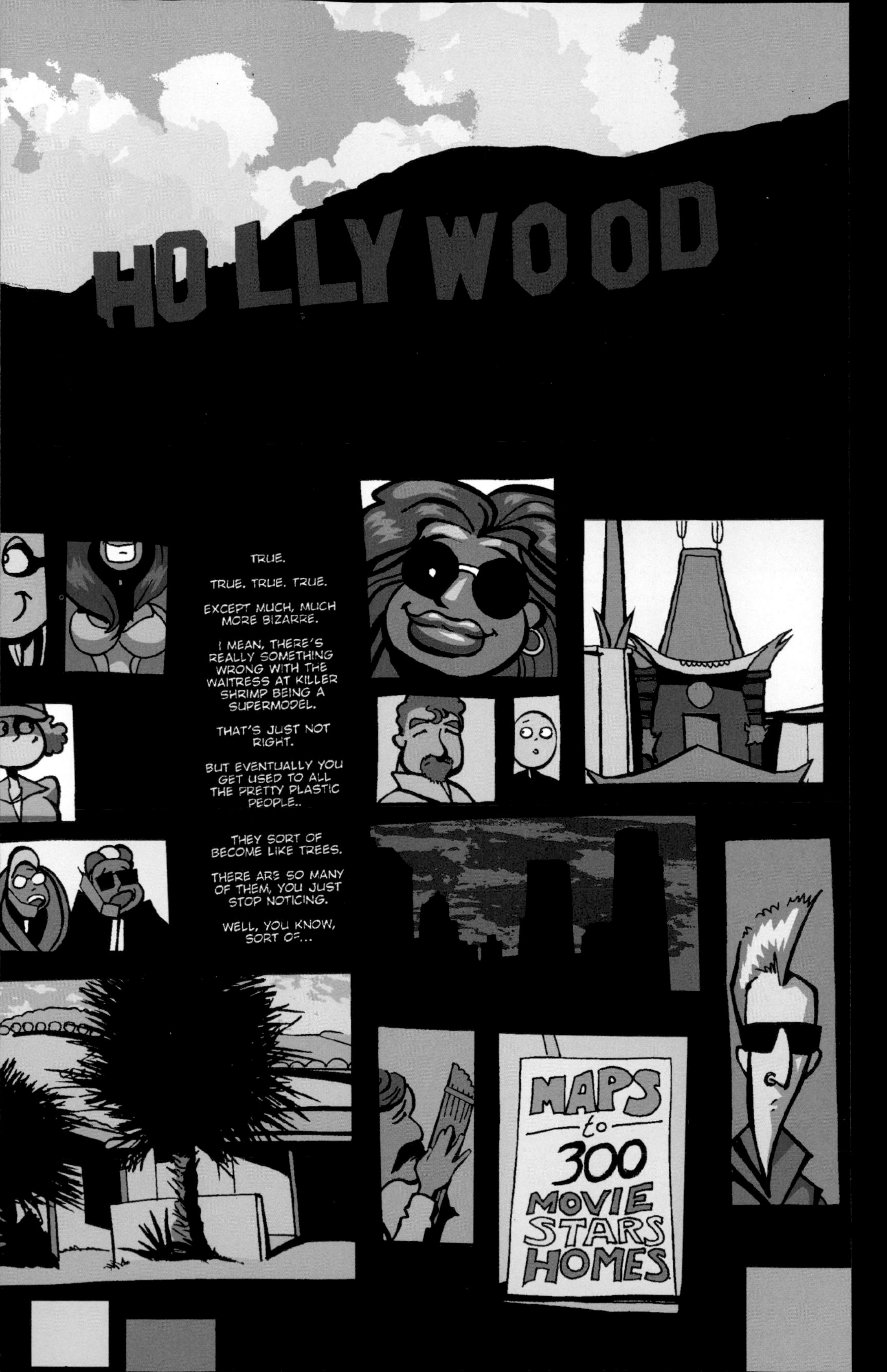
HOLLYWOOD
TRUE.
TRUE. TRUE. TRUE.
EXCEPT MUCH, MUCH MORE BIZARRE.
I MEAN, THERE'S REALLY SOMETHING WRONG WITH THE WAITRESS AT KILLER SHRIMP BEING A SUPERMODEL.
THAT'S JUST NOT RIGHT.
BUT EVENTUALLY YOU GET USED TO ALL THE PRETTY PLASTIC PEOPLE..
THEY SORT OF BECOME LIKE TREES.
THERE ARE SO MANY OF THEM, YOU JUST STOP NOTICING.
WELL, YOU KNOW, SORT OF...
MAPS to 300 MOVIE STARS HOMES

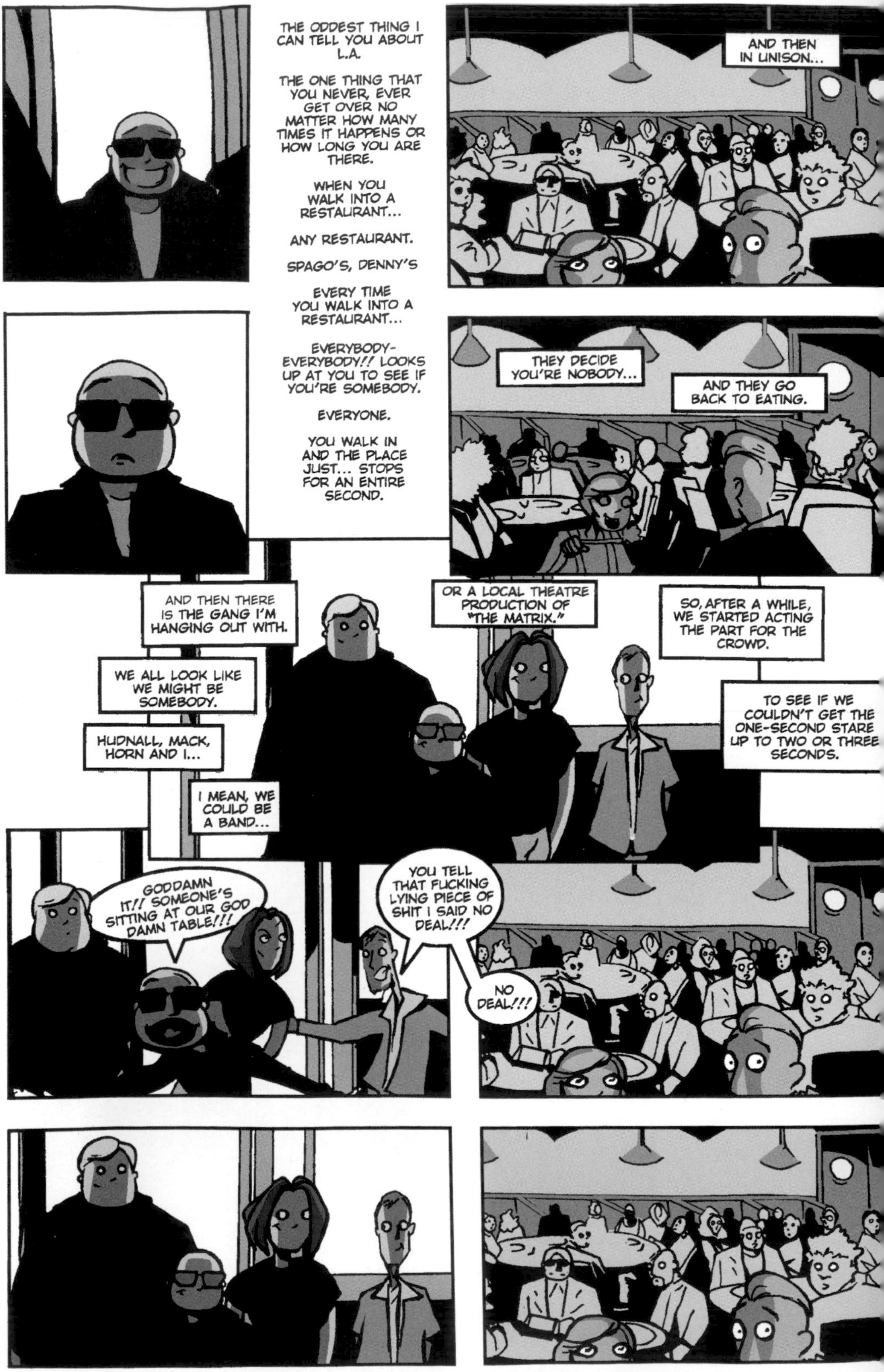

THE ODDEST THING I CAN TELL YOU ABOUT L.A.
THE ONE THING THAT YOU NEVER, EVER GET OVER NO MATTER HOW MANY TIMES IT HAPPENS OR HOW LONG YOU ARE THERE.
WHEN YOU WALK INTO A RESTAURANT...
ANY RESTAURANT.
SPAGO'S, DENNY'S
EVERY TIME YOU WALK INTO A RESTAURANT...
EVERYBODY- EVERYBODY!! LOOKS UP AT YOU TO SEE IF YOU'RE SOMEBODY.
EVERYONE.
YOU WALK IN AND THE PLACE JUST... STOPS FOR AN ENTIRE SECOND.
AND THEN IN UNISON...
THEY DECIDE YOU'RE NOBODY...
AND THEY GO BACK TO EATING.
AND THEN THERE IS THE GANG I'M HANGING OUT WITH.
WE ALL LOOK LIKE WE MIGHT BE SOMEBODY.
HUDNALL, MACK, HORN AND I...
I MEAN, WE COULD BE A BAND...
OR A LOCAL THEATRE PRODUCTION OF "THE MATRIX."
SO, AFTER A WHILE, WE STARTED ACTING THE PART FOR THE CROWD.
TO SEE IF WE COULDN'T GET THE ONE-SECOND STARE UP TO TWO OR THREE SECONDS.
GODDAMN IT!! SOMEONE'S SITTING AT OUR GOD DAMN TABLE!!!
YOU TELL THAT FUCKING LYING PIECE OF SHIT I SAID NO DEAL!!!
NO DEAL!!!

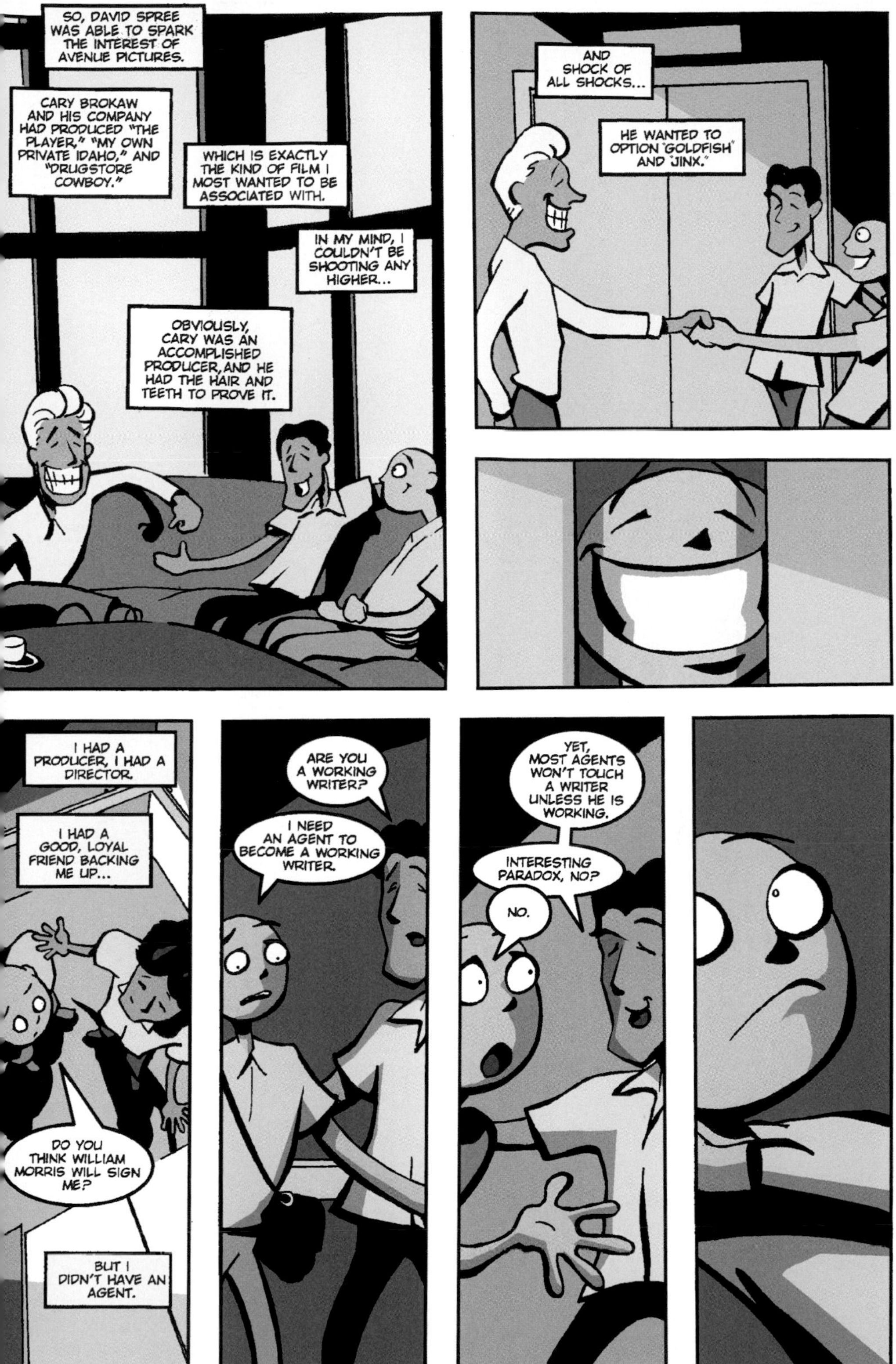
SO, DAVID SPREE WAS ABLE TO SPARK THE INTEREST OF AVENUE PICTURES.
CARY BROKAW AND HIS COMPANY HAD PRODUCED "THE PLAYER," "MY OWN PRIVATE IDAHO," AND "DRUGSTORE COWBOY."
WHICH IS EXACTLY THE KIND OF FILM I MOST WANTED TO BE ASSOCIATED WITH.
IN MY MIND, I COULDN'T BE SHOOTING ANY HIGHER...
OBVIOUSLY, CARY WAS AN ACCOMPLISHED PRODUCER, AND HE HAD THE HAIR AND TEETH TO PROVE IT.
AND SHOCK OF ALL SHOCKS...
HE WANTED TO OPTION "GOLDFISH" AND "JINX."
I HAD A PRODUCER, I HAD A DIRECTOR.
I HAD A GOOD, LOYAL FRIEND BACKING ME UP...
DO YOU THINK WILLIAM MORRIS WILL SIGN ME?
BUT I DIDN'T HAVE AN AGENT.
ARE YOU A WORKING WRITER?
I NEED AN AGENT TO BECOME A WORKING WRITER.
YET, MOST AGENTS WON'T TOUCH A WRITER UNLESS HE IS WORKING.
INTERESTING PARADOX, NO?
NO.

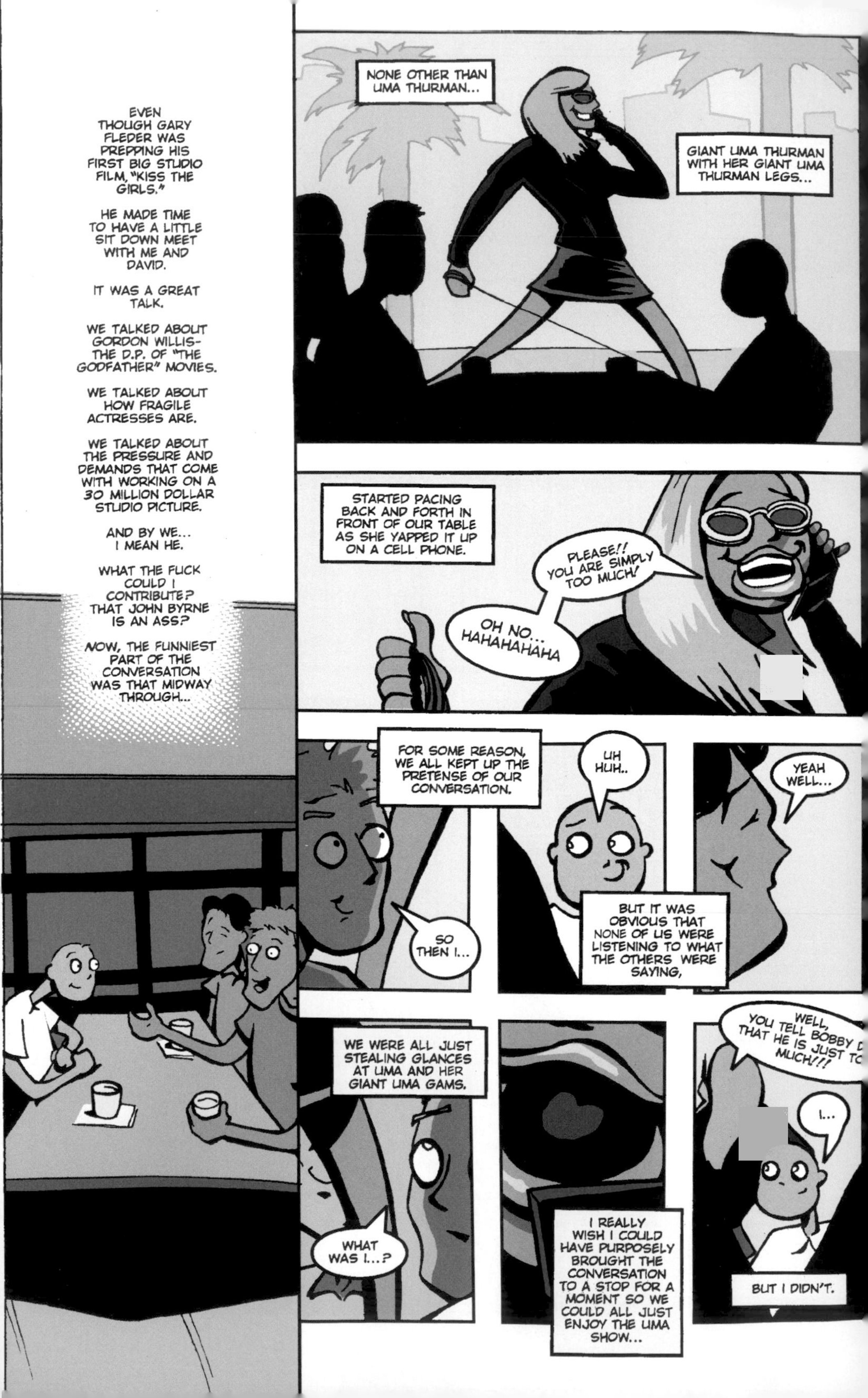
EVEN THOUGH GARY FLEDER WAS PREPPING HIS FIRST BIG STUDIO FILM, "KISS THE GIRLS."
HE MADE TIME TO HAVE A LITTLE SIT DOWN MEET WITH ME AND DAVID.
IT WAS A GREAT TALK.
WE TALKED ABOUT GORDON WILLIS-THE D.P. OF "THE GODFATHER" MOVIES.
WE TALKED ABOUT HOW FRAGILE ACTRESSES ARE.
WE TALKED ABOUT THE PRESSURE AND DEMANDS THAT COME WITH WORKING ON A 30 MILLION DOLLAR STUDIO PICTURE.
AND BY WE... I MEAN HE.
WHAT THE FUCK COULD I CONTRIBUTE? THAT JOHN BYRNE IS AN ASS?
NOW, THE FUNNIEST PART OF THE CONVERSATION WAS THAT MIDWAY THROUGH...
NONE OTHER THAN UMA THURMAN...
GIANT UMA THURMAN WITH HER GIANT UMA THURMAN LEGS...
STARTED PACING BACK AND FORTH IN FRONT OF OUR TABLE AS SHE YAPPED IT UP ON A CELL PHONE.
PLEASE!! YOU ARE SIMPLY TOO MUCH!
OH NO... HAHAHAHAHA
FOR SOME REASON, WE ALL KEPT UP THE PRETENSE OF OUR CONVERSATION.
SO THEN I...
UH HUH..
BUT IT WAS OBVIOUS THAT NONE OF US WERE LISTENING TO WHAT THE OTHERS WERE SAYING,
YEAH WELL...
WE WERE ALL JUST STEALING GLANCES AT UMA AND HER GIANT UMA GAMS.
WHAT WAS I...?
I REALLY WISH I COULD HAVE PURPOSELY BROUGHT THE CONVERSATION TO A STOP FOR A MOMENT SO WE COULD ALL JUST ENJOY THE UMA SHOW...
WELL, YOU TELL BOBBY D THAT HE IS JUST TO MUCH!!!
I...
BUT I DIDN'T.

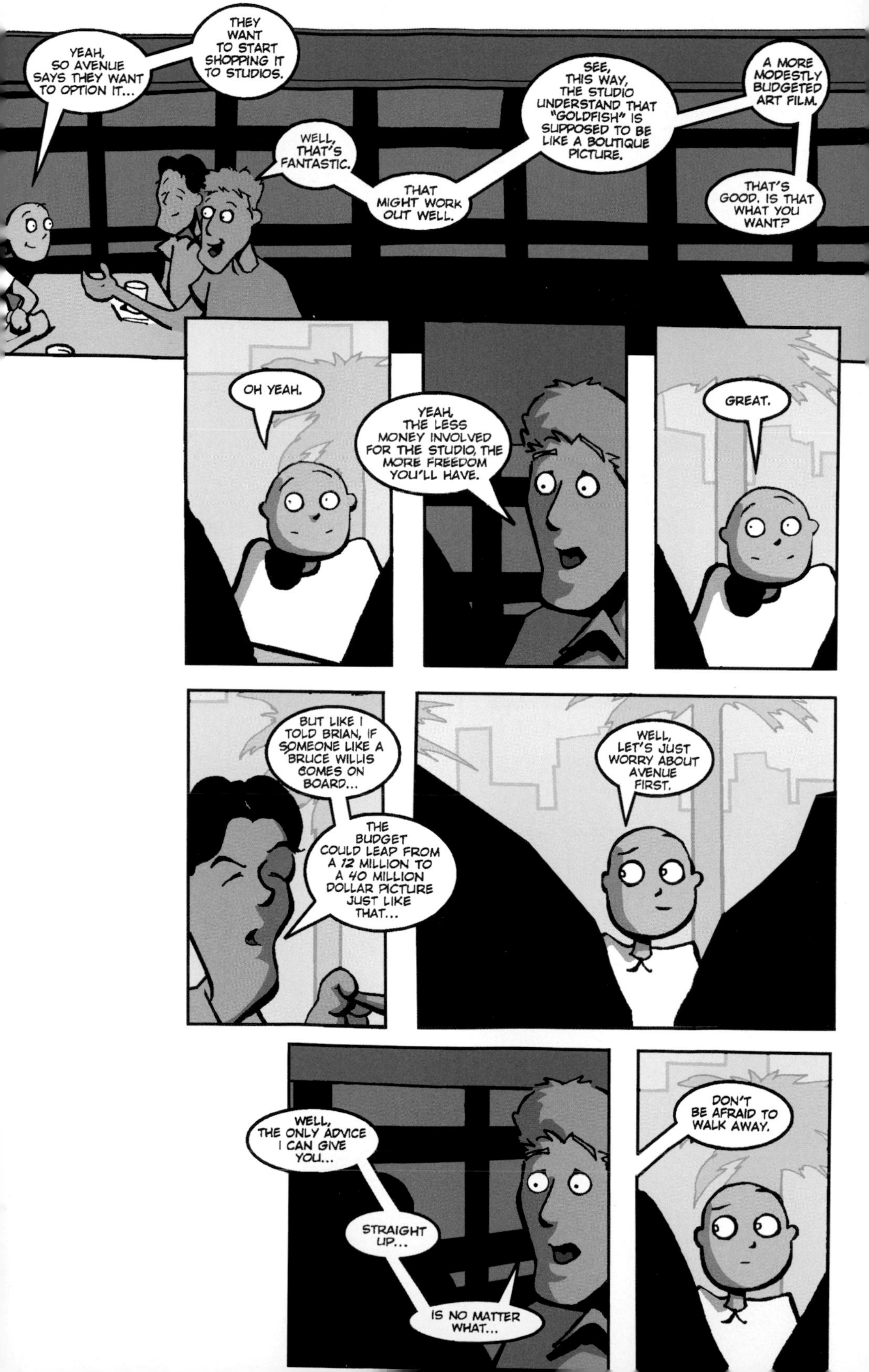
YEAH, SO AVENUE SAYS THEY WANT TO OPTION IT...
THEY WANT TO START SHOPPING IT TO STUDIOS.
WELL, THAT'S FANTASTIC.
THAT MIGHT WORK OUT WELL.
SEE, THIS WAY, THE STUDIO UNDERSTAND THAT "GOLDFISH" IS SUPPOSED TO BE LIKE A BOUTIQUE PICTURE.
A MORE MODESTLY BUDGETED ART FILM.
THAT'S GOOD. IS THAT WHAT YOU WANT?
OH YEAH.
YEAH, THE LESS MONEY INVOLVED FOR THE STUDIO, THE MORE FREEDOM YOU'LL HAVE.
GREAT.
BUT LIKE I TOLD BRIAN, IF SOMEONE LIKE A BRUCE WILLIS COMES ON BOARD...
THE BUDGET COULD LEAP FROM A 12 MILLION TO A 40 MILLION DOLLAR PICTURE JUST LIKE THAT...
WELL, LET'S JUST WORRY ABOUT AVENUE FIRST.
WELL, THE ONLY ADVICE I CAN GIVE YOU...
STRAIGHT UP...
IS NO MATTER WHAT...
DON'T BE AFRAID TO WALK AWAY.

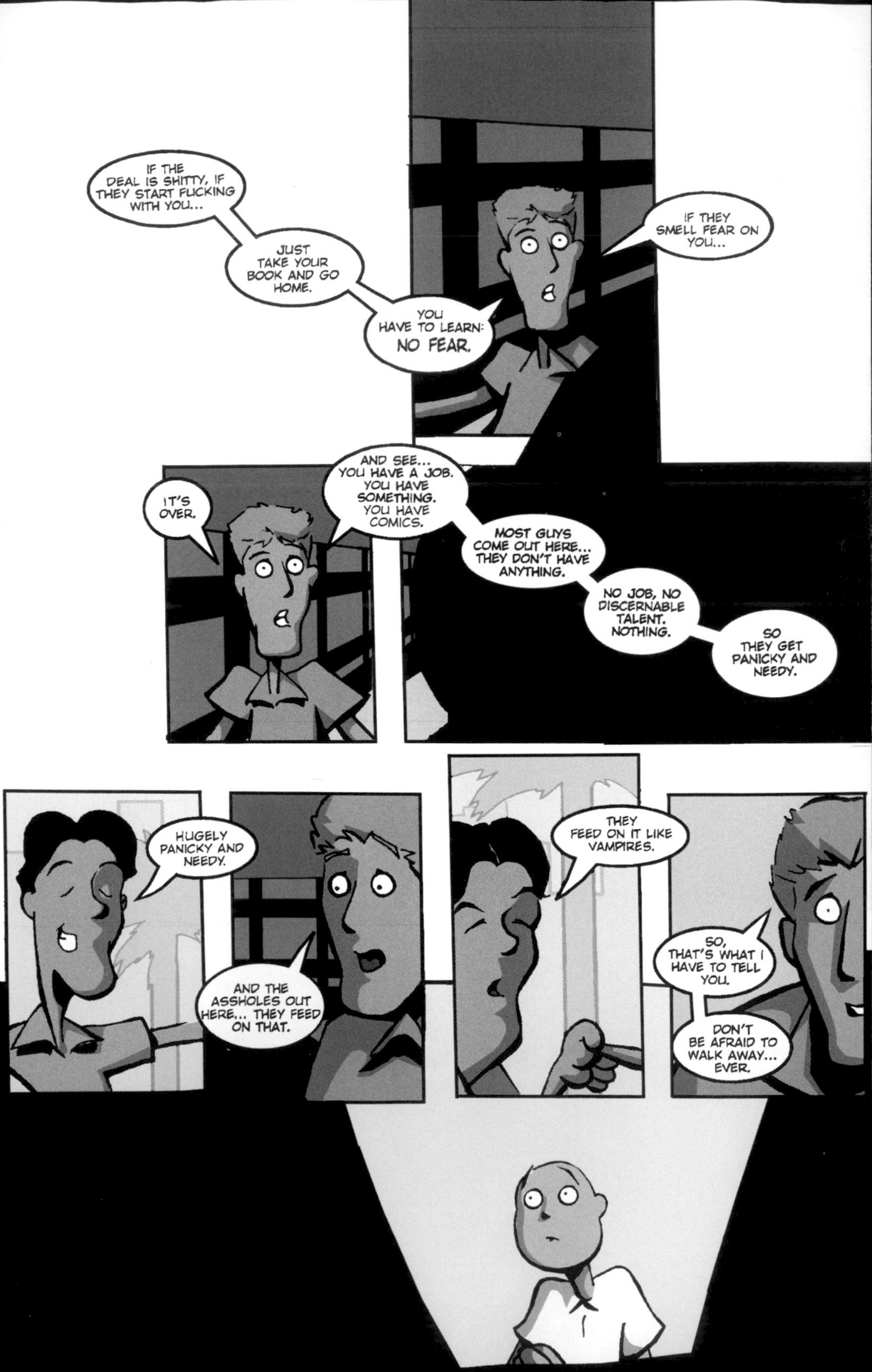
IF THE DEAL IS SHITTY, IF THEY START FUCKING WITH YOU...
JUST TAKE YOUR BOOK AND GO HOME.
YOU HAVE TO LEARN: NO FEAR.
IF THEY SMELL FEAR ON YOU...
IT'S OVER.
AND SEE... YOU HAVE A JOB. YOU HAVE SOMETHING. YOU HAVE COMICS.
MOST GUYS COME OUT HERE... THEY DON'T HAVE ANYTHING.
NO JOB, NO DISCERNABLE TALENT. NOTHING.
SO THEY GET PANICKY AND NEEDY.
HUGELY PANICKY AND NEEDY.
AND THE ASSHOLES OUT HERE... THEY FEED ON THAT.
THEY FEED ON IT LIKE VAMPIRES.
SO, THAT'S WHAT I HAVE TO TELL YOU.
DON'T BE AFRAID TO WALK AWAY... EVER.

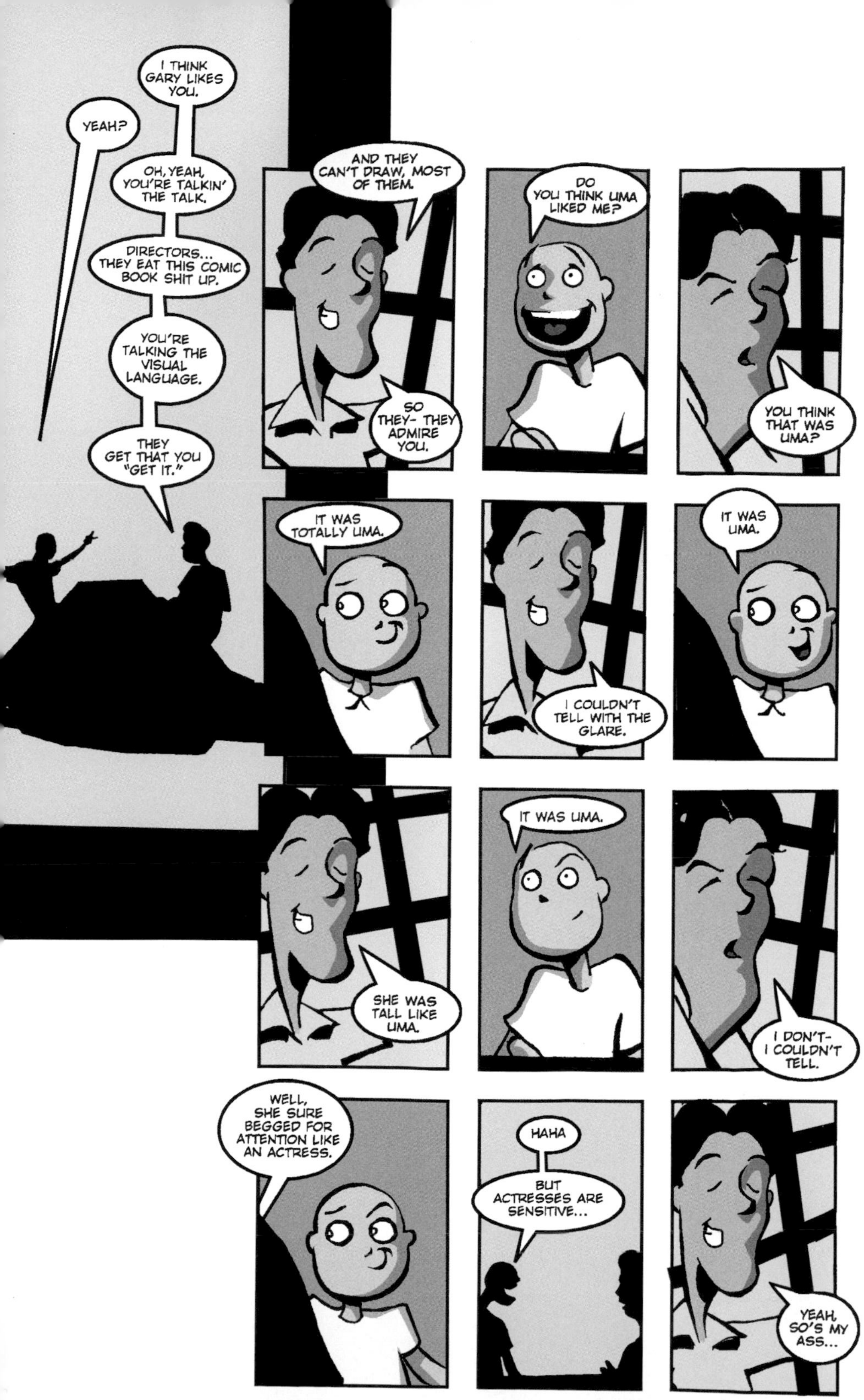
I THINK GARY LIKES YOU.
YEAH?
OH, YEAH, YOU'RE TALKIN' THE TALK.
DIRECTORS... THEY EAT THIS COMIC BOOK SHIT UP.
YOU'RE TALKING THE VISUAL LANGUAGE.
THEY GET THAT YOU "GET IT."
AND THEY CAN'T DRAW, MOST OF THEM.
SO THEY- THEY ADMIRE YOU.
DO YOU THINK UMA LIKED ME?
YOU THINK THAT WAS UMA?
IT WAS TOTALLY UMA.
I COULDN'T TELL WITH THE GLARE.
IT WAS UMA.
SHE WAS TALL LIKE UMA.
IT WAS UMA.
I DON'T- I COULDN'T TELL.
WELL, SHE SURE BEGGED FOR ATTENTION LIKE AN ACTRESS.
HAHA
BUT ACTRESSES ARE SENSITIVE...
YEAH, SO'S MY ASS...

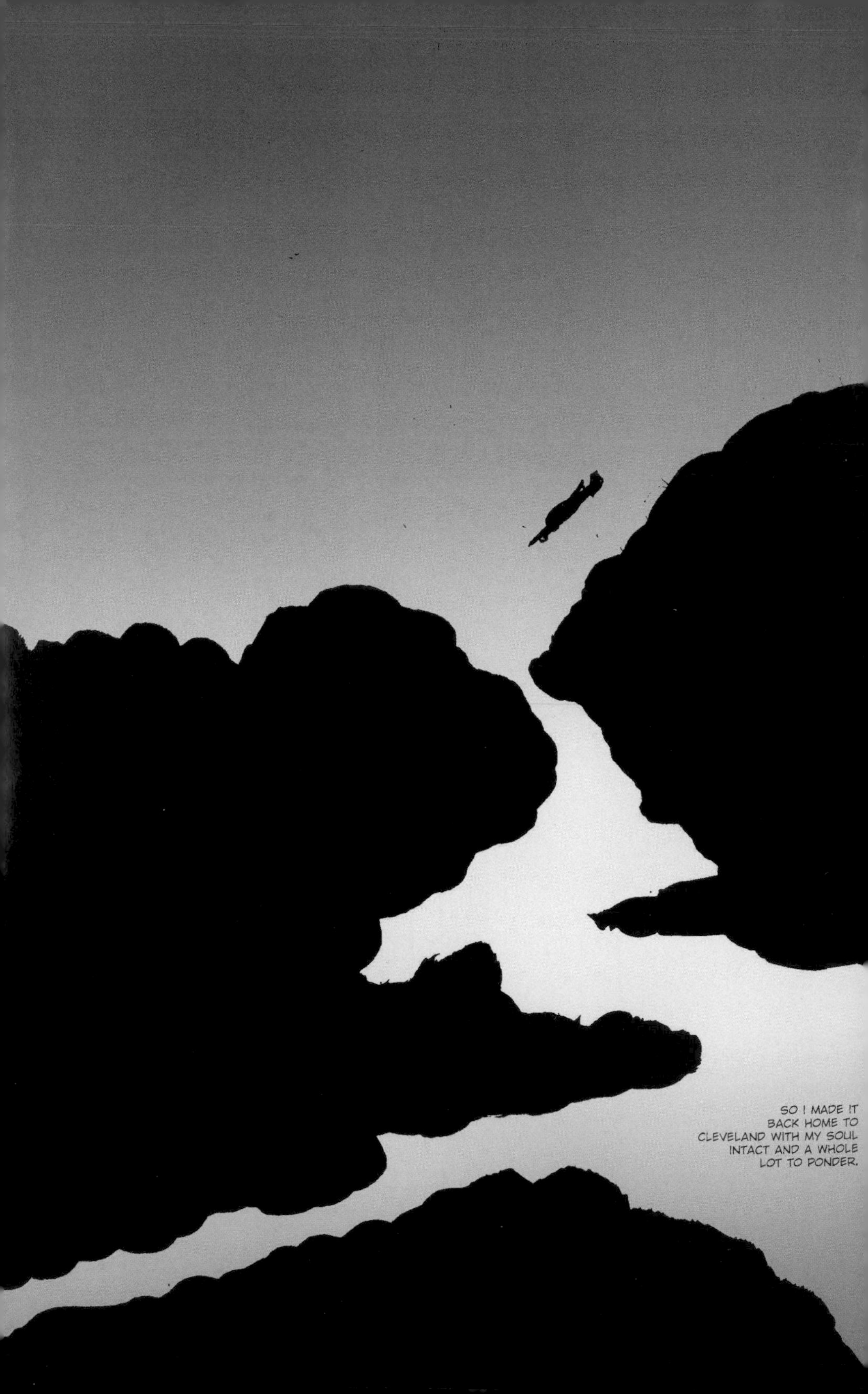
SO I MADE IT BACK HOME TO CLEVELAND WITH MY SOUL INTACT AND A WHOLE LOT TO PONDER.

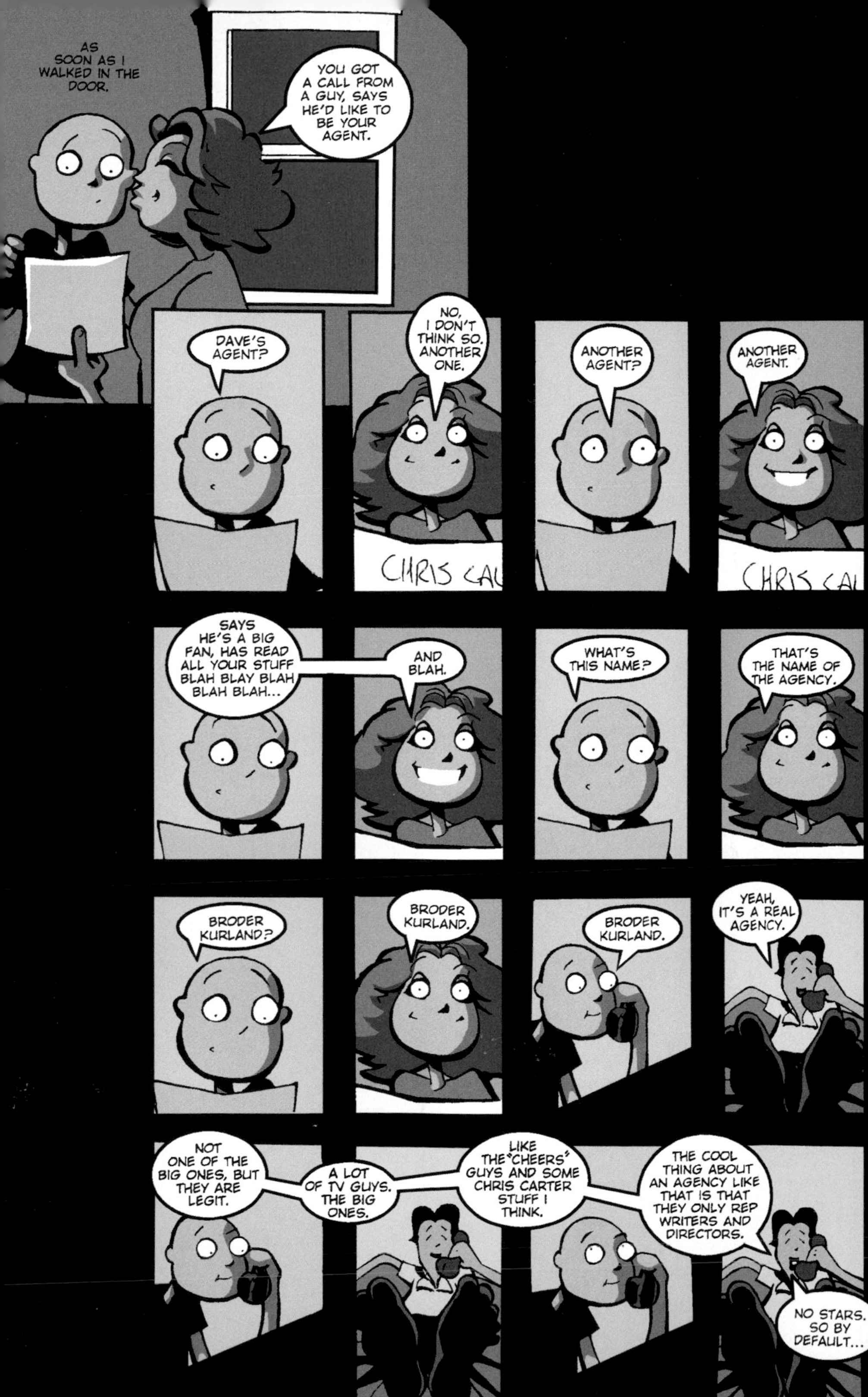
AS SOON AS I WALKED IN THE DOOR.
YOU GOT A CALL FROM A GUY, SAYS HE'D LIKE TO BE YOUR AGENT.
DAVE'S AGENT?
NO, I DON'T THINK SO. ANOTHER ONE.
CHRIS CAL
ANOTHER AGENT?
ANOTHER AGENT.
CHRIS CAL
SAYS HE'S A BIG FAN, HAS READ ALL YOUR STUFF BLAH BLAY BLAH BLAH BLAH...
AND BLAH.
WHAT'S THIS NAME?
THAT'S THE NAME OF THE AGENCY.
BRODER KURLAND?
BRODER KURLAND.
BRODER KURLAND.
YEAH, IT'S A REAL AGENCY.
NOT ONE OF THE BIG ONES, BUT THEY ARE LEGIT.
A LOT OF TV GUYS. THE BIG ONES.
LIKE THE "CHEERS" GUYS AND SOME CHRIS CARTER STUFF I THINK.
THE COOL THING ABOUT AN AGENCY LIKE THAT IS THAT THEY ONLY REP WRITERS AND DIRECTORS.
NO STARS. SO BY DEFAULT...

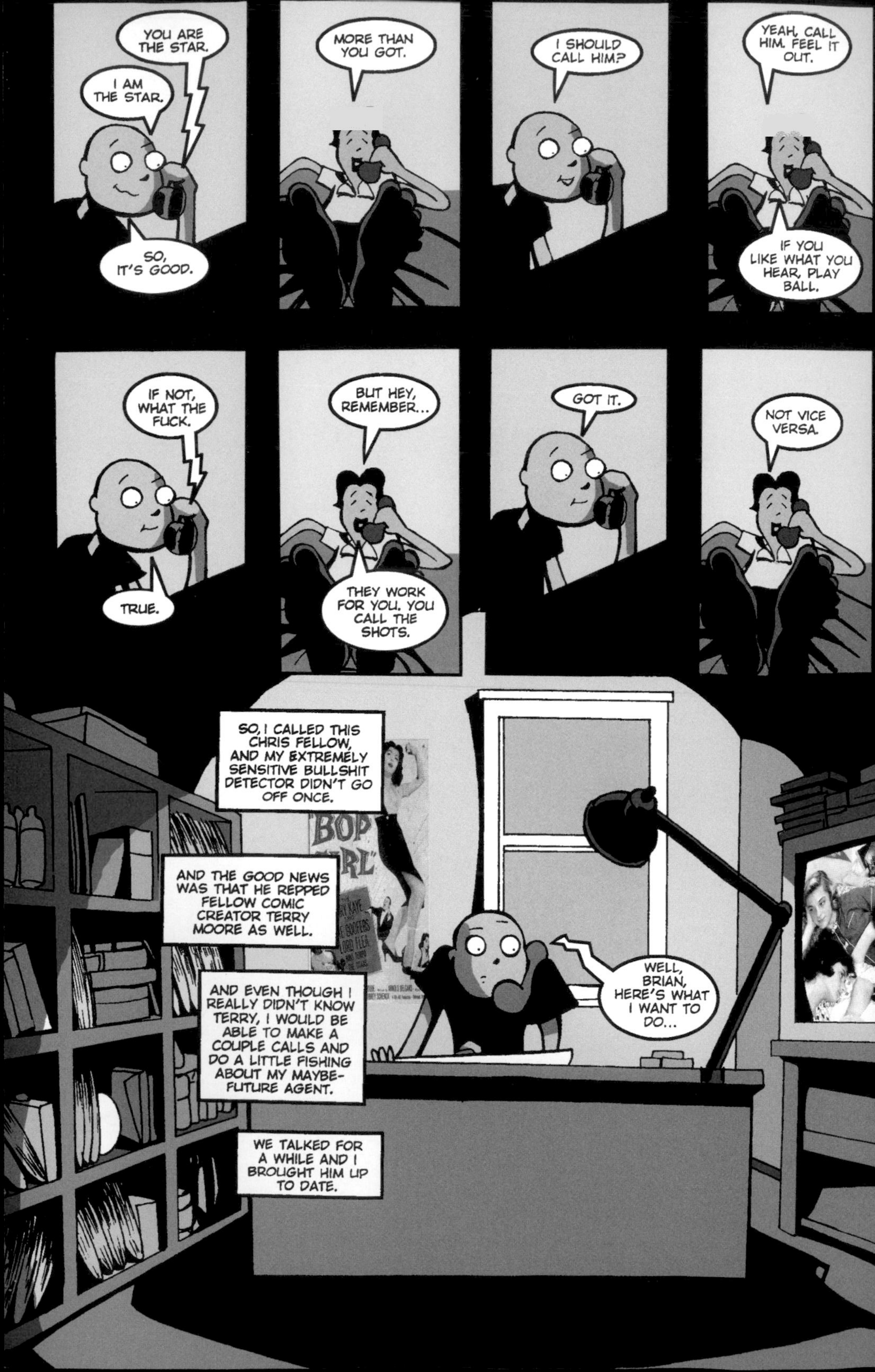
I AM THE STAR.
YOU ARE THE STAR.
SO, IT'S GOOD.
MORE THAN YOU GOT.
I SHOULD CALL HIM?
YEAH, CALL HIM. FEEL IT OUT.
IF YOU LIKE WHAT YOU HEAR, PLAY BALL.
IF NOT, WHAT THE FUCK.
TRUE.
BUT HEY, REMEMBER...
THEY WORK FOR YOU. YOU CALL THE SHOTS.
GOT IT.
NOT VICE VERSA.
SO, I CALLED THIS CHRIS FELLOW, AND MY EXTREMELY SENSITIVE BULLSHIT DETECTOR DIDN'T GO OFF ONCE.
AND THE GOOD NEWS WAS THAT HE REPPED FELLOW COMIC CREATOR TERRY MOORE AS WELL.
AND EVEN THOUGH I REALLY DIDN'T KNOW TERRY, I WOULD BE ABLE TO MAKE A COUPLE CALLS AND DO A LITTLE FISHING ABOUT MY MAYBE-FUTURE AGENT.
WE TALKED FOR A WHILE AND I BROUGHT HIM UP TO DATE.
WELL, BRIAN, HERE'S WHAT I WANT TO DO...

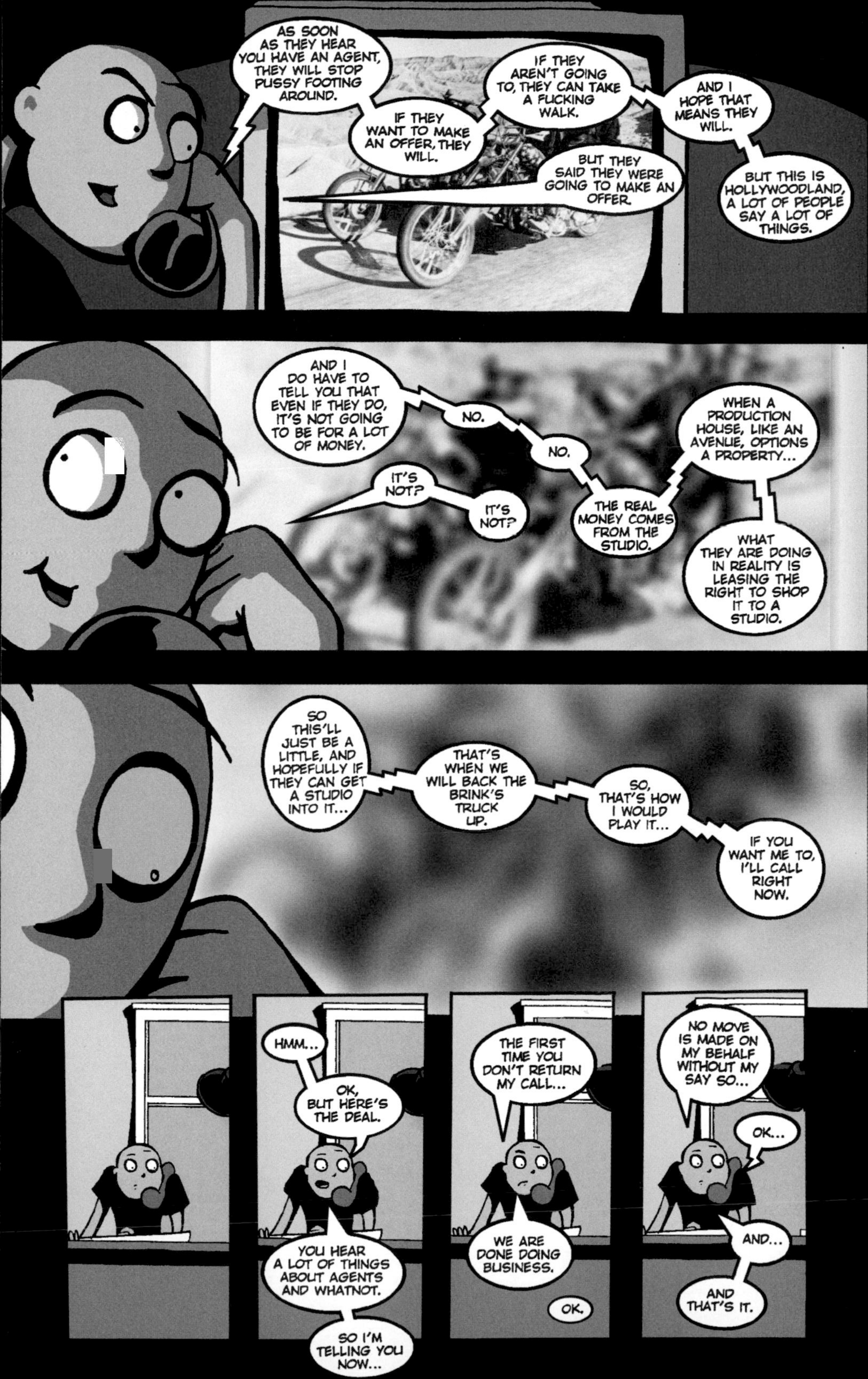
AS SOON AS THEY HEAR YOU HAVE AN AGENT, THEY WILL STOP PUSSY FOOTING AROUND.
IF THEY WANT TO MAKE AN OFFER, THEY WILL.
IF THEY AREN'T GOING TO, THEY CAN TAKE A FUCKING WALK.
AND I HOPE THAT MEANS THEY WILL.
BUT THEY SAID THEY WERE GOING TO MAKE AN OFFER.
BUT THIS IS HOLLYWOODLAND, A LOT OF PEOPLE SAY A LOT OF THINGS.
AND I DO HAVE TO TELL YOU THAT EVEN IF THEY DO, IT'S NOT GOING TO BE FOR A LOT OF MONEY.
IT'S NOT?
NO.
IT'S NOT?
NO.
WHEN A PRODUCTION HOUSE, LIKE AN AVENUE, OPTIONS A PROPERTY...
THE REAL MONEY COMES FROM THE STUDIO.
WHAT THEY ARE DOING IN REALITY IS LEASING THE RIGHT TO SHOP IT TO A STUDIO.
SO THIS'LL JUST BE A LITTLE, AND HOPEFULLY IF THEY CAN GET A STUDIO INTO IT...
THAT'S WHEN WE WILL BACK THE BRINK'S TRUCK UP.
SO, THAT'S HOW I WOULD PLAY IT...
IF YOU WANT ME TO, I'LL CALL RIGHT NOW.
HMM...
OK, BUT HERE'S THE DEAL.
YOU HEAR A LOT OF THINGS ABOUT AGENTS AND WHATNOT.
SO I'M TELLING YOU NOW...
THE FIRST TIME YOU DON'T RETURN MY CALL...
WE ARE DONE DOING BUSINESS.
OK.
NO MOVE IS MADE ON MY BEHALF WITHOUT MY SAY SO...
OK...
AND...
AND THAT'S IT.

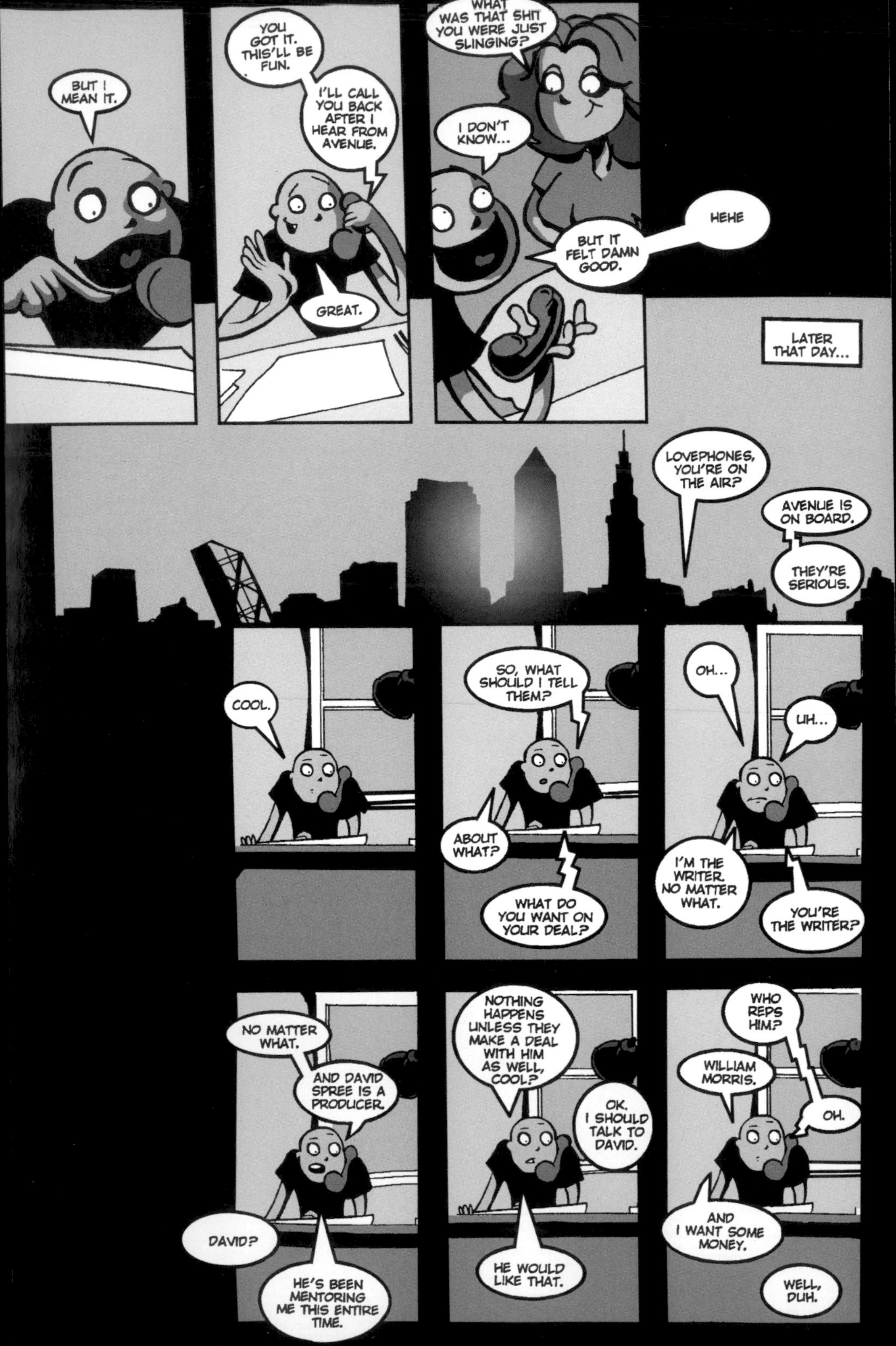
BUT I MEAN IT.
YOU GOT IT. THIS'LL BE FUN.
I'LL CALL YOU BACK AFTER I HEAR FROM AVENUE.
GREAT.
WHAT WAS THAT SHIT YOU WERE JUST SLINGING?
I DON'T KNOW...
BUT IT FELT DAMN GOOD.
HEHE
LATER THAT DAY...
LOVEPHONES, YOU'RE ON THE AIR?
AVENUE IS ON BOARD.
THEY'RE SERIOUS.
COOL.
SO, WHAT SHOULD I TELL THEM?
ABOUT WHAT?
WHAT DO YOU WANT ON YOUR DEAL?
OH...
UH...
I'M THE WRITER. NO MATTER WHAT.
YOU'RE THE WRITER?
NO MATTER WHAT.
AND DAVID SPREE IS A PRODUCER.
DAVID?
HE'S BEEN MENTORING ME THIS ENTIRE TIME.
NOTHING HAPPENS UNLESS THEY MAKE A DEAL WITH HIM AS WELL, COOL?
OK. I SHOULD TALK TO DAVID.
HE WOULD LIKE THAT.
WHO REPS HIM?
WILLIAM MORRIS.
OH.
AND I WANT SOME MONEY.
WELL, DUH.

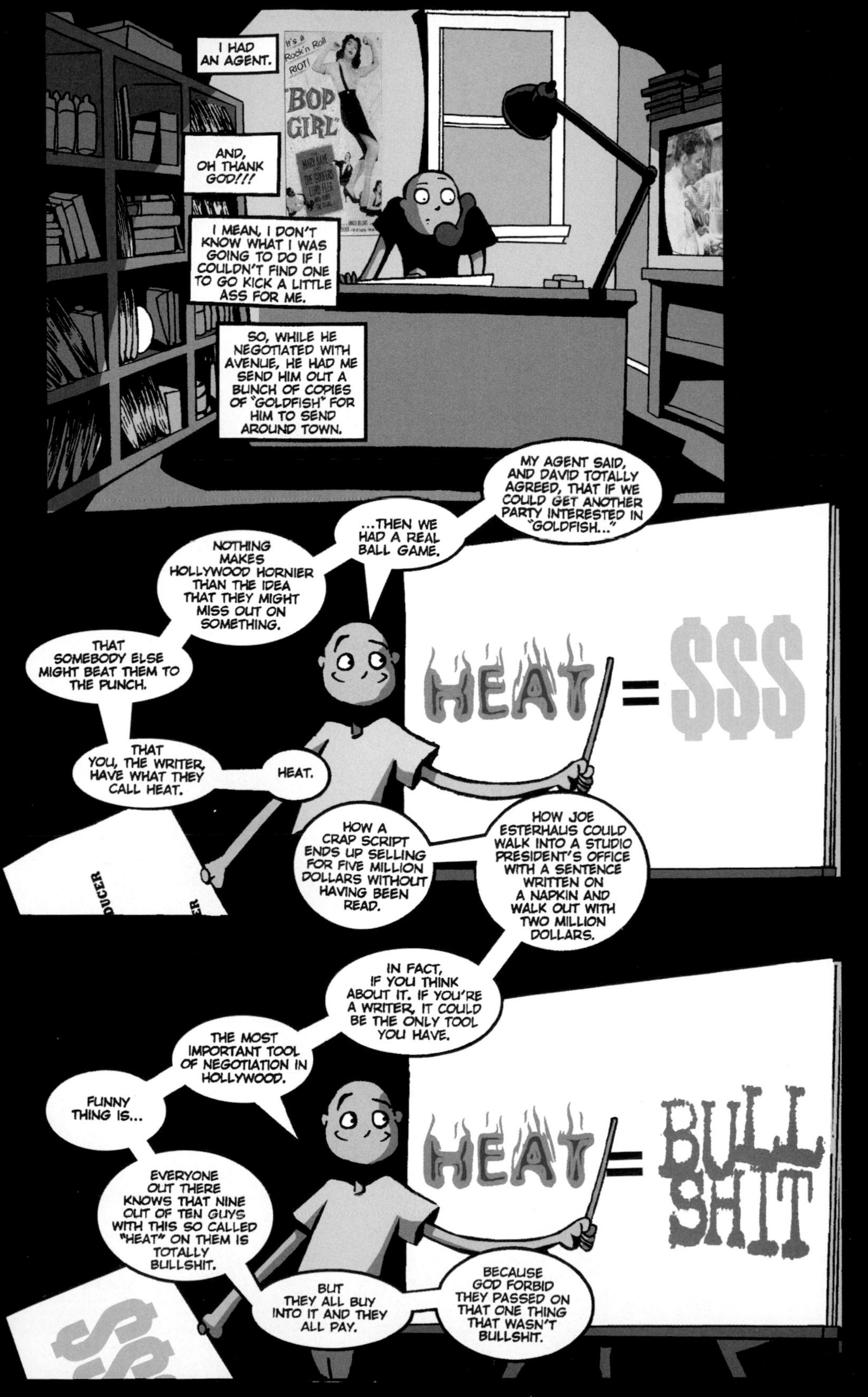
I HAD AN AGENT.
AND, OH THANK GOD!!!
I MEAN, I DON'T KNOW WHAT I WAS GOING TO DO IF I COULDN'T FIND ONE TO GO KICK A LITTLE ASS FOR ME.
SO, WHILE HE NEGOTIATED WITH AVENUE, HE HAD ME SEND HIM OUT A BUNCH OF COPIES OF "GOLDFISH" FOR HIM TO SEND AROUND TOWN.
It's a Rock'n Roll RIOT!
"BOP GIRL"
MY AGENT SAID, AND DAVID TOTALLY AGREED, THAT IF WE COULD GET ANOTHER PARTY INTERESTED IN "GOLDFISH..."
...THEN WE HAD A REAL BALL GAME.
NOTHING MAKES HOLLYWOOD HORNIER THAN THE IDEA THAT THEY MIGHT MISS OUT ON SOMETHING.
THAT SOMEBODY ELSE MIGHT BEAT THEM TO THE PUNCH.
THAT YOU, THE WRITER, HAVE WHAT THEY CALL HEAT.
HEAT.
HEAT = $$$
HOW A CRAP SCRIPT ENDS UP SELLING FOR FIVE MILLION DOLLARS WITHOUT HAVING BEEN READ.
HOW JOE ESTERHAUS COULD WALK INTO A STUDIO PRESIDENT'S OFFICE WITH A SENTENCE WRITTEN ON A NAPKIN AND WALK OUT WITH TWO MILLION DOLLARS.
IN FACT, IF YOU THINK ABOUT IT. IF YOU'RE A WRITER, IT COULD BE THE ONLY TOOL YOU HAVE.
THE MOST IMPORTANT TOOL OF NEGOTIATION IN HOLLYWOOD.
FUNNY THING IS...
HEAT = BULL SHIT
EVERYONE OUT THERE KNOWS THAT NINE OUT OF TEN GUYS WITH THIS SO CALLED "HEAT" ON THEM IS TOTALLY BULLSHIT.
BUT THEY ALL BUY INTO IT AND THEY ALL PAY.
BECAUSE GOD FORBID THEY PASSED ON THAT ONE THING THAT WASN'T BULLSHIT.

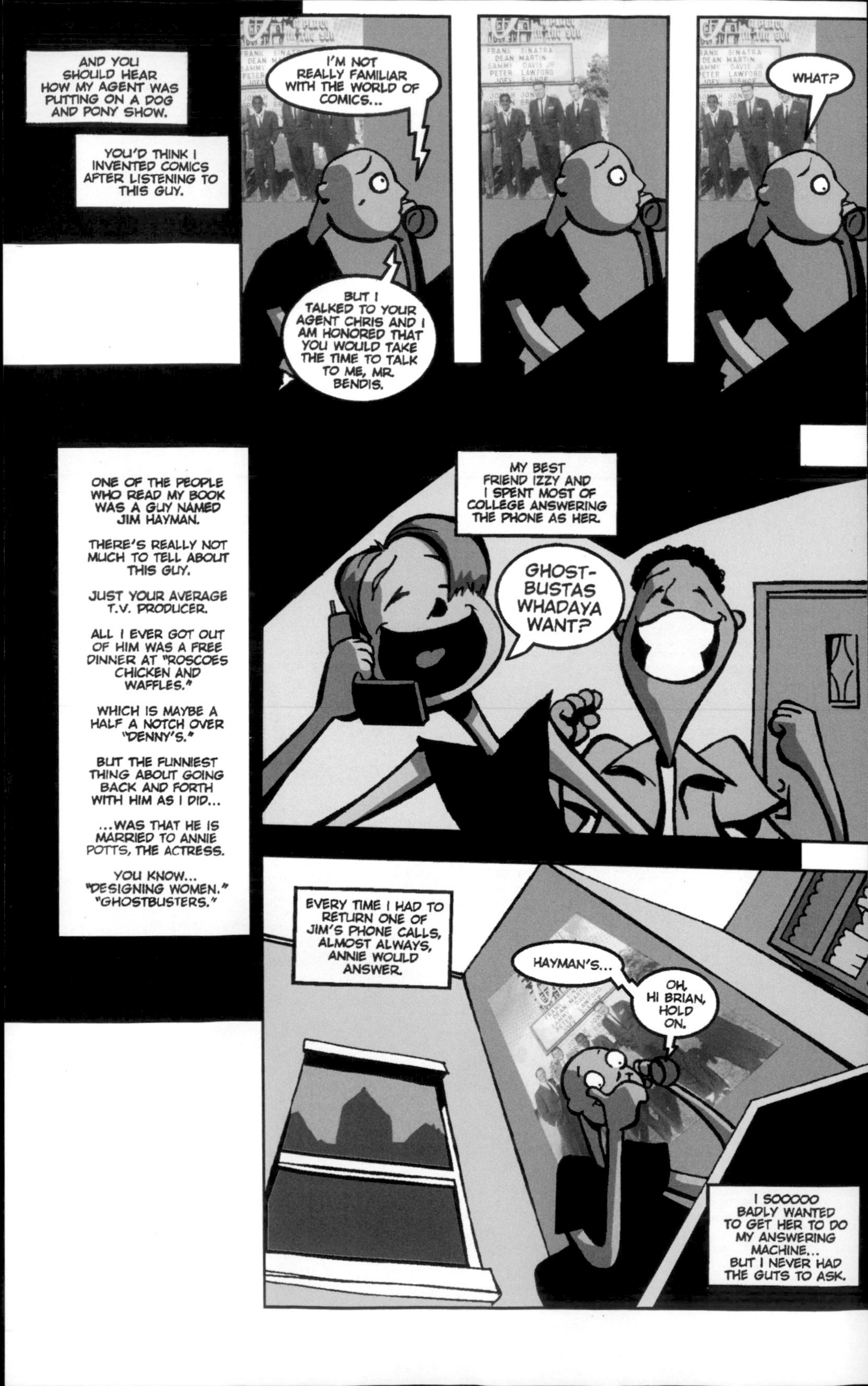
AND YOU SHOULD HEAR HOW MY AGENT WAS PUTTING ON A DOG AND PONY SHOW.
YOU'D THINK I INVENTED COMICS AFTER LISTENING TO THIS GUY.
I'M NOT REALLY FAMILIAR WITH THE WORLD OF COMICS...
BUT I TALKED TO YOUR AGENT CHRIS AND I AM HONORED THAT YOU WOULD TAKE THE TIME TO TALK TO ME, MR. BENDIS.
FRANK SINATRA
DEAN MARTIN
SAMMY DAVIS JR
PETER LAWFORD
JOEY BISHOP
WHAT?
ONE OF THE PEOPLE WHO READ MY BOOK WAS A GUY NAMED JIM HAYMAN.
THERE'S REALLY NOT MUCH TO TELL ABOUT THIS GUY.
JUST YOUR AVERAGE T.V. PRODUCER.
ALL I EVER GOT OUT OF HIM WAS A FREE DINNER AT "ROSCOES CHICKEN AND WAFFLES."
WHICH IS MAYBE A HALF A NOTCH OVER "DENNY'S."
BUT THE FUNNIEST THING ABOUT GOING BACK AND FORTH WITH HIM AS I DID...
...WAS THAT HE IS MARRIED TO ANNIE POTTS, THE ACTRESS.
YOU KNOW... "DESIGNING WOMEN." "GHOSTBUSTERS."
MY BEST FRIEND IZZY AND I SPENT MOST OF COLLEGE ANSWERING THE PHONE AS HER.
GHOST-BUSTAS WHADAYA WANT?
EVERY TIME I HAD TO RETURN ONE OF JIM'S PHONE CALLS, ALMOST ALWAYS, ANNIE WOULD ANSWER.
HAYMAN'S...
OH, HI BRIAN, HOLD ON.
I SOOOOO BADLY WANTED TO GET HER TO DO MY ANSWERING MACHINE... BUT I NEVER HAD THE GUTS TO ASK.

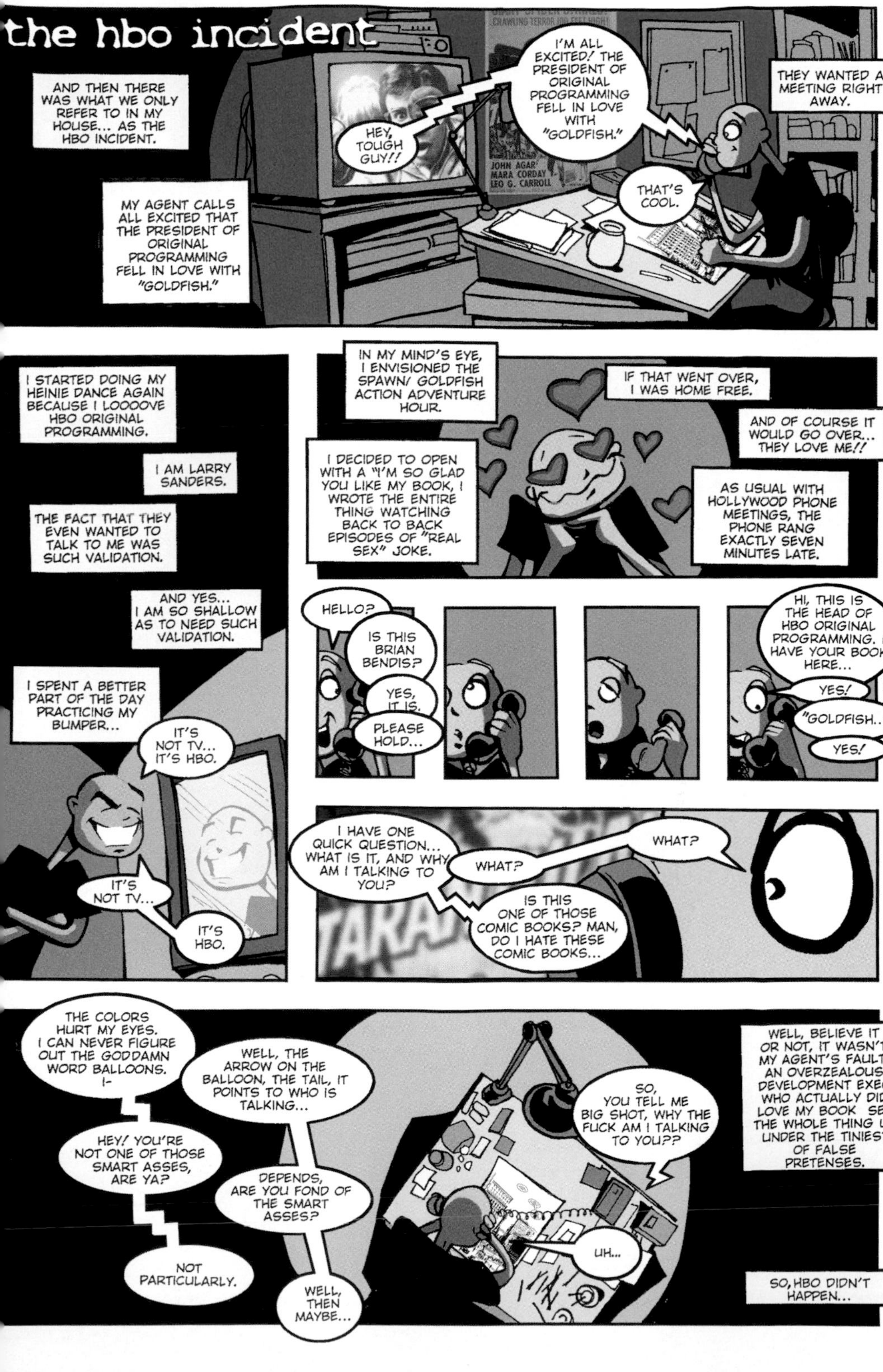
the hbo incident
AND THEN THERE WAS WHAT WE ONLY REFER TO IN MY HOUSE... AS THE HBO INCIDENT.
MY AGENT CALLS ALL EXCITED THAT THE PRESIDENT OF ORIGINAL PROGRAMMING FELL IN LOVE WITH "GOLDFISH."
HEY, TOUGH GUY!!
I'M ALL EXCITED! THE PRESIDENT OF ORIGINAL PROGRAMMING FELL IN LOVE WITH "GOLDFISH."
THAT'S COOL.
THEY WANTED A MEETING RIGHT AWAY.
JOHN AGAR
MARA CORDAY
LEO G. CARROLL
I STARTED DOING MY HEINIE DANCE AGAIN BECAUSE I LOOOOVE HBO ORIGINAL PROGRAMMING.
I AM LARRY SANDERS.
THE FACT THAT THEY EVEN WANTED TO TALK TO ME WAS SUCH VALIDATION.
AND YES... I AM SO SHALLOW AS TO NEED SUCH VALIDATION.
I SPENT A BETTER PART OF THE DAY PRACTICING MY BUMPER...
IT'S NOT TV... IT'S HBO.
IT'S NOT TV...
IT'S HBO.
IN MY MIND'S EYE, I ENVISIONED THE SPAWN/ GOLDFISH ACTION ADVENTURE HOUR.
IF THAT WENT OVER, I WAS HOME FREE.
AND OF COURSE IT WOULD GO OVER... THEY LOVE ME!!
I DECIDED TO OPEN WITH A "I'M SO GLAD YOU LIKE MY BOOK, I WROTE THE ENTIRE THING WATCHING BACK TO BACK EPISODES OF "REAL SEX" JOKE.
AS USUAL WITH HOLLYWOOD PHONE MEETINGS, THE PHONE RANG EXACTLY SEVEN MINUTES LATE.
HELLO?
IS THIS BRIAN BENDIS?
YES, IT IS.
PLEASE HOLD...
HI, THIS IS THE HEAD OF HBO ORIGINAL PROGRAMMING. I HAVE YOUR BOOK HERE...
YES!
"GOLDFISH..."
YES!
I HAVE ONE QUICK QUESTION... WHAT IS IT, AND WHY AM I TALKING TO YOU?
WHAT?
WHAT?
IS THIS ONE OF THOSE COMIC BOOKS? MAN, DO I HATE THESE COMIC BOOKS...
THE COLORS HURT MY EYES. I CAN NEVER FIGURE OUT THE GODDAMN WORD BALLOONS. I-
WELL, THE ARROW ON THE BALLOON, THE TAIL, IT POINTS TO WHO IS TALKING...
HEY! YOU'RE NOT ONE OF THOSE SMART ASSES, ARE YA?
DEPENDS, ARE YOU FOND OF THE SMART ASSES?
NOT PARTICULARLY.
WELL, THEN MAYBE...
SO, YOU TELL ME BIG SHOT, WHY THE FUCK AM I TALKING TO YOU??
UH...
WELL, BELIEVE IT OR NOT, IT WASN'T MY AGENT'S FAULT. AN OVERZEALOUS DEVELOPMENT EXEC WHO ACTUALLY DID LOVE MY BOOK SET THE WHOLE THING UP UNDER THE TINIEST OF FALSE PRETENSES.
SO, HBO DIDN'T HAPPEN...

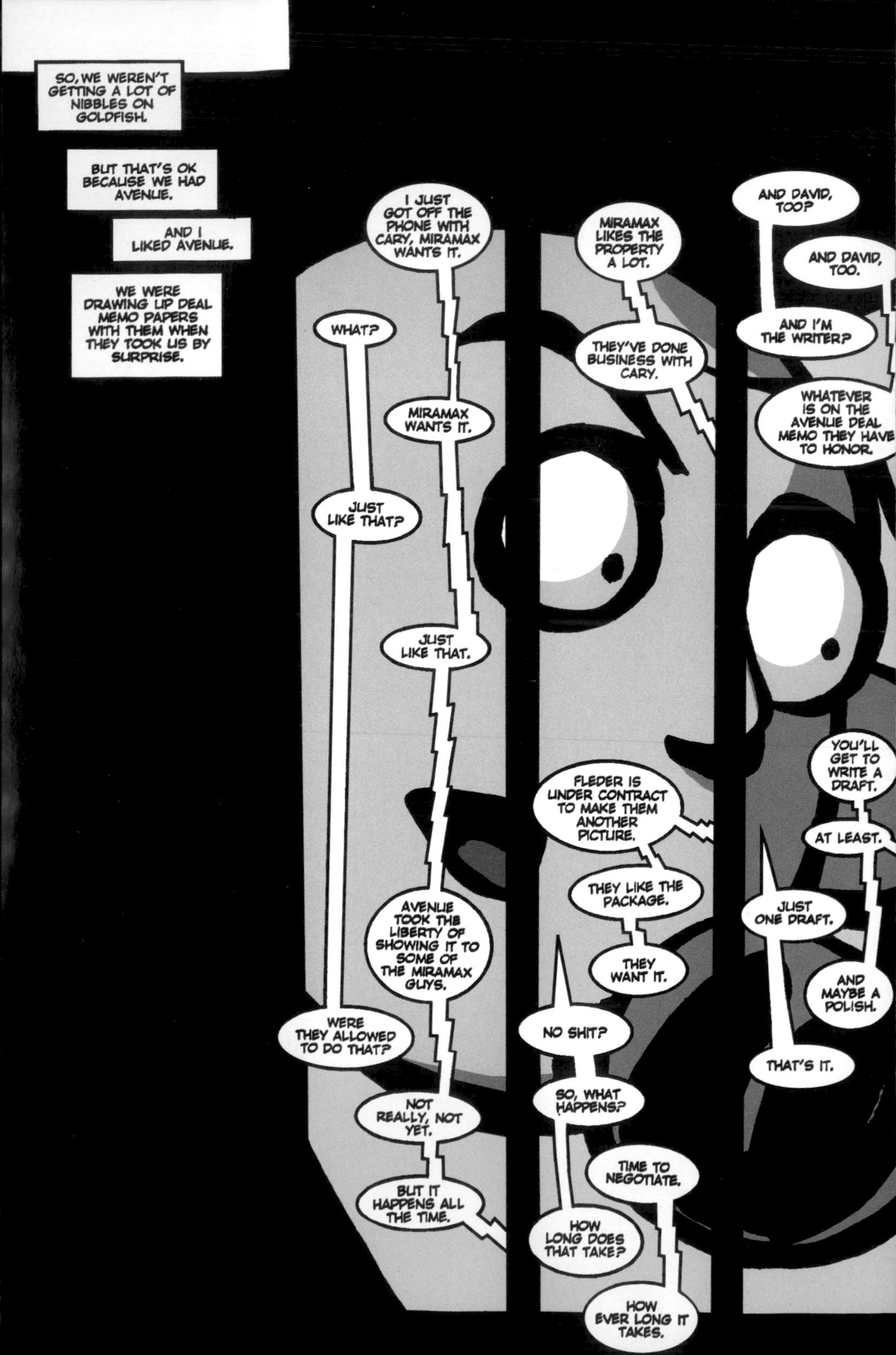
SO, WE WEREN'T GETTING A LOT OF NIBBLES ON GOLDFISH.
BUT THAT'S OK BECAUSE WE HAD AVENUE.
AND I LIKED AVENUE.
WE WERE DRAWING UP DEAL MEMO PAPERS WITH THEM WHEN THEY TOOK US BY SURPRISE.
I JUST GOT OFF THE PHONE WITH CARY, MIRAMAX WANTS IT.
WHAT?
MIRAMAX WANTS IT.
JUST LIKE THAT?
JUST LIKE THAT.
AVENUE TOOK THE LIBERTY OF SHOWING IT TO SOME OF THE MIRAMAX GUYS.
WERE THEY ALLOWED TO DO THAT?
NOT REALLY, NOT YET.
BUT IT HAPPENS ALL THE TIME.
MIRAMAX LIKES THE PROPERTY A LOT.
THEY'VE DONE BUSINESS WITH CARY.
FLEDER IS UNDER CONTRACT TO MAKE THEM ANOTHER PICTURE.
THEY LIKE THE PACKAGE.
THEY WANT IT.
NO SHIT?
SO, WHAT HAPPENS?
TIME TO NEGOTIATE.
HOW LONG DOES THAT TAKE?
HOW EVER LONG IT TAKES.
AND DAVID, TOO?
AND DAVID, TOO.
AND I'M THE WRITER?
WHATEVER IS ON THE AVENUE DEAL MEMO THEY HAVE TO HONOR.
YOU'LL GET TO WRITE A DRAFT.
AT LEAST.
JUST ONE DRAFT.
AND MAYBE A POLISH.
THAT'S IT.

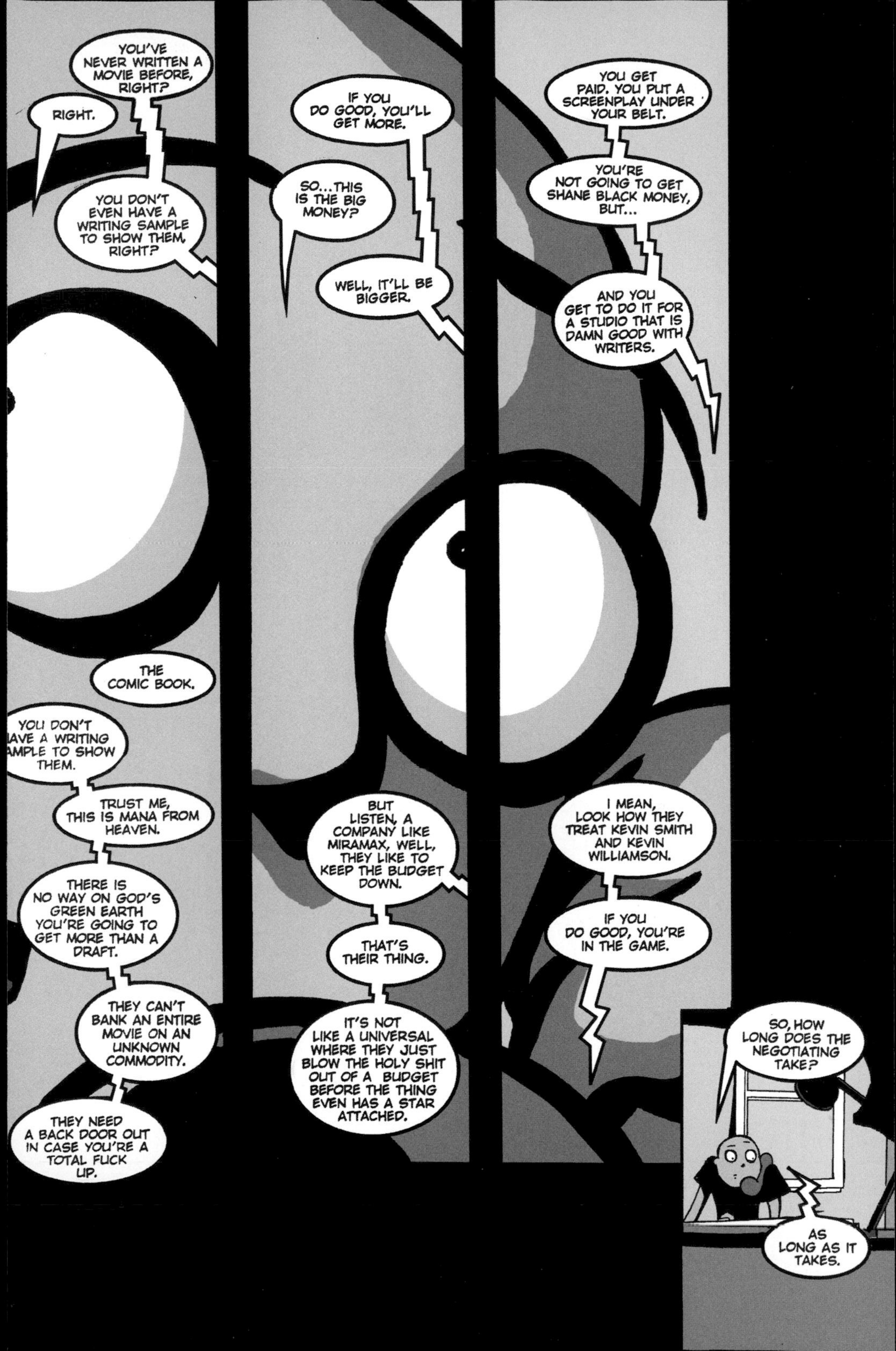
YOU'VE NEVER WRITTEN A MOVIE BEFORE, RIGHT?
RIGHT.
YOU DON'T EVEN HAVE A WRITING SAMPLE TO SHOW THEM, RIGHT?
IF YOU DO GOOD, YOU'LL GET MORE.
SO...THIS IS THE BIG MONEY?
WELL, IT'LL BE BIGGER.
YOU GET PAID. YOU PUT A SCREENPLAY UNDER YOUR BELT.
YOU'RE NOT GOING TO GET SHANE BLACK MONEY, BUT...
AND YOU GET TO DO IT FOR A STUDIO THAT IS DAMN GOOD WITH WRITERS.
THE COMIC BOOK.
YOU DON'T IAVE A WRITING AMPLE TO SHOW THEM.
TRUST ME, THIS IS MANA FROM HEAVEN.
THERE IS NO WAY ON GOD'S GREEN EARTH YOU'RE GOING TO GET MORE THAN A DRAFT.
THEY CAN'T BANK AN ENTIRE MOVIE ON AN UNKNOWN COMMODITY.
THEY NEED A BACK DOOR OUT IN CASE YOU'RE A TOTAL FUCK UP.
BUT LISTEN, A COMPANY LIKE MIRAMAX, WELL, THEY LIKE TO KEEP THE BUDGET DOWN.
THAT'S THEIR THING.
IT'S NOT LIKE A UNIVERSAL WHERE THEY JUST BLOW THE HOLY SHIT OUT OF A BUDGET BEFORE THE THING EVEN HAS A STAR ATTACHED.
I MEAN, LOOK HOW THEY TREAT KEVIN SMITH AND KEVIN WILLIAMSON.
IF YOU DO GOOD, YOU'RE IN THE GAME.
SO, HOW LONG DOES THE NEGOTIATING TAKE?
AS LONG AS IT TAKES.

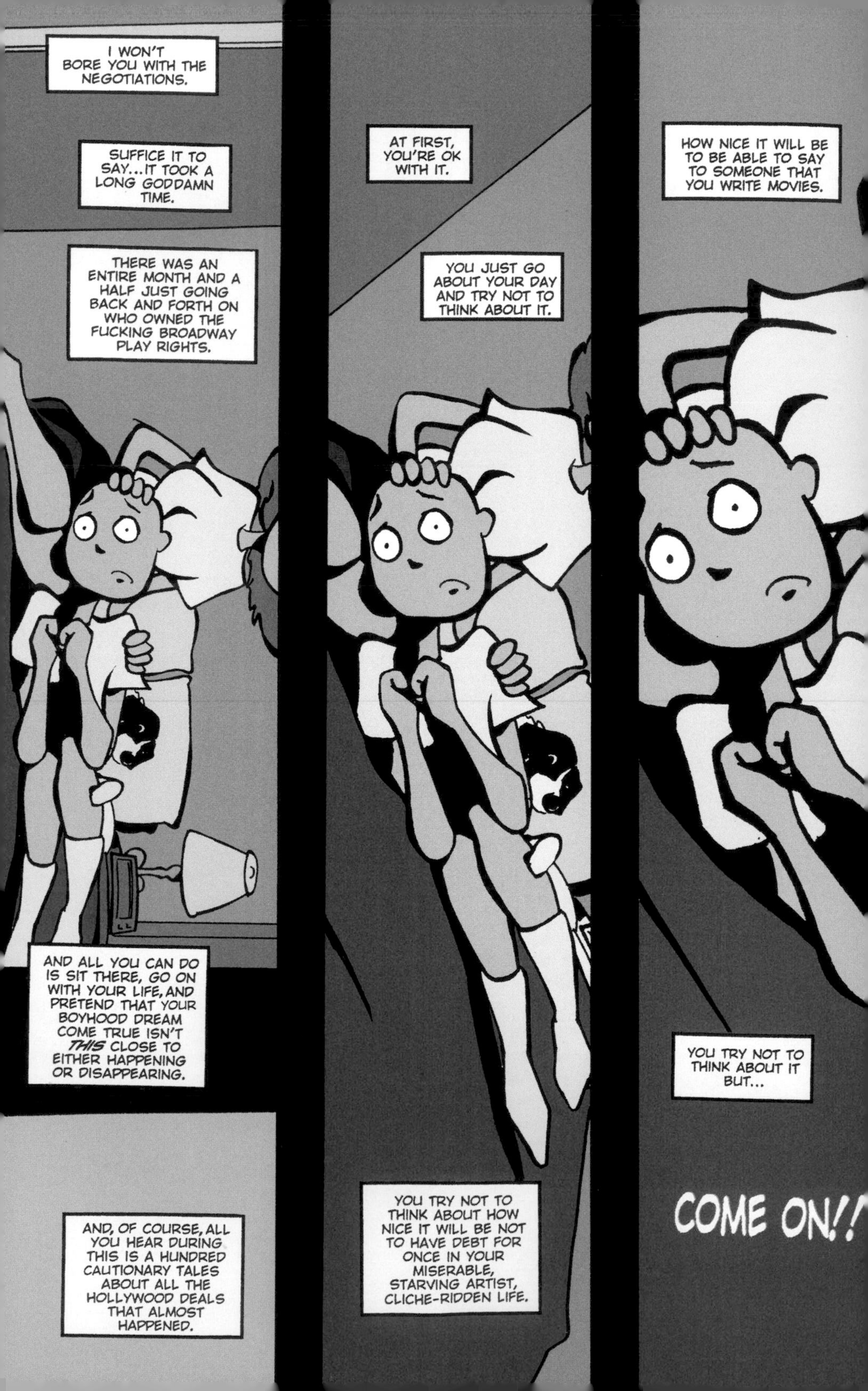
I WON'T BORE YOU WITH THE NEGOTIATIONS.
SUFFICE IT TO SAY...IT TOOK A LONG GODDAMN TIME.
THERE WAS AN ENTIRE MONTH AND A HALF JUST GOING BACK AND FORTH ON WHO OWNED THE FUCKING BROADWAY PLAY RIGHTS.
AND ALL YOU CAN DO IS SIT THERE, GO ON WITH YOUR LIFE, AND PRETEND THAT YOUR BOYHOOD DREAM COME TRUE ISN'T *THIS* CLOSE TO EITHER HAPPENING OR DISAPPEARING.
AND, OF COURSE, ALL YOU HEAR DURING THIS IS A HUNDRED CAUTIONARY TALES ABOUT ALL THE HOLLYWOOD DEALS THAT ALMOST HAPPENED.
AT FIRST, YOU'RE OK WITH IT.
YOU JUST GO ABOUT YOUR DAY AND TRY NOT TO THINK ABOUT IT.
YOU TRY NOT TO THINK ABOUT HOW NICE IT WILL BE NOT TO HAVE DEBT FOR ONCE IN YOUR MISERABLE, STARVING ARTIST, CLICHE-RIDDEN LIFE.
HOW NICE IT WILL BE TO BE ABLE TO SAY TO SOMEONE THAT YOU WRITE MOVIES.
YOU TRY NOT TO THINK ABOUT IT BUT...
COME ON!!

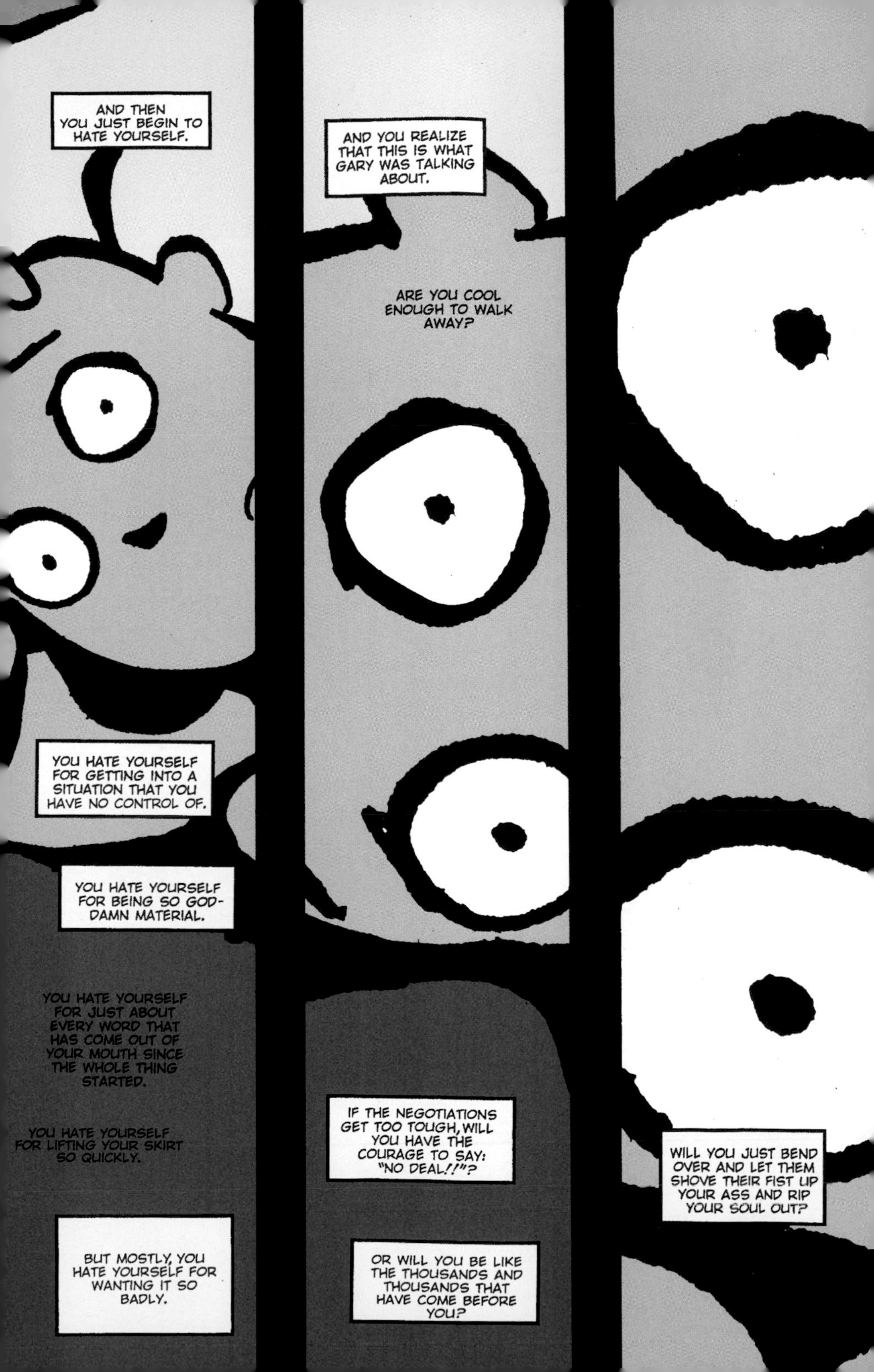
AND THEN YOU JUST BEGIN TO HATE YOURSELF.
YOU HATE YOURSELF FOR GETTING INTO A SITUATION THAT YOU HAVE NO CONTROL OF.
YOU HATE YOURSELF FOR BEING SO GOD-DAMN MATERIAL.
YOU HATE YOURSELF FOR JUST ABOUT EVERY WORD THAT HAS COME OUT OF YOUR MOUTH SINCE THE WHOLE THING STARTED.
YOU HATE YOURSELF FOR LIFTING YOUR SKIRT SO QUICKLY.
BUT MOSTLY, YOU HATE YOURSELF FOR WANTING IT SO BADLY.
AND YOU REALIZE THAT THIS IS WHAT GARY WAS TALKING ABOUT.
ARE YOU COOL ENOUGH TO WALK AWAY?
IF THE NEGOTIATIONS GET TOO TOUGH, WILL YOU HAVE THE COURAGE TO SAY: "NO DEAL!!"?
OR WILL YOU BE LIKE THE THOUSANDS AND THOUSANDS THAT HAVE COME BEFORE YOU?
WILL YOU JUST BEND OVER AND LET THEM SHOVE THEIR FIST UP YOUR ASS AND RIP YOUR SOUL OUT?

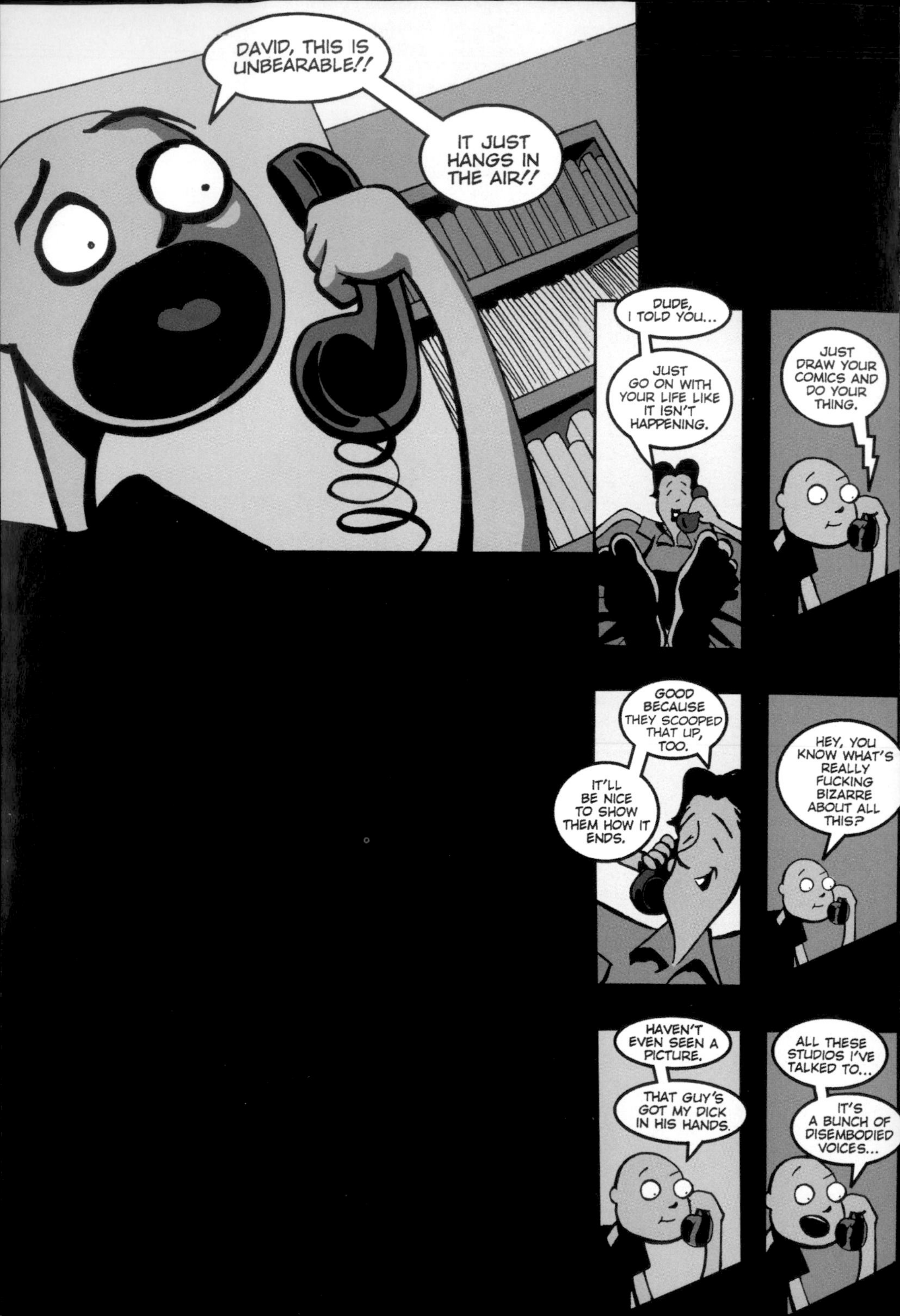

DAVID, THIS IS UNBEARABLE!!
IT JUST HANGS IN THE AIR!!
DUDE, I TOLD YOU...
JUST GO ON WITH YOUR LIFE LIKE IT ISN'T HAPPENING.
JUST DRAW YOUR COMICS AND DO YOUR THING.
GOOD BECAUSE THEY SCOOPED THAT UP, TOO.
IT'LL BE NICE TO SHOW THEM HOW IT ENDS.
HEY, YOU KNOW WHAT'S REALLY FUCKING BIZARRE ABOUT ALL THIS?
HAVEN'T EVEN SEEN A PICTURE.
THAT GUY'S GOT MY DICK IN HIS HANDS.
ALL THESE STUDIOS I'VE TALKED TO...
IT'S A BUNCH OF DISEMBODIED VOICES...

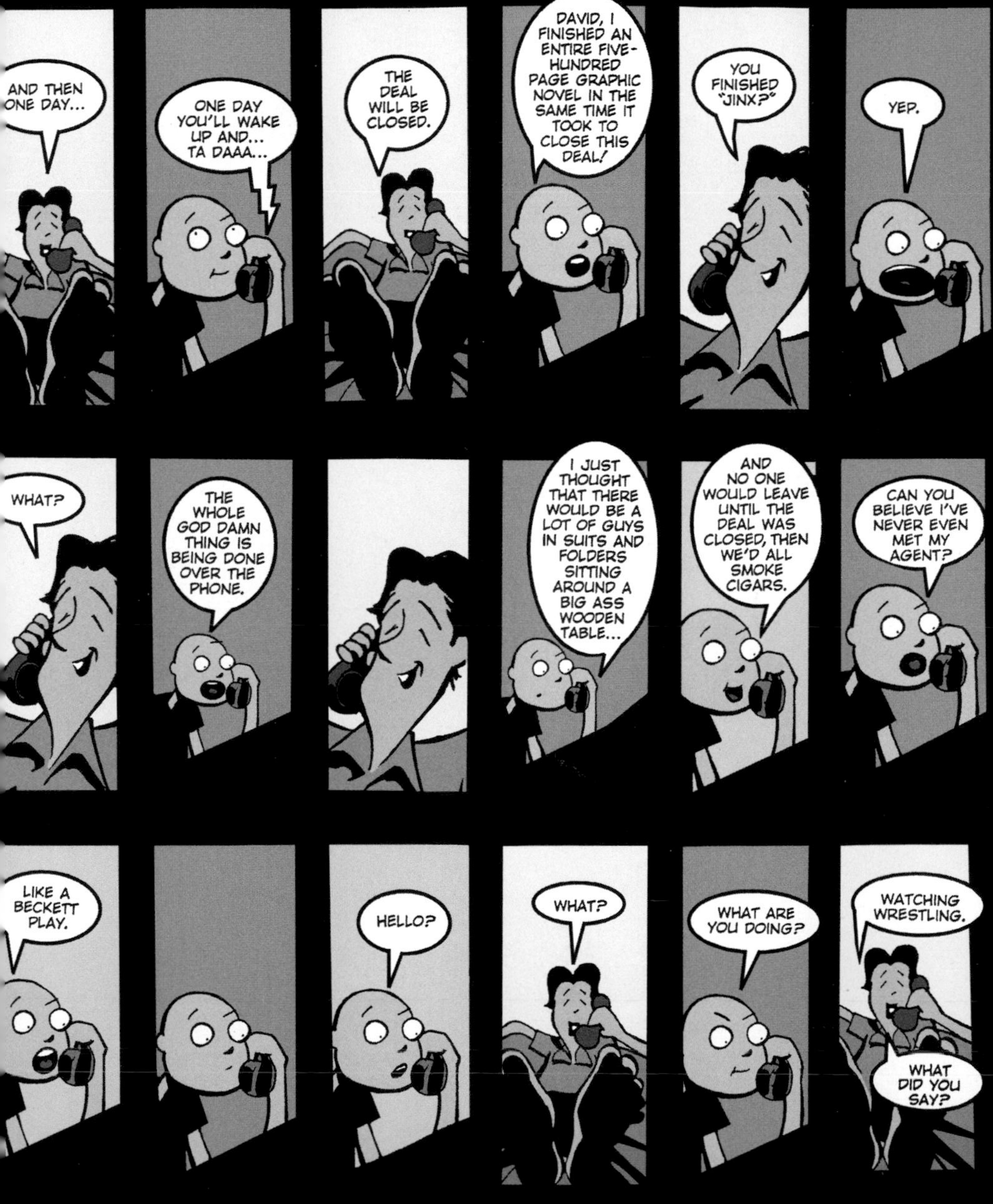
AND THEN ONE DAY...
ONE DAY YOU'LL WAKE UP AND... TA DAAA...
THE DEAL WILL BE CLOSED.
DAVID, I FINISHED AN ENTIRE FIVE-HUNDRED PAGE GRAPHIC NOVEL IN THE SAME TIME IT TOOK TO CLOSE THIS DEAL!
YOU FINISHED "JINX?"
YEP.
WHAT?
THE WHOLE GOD DAMN THING IS BEING DONE OVER THE PHONE.
I JUST THOUGHT THAT THERE WOULD BE A LOT OF GUYS IN SUITS AND FOLDERS SITTING AROUND A BIG ASS WOODEN TABLE...
AND NO ONE WOULD LEAVE UNTIL THE DEAL WAS CLOSED, THEN WE'D ALL SMOKE CIGARS.
CAN YOU BELIEVE I'VE NEVER EVEN MET MY AGENT?
LIKE A BECKETT PLAY.
HELLO?
WHAT?
WHAT ARE YOU DOING?
WATCHING WRESTLING.
WHAT DID YOU SAY?

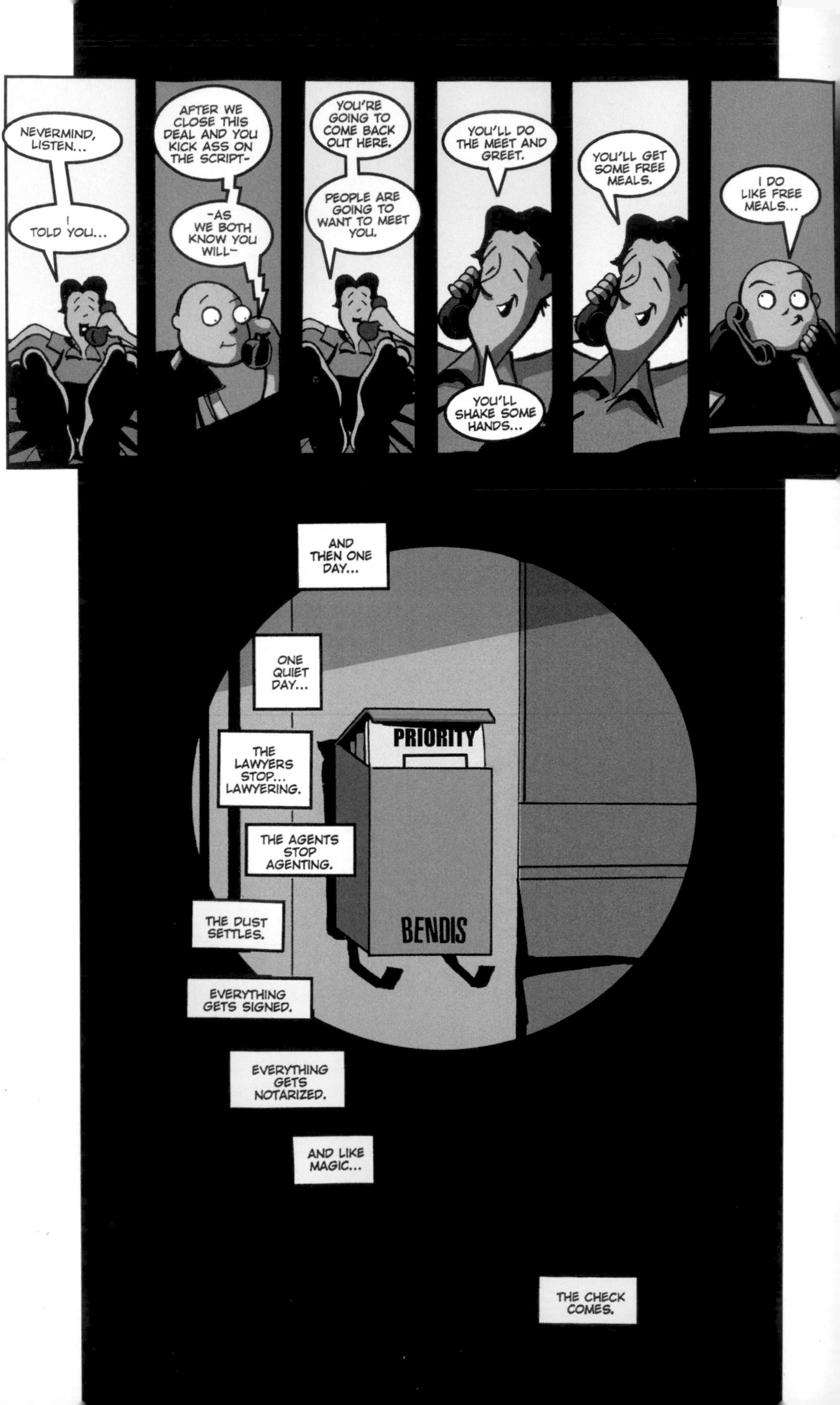
NEVERMIND, LISTEN...
I TOLD YOU...
AFTER WE CLOSE THIS DEAL AND YOU KICK ASS ON THE SCRIPT-
-AS WE BOTH KNOW YOU WILL-
YOU'RE GOING TO COME BACK OUT HERE.
PEOPLE ARE GOING TO WANT TO MEET YOU.
YOU'LL DO THE MEET AND GREET.
YOU'LL SHAKE SOME HANDS...
YOU'LL GET SOME FREE MEALS.
I DO LIKE FREE MEALS...
AND THEN ONE DAY...
ONE QUIET DAY...
PRIORITY
THE LAWYERS STOP... LAWYERING.
THE AGENTS STOP AGENTING.
THE DUST SETTLES.
BENDIS
EVERYTHING GETS SIGNED.
EVERYTHING GETS NOTARIZED.
AND LIKE MAGIC...
THE CHECK COMES.

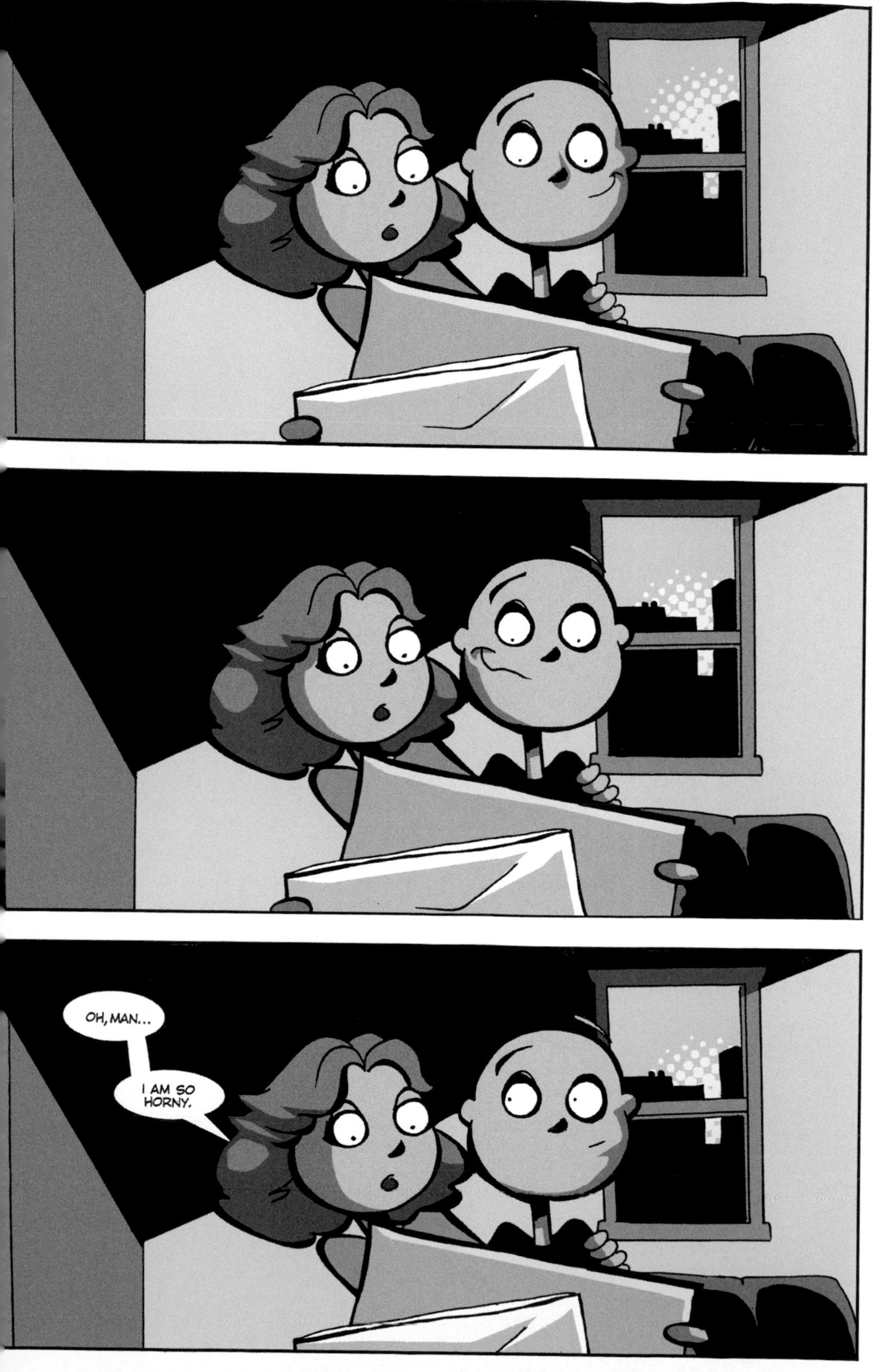
OH, MAN...
I AM SO HORNY.

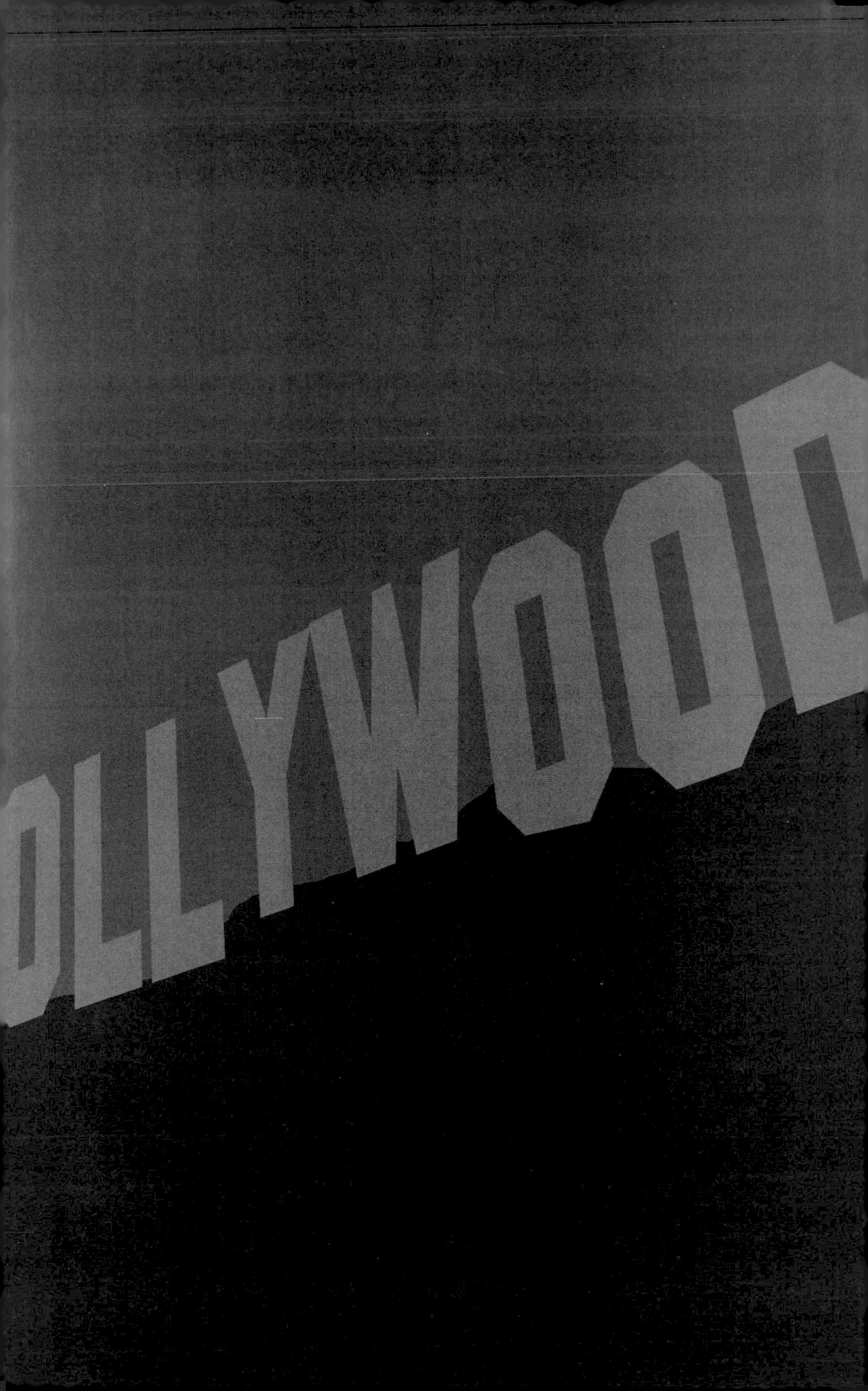
OLLYWOOD

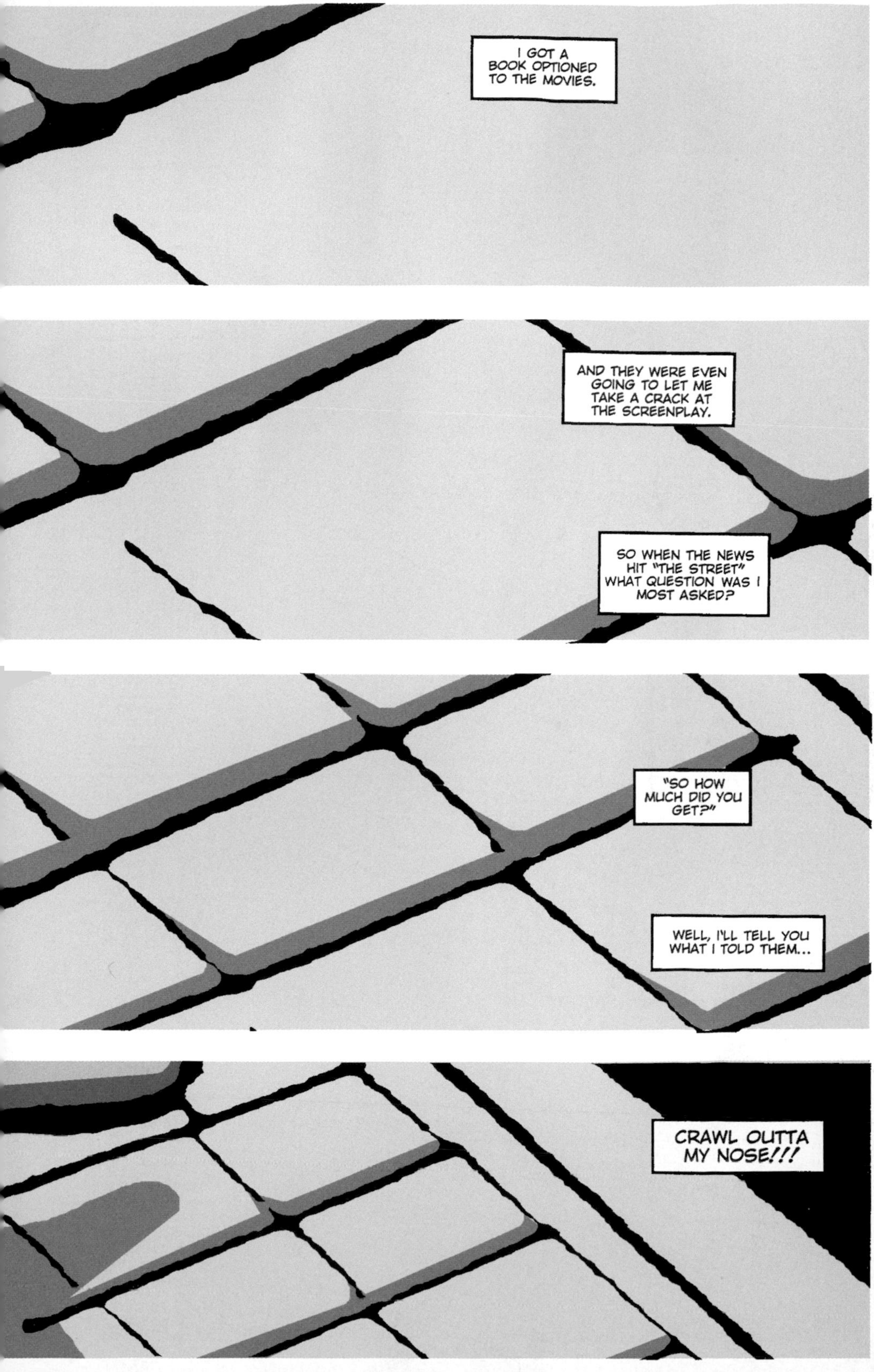
I GOT A BOOK OPTIONED TO THE MOVIES.
AND THEY WERE EVEN GOING TO LET ME TAKE A CRACK AT THE SCREENPLAY.
SO WHEN THE NEWS HIT "THE STREET" WHAT QUESTION WAS I MOST ASKED?
"SO HOW MUCH DID YOU GET?"
WELL, I'LL TELL YOU WHAT I TOLD THEM...
CRAWL OUTTA MY NOSE!!!

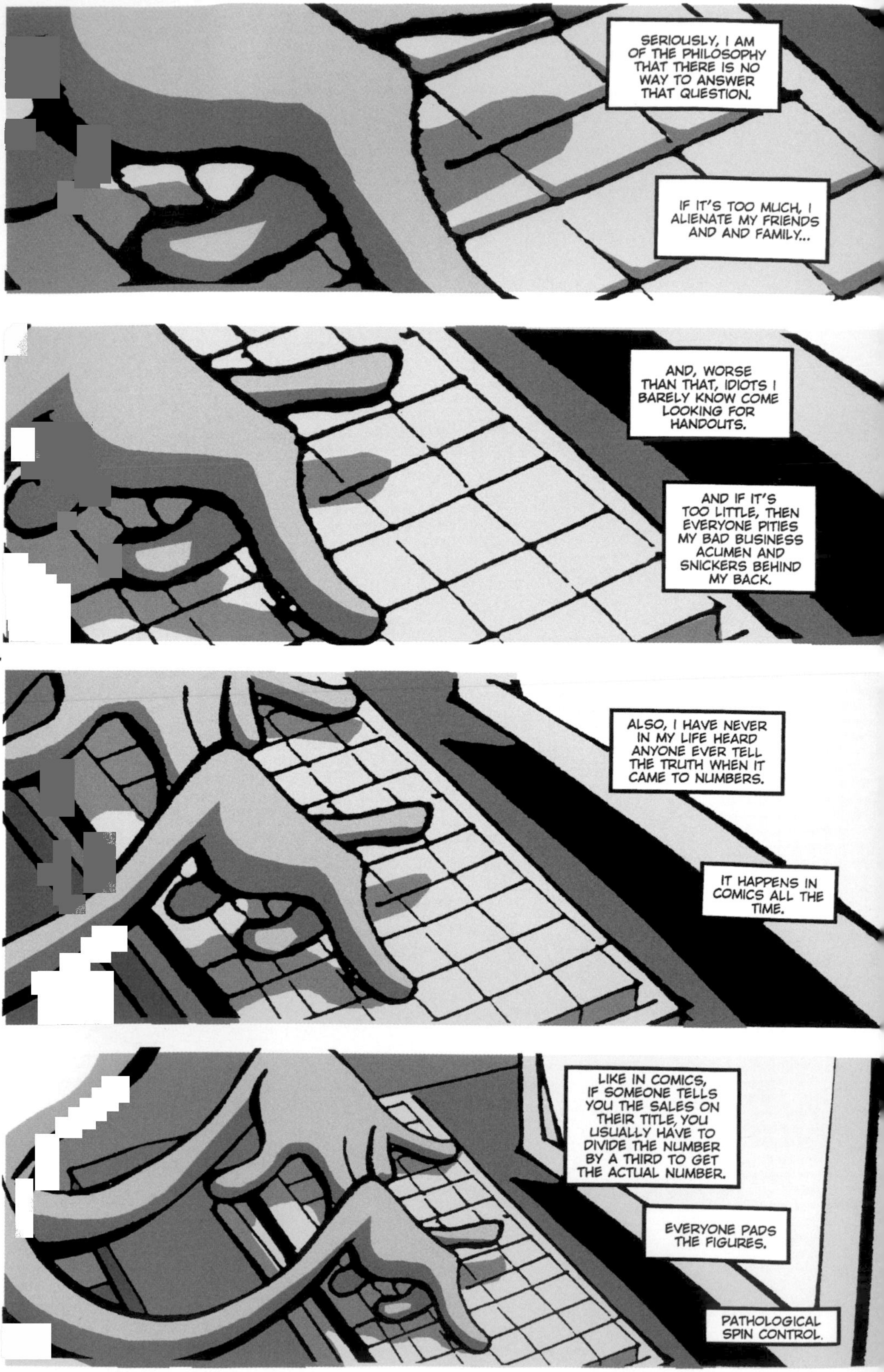
SERIOUSLY, I AM OF THE PHILOSOPHY THAT THERE IS NO WAY TO ANSWER THAT QUESTION.
IF IT'S TOO MUCH, I ALIENATE MY FRIENDS AND AND FAMILY...
AND, WORSE THAN THAT, IDIOTS I BARELY KNOW COME LOOKING FOR HANDOUTS.
AND IF IT'S TOO LITTLE, THEN EVERYONE PITIES MY BAD BUSINESS ACUMEN AND SNICKERS BEHIND MY BACK.
ALSO, I HAVE NEVER IN MY LIFE HEARD ANYONE EVER TELL THE TRUTH WHEN IT CAME TO NUMBERS.
IT HAPPENS IN COMICS ALL THE TIME.
LIKE IN COMICS, IF SOMEONE TELLS YOU THE SALES ON THEIR TITLE, YOU USUALLY HAVE TO DIVIDE THE NUMBER BY A THIRD TO GET THE ACTUAL NUMBER.
EVERYONE PADS THE FIGURES.
PATHOLOGICAL SPIN CONTROL.

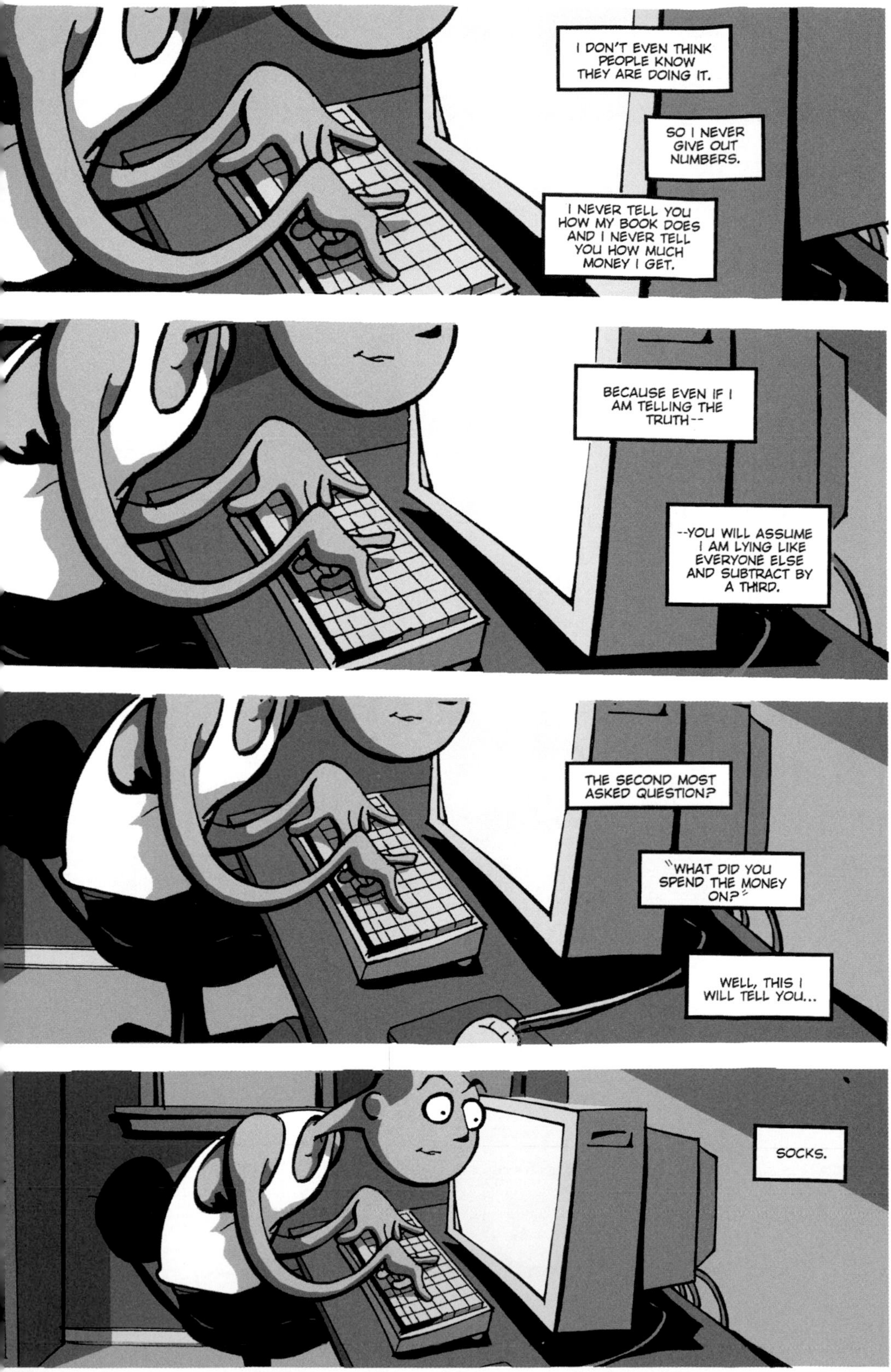
I DON'T EVEN THINK PEOPLE KNOW THEY ARE DOING IT.
SO I NEVER GIVE OUT NUMBERS.
I NEVER TELL YOU HOW MY BOOK DOES AND I NEVER TELL YOU HOW MUCH MONEY I GET.
BECAUSE EVEN IF I AM TELLING THE TRUTH--
--YOU WILL ASSUME I AM LYING LIKE EVERYONE ELSE AND SUBTRACT BY A THIRD.
THE SECOND MOST ASKED QUESTION?
"WHAT DID YOU SPEND THE MONEY ON?"
WELL, THIS I WILL TELL YOU...
SOCKS.

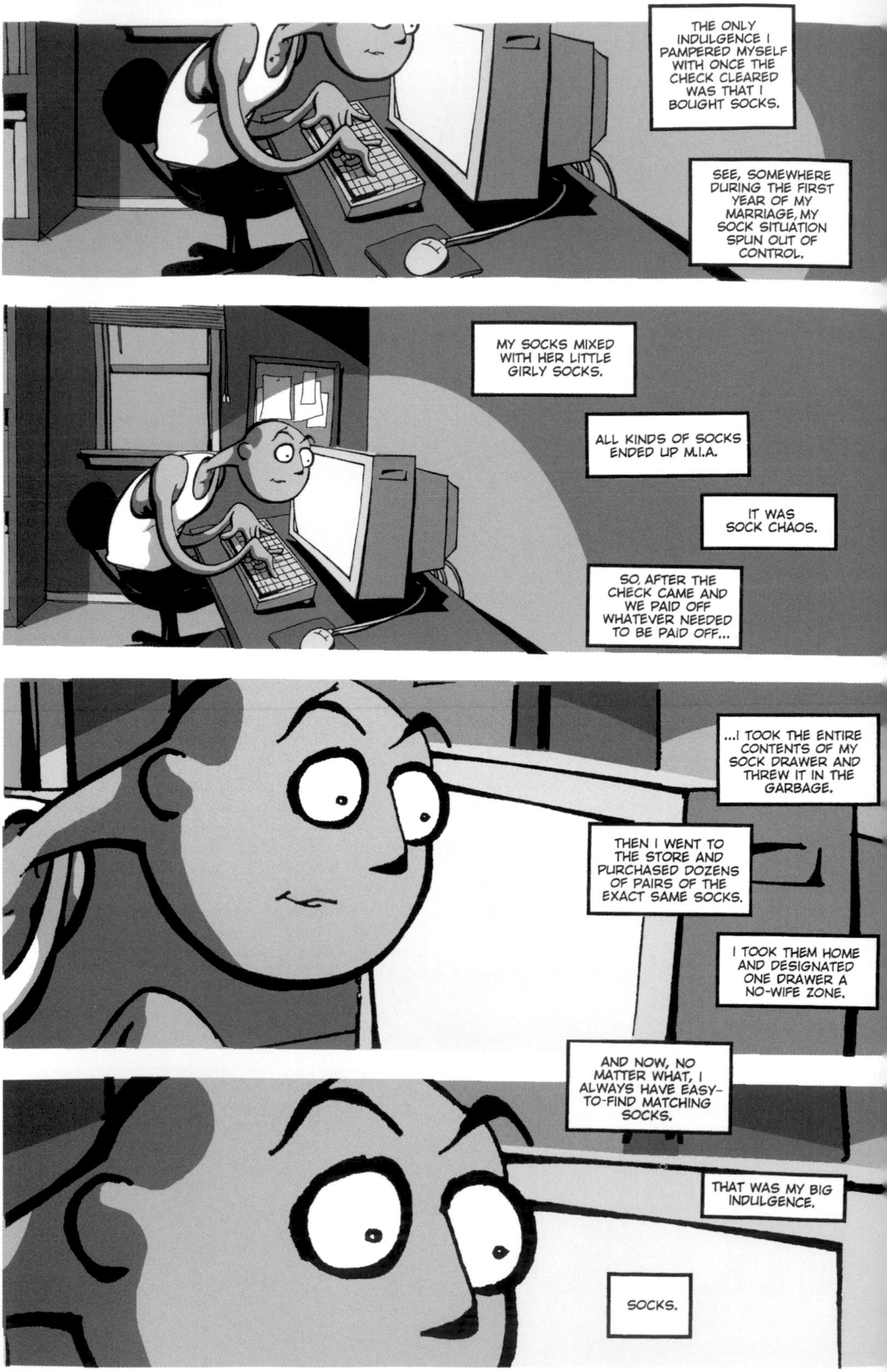

THE ONLY INDULGENCE I PAMPERED MYSELF WITH ONCE THE CHECK CLEARED WAS THAT I BOUGHT SOCKS.
SEE, SOMEWHERE DURING THE FIRST YEAR OF MY MARRIAGE, MY SOCK SITUATION SPUN OUT OF CONTROL.
MY SOCKS MIXED WITH HER LITTLE GIRLY SOCKS.
ALL KINDS OF SOCKS ENDED UP M.I.A.
IT WAS SOCK CHAOS.
SO, AFTER THE CHECK CAME AND WE PAID OFF WHATEVER NEEDED TO BE PAID OFF...
...I TOOK THE ENTIRE CONTENTS OF MY SOCK DRAWER AND THREW IT IN THE GARBAGE.
THEN I WENT TO THE STORE AND PURCHASED DOZENS OF PAIRS OF THE EXACT SAME SOCKS.
I TOOK THEM HOME AND DESIGNATED ONE DRAWER A NO-WIFE ZONE.
AND NOW, NO MATTER WHAT, I ALWAYS HAVE EASY-TO-FIND MATCHING SOCKS.
THAT WAS MY BIG INDULGENCE.
SOCKS.

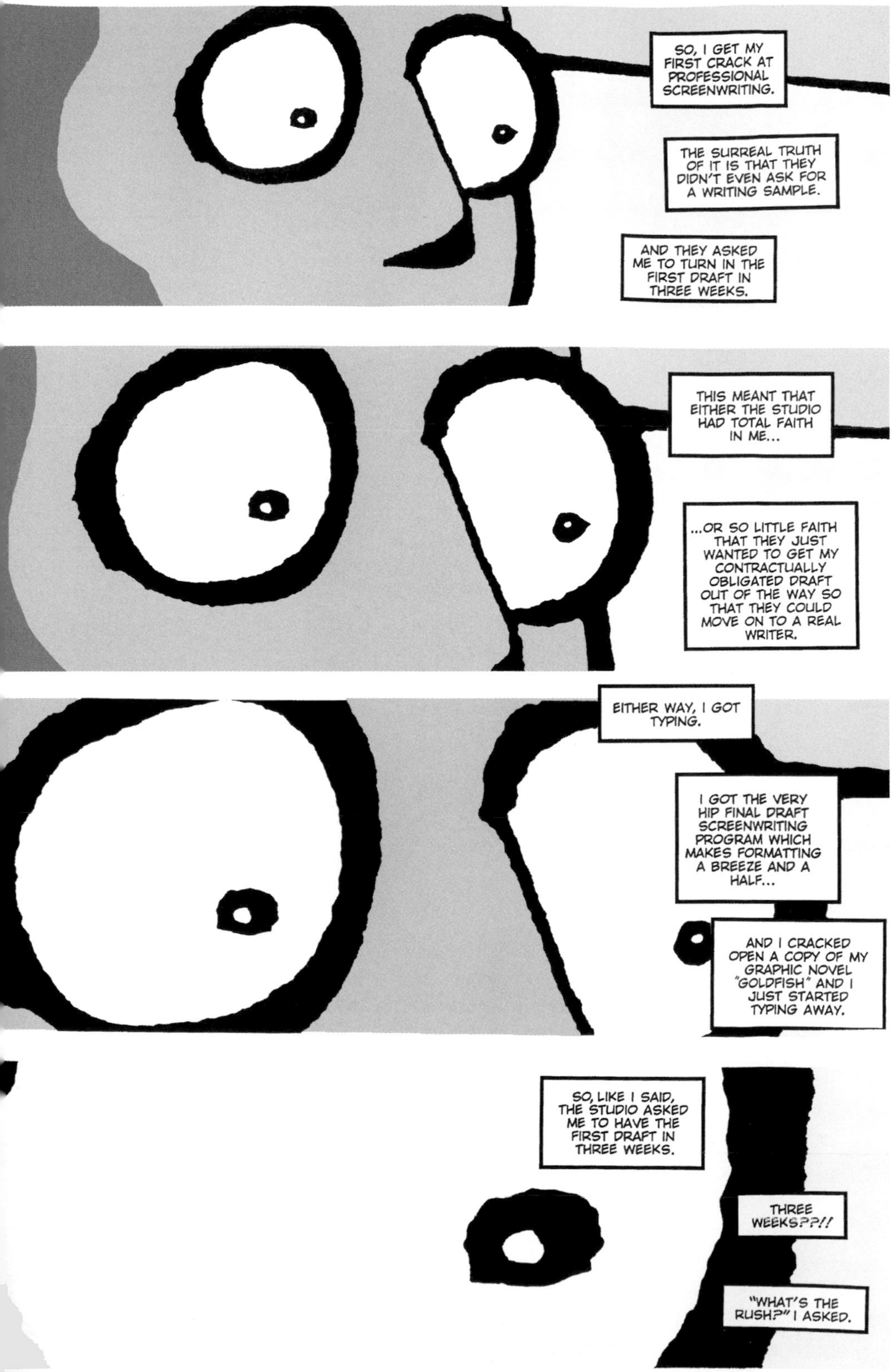
SO, I GET MY FIRST CRACK AT PROFESSIONAL SCREENWRITING.
THE SURREAL TRUTH OF IT IS THAT THEY DIDN'T EVEN ASK FOR A WRITING SAMPLE.
AND THEY ASKED ME TO TURN IN THE FIRST DRAFT IN THREE WEEKS.
THIS MEANT THAT EITHER THE STUDIO HAD TOTAL FAITH IN ME...
...OR SO LITTLE FAITH THAT THEY JUST WANTED TO GET MY CONTRACTUALLY OBLIGATED DRAFT OUT OF THE WAY SO THAT THEY COULD MOVE ON TO A REAL WRITER.
EITHER WAY, I GOT TYPING.
I GOT THE VERY HIP FINAL DRAFT SCREENWRITING PROGRAM WHICH MAKES FORMATTING A BREEZE AND A HALF...
AND I CRACKED OPEN A COPY OF MY GRAPHIC NOVEL "GOLDFISH" AND I JUST STARTED TYPING AWAY.
SO, LIKE I SAID, THE STUDIO ASKED ME TO HAVE THE FIRST DRAFT IN THREE WEEKS.
THREE WEEKS??!!
"WHAT'S THE RUSH?" I ASKED.

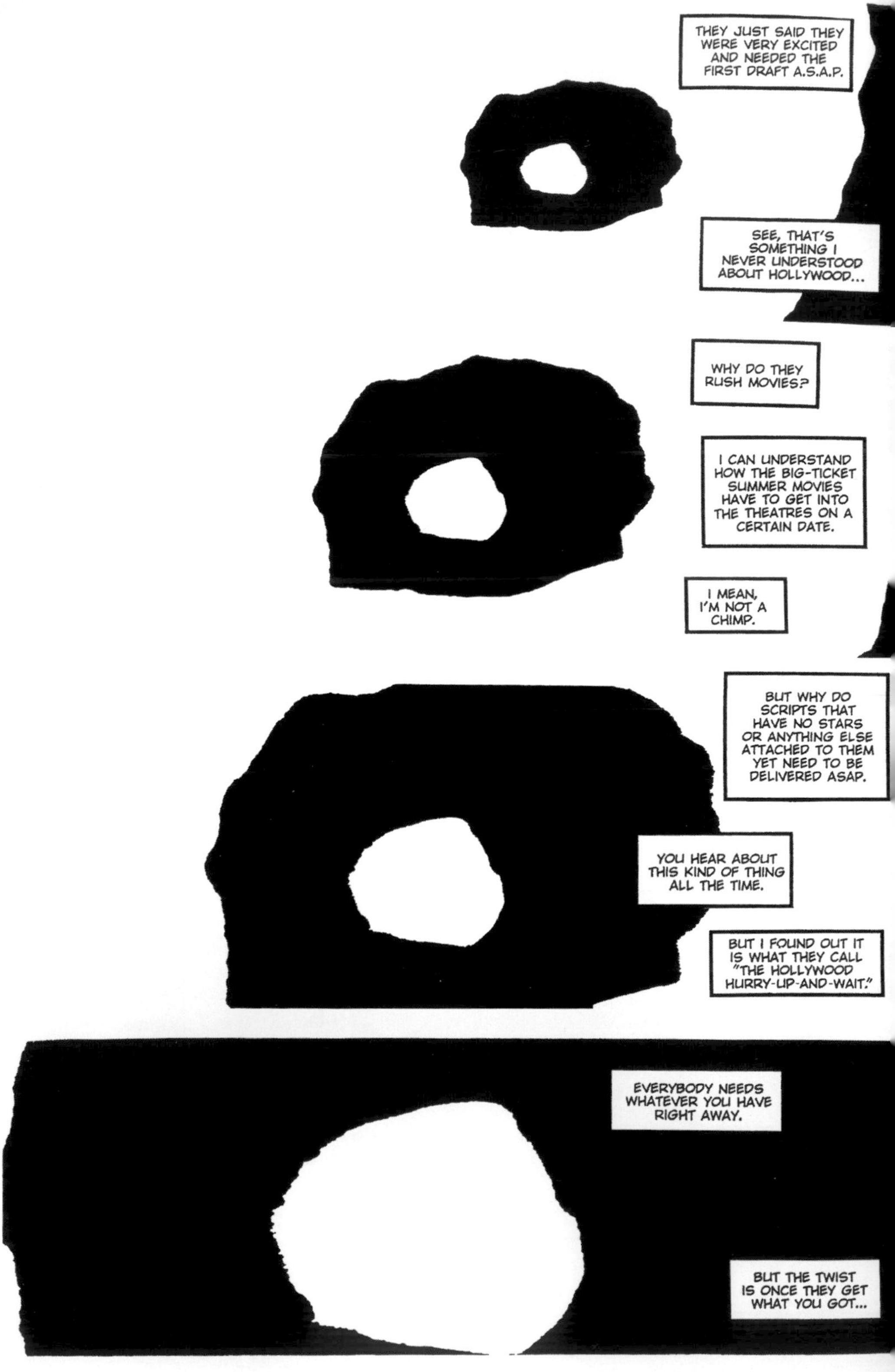
THEY JUST SAID THEY WERE VERY EXCITED AND NEEDED THE FIRST DRAFT A.S.A.P.
SEE, THAT'S SOMETHING I NEVER UNDERSTOOD ABOUT HOLLYWOOD...
WHY DO THEY RUSH MOVIES?
I CAN UNDERSTAND HOW THE BIG-TICKET SUMMER MOVIES HAVE TO GET INTO THE THEATRES ON A CERTAIN DATE.
I MEAN, I'M NOT A CHIMP.
BUT WHY DO SCRIPTS THAT HAVE NO STARS OR ANYTHING ELSE ATTACHED TO THEM YET NEED TO BE DELIVERED ASAP.
YOU HEAR ABOUT THIS KIND OF THING ALL THE TIME.
BUT I FOUND OUT IT IS WHAT THEY CALL "THE HOLLYWOOD HURRY-UP-AND-WAIT."
EVERYBODY NEEDS WHATEVER YOU HAVE RIGHT AWAY.
BUT THE TWIST IS ONCE THEY GET WHAT YOU GOT...

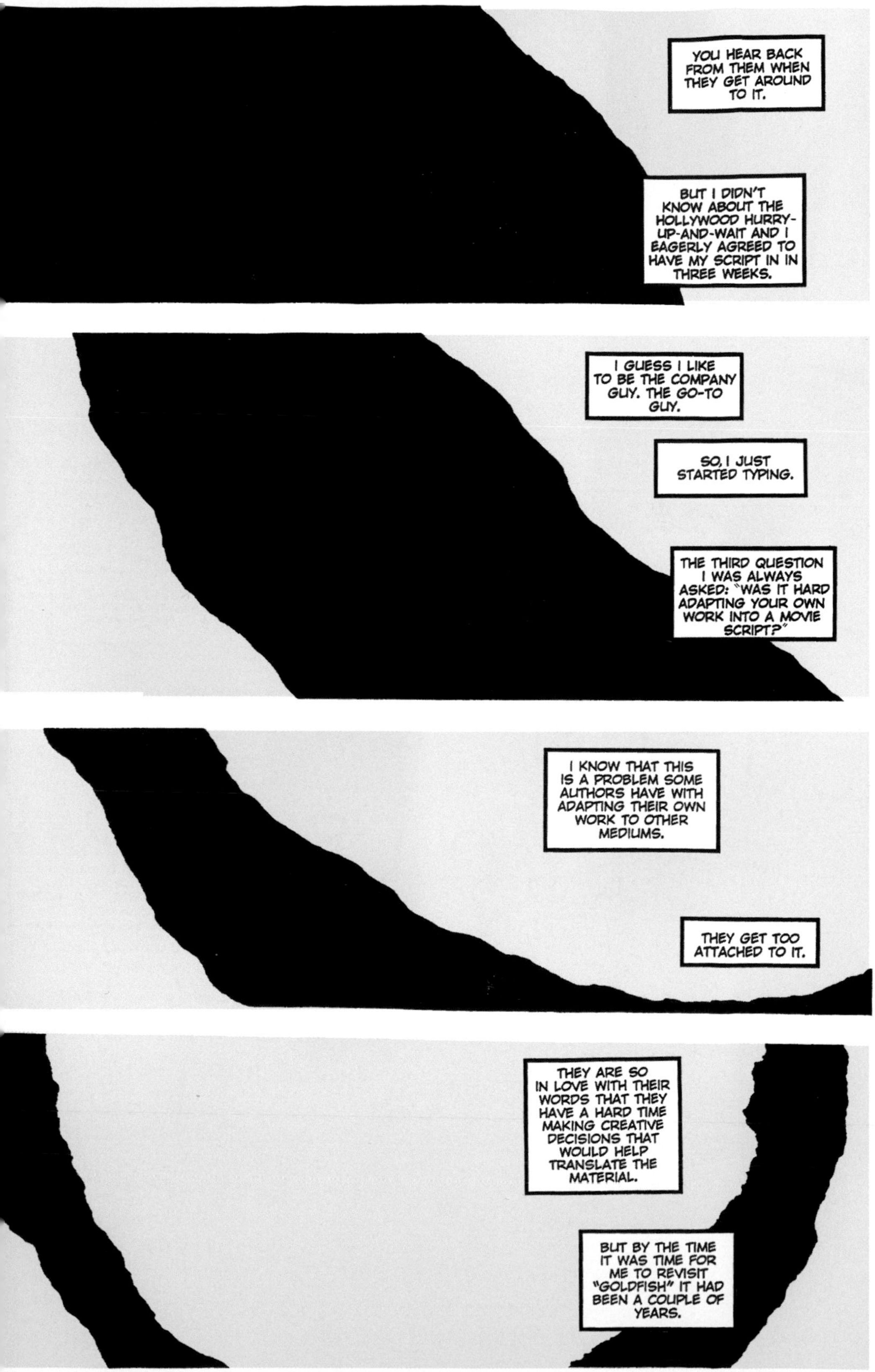
YOU HEAR BACK FROM THEM WHEN THEY GET AROUND TO IT.
BUT I DIDN'T KNOW ABOUT THE HOLLYWOOD HURRY-UP-AND-WAIT AND I EAGERLY AGREED TO HAVE MY SCRIPT IN IN THREE WEEKS.
I GUESS I LIKE TO BE THE COMPANY GUY. THE GO-TO GUY.
SO, I JUST STARTED TYPING.
THE THIRD QUESTION I WAS ALWAYS ASKED: "WAS IT HARD ADAPTING YOUR OWN WORK INTO A MOVIE SCRIPT?"
I KNOW THAT THIS IS A PROBLEM SOME AUTHORS HAVE WITH ADAPTING THEIR OWN WORK TO OTHER MEDIUMS.
THEY GET TOO ATTACHED TO IT.
THEY ARE SO IN LOVE WITH THEIR WORDS THAT THEY HAVE A HARD TIME MAKING CREATIVE DECISIONS THAT WOULD HELP TRANSLATE THE MATERIAL.
BUT BY THE TIME IT WAS TIME FOR ME TO REVISIT "GOLDFISH" IT HAD BEEN A COUPLE OF YEARS.

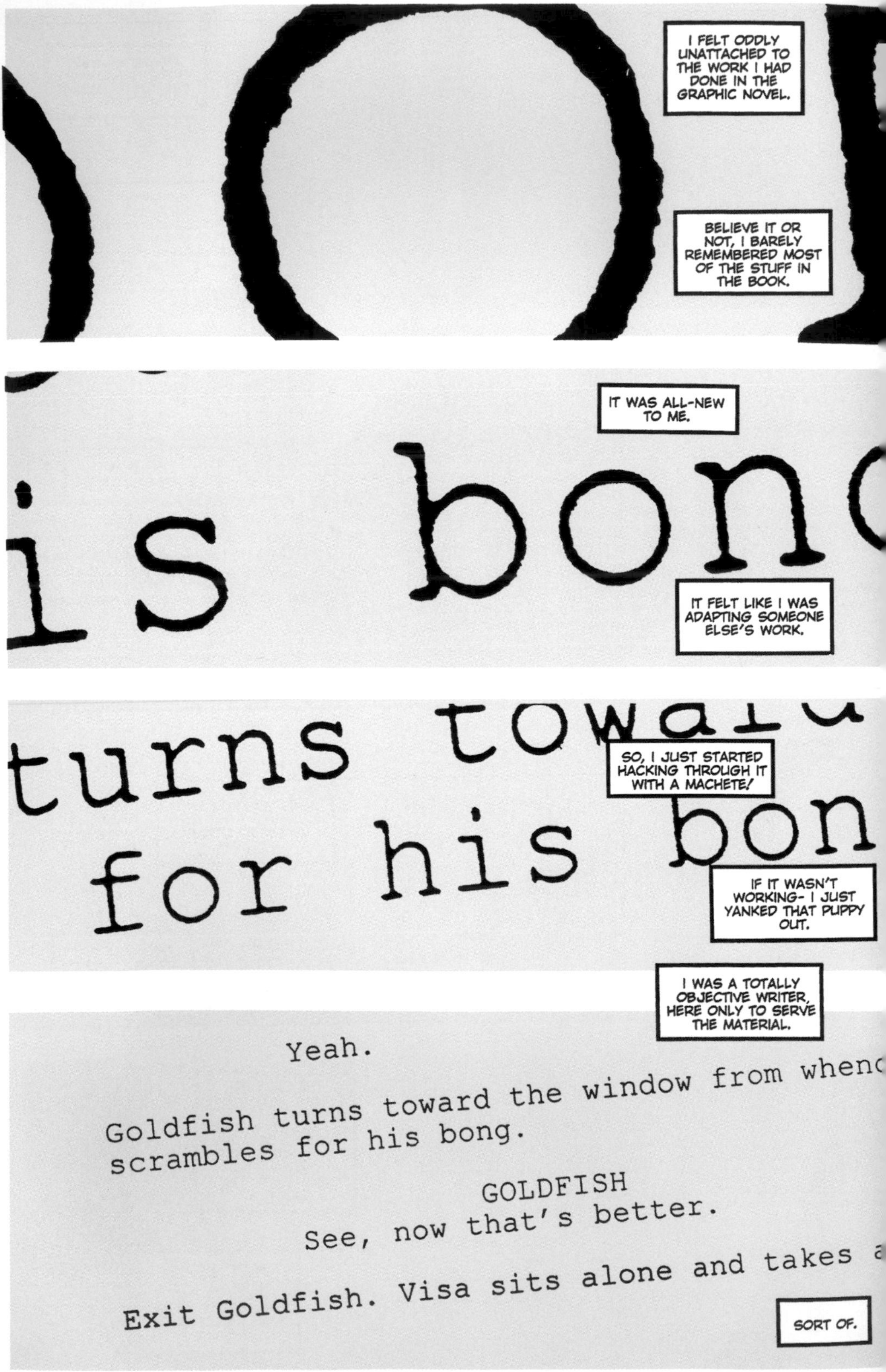
I FELT ODDLY UNATTACHED TO THE WORK I HAD DONE IN THE GRAPHIC NOVEL.
BELIEVE IT OR NOT, I BARELY REMEMBERED MOST OF THE STUFF IN THE BOOK.
IT WAS ALL-NEW TO ME.
is bon
IT FELT LIKE I WAS ADAPTING SOMEONE ELSE'S WORK.
turns towa
SO, I JUST STARTED HACKING THROUGH IT WITH A MACHETE!
for his bon
IF IT WASN'T WORKING- I JUST YANKED THAT PUPPY OUT.
I WAS A TOTALLY OBJECTIVE WRITER, HERE ONLY TO SERVE THE MATERIAL.
Yeah.
Goldfish turns toward the window from whenc
scrambles for his bong.
GOLDFISH
See, now that's better.
Exit Goldfish. Visa sits alone and takes a
SORT OF.

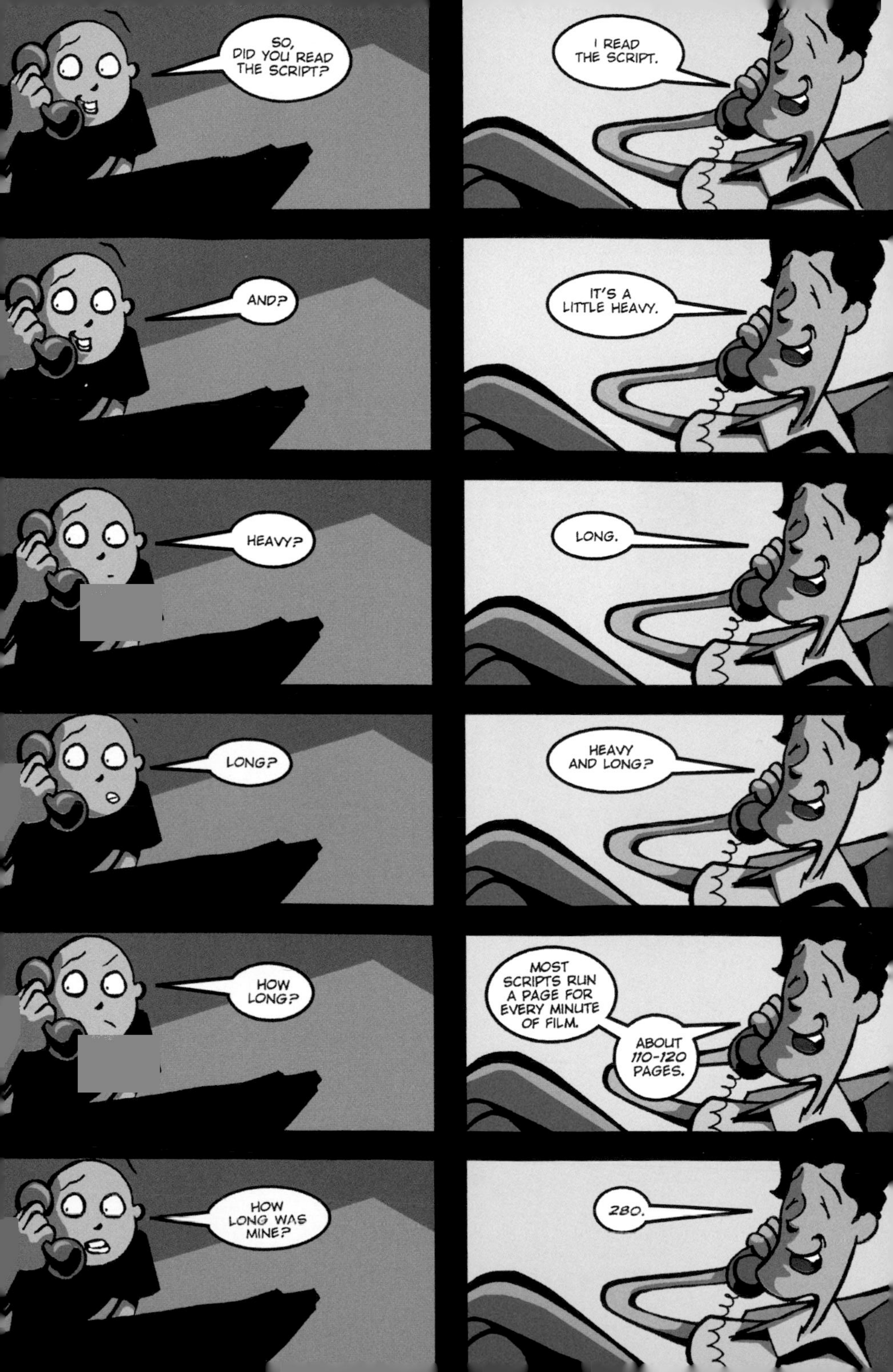
SO, DID YOU READ THE SCRIPT?
I READ THE SCRIPT.
AND?
IT'S A LITTLE HEAVY.
HEAVY?
LONG.
LONG?
HEAVY AND LONG?
HOW LONG?
MOST SCRIPTS RUN A PAGE FOR EVERY MINUTE OF FILM.
ABOUT 110-120 PAGES.
HOW LONG WAS MINE?
280.

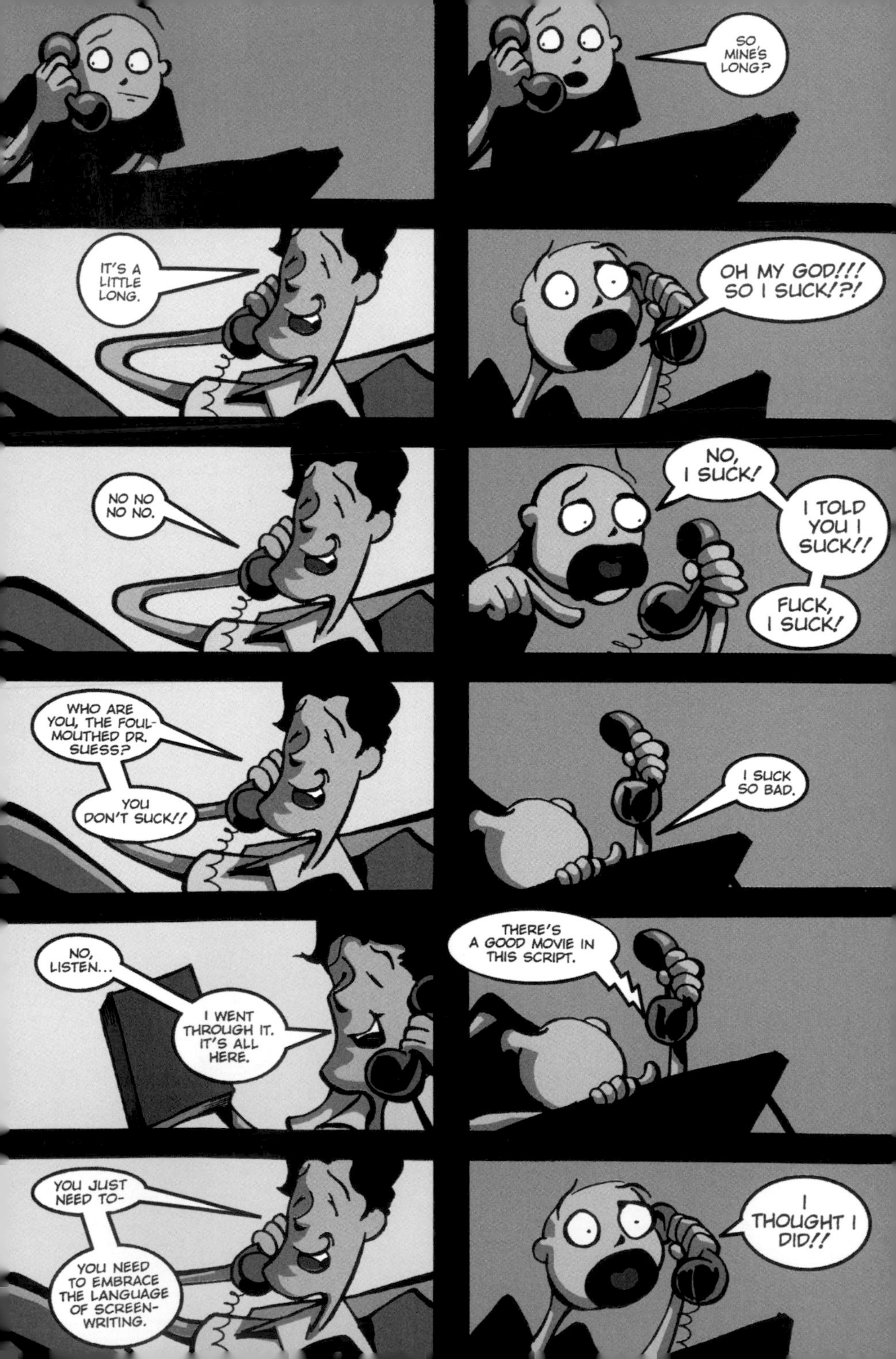
SO MINE'S LONG?
IT'S A LITTLE LONG.
OH MY GOD!!! SO I SUCK!?!
NO NO NO NO.
NO, I SUCK!
I TOLD YOU I SUCK!!
FUCK, I SUCK!
WHO ARE YOU, THE FOUL-MOUTHED DR. SUESS?
YOU DON'T SUCK!!
I SUCK SO BAD.
NO, LISTEN...
I WENT THROUGH IT. IT'S ALL HERE.
THERE'S A GOOD MOVIE IN THIS SCRIPT.
YOU JUST NEED TO-
YOU NEED TO EMBRACE THE LANGUAGE OF SCREEN-WRITING.
I THOUGHT I DID!!

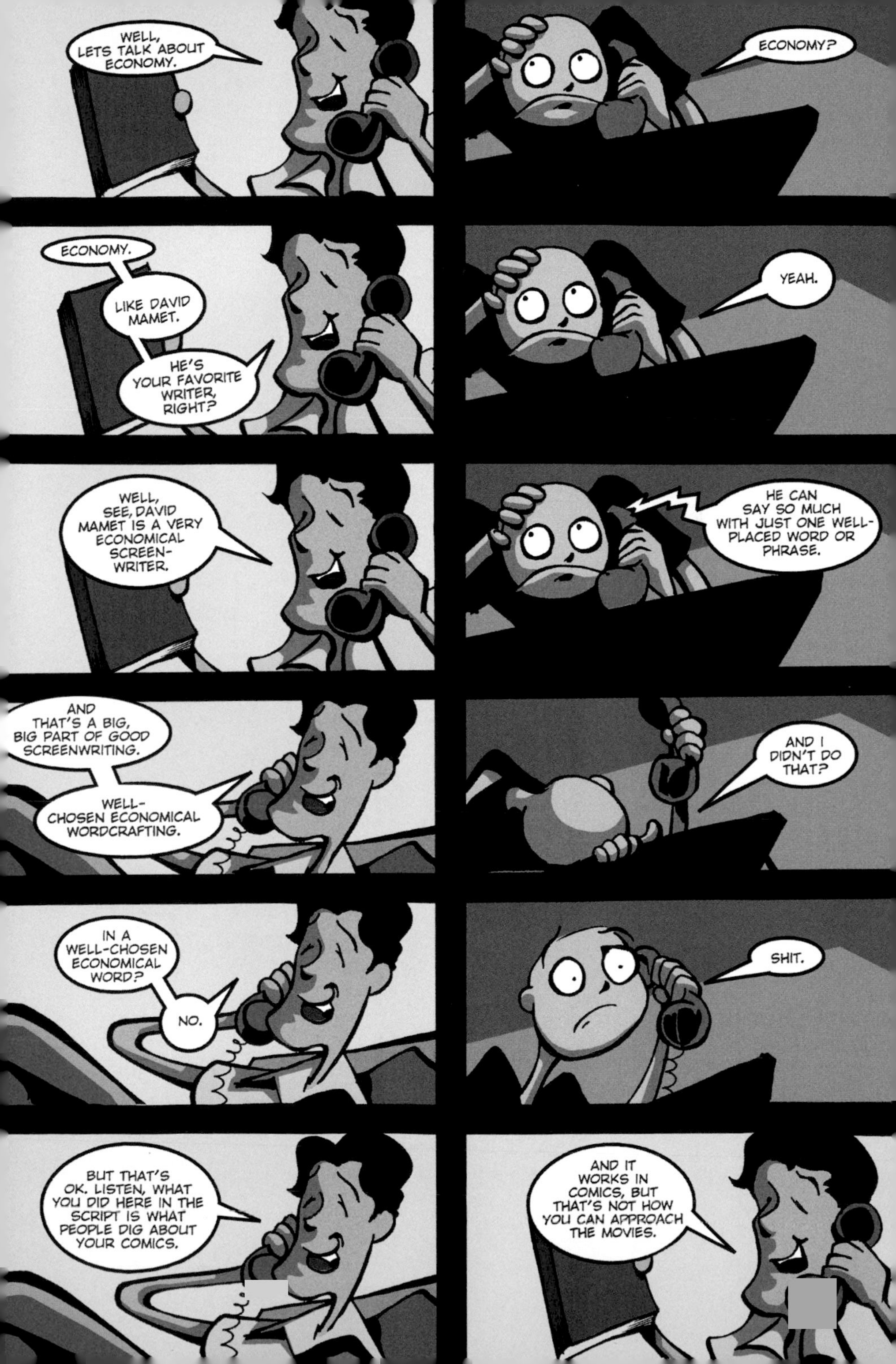
WELL, LETS TALK ABOUT ECONOMY.
ECONOMY?
ECONOMY.
LIKE DAVID MAMET.
HE'S YOUR FAVORITE WRITER, RIGHT?
YEAH.
WELL, SEE, DAVID MAMET IS A VERY ECONOMICAL SCREEN-WRITER.
HE CAN SAY SO MUCH WITH JUST ONE WELL-PLACED WORD OR PHRASE.
AND THAT'S A BIG, BIG PART OF GOOD SCREENWRITING.
WELL-CHOSEN ECONOMICAL WORDCRAFTING.
AND I DIDN'T DO THAT?
IN A WELL-CHOSEN ECONOMICAL WORD?
NO.
SHIT.
BUT THAT'S OK. LISTEN, WHAT YOU DID HERE IN THE SCRIPT IS WHAT PEOPLE DIG ABOUT YOUR COMICS.
AND IT WORKS IN COMICS, BUT THAT'S NOT HOW YOU CAN APPROACH THE MOVIES.

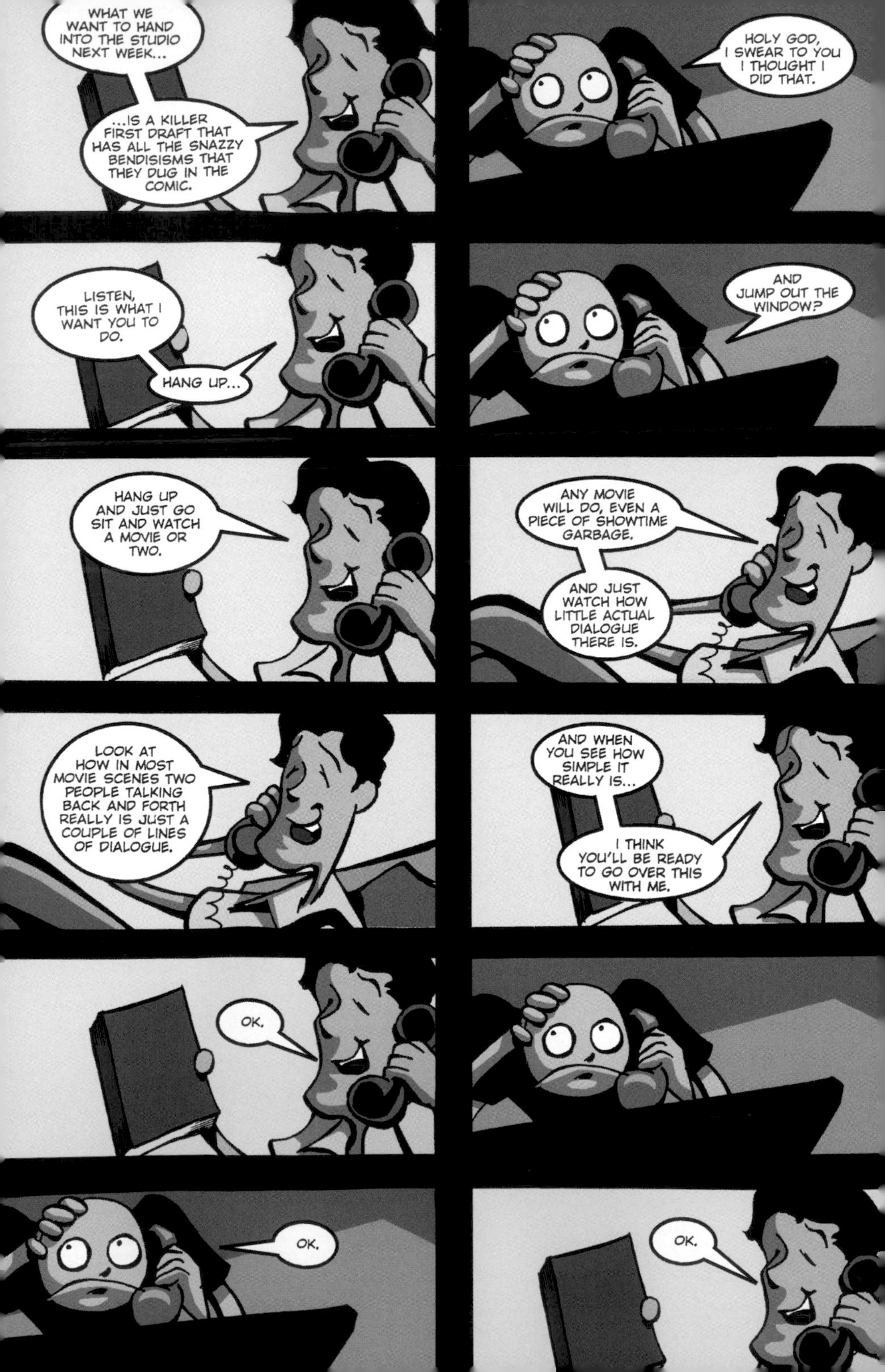
WHAT WE WANT TO HAND INTO THE STUDIO NEXT WEEK...
...IS A KILLER FIRST DRAFT THAT HAS ALL THE SNAZZY BENDISISMS THAT THEY DUG IN THE COMIC.
HOLY GOD, I SWEAR TO YOU I THOUGHT I DID THAT.
LISTEN, THIS IS WHAT I WANT YOU TO DO.
HANG UP...
AND JUMP OUT THE WINDOW?
HANG UP AND JUST GO SIT AND WATCH A MOVIE OR TWO.
ANY MOVIE WILL DO, EVEN A PIECE OF SHOWTIME GARBAGE.
AND JUST WATCH HOW LITTLE ACTUAL DIALOGUE THERE IS.
LOOK AT HOW IN MOST MOVIE SCENES TWO PEOPLE TALKING BACK AND FORTH REALLY IS JUST A COUPLE OF LINES OF DIALOGUE.
AND WHEN YOU SEE HOW SIMPLE IT REALLY IS...
I THINK YOU'LL BE READY TO GO OVER THIS WITH ME.
OK.
OK.
OK.

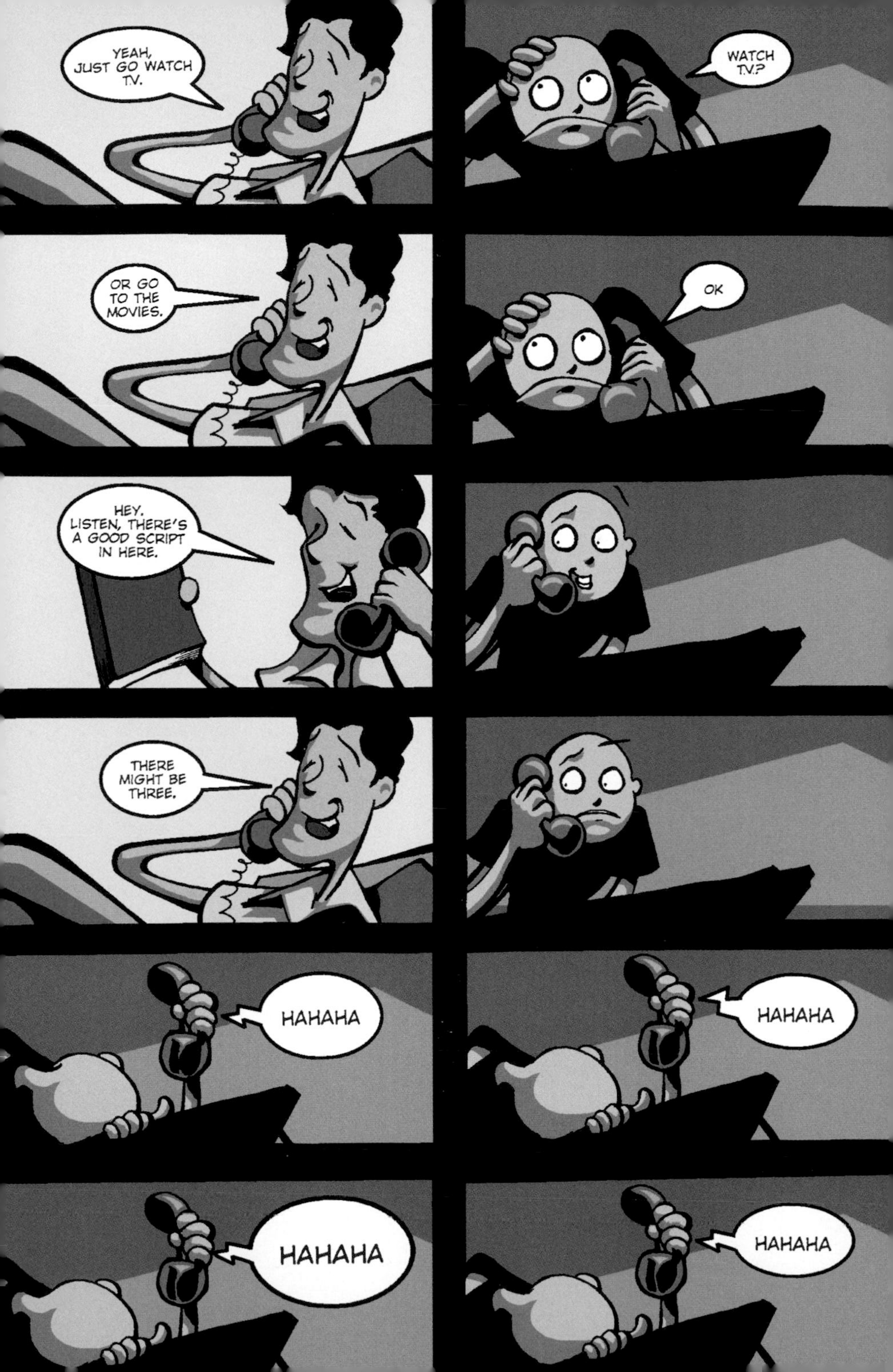
YEAH, JUST GO WATCH T.V.
WATCH T.V.?
OR GO TO THE MOVIES.
OK
HEY. LISTEN, THERE'S A GOOD SCRIPT IN HERE.
THERE MIGHT BE THREE.
HAHAHA
HAHAHA
HAHAHA
HAHAHA

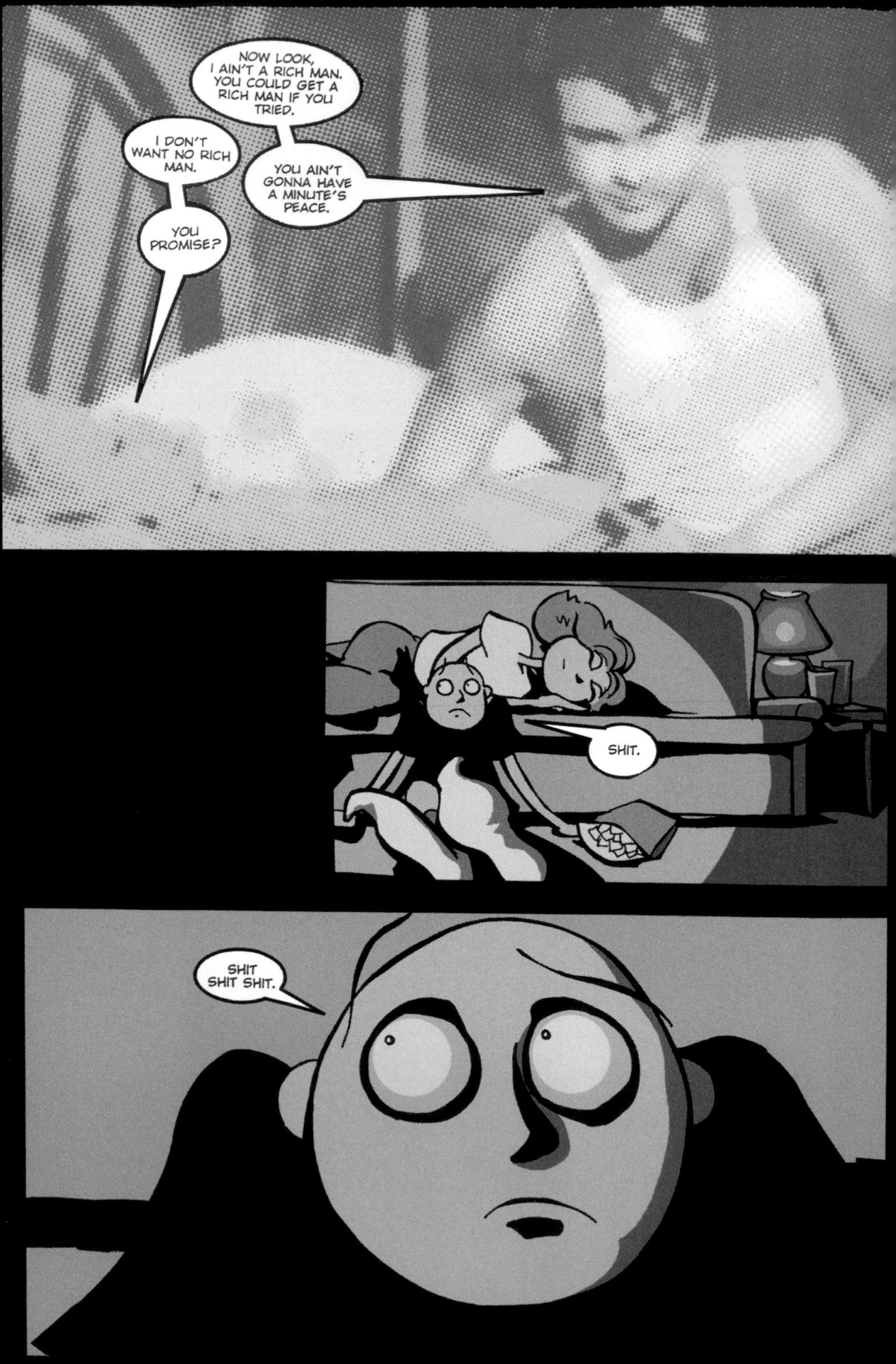
NOW LOOK, I AIN'T A RICH MAN. YOU COULD GET A RICH MAN IF YOU TRIED.
I DON'T WANT NO RICH MAN.
YOU AIN'T GONNA HAVE A MINUTE'S PEACE.
YOU PROMISE?
SHIT.
SHIT SHIT SHIT.

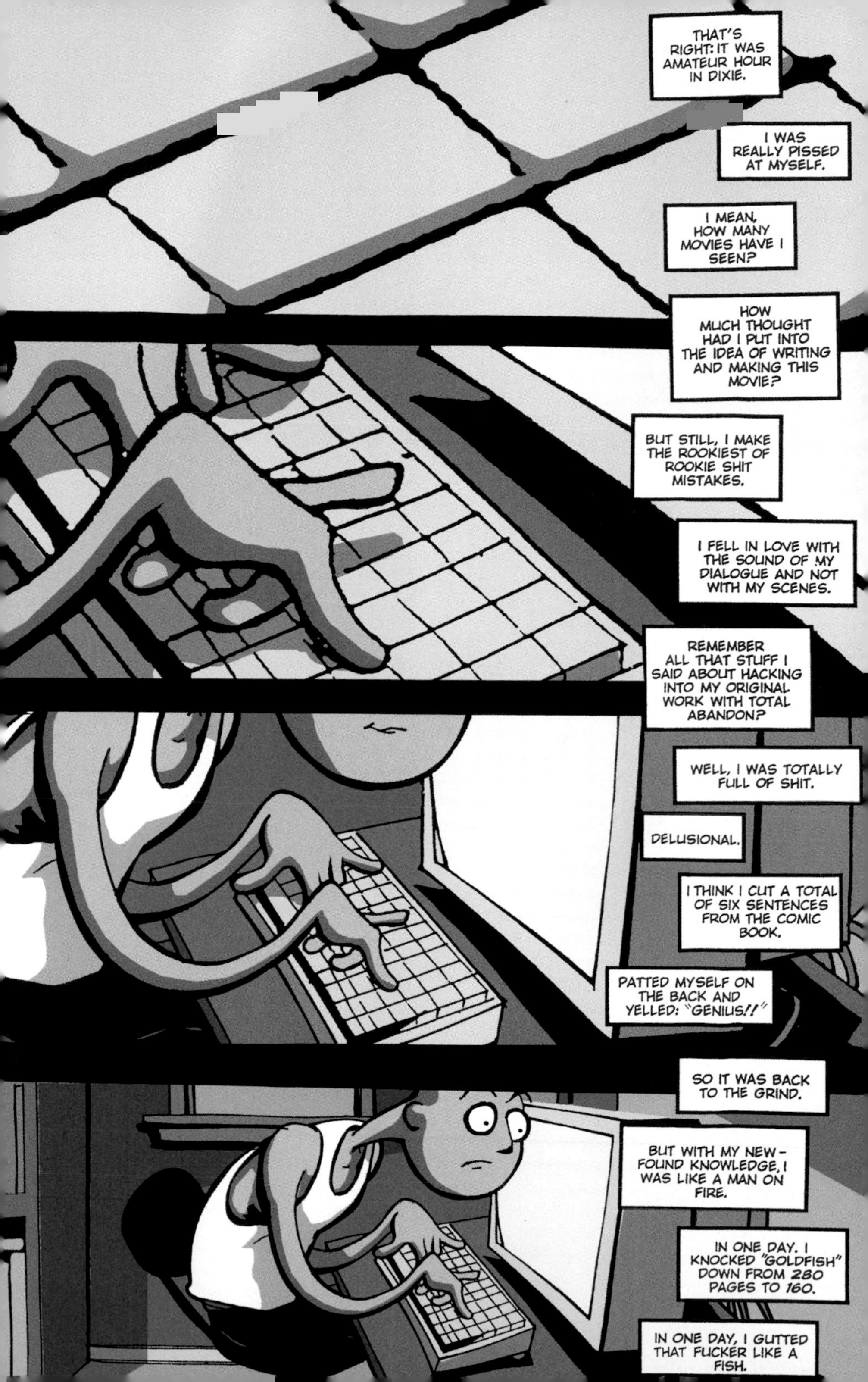
THAT'S RIGHT: IT WAS AMATEUR HOUR IN DIXIE.
I WAS REALLY PISSED AT MYSELF.
I MEAN, HOW MANY MOVIES HAVE I SEEN?
HOW MUCH THOUGHT HAD I PUT INTO THE IDEA OF WRITING AND MAKING THIS MOVIE?
BUT STILL, I MAKE THE ROOKIEST OF ROOKIE SHIT MISTAKES.
I FELL IN LOVE WITH THE SOUND OF MY DIALOGUE AND NOT WITH MY SCENES.
REMEMBER ALL THAT STUFF I SAID ABOUT HACKING INTO MY ORIGINAL WORK WITH TOTAL ABANDON?
WELL, I WAS TOTALLY FULL OF SHIT.
DELUSIONAL.
I THINK I CUT A TOTAL OF SIX SENTENCES FROM THE COMIC BOOK.
PATTED MYSELF ON THE BACK AND YELLED: "GENIUS!!"
SO IT WAS BACK TO THE GRIND.
BUT WITH MY NEW-FOUND KNOWLEDGE, I WAS LIKE A MAN ON FIRE.
IN ONE DAY. I KNOCKED "GOLDFISH" DOWN FROM 280 PAGES TO 160.
IN ONE DAY, I GUTTED THAT FUCKER LIKE A FISH.

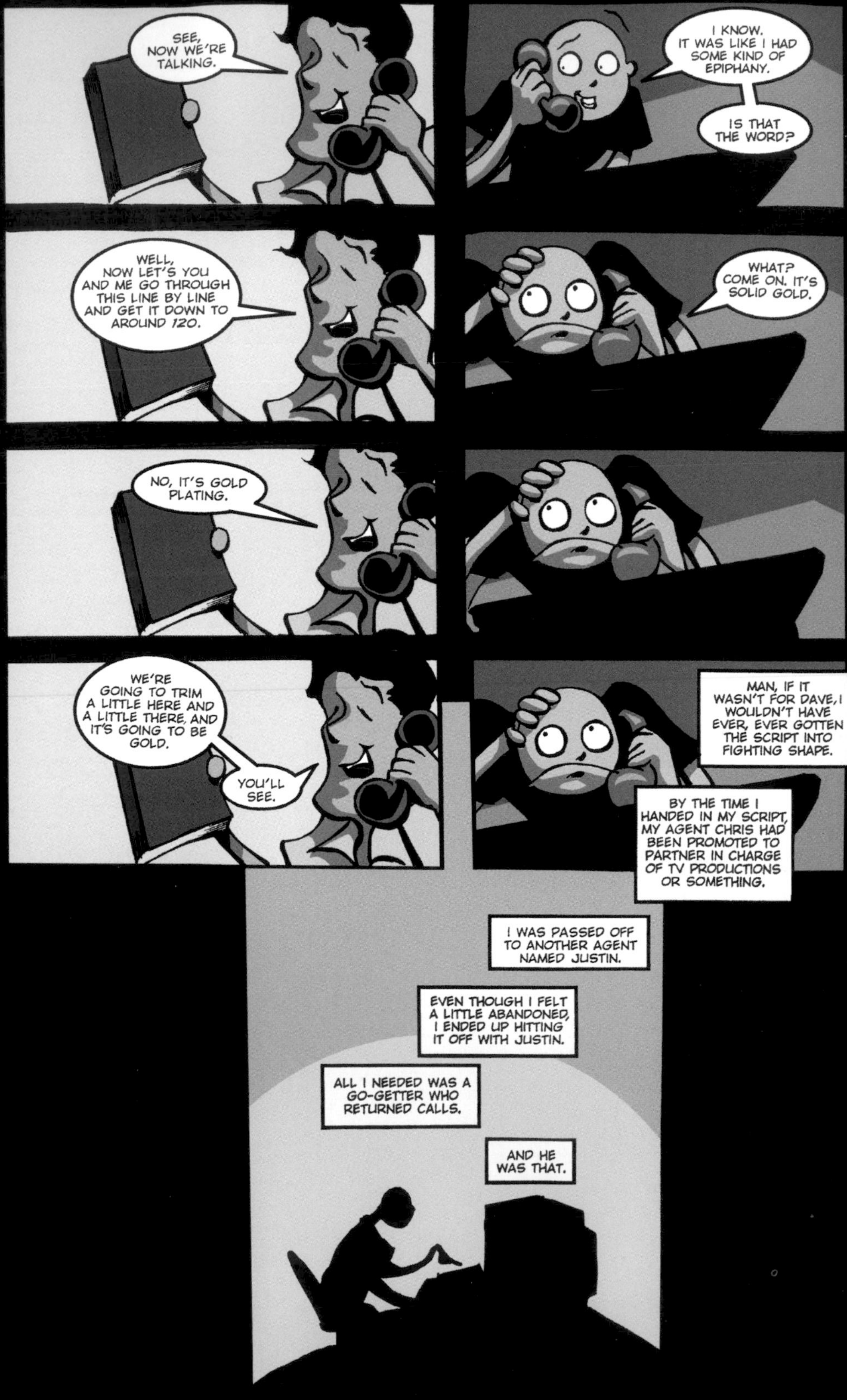
SEE, NOW WE'RE TALKING.
I KNOW. IT WAS LIKE I HAD SOME KIND OF EPIPHANY.
IS THAT THE WORD?
WELL, NOW LET'S YOU AND ME GO THROUGH THIS LINE BY LINE AND GET IT DOWN TO AROUND 120.
WHAT? COME ON. IT'S SOLID GOLD.
NO, IT'S GOLD PLATING.
WE'RE GOING TO TRIM A LITTLE HERE AND A LITTLE THERE, AND IT'S GOING TO BE GOLD.
YOU'LL SEE.
MAN, IF IT WASN'T FOR DAVE, I WOULDN'T HAVE EVER, EVER GOTTEN THE SCRIPT INTO FIGHTING SHAPE.
BY THE TIME I HANDED IN MY SCRIPT, MY AGENT CHRIS HAD BEEN PROMOTED TO PARTNER IN CHARGE OF TV PRODUCTIONS OR SOMETHING.
I WAS PASSED OFF TO ANOTHER AGENT NAMED JUSTIN.
EVEN THOUGH I FELT A LITTLE ABANDONED, I ENDED UP HITTING IT OFF WITH JUSTIN.
ALL I NEEDED WAS A GO-GETTER WHO RETURNED CALLS.
AND HE WAS THAT.

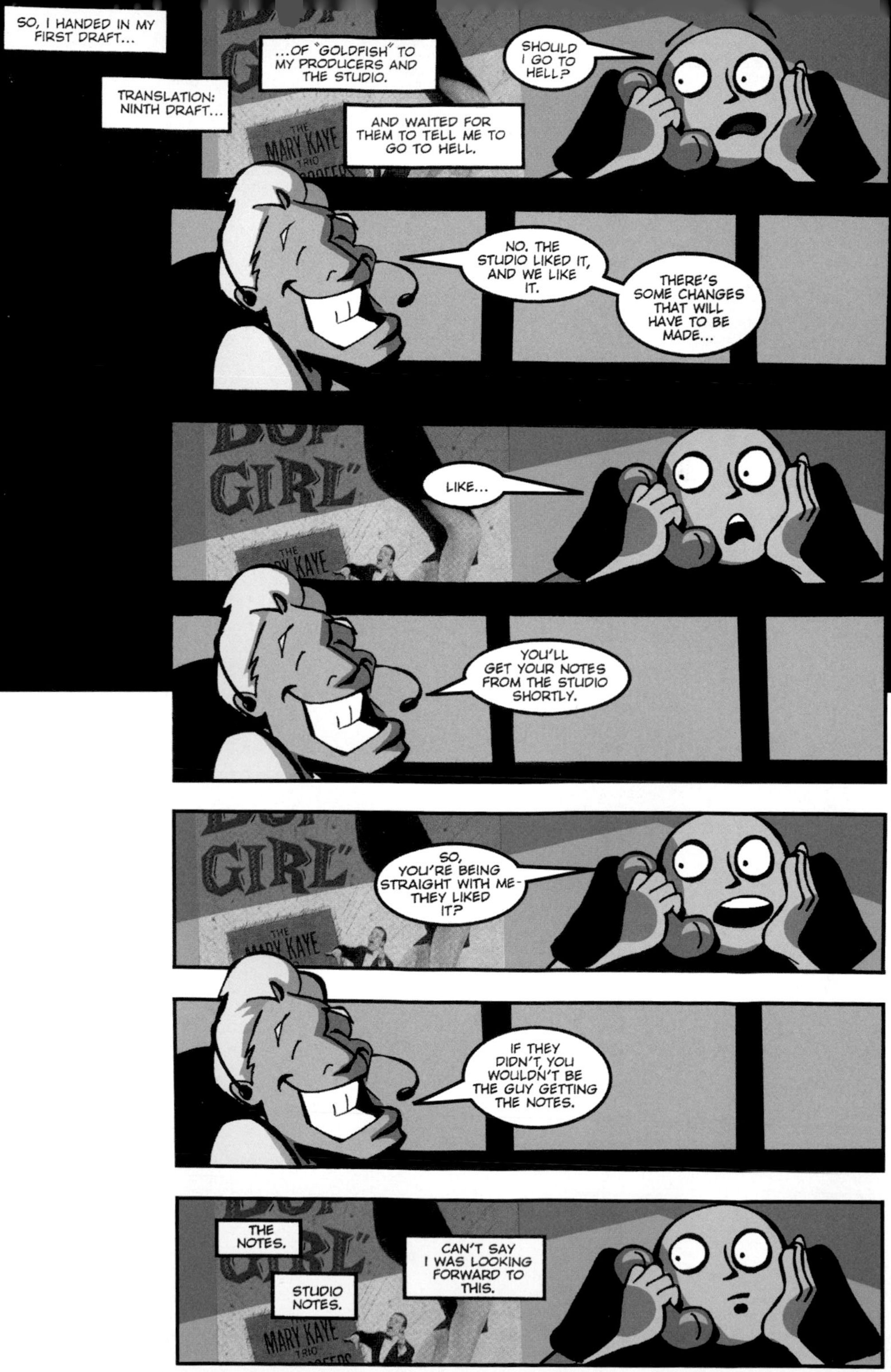
SO, I HANDED IN MY FIRST DRAFT...
TRANSLATION: NINTH DRAFT...
...OF "GOLDFISH" TO MY PRODUCERS AND THE STUDIO.
AND WAITED FOR THEM TO TELL ME TO GO TO HELL.
SHOULD I GO TO HELL?
NO. THE STUDIO LIKED IT, AND WE LIKE IT.
THERE'S SOME CHANGES THAT WILL HAVE TO BE MADE...
LIKE...
YOU'LL GET YOUR NOTES FROM THE STUDIO SHORTLY.
SO, YOU'RE BEING STRAIGHT WITH ME- THEY LIKED IT?
IF THEY DIDN'T, YOU WOULDN'T BE THE GUY GETTING THE NOTES.
THE NOTES.
STUDIO NOTES.
CAN'T SAY I WAS LOOKING FORWARD TO THIS.

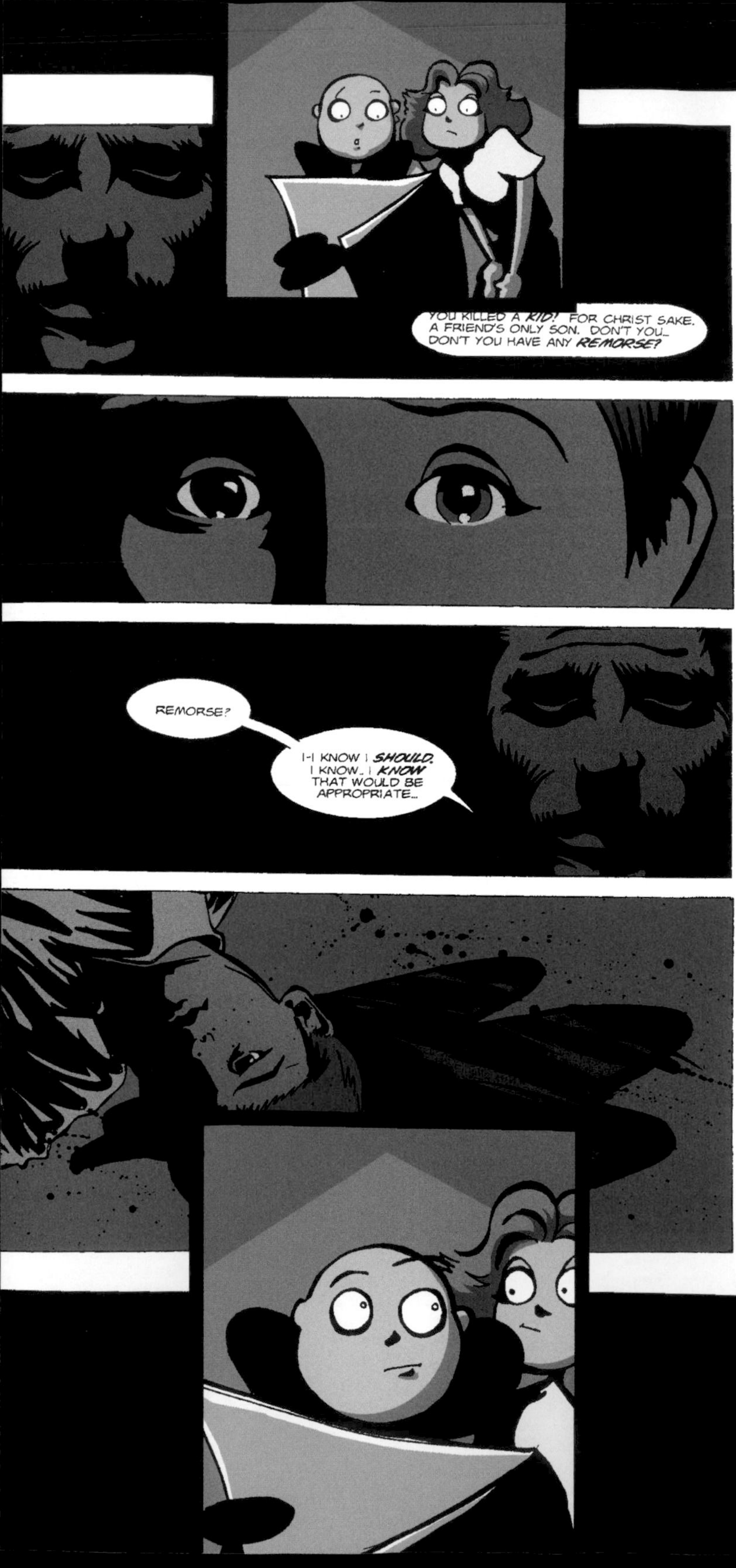
YOU KILLED A *KID!* FOR CHRIST SAKE. A FRIEND'S ONLY SON. DON'T YOU... DON'T YOU HAVE ANY *REMORSE?*
REMORSE?
I-I KNOW I *SHOULD.* I KNOW.. I *KNOW* THAT WOULD BE APPROPRIATE...

BUT TO MY SURPRISE...

THE NOTES MADE A LOT OF SENSE.

THE BIG PLOT CONCERN WAS THAT I KILLED GOLDFISH'S KID AT THE END OF THE THIRD ACT.

LIKE I DID IN THE BOOK.

THEY EXPLAINED THAT KILLING THE KID BEFORE GOLDFISH GETS TO HIM WORKS IN BOOK FORM...

BUT IN MOVIE FORM, ALL YOU ACCOMPLISH BY KILLING THE KID IS DENYING THE AUDIENCE THE MAGIC REUNION MOMENT YOU'VE BEEN PROMISING THEM SINCE THE FILM STARTED.

I HAD TO SAY THAT THIS MADE DAMN GOOD SENSE.

THEY ALSO THOUGHT IT WOULDN'T KILL ME TO SHAVE TEN PAGES OFF IT. AT *119,* IT CAME IN A LITTLE LONG.

LITTLE DID THEY KNOW...

SO, I DID ANOTHER POLISH...

GOT ANOTHER CHECK...

AND EVERYBODY INVOLVED SEEMED TO BE ABLE TO SMILE AND LOOK ME IN THE EYE.

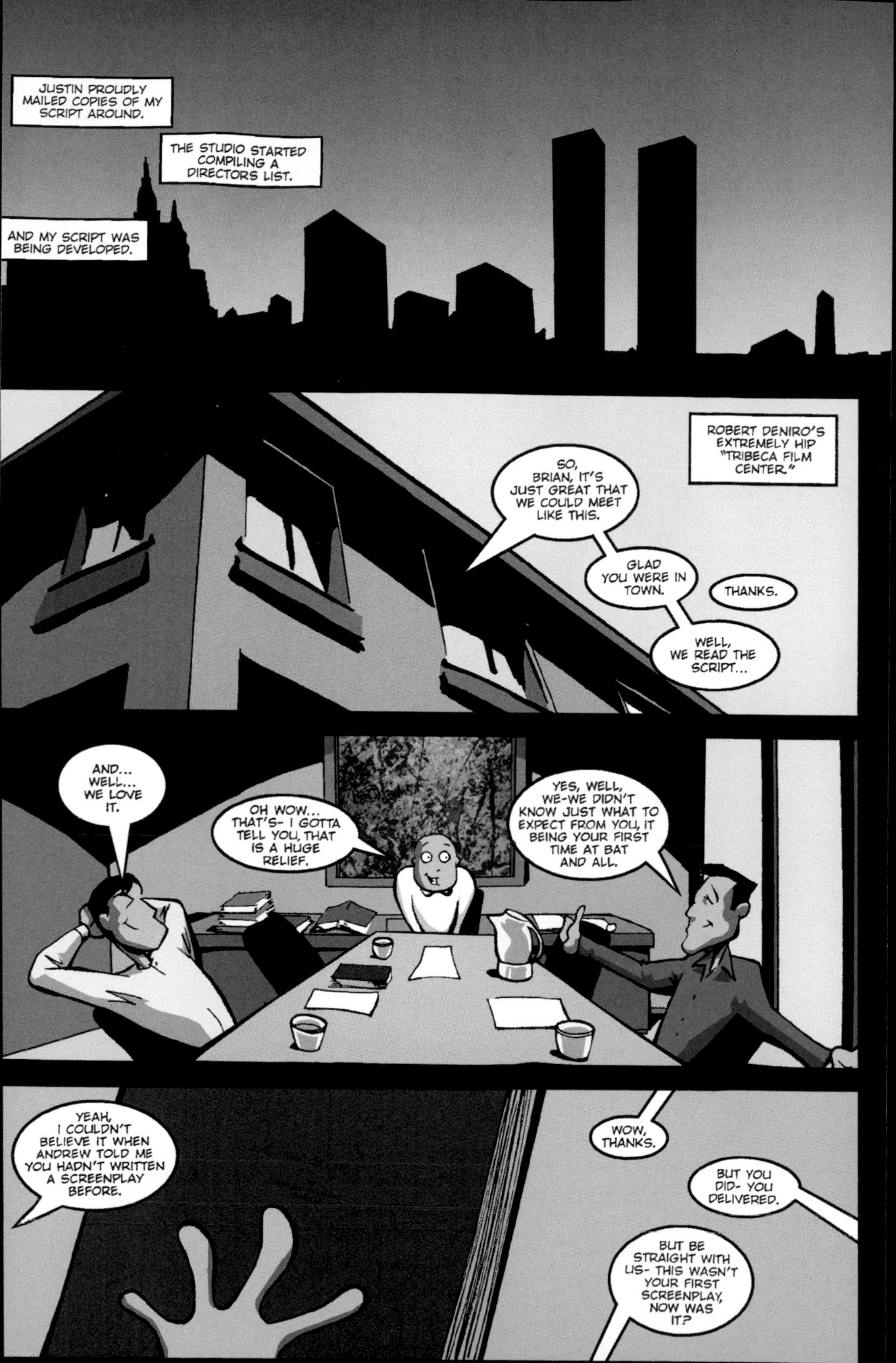
JUSTIN PROUDLY MAILED COPIES OF MY SCRIPT AROUND.
THE STUDIO STARTED COMPILING A DIRECTORS LIST.
AND MY SCRIPT WAS BEING DEVELOPED.
ROBERT DENIRO'S EXTREMELY HIP "TRIBECA FILM CENTER."
SO, BRIAN, IT'S JUST GREAT THAT WE COULD MEET LIKE THIS.
GLAD YOU WERE IN TOWN.
THANKS.
WELL, WE READ THE SCRIPT...
AND... WELL... WE LOVE IT.
OH WOW... THAT'S- I GOTTA TELL YOU, THAT IS A HUGE RELIEF.
YES, WELL, WE-WE DIDN'T KNOW JUST WHAT TO EXPECT FROM YOU, IT BEING YOUR FIRST TIME AT BAT AND ALL.
YEAH, I COULDN'T BELIEVE IT WHEN ANDREW TOLD ME YOU HADN'T WRITTEN A SCREENPLAY BEFORE.
WOW, THANKS.
BUT YOU DID- YOU DELIVERED.
BUT BE STRAIGHT WITH US- THIS WASN'T YOUR FIRST SCREENPLAY, NOW WAS IT?

CORDIALLY INVITE

TO A SPECIAL SCREENING

AFTER MY MEETING WITH THE NEW YORK GUYS I STARTED RECEIVING INVITATIONS TO ALL THE BIG HOLLYWOOD PREMIERES AND PARTIES THAT THE STUDIO HOSTED.

I WAS INVITED TO THE PREMIERES OF "SCREAM 2," "HALLOWEEN H20," AND "GOOD WILL HUNTING."

I ALWAYS GOT THE INVITATION LIKE FOUR DAYS BEFORE THE EVENT.

SO, EVEN IF I WAS DYING TO GO, IT WOULD HAVE BEEN ONE HUGE EXPENSIVE PAIN IN THE ASS JUST TO SEE JAIMIE LEE CURTIS OUTRUN FATHER TIME BEFORE EVERYBODY ELSE.

SO, I FORWARDED THE INVITES TO MARC ANDREYKO, WHO I HAD STARTED WORKING ON "TORSO" WITH.

MARC WAS A FELLOW CLEVELANDER WHO HAD HEAD OUT WEST TO SEEK HIS FORTUNE.

AND HE WAS DOING PRETTY WELL.

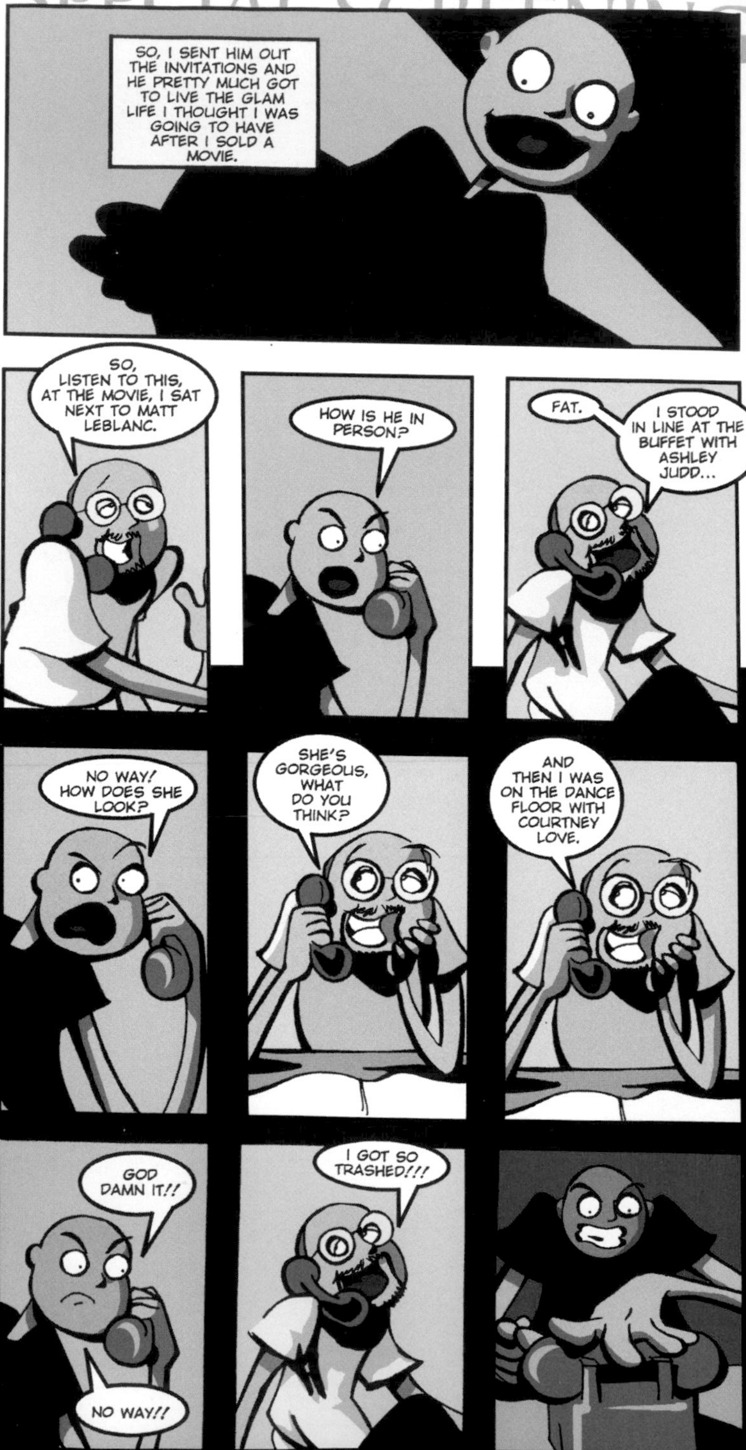
SO, I SENT HIM OUT THE INVITATIONS AND HE PRETTY MUCH GOT TO LIVE THE GLAM LIFE I THOUGHT I WAS GOING TO HAVE AFTER I SOLD A MOVIE.
SO, LISTEN TO THIS, AT THE MOVIE, I SAT NEXT TO MATT LEBLANC.
HOW IS HE IN PERSON?
FAT.
I STOOD IN LINE AT THE BUFFET WITH ASHLEY JUDD...
NO WAY! HOW DOES SHE LOOK?
SHE'S GORGEOUS, WHAT DO YOU THINK?
AND THEN I WAS ON THE DANCE FLOOR WITH COURTNEY LOVE.
GOD DAMN IT!!
NO WAY!!
I GOT SO TRASHED!!!

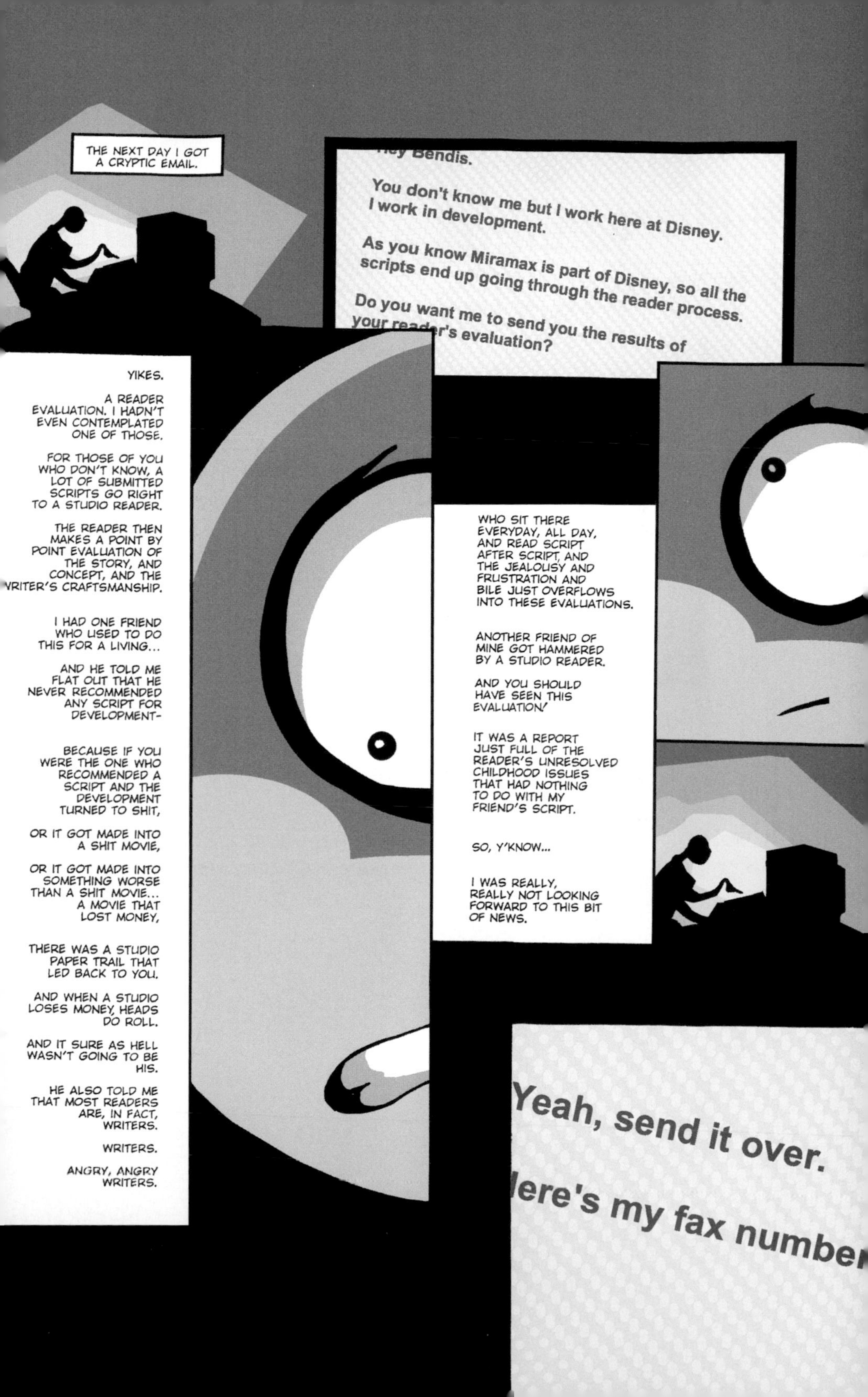
THE NEXT DAY I GOT A CRYPTIC EMAIL.
Hey Bendis.
You don't know me but I work here at Disney. I work in development.
As you know Miramax is part of Disney, so all the scripts end up going through the reader process.
Do you want me to send you the results of your reader's evaluation?
YIKES.
A READER EVALUATION. I HADN'T EVEN CONTEMPLATED ONE OF THOSE.
FOR THOSE OF YOU WHO DON'T KNOW, A LOT OF SUBMITTED SCRIPTS GO RIGHT TO A STUDIO READER.
THE READER THEN MAKES A POINT BY POINT EVALUATION OF THE STORY, AND CONCEPT, AND THE WRITER'S CRAFTSMANSHIP.
I HAD ONE FRIEND WHO USED TO DO THIS FOR A LIVING...
AND HE TOLD ME FLAT OUT THAT HE NEVER RECOMMENDED ANY SCRIPT FOR DEVELOPMENT-
BECAUSE IF YOU WERE THE ONE WHO RECOMMENDED A SCRIPT AND THE DEVELOPMENT TURNED TO SHIT,
OR IT GOT MADE INTO A SHIT MOVIE,
OR IT GOT MADE INTO SOMETHING WORSE THAN A SHIT MOVIE... A MOVIE THAT LOST MONEY,
THERE WAS A STUDIO PAPER TRAIL THAT LED BACK TO YOU.
AND WHEN A STUDIO LOSES MONEY, HEADS DO ROLL.
AND IT SURE AS HELL WASN'T GOING TO BE HIS.
HE ALSO TOLD ME THAT MOST READERS ARE, IN FACT, WRITERS.
WRITERS.
ANGRY, ANGRY WRITERS.
WHO SIT THERE EVERYDAY, ALL DAY, AND READ SCRIPT AFTER SCRIPT, AND THE JEALOUSY AND FRUSTRATION AND BILE JUST OVERFLOWS INTO THESE EVALUATIONS.
ANOTHER FRIEND OF MINE GOT HAMMERED BY A STUDIO READER.
AND YOU SHOULD HAVE SEEN THIS EVALUATION!
IT WAS A REPORT JUST FULL OF THE READER'S UNRESOLVED CHILDHOOD ISSUES THAT HAD NOTHING TO DO WITH MY FRIEND'S SCRIPT.
SO, Y'KNOW...
I WAS REALLY, REALLY NOT LOOKING FORWARD TO THIS BIT OF NEWS.
Yeah, send it over.
Here's my fax number

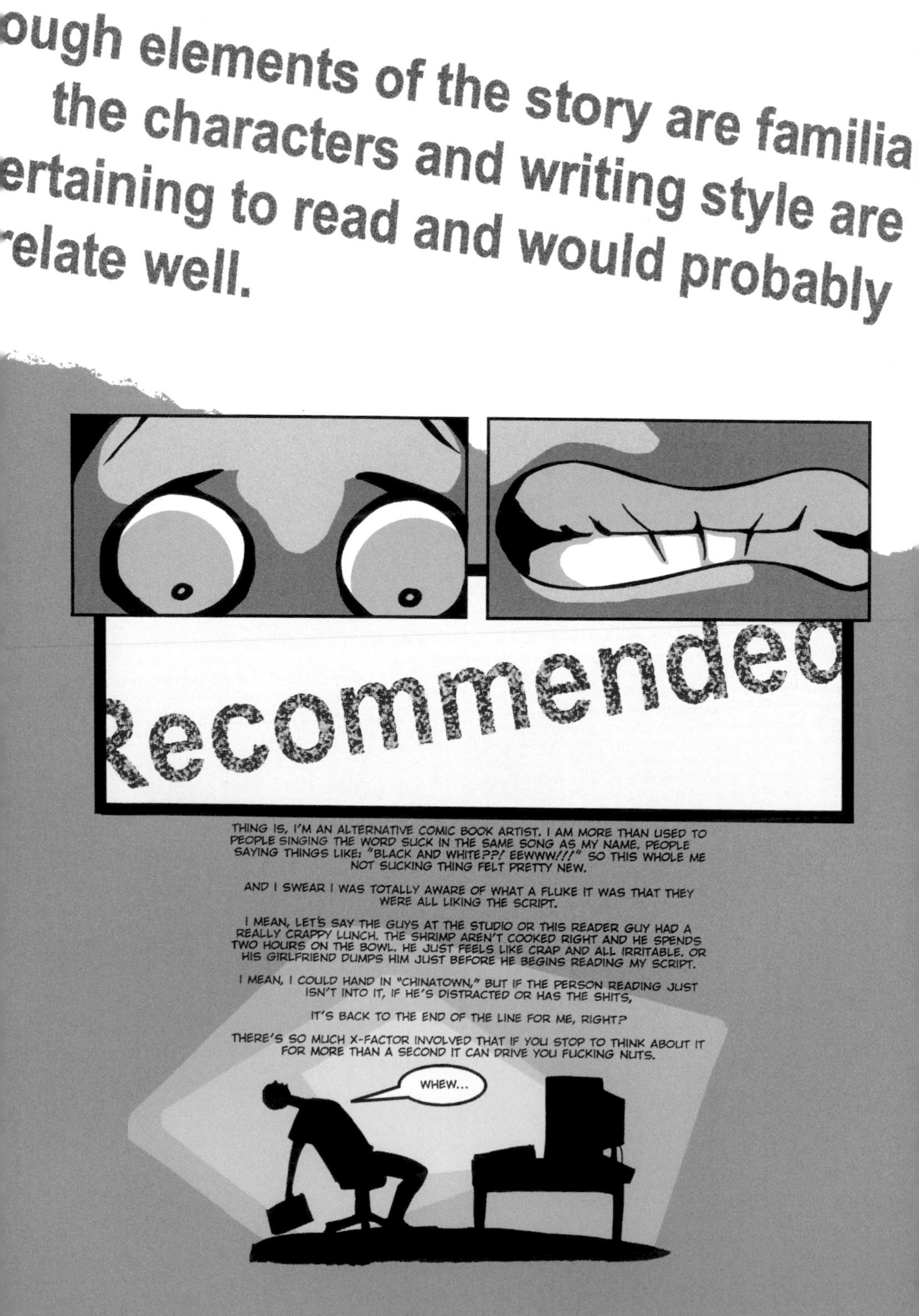
ough elements of the story are familia
the characters and writing style are
ertaining to read and would probably
relate well.
Recommended
THING IS, I'M AN ALTERNATIVE COMIC BOOK ARTIST. I AM MORE THAN USED TO PEOPLE SINGING THE WORD SUCK IN THE SAME SONG AS MY NAME. PEOPLE SAYING THINGS LIKE: "BLACK AND WHITE??! EEWWW!!!" SO THIS WHOLE ME NOT SUCKING THING FELT PRETTY NEW.
AND I SWEAR I WAS TOTALLY AWARE OF WHAT A FLUKE IT WAS THAT THEY WERE ALL LIKING THE SCRIPT.
I MEAN, LET'S SAY THE GUYS AT THE STUDIO OR THIS READER GUY HAD A REALLY CRAPPY LUNCH. THE SHRIMP AREN'T COOKED RIGHT AND HE SPENDS TWO HOURS ON THE BOWL. HE JUST FEELS LIKE CRAP AND ALL IRRITABLE. OR HIS GIRLFRIEND DUMPS HIM JUST BEFORE HE BEGINS READING MY SCRIPT.
I MEAN, I COULD HAND IN "CHINATOWN," BUT IF THE PERSON READING JUST ISN'T INTO IT, IF HE'S DISTRACTED OR HAS THE SHITS,
IT'S BACK TO THE END OF THE LINE FOR ME, RIGHT?
THERE'S SO MUCH X-FACTOR INVOLVED THAT IF YOU STOP TO THINK ABOUT IT FOR MORE THAN A SECOND IT CAN DRIVE YOU FUCKING NUTS.
WHEW...

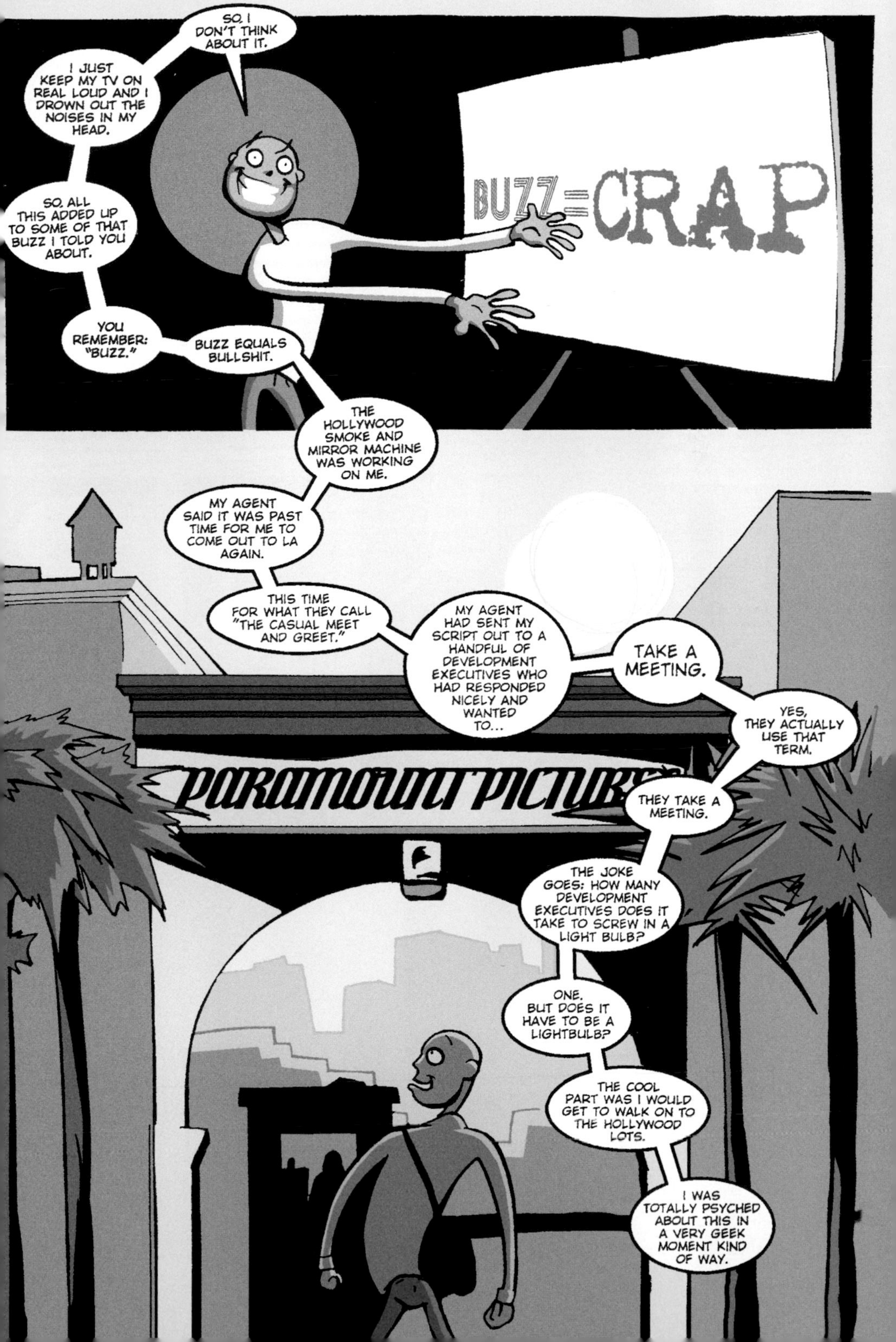
I JUST KEEP MY TV ON REAL LOUD AND I DROWN OUT THE NOISES IN MY HEAD.
SO, I DON'T THINK ABOUT IT.
BUZZ=CRAP
SO, ALL THIS ADDED UP TO SOME OF THAT BUZZ I TOLD YOU ABOUT.
YOU REMEMBER: "BUZZ."
BUZZ EQUALS BULLSHIT.
THE HOLLYWOOD SMOKE AND MIRROR MACHINE WAS WORKING ON ME.
MY AGENT SAID IT WAS PAST TIME FOR ME TO COME OUT TO LA AGAIN.
THIS TIME FOR WHAT THEY CALL "THE CASUAL MEET AND GREET."
MY AGENT HAD SENT MY SCRIPT OUT TO A HANDFUL OF DEVELOPMENT EXECUTIVES WHO HAD RESPONDED NICELY AND WANTED TO...
TAKE A MEETING.
YES, THEY ACTUALLY USE THAT TERM.
THEY TAKE A MEETING.
THE JOKE GOES: HOW MANY DEVELOPMENT EXECUTIVES DOES IT TAKE TO SCREW IN A LIGHT BULB?
ONE. BUT DOES IT HAVE TO BE A LIGHTBULB?
THE COOL PART WAS I WOULD GET TO WALK ON TO THE HOLLYWOOD LOTS.
I WAS TOTALLY PSYCHED ABOUT THIS IN A VERY GEEK MOMENT KIND OF WAY.

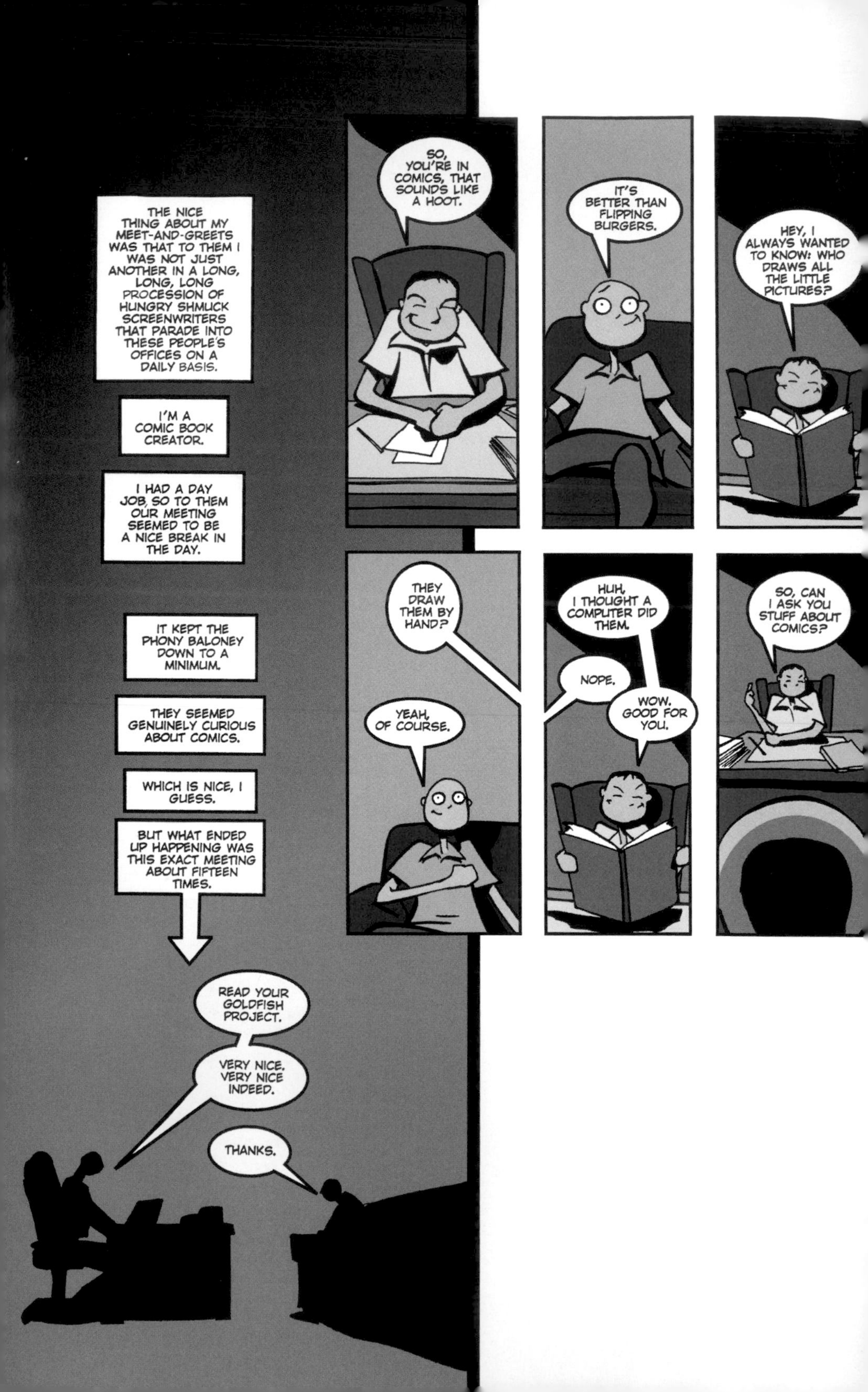
THE NICE THING ABOUT MY MEET-AND-GREETS WAS THAT TO THEM I WAS NOT JUST ANOTHER IN A LONG, LONG, LONG PROCESSION OF HUNGRY SHMUCK SCREENWRITERS THAT PARADE INTO THESE PEOPLE'S OFFICES ON A DAILY BASIS.
I'M A COMIC BOOK CREATOR.
I HAD A DAY JOB, SO TO THEM OUR MEETING SEEMED TO BE A NICE BREAK IN THE DAY.
SO, YOU'RE IN COMICS, THAT SOUNDS LIKE A HOOT.
IT'S BETTER THAN FLIPPING BURGERS.
HEY, I ALWAYS WANTED TO KNOW: WHO DRAWS ALL THE LITTLE PICTURES?
IT KEPT THE PHONY BALONEY DOWN TO A MINIMUM.
THEY SEEMED GENUINELY CURIOUS ABOUT COMICS.
WHICH IS NICE, I GUESS.
BUT WHAT ENDED UP HAPPENING WAS THIS EXACT MEETING ABOUT FIFTEEN TIMES.
YEAH, OF COURSE.
THEY DRAW THEM BY HAND?
NOPE.
HUH, I THOUGHT A COMPUTER DID THEM.
WOW. GOOD FOR YOU.
SO, CAN I ASK YOU STUFF ABOUT COMICS?
READ YOUR GOLDFISH PROJECT.
VERY NICE. VERY NICE INDEED.
THANKS.

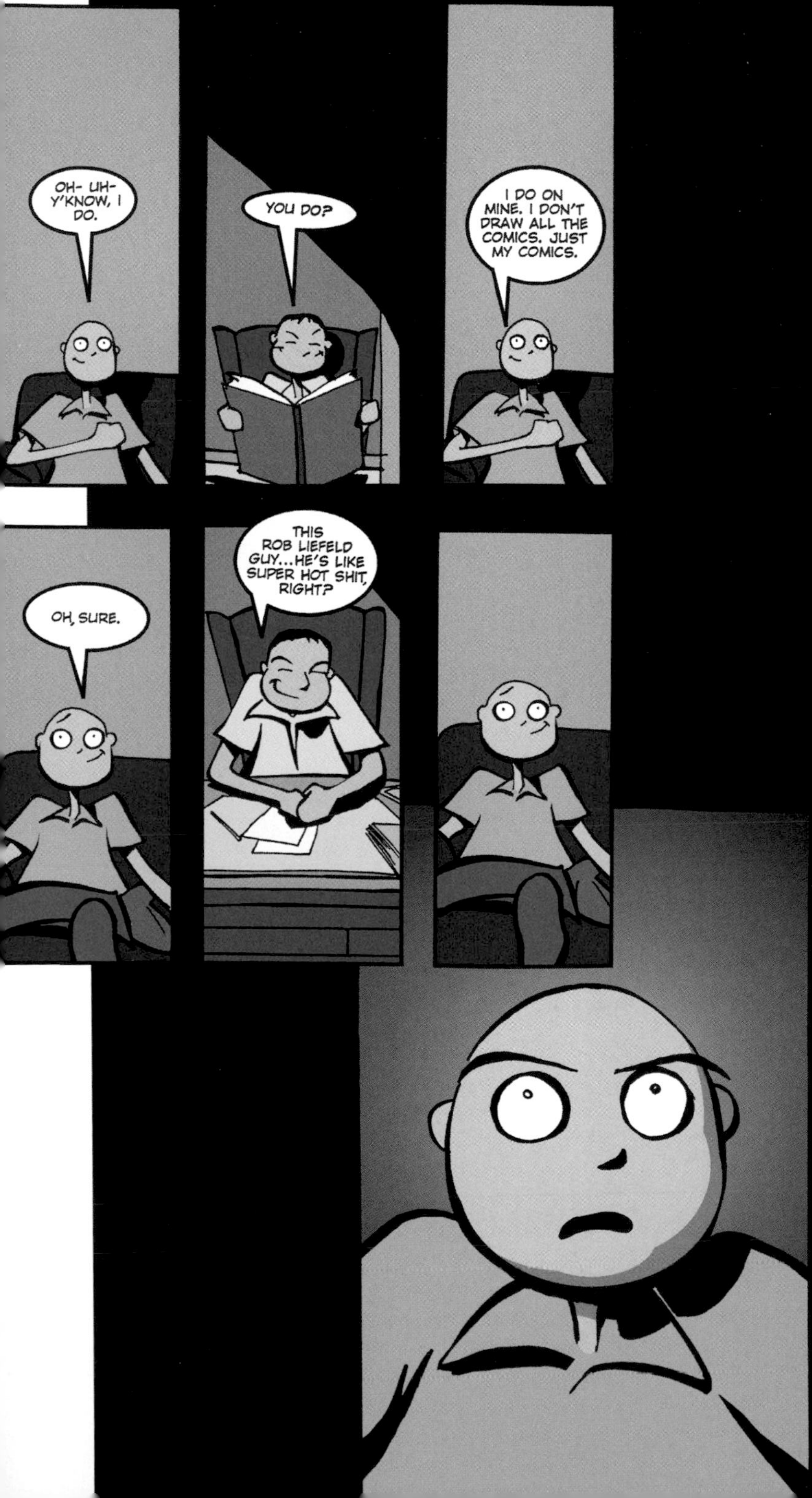
OH- UH- Y'KNOW, I DO.
YOU DO?
I DO ON MINE. I DON'T DRAW ALL THE COMICS. JUST MY COMICS.
OH, SURE.
THIS ROB LIEFELD GUY...HE'S LIKE SUPER HOT SHIT, RIGHT?

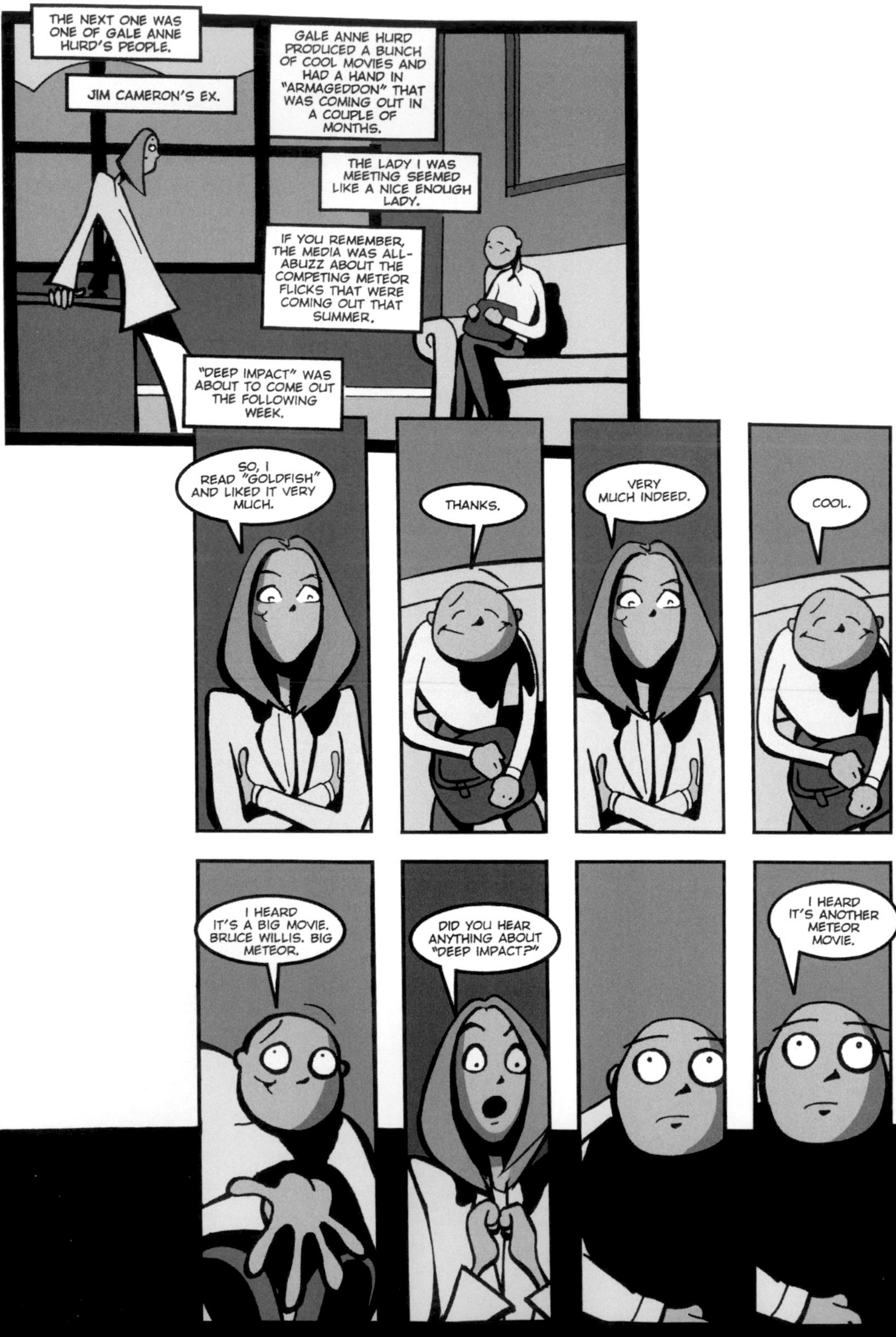
THE NEXT ONE WAS ONE OF GALE ANNE HURD'S PEOPLE.
JIM CAMERON'S EX.
GALE ANNE HURD PRODUCED A BUNCH OF COOL MOVIES AND HAD A HAND IN "ARMAGEDDON" THAT WAS COMING OUT IN A COUPLE OF MONTHS.
THE LADY I WAS MEETING SEEMED LIKE A NICE ENOUGH LADY.
IF YOU REMEMBER, THE MEDIA WAS ALL-ABUZZ ABOUT THE COMPETING METEOR FLICKS THAT WERE COMING OUT THAT SUMMER.
"DEEP IMPACT" WAS ABOUT TO COME OUT THE FOLLOWING WEEK.
SO, I READ "GOLDFISH" AND LIKED IT VERY MUCH.
THANKS.
VERY MUCH INDEED.
COOL.
I HEARD IT'S A BIG MOVIE. BRUCE WILLIS. BIG METEOR.
DID YOU HEAR ANYTHING ABOUT "DEEP IMPACT?"
I HEARD IT'S ANOTHER METEOR MOVIE.

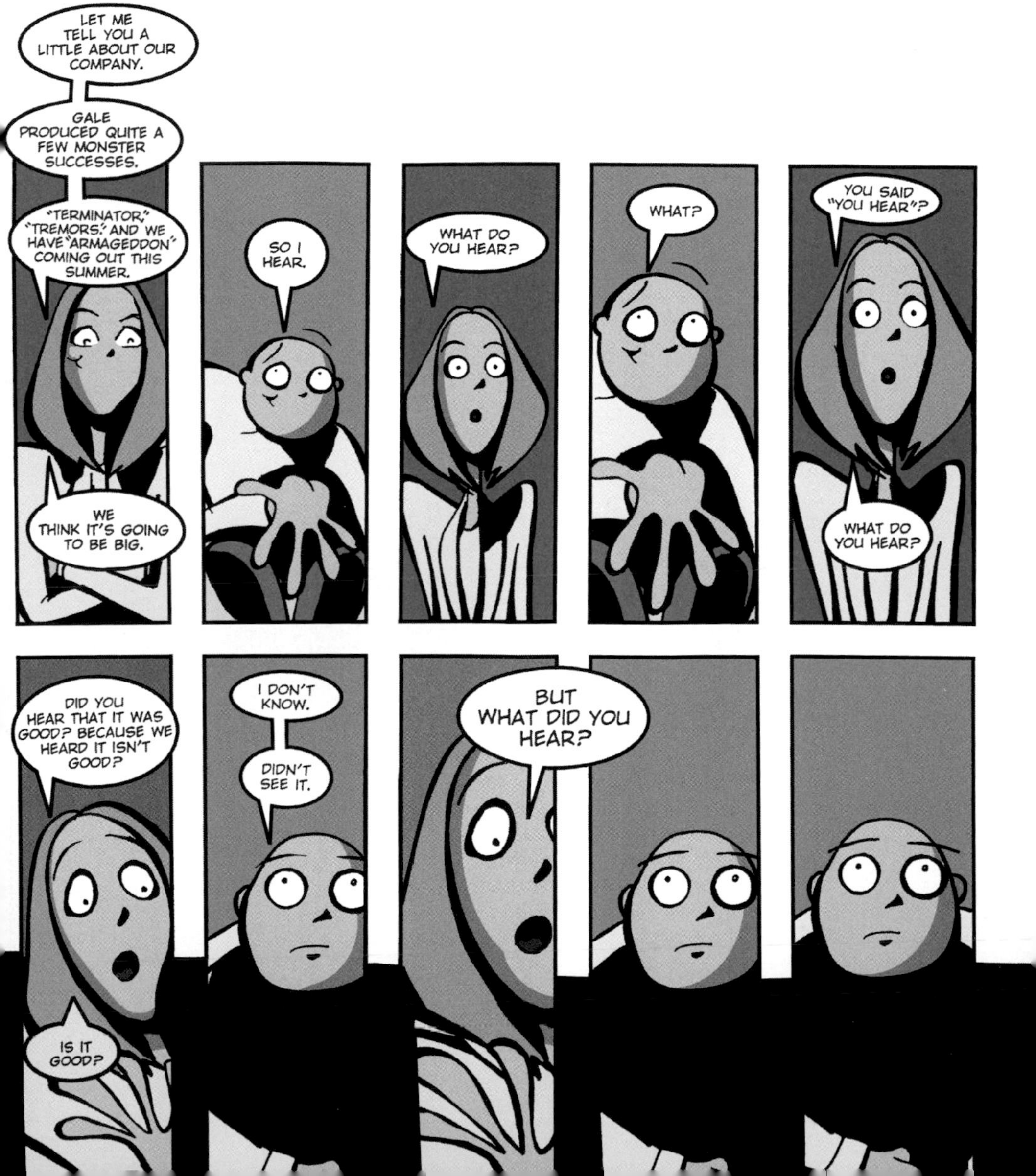
LET ME TELL YOU A LITTLE ABOUT OUR COMPANY.
GALE PRODUCED QUITE A FEW MONSTER SUCCESSES.
"TERMINATOR," "TREMORS," AND WE HAVE "ARMAGEDDON" COMING OUT THIS SUMMER.
WE THINK IT'S GOING TO BE BIG.
SO I HEAR.
WHAT DO YOU HEAR?
WHAT?
YOU SAID "YOU HEAR"?
WHAT DO YOU HEAR?
DID YOU HEAR THAT IT WAS GOOD? BECAUSE WE HEARD IT ISN'T GOOD?
IS IT GOOD?
I DON'T KNOW.
DIDN'T SEE IT.
BUT WHAT DID YOU HEAR?

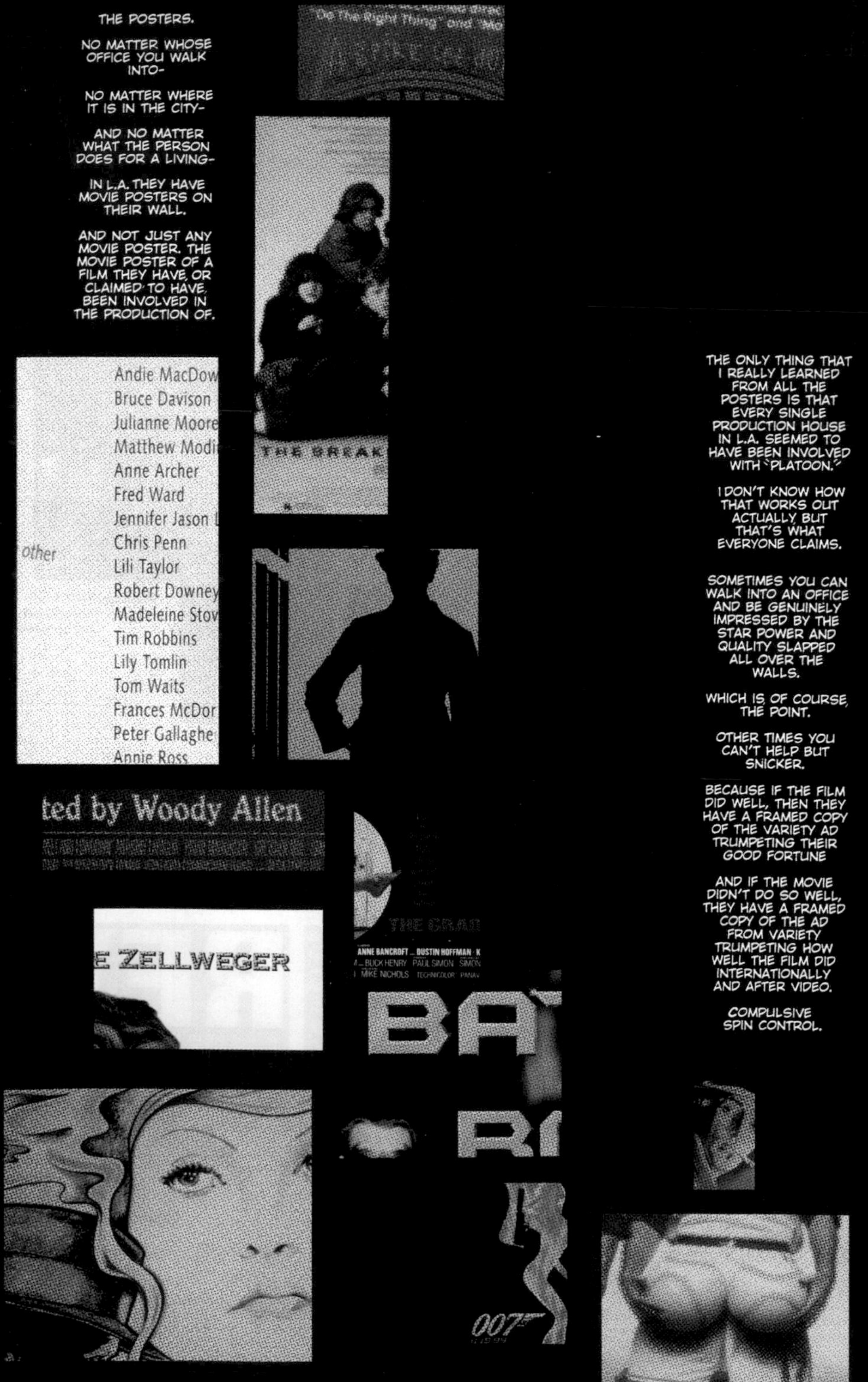

THE POSTERS.

NO MATTER WHOSE
OFFICE YOU WALK
INTO—

NO MATTER WHERE
IT IS IN THE CITY—

AND NO MATTER
WHAT THE PERSON
DOES FOR A LIVING—

IN L.A. THEY HAVE
MOVIE POSTERS ON
THEIR WALL.

AND NOT JUST ANY
MOVIE POSTER. THE
MOVIE POSTER OF A
FILM THEY HAVE, OR
CLAIMED TO HAVE
BEEN INVOLVED IN
THE PRODUCTION OF.

Andie MacDow
Bruce Davison
Julianne Moore
Matthew Modi
Anne Archer
Fred Ward
Jennifer Jason L
Chris Penn
Lili Taylor
Robert Downey
Madeleine Stov
Tim Robbins
Lily Tomlin
Tom Waits
Frances McDor
Peter Gallaghe
Annie Ross

other

THE BREAK

THE ONLY THING THAT
I REALLY LEARNED
FROM ALL THE
POSTERS IS THAT
EVERY SINGLE
PRODUCTION HOUSE
IN L.A. SEEMED TO
HAVE BEEN INVOLVED
WITH `PLATOON.´

I DON'T KNOW HOW
THAT WORKS OUT
ACTUALLY, BUT
THAT'S WHAT
EVERYONE CLAIMS.

SOMETIMES YOU CAN
WALK INTO AN OFFICE
AND BE GENUINELY
IMPRESSED BY THE
STAR POWER AND
QUALITY SLAPPED
ALL OVER THE
WALLS.

WHICH IS OF COURSE,
THE POINT.

OTHER TIMES YOU
CAN'T HELP BUT
SNICKER.

BECAUSE IF THE FILM
DID WELL, THEN THEY
HAVE A FRAMED COPY
OF THE VARIETY AD
TRUMPETING THEIR
GOOD FORTUNE

AND IF THE MOVIE
DIDN'T DO SO WELL,
THEY HAVE A FRAMED
COPY OF THE AD
FROM VARIETY
TRUMPETING HOW
WELL THE FILM DID
INTERNATIONALLY
AND AFTER VIDEO.

COMPULSIVE
SPIN CONTROL.

ted by Woody Allen

THE GRA

ANNE BANCROFT ... DUSTIN HOFFMAN · K
... BUCK HENRY PAUL SIMON SIMON ..
· MIKE NICHOLS TECHNICOLOR PANAV ...

E ZELLWEGER

007

THE SONY LOT IS A PRETTY INTERESTING PLACE.
IT IS A NEW STUDIO LOT AND THEY BUILT IT BIG.
REALLY BIG. GODZILLA BIG.
IN FACT, I WAS THERE THE SUMMER THEY WERE PROMOTING "GODZILLA."
EVERY SQUARE INCH OF THE CITY WAS COVERED IN GIANT "GODZILLA'S FOOT IS BIGGER THAN THIS" SIGNS.
THEY WERE PRETTY MUCH PISSING EVERYONE ELSE IN THE INDUSTRY OFF, AND I THINK THAT'S WHAT THE POINT OF THE SIGNS WERE TO BEGIN WITH.
NOW MOST STUDIOS, WHEN YOU WALK DOWN THE HALLWAYS, TREAT YOU TO THE MOVIE POSTERS OF THIER GREATEST MOMENTS IN MOTION PICTURE HISTORY.
WHEN YOU WALK DOWN THE HALLS AT SONY THEY GLADLY DISPLAY EACH AND EVERY MOVIE POSTER IN THE LIBRARY NO MATTER HOW SHIT ASS BAD THE MOVIE IS.
IN FACT, THERE'S THIS ONE BUILDING THAT IS LITERALLY A WALK OF SHAME.
YOU GET TWO BURT REYNOLDS PICTURES FROM THE MID EIGHTIES, "KRULL," "HARD BODIES," AND AS I WALKED UP TO THE DOOR OF THE OFFICE I HAD THE NEXT MEETING WITH
THERE SHE WAS... "SHEENA, QUEEN OF THE JUNGLE."
DE NIRO
GUN CRAZY
PROF
KED
NCH
A BRI
BUT I DIDN'T KNOW THAT THESE WERE JUST RAMDOMLY PLACED POSTERS.
I THOUGHT I WAS LOOKING AT THE PRODUCT OF THE FILM COMPANY I WAS GOING INTO, AND I WAS VERY CLOSE TO THROWING UP RIGHT THERE ON THE CARPET.

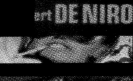

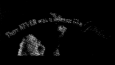

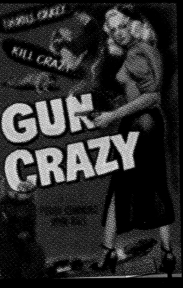

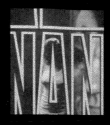

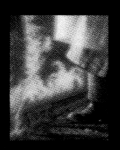

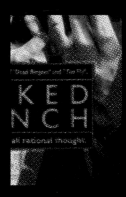

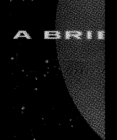

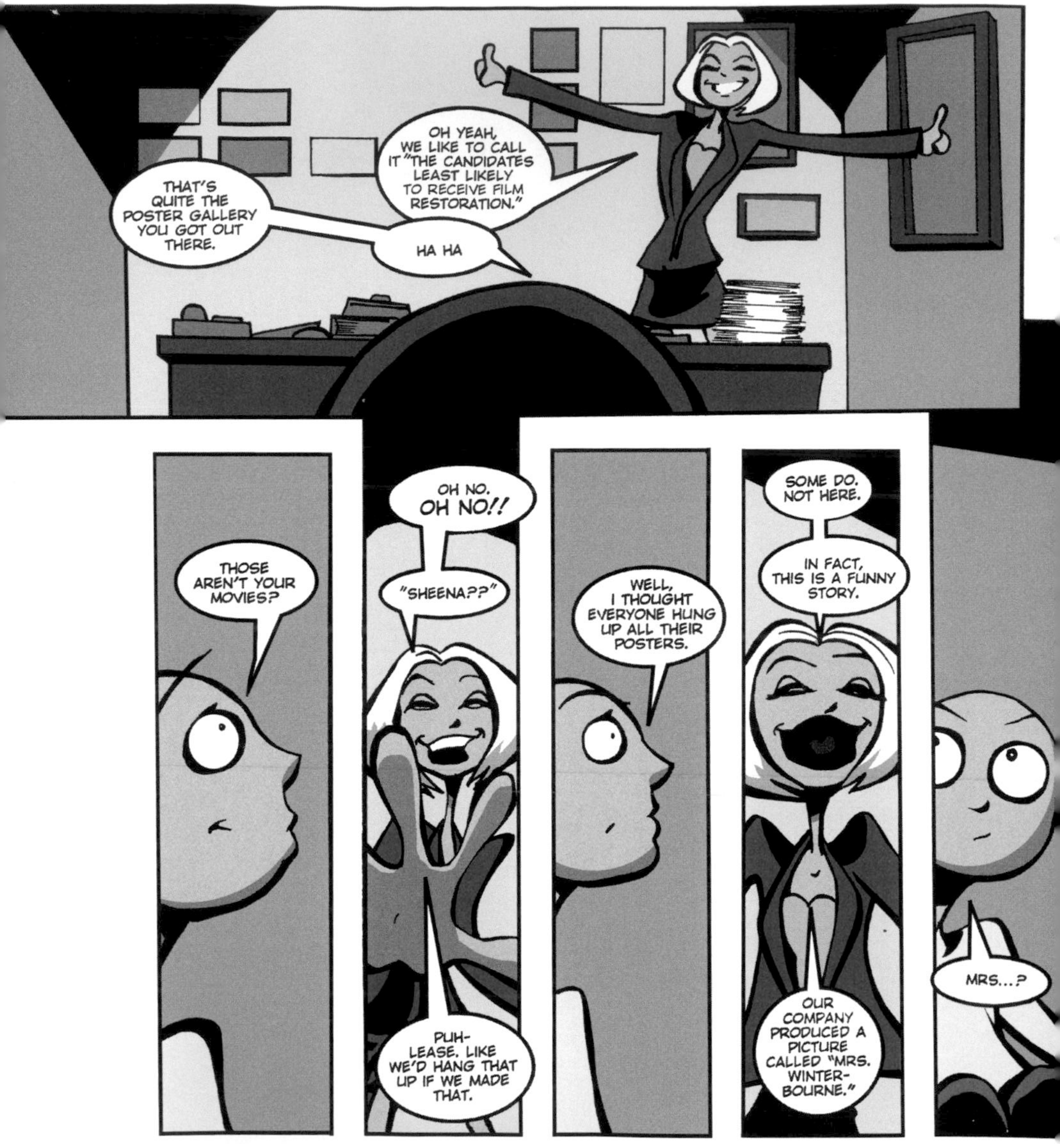
THAT'S QUITE THE POSTER GALLERY YOU GOT OUT THERE.
OH YEAH, WE LIKE TO CALL IT "THE CANDIDATES LEAST LIKELY TO RECEIVE FILM RESTORATION."
HA HA
THOSE AREN'T YOUR MOVIES?
OH NO. OH NO!!
"SHEENA??"
PUH-LEASE. LIKE WE'D HANG THAT UP IF WE MADE THAT.
WELL, I THOUGHT EVERYONE HUNG UP ALL THEIR POSTERS.
SOME DO. NOT HERE.
IN FACT, THIS IS A FUNNY STORY.
OUR COMPANY PRODUCED A PICTURE CALLED "MRS. WINTER-BOURNE."
MRS...?

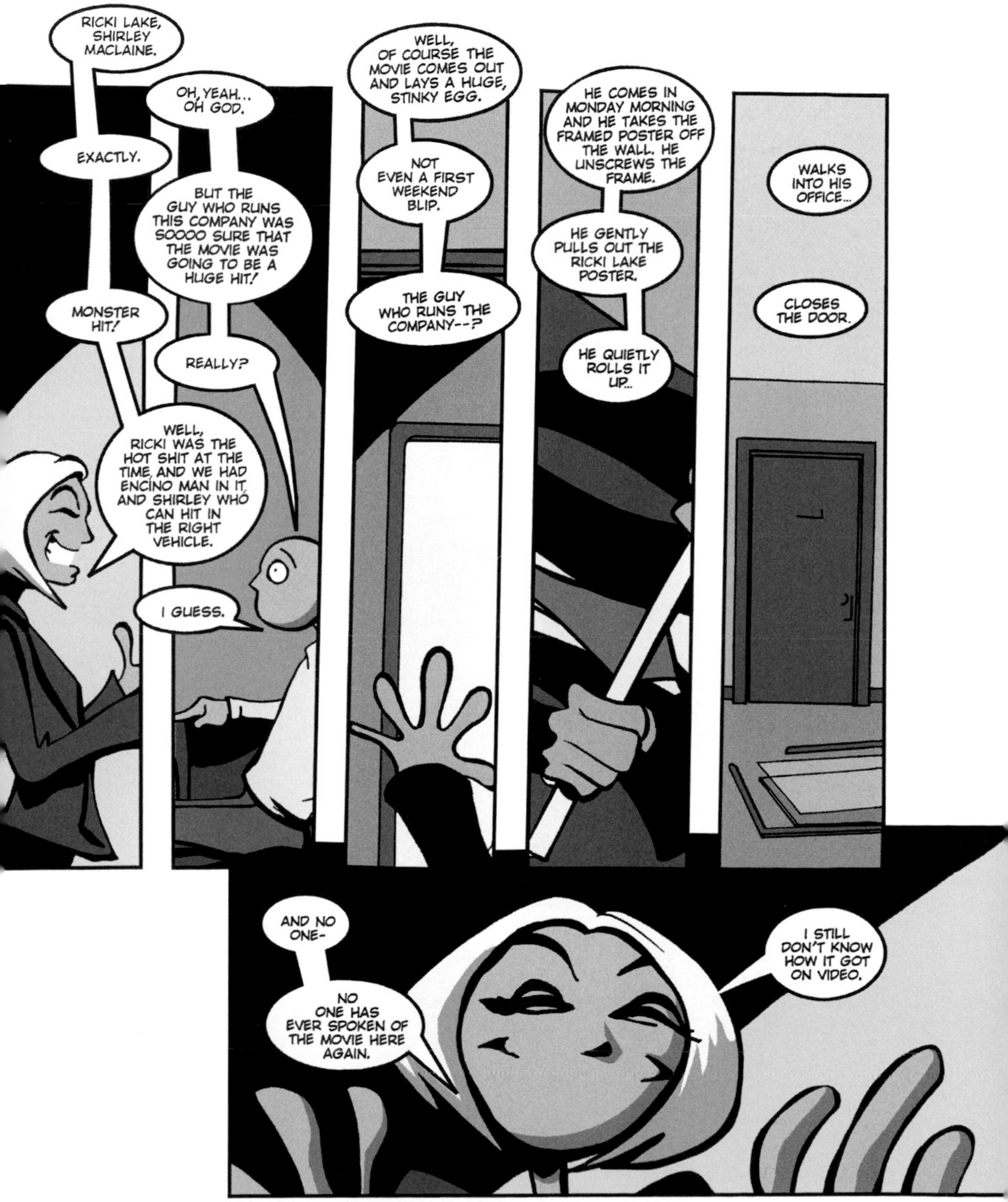
RICKI LAKE, SHIRLEY MACLAINE.
OH, YEAH... OH GOD.
EXACTLY.
BUT THE GUY WHO RUNS THIS COMPANY WAS SOOOO SURE THAT THE MOVIE WAS GOING TO BE A HUGE HIT!
MONSTER HIT!
REALLY?
WELL, RICKI WAS THE HOT SHIT AT THE TIME, AND WE HAD ENCINO MAN IN IT, AND SHIRLEY WHO CAN HIT IN THE RIGHT VEHICLE.
I GUESS.
WELL, OF COURSE THE MOVIE COMES OUT AND LAYS A HUGE, STINKY EGG.
NOT EVEN A FIRST WEEKEND BLIP.
THE GUY WHO RUNS THE COMPANY--?
HE COMES IN MONDAY MORNING AND HE TAKES THE FRAMED POSTER OFF THE WALL. HE UNSCREWS THE FRAME.
HE GENTLY PULLS OUT THE RICKI LAKE POSTER.
HE QUIETLY ROLLS IT UP...
WALKS INTO HIS OFFICE...
CLOSES THE DOOR.
AND NO ONE-
NO ONE HAS EVER SPOKEN OF THE MOVIE HERE AGAIN.
I STILL DON'T KNOW HOW IT GOT ON VIDEO.

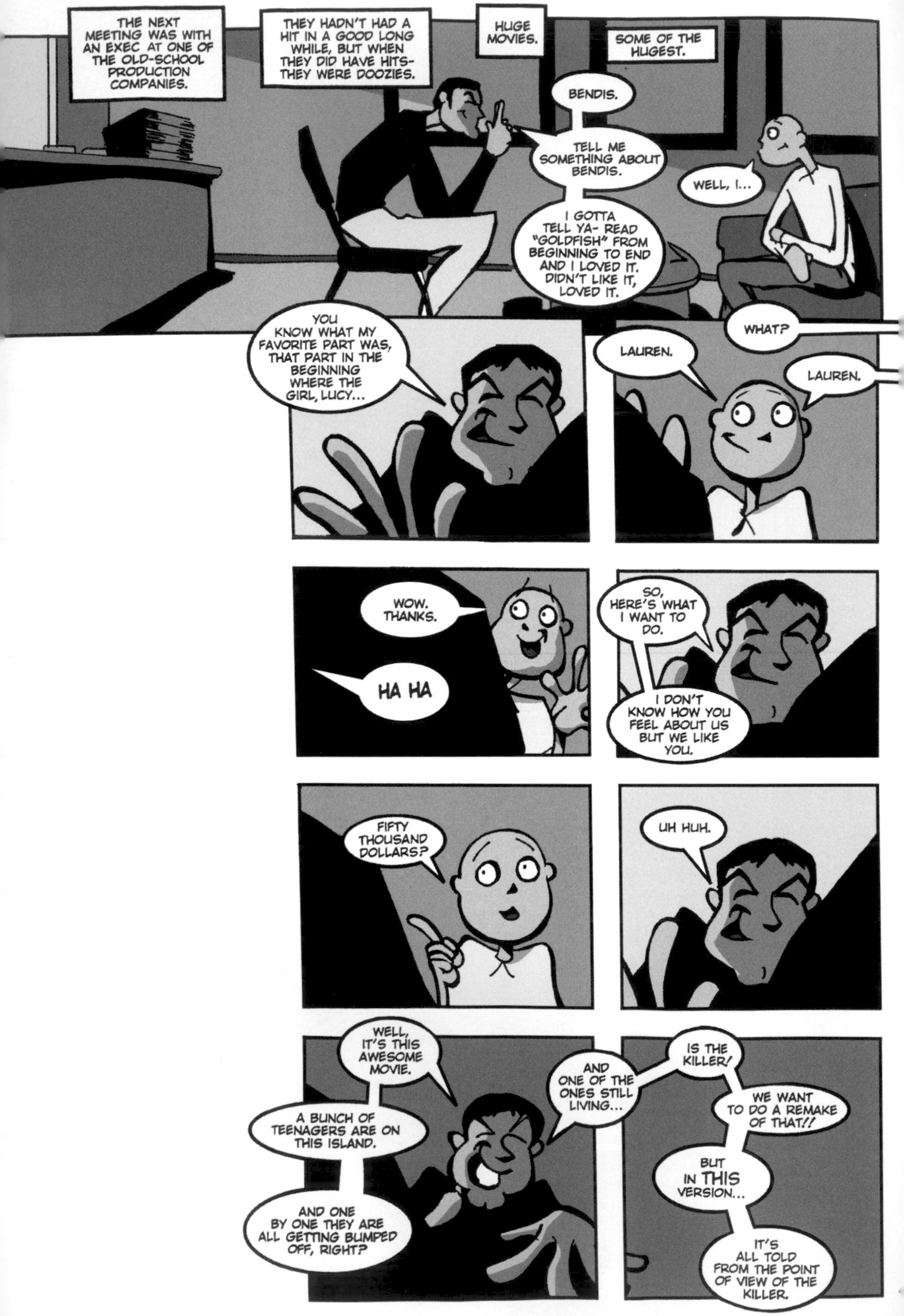
THE NEXT MEETING WAS WITH AN EXEC AT ONE OF THE OLD-SCHOOL PRODUCTION COMPANIES.
THEY HADN'T HAD A HIT IN A GOOD LONG WHILE, BUT WHEN THEY DID HAVE HITS- THEY WERE DOOZIES.
HUGE MOVIES.
SOME OF THE HUGEST.
BENDIS.
TELL ME SOMETHING ABOUT BENDIS.
WELL, I...
I GOTTA TELL YA- READ "GOLDFISH" FROM BEGINNING TO END AND I LOVED IT. DIDN'T LIKE IT, LOVED IT.
YOU KNOW WHAT MY FAVORITE PART WAS, THAT PART IN THE BEGINNING WHERE THE GIRL, LUCY...
LAUREN.
WHAT?
LAUREN.
WOW. THANKS.
HA HA
SO, HERE'S WHAT I WANT TO DO.
I DON'T KNOW HOW YOU FEEL ABOUT US BUT WE LIKE YOU.
FIFTY THOUSAND DOLLARS?
UH HUH.
WELL, IT'S THIS AWESOME MOVIE.
A BUNCH OF TEENAGERS ARE ON THIS ISLAND.
AND ONE BY ONE THEY ARE ALL GETTING BUMPED OFF, RIGHT?
AND ONE OF THE ONES STILL LIVING...
IS THE KILLER!
WE WANT TO DO A REMAKE OF THAT!!
BUT IN THIS VERSION...
IT'S ALL TOLD FROM THE POINT OF VIEW OF THE KILLER.

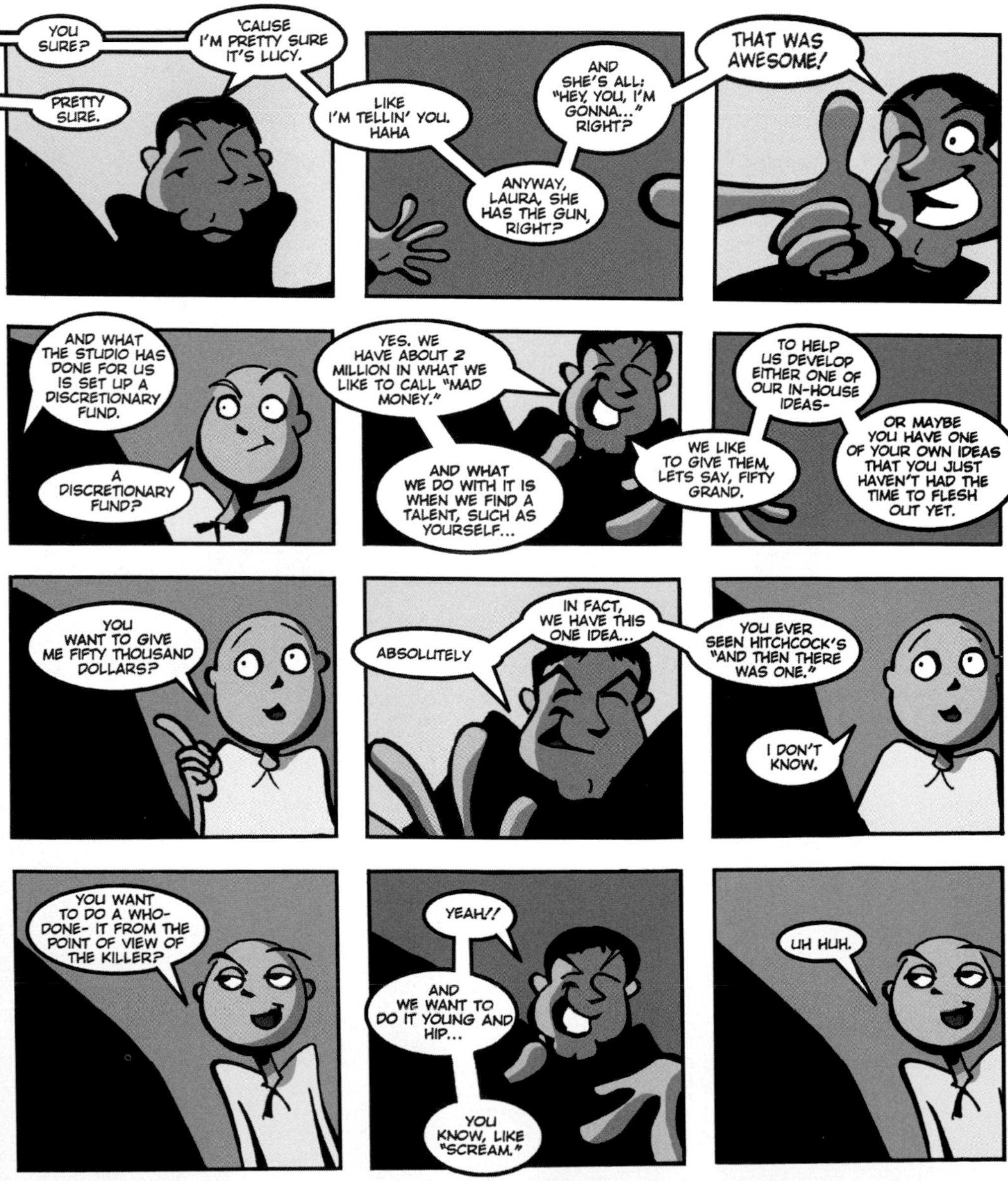
YOU SURE?
'CAUSE I'M PRETTY SURE IT'S LUCY.
PRETTY SURE.
LIKE I'M TELLIN' YOU. HAHA
ANYWAY, LAURA, SHE HAS THE GUN, RIGHT?
AND SHE'S ALL: "HEY, YOU, I'M GONNA..." RIGHT?
THAT WAS AWESOME!
AND WHAT THE STUDIO HAS DONE FOR US IS SET UP A DISCRETIONARY FUND.
A DISCRETIONARY FUND?
YES. WE HAVE ABOUT 2 MILLION IN WHAT WE LIKE TO CALL "MAD MONEY."
AND WHAT WE DO WITH IT IS WHEN WE FIND A TALENT, SUCH AS YOURSELF...
WE LIKE TO GIVE THEM, LETS SAY, FIFTY GRAND.
TO HELP US DEVELOP EITHER ONE OF OUR IN-HOUSE IDEAS-
OR MAYBE YOU HAVE ONE OF YOUR OWN IDEAS THAT YOU JUST HAVEN'T HAD THE TIME TO FLESH OUT YET.
YOU WANT TO GIVE ME FIFTY THOUSAND DOLLARS?
ABSOLUTELY
IN FACT, WE HAVE THIS ONE IDEA...
YOU EVER SEEN HITCHCOCK'S "AND THEN THERE WAS ONE."
I DON'T KNOW.
YOU WANT TO DO A WHO-DONE- IT FROM THE POINT OF VIEW OF THE KILLER?
YEAH!!
AND WE WANT TO DO IT YOUNG AND HIP...
YOU KNOW, LIKE "SCREAM."
UH HUH.

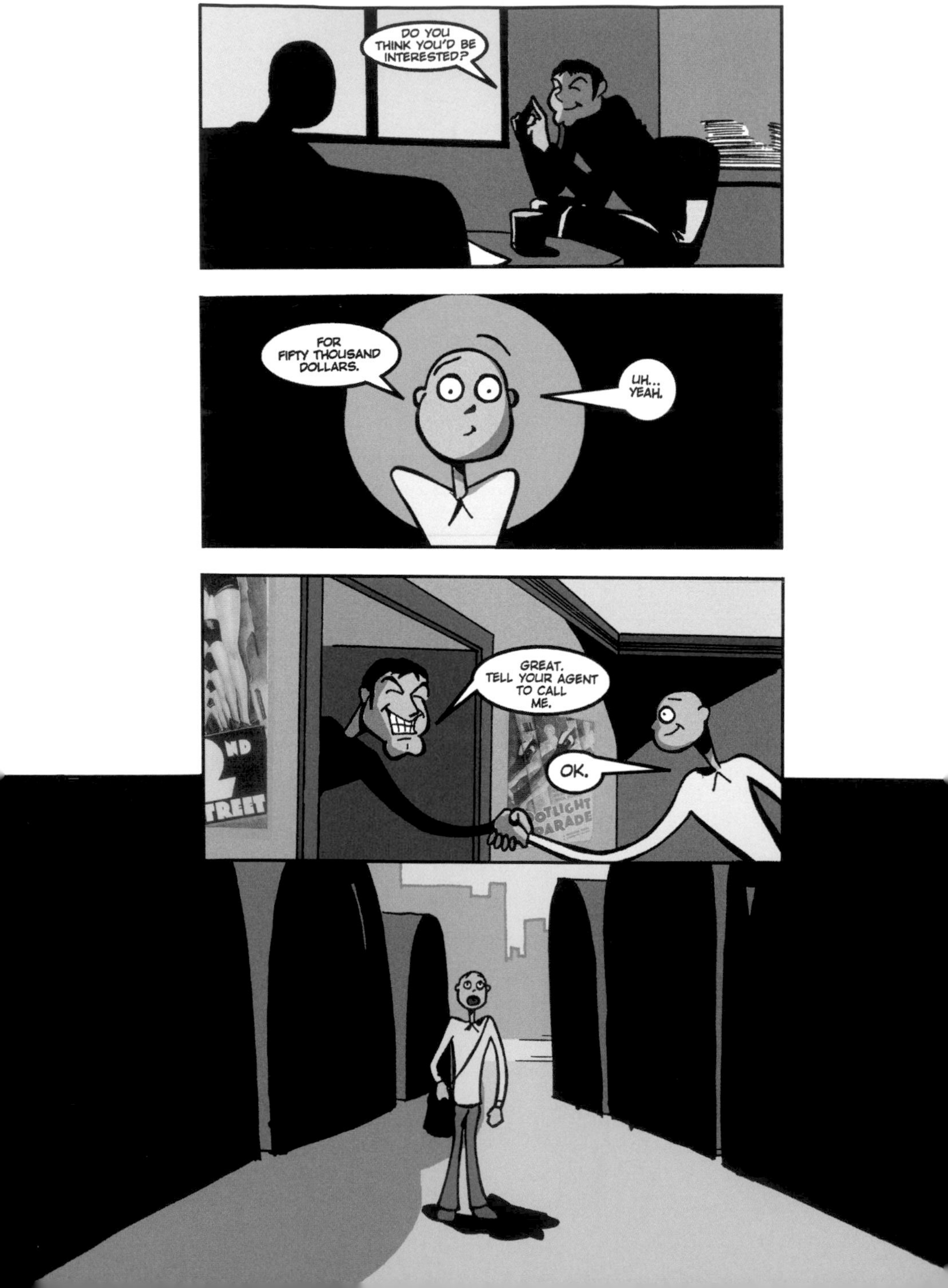
DO YOU THINK YOU'D BE INTERESTED?
FOR FIFTY THOUSAND DOLLARS.
UH... YEAH.
GREAT. TELL YOUR AGENT TO CALL ME.
OK.

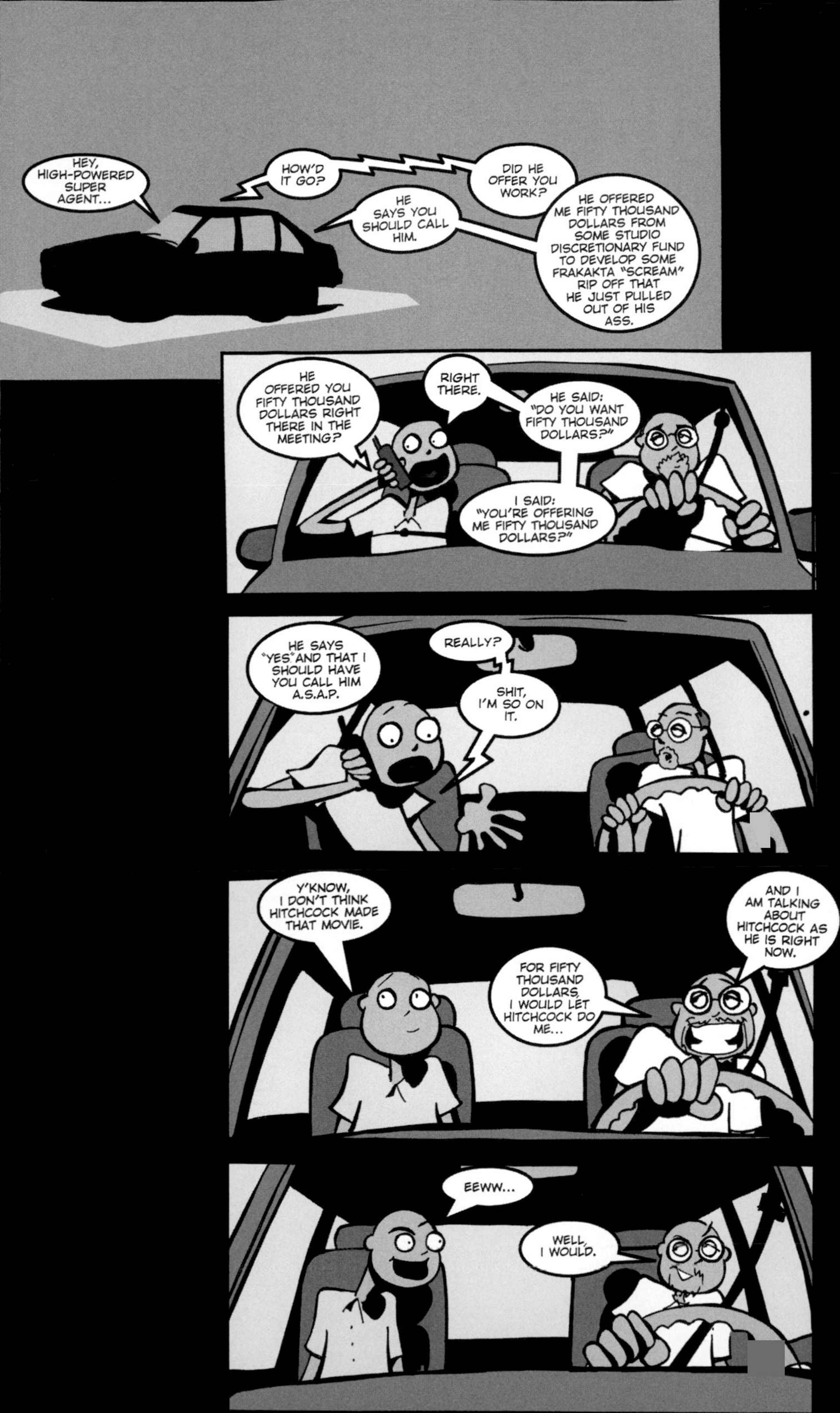
HEY, HIGH-POWERED SUPER AGENT...
HOW'D IT GO?
DID HE OFFER YOU WORK?
HE SAYS YOU SHOULD CALL HIM.
HE OFFERED ME FIFTY THOUSAND DOLLARS FROM SOME STUDIO DISCRETIONARY FUND TO DEVELOP SOME FRAKAKTA "SCREAM" RIP OFF THAT HE JUST PULLED OUT OF HIS ASS.
HE OFFERED YOU FIFTY THOUSAND DOLLARS RIGHT THERE IN THE MEETING?
RIGHT THERE.
HE SAID: "DO YOU WANT FIFTY THOUSAND DOLLARS?"
I SAID: "YOU'RE OFFERING ME FIFTY THOUSAND DOLLARS?"
HE SAYS "YES" AND THAT I SHOULD HAVE YOU CALL HIM A.S.A.P.
REALLY?
SHIT, I'M SO ON IT.
Y'KNOW, I DON'T THINK HITCHCOCK MADE THAT MOVIE.
FOR FIFTY THOUSAND DOLLARS, I WOULD LET HITCHCOCK DO ME...
AND I AM TALKING ABOUT HITCHCOCK AS HE IS RIGHT NOW.
EEWW...
WELL, I WOULD.

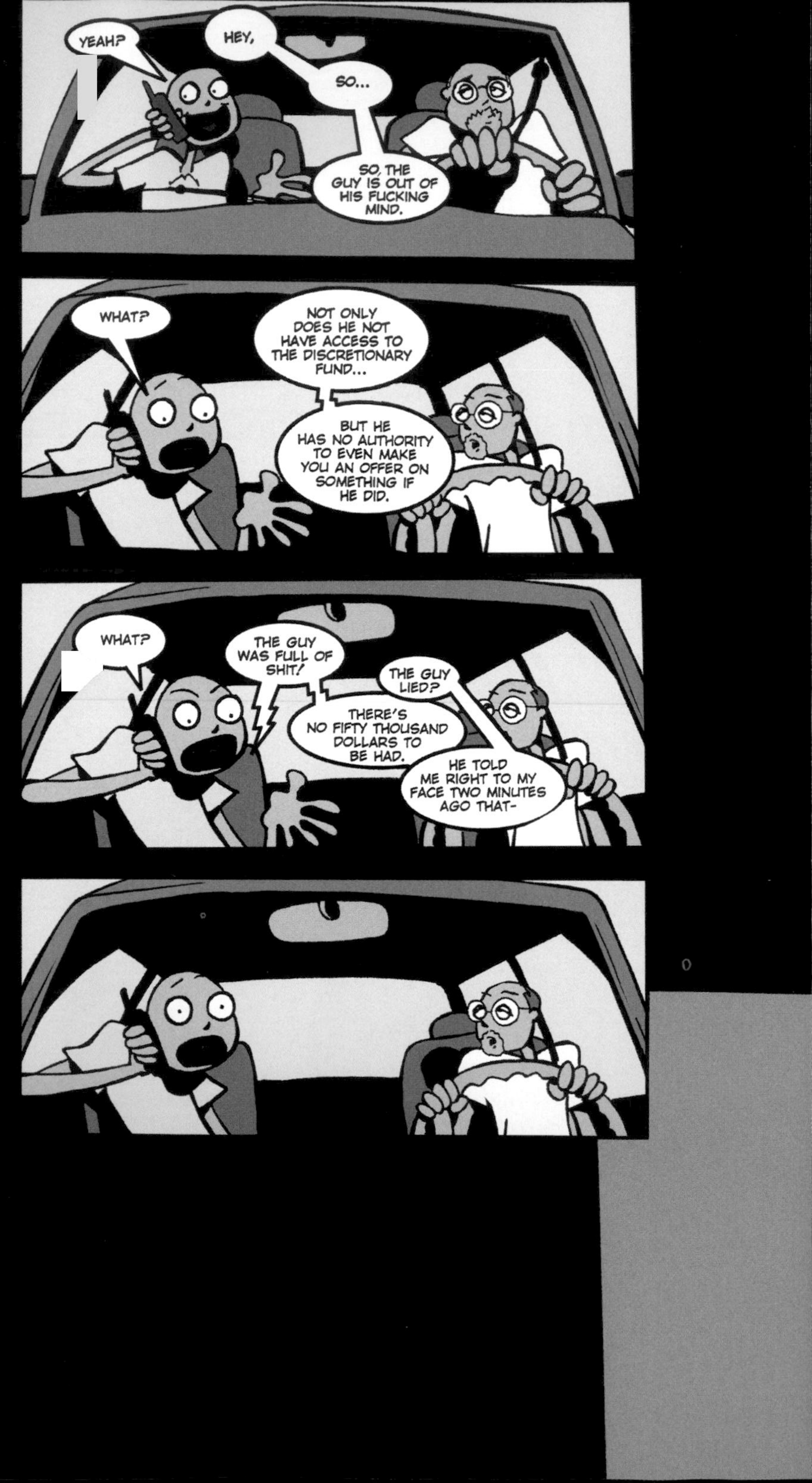
YEAH?
HEY,
SO...
SO, THE GUY IS OUT OF HIS FUCKING MIND.
WHAT?
NOT ONLY DOES HE NOT HAVE ACCESS TO THE DISCRETIONARY FUND...
BUT HE HAS NO AUTHORITY TO EVEN MAKE YOU AN OFFER ON SOMETHING IF HE DID.
WHAT?
THE GUY WAS FULL OF SHIT!
THERE'S NO FIFTY THOUSAND DOLLARS TO BE HAD.
THE GUY LIED?
HE TOLD ME RIGHT TO MY FACE TWO MINUTES AGO THAT-

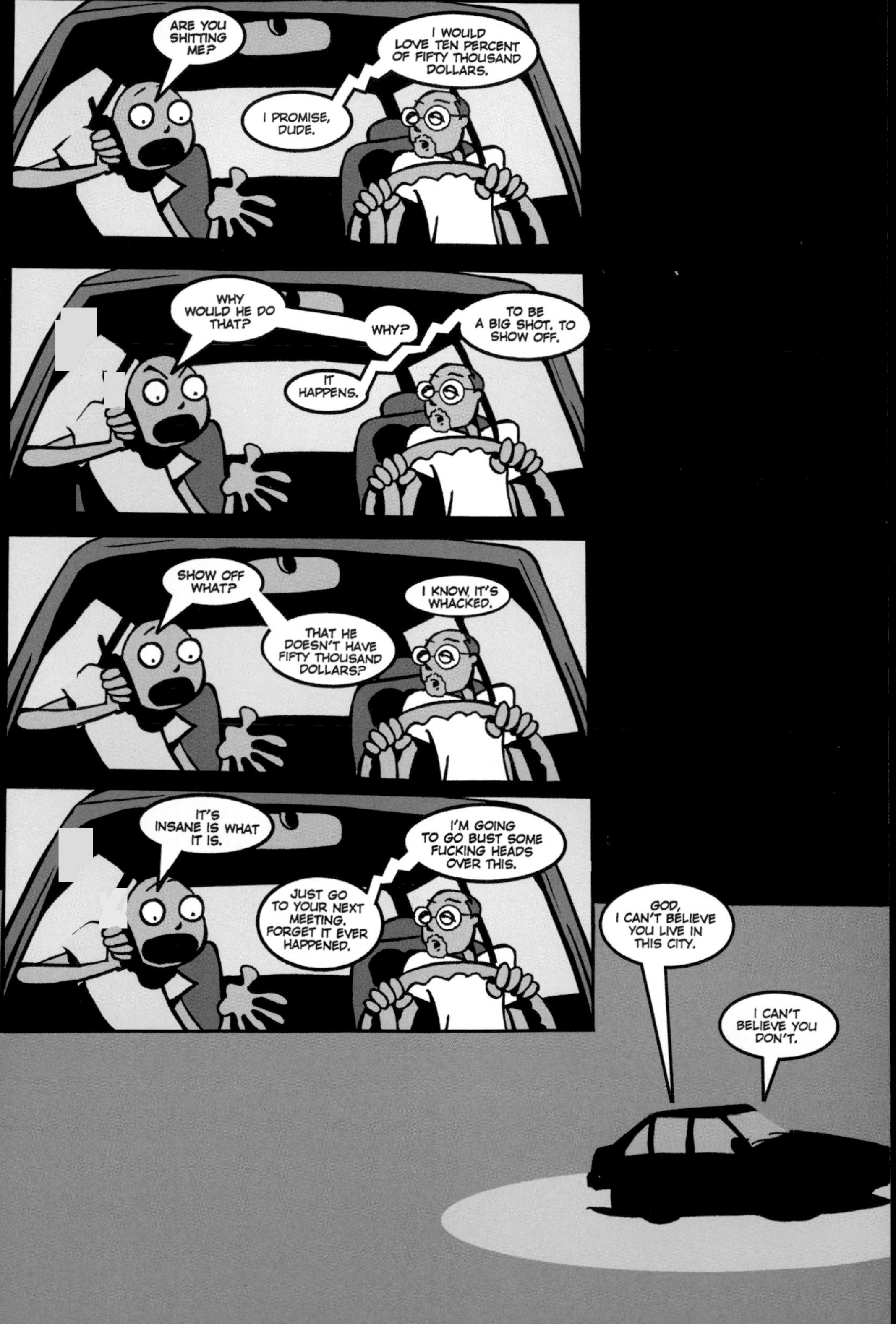

ARE YOU SHITTING ME?
I WOULD LOVE TEN PERCENT OF FIFTY THOUSAND DOLLARS.
I PROMISE, DUDE.
WHY WOULD HE DO THAT?
WHY?
TO BE A BIG SHOT. TO SHOW OFF.
IT HAPPENS.
SHOW OFF WHAT?
THAT HE DOESN'T HAVE FIFTY THOUSAND DOLLARS?
I KNOW, IT'S WHACKED.
IT'S INSANE IS WHAT IT IS.
I'M GOING TO GO BUST SOME FUCKING HEADS OVER THIS.
JUST GO TO YOUR NEXT MEETING. FORGET IT EVER HAPPENED.
GOD, I CAN'T BELIEVE YOU LIVE IN THIS CITY.
I CAN'T BELIEVE YOU DON'T.

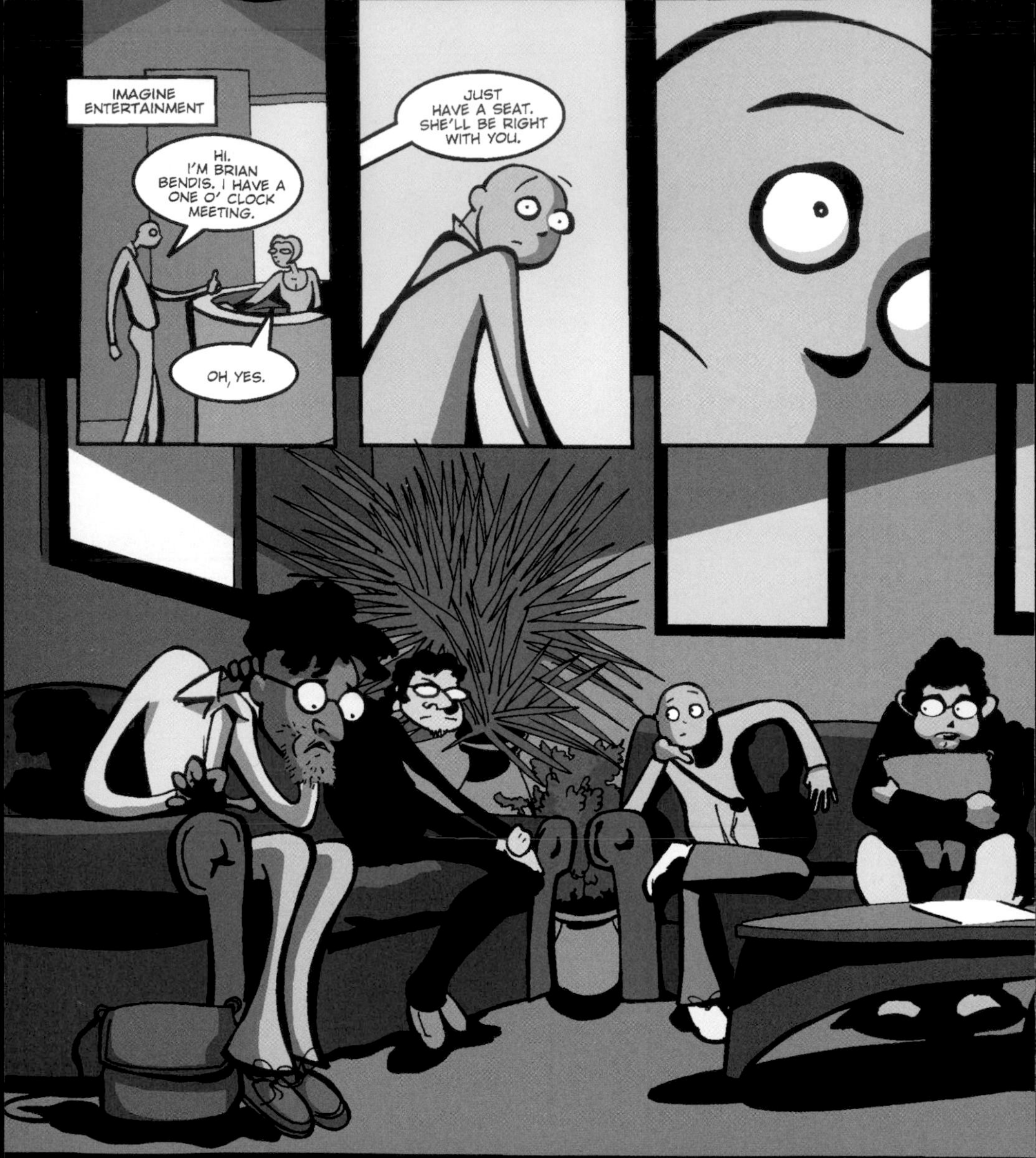
IMAGINE ENTERTAINMENT
HI. I'M BRIAN BENDIS. I HAVE A ONE O' CLOCK MEETING.
OH, YES.
JUST HAVE A SEAT. SHE'LL BE RIGHT WITH YOU.

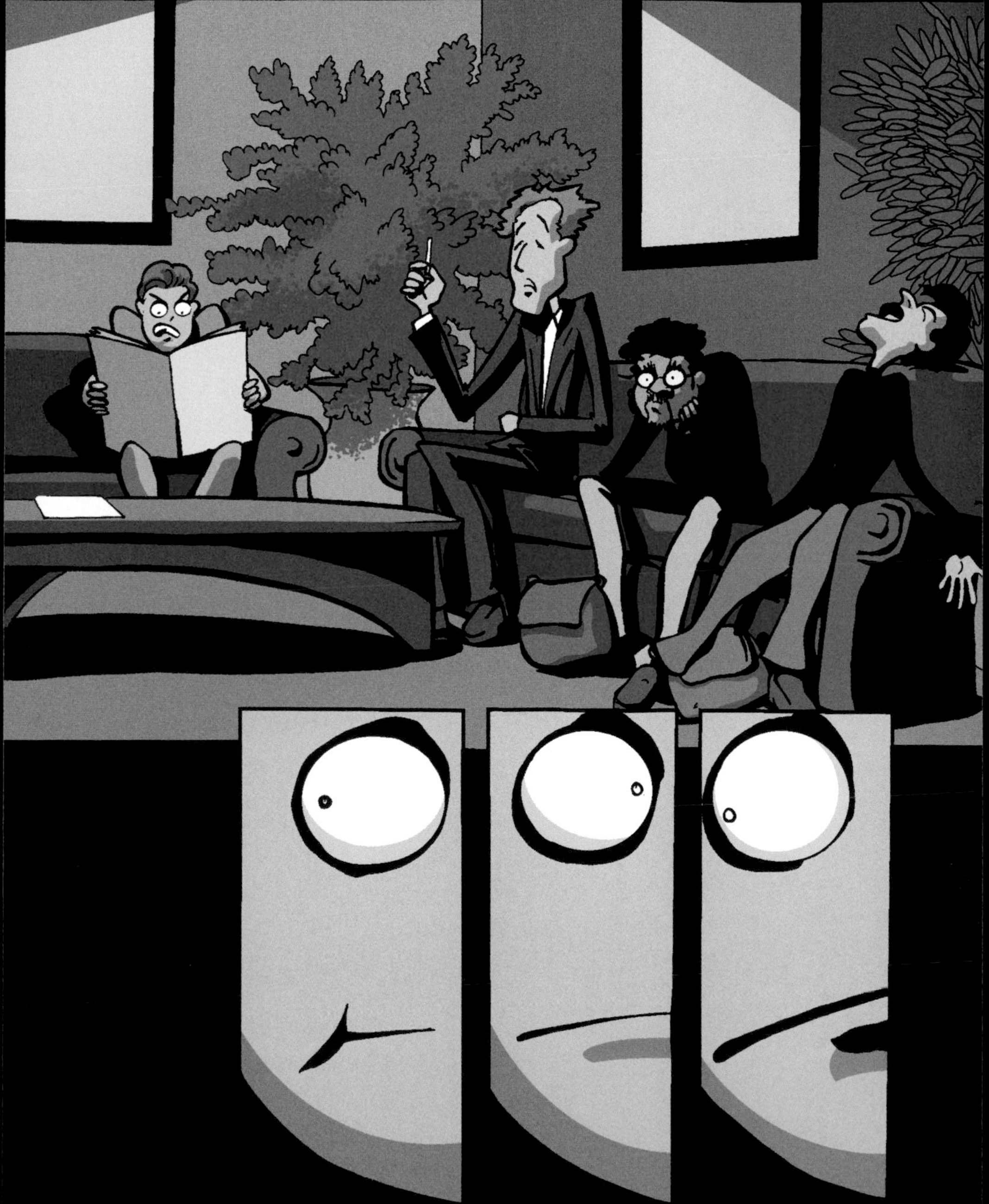

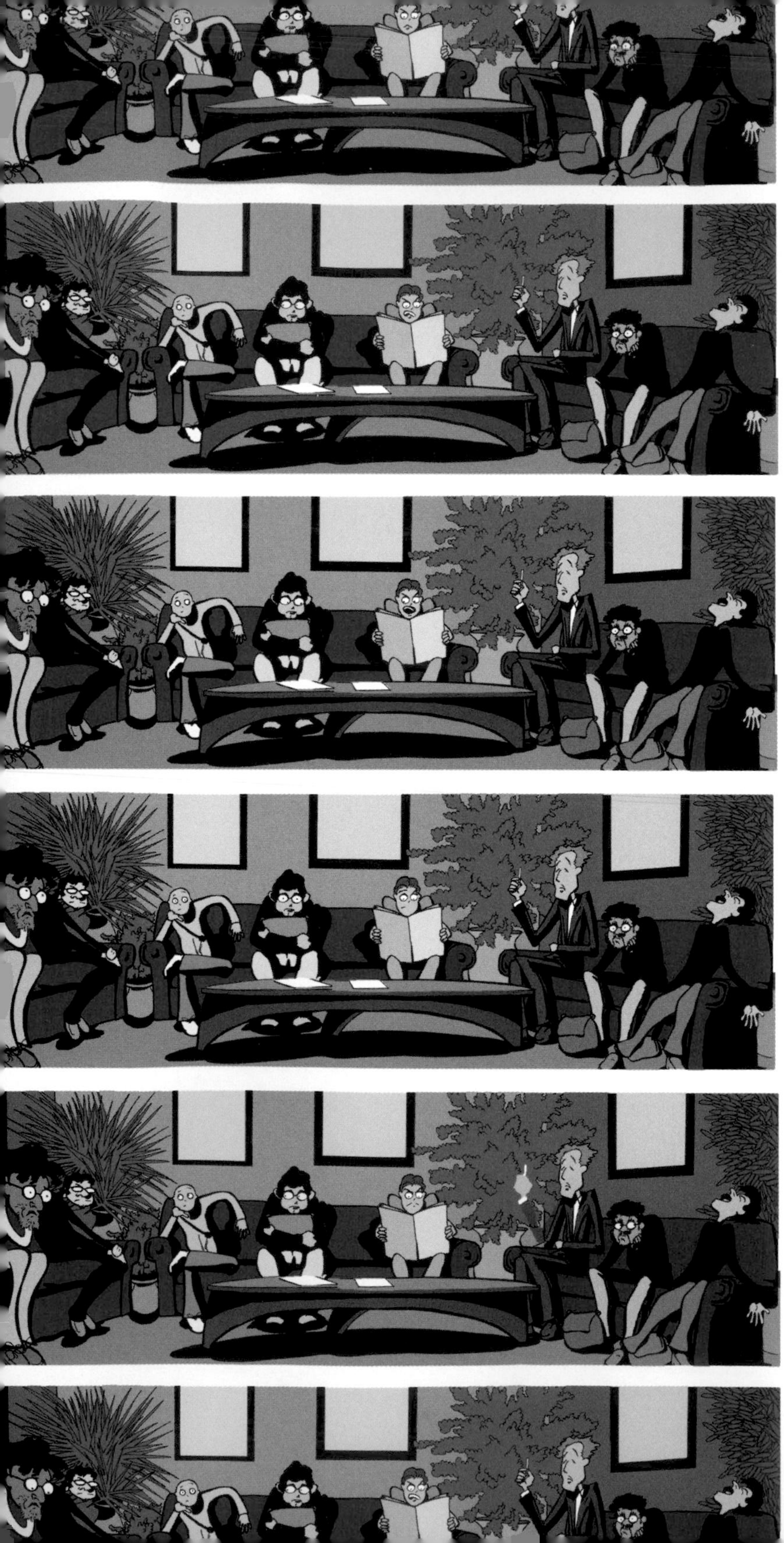

SO, I AM SITTING IN THIS ROOM FILLED WITH THESE GUYS THAT ALL LOOKED LIKE THEY MIGHT BE A COEN BROTHER.

YOU KNOW THEY ARE WRITERS BECAUSE THEY ARE THE ONLY PEOPLE IN L.A. THAT DON'T HAVE A TAN, A SHAVE, OR A REASON TO LIVE.

JUST SWEATY, DISHEVELED, CURLY-HAIRED GUYS IN SPORTS COATS AND A FIVE O'CLOCK SHADOW...

THEY SIT THERE AND THEY THUMB THROUGH THE TRADES CURSING EVERYONE IN THE WORLD WHO IS DOING BETTER THAN THEM.

THEY CLUTCH ONTO THEIR MANDATORY WRITER'S CASE.

AND THEY ALL STINK OF NICOTINE, CAFFEINE, AND HUMAN DESPERATION.

BECAUSE IF THEY DON'T SELL WHATEVER IS IN THAT LITTLE CASE OF THEIRS, IT'S BACK TO THE CARPET BARN OR THE KFC OR WHERE EVER IT IS THEY WORK.

THEY ARE JUST ALL WOUND UP AND READY FOR THE FALL.

THIS IS THE LIFE OF A HOLLYWOOD WRITER.

IF THEY DON'T SELL WHATEVER THEY HAVE IN THEIR LITTLE BAGS, IT'S ANOTHER MONTH OF FOOD STAMPS AND BLOOD BANK.

AND I THOUGHT HOW WHACKED IT IS.

THEY SAY THERE ARE *40,000* SCRIPTS REGISTERED EVERY YEAR IN THE WRITER'S GUILD.

THERE ARE ONLY *200-250* MAINSTREAM MOVIES MADE A YEAR, AND HALF OF THOSE ARE FROM PREEXISTING SOURCES.

SO OUT OF THE *40,000* PEOPLE RUNNING AROUND TOWN WITH THEIR LITTLE SCRIPT IN THEIR LITTLE BAGS ONLY *100* MIGHT GET TO SELL THEIRS.

IT'S LIKE THE LOTTERY...

ONLY WITH THE ADDED BONUS OF REJECTION AND HUMILIATION.

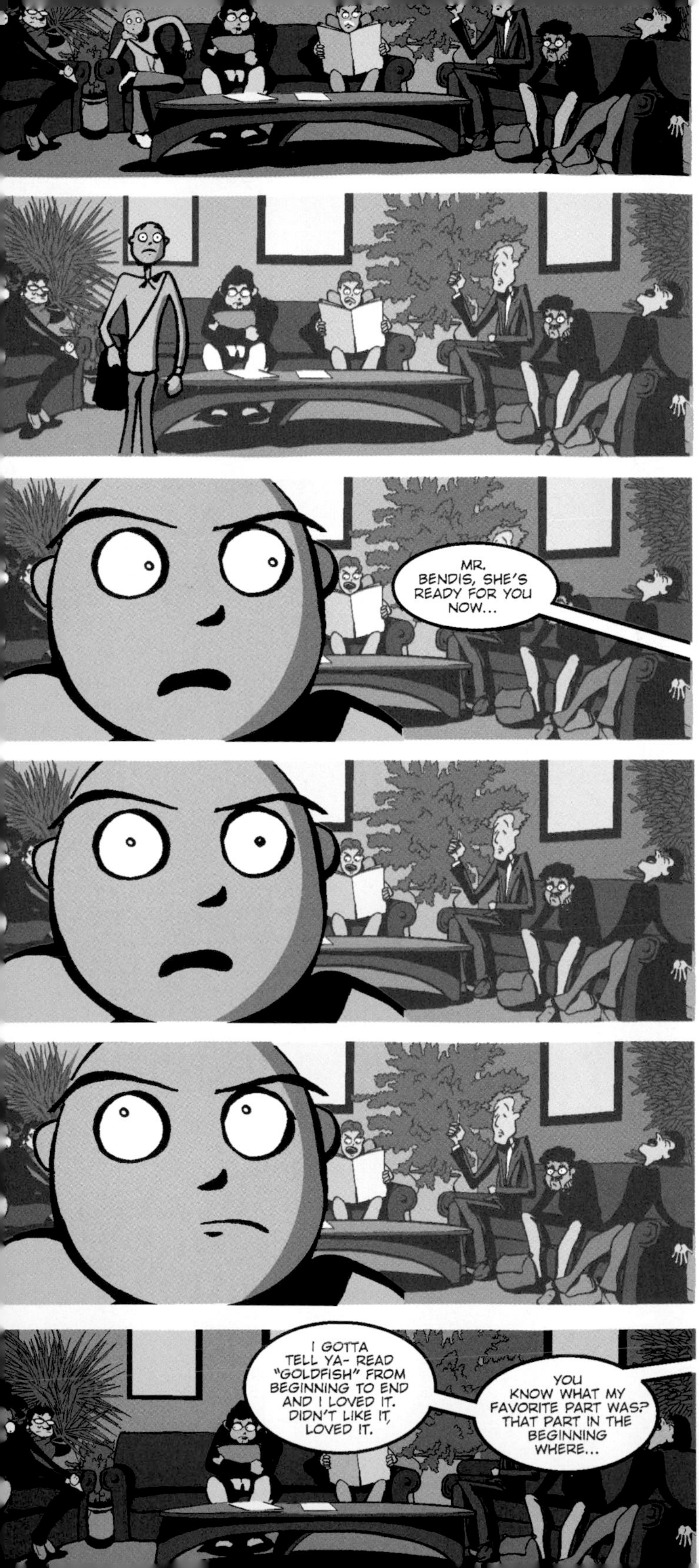
MR. BENDIS, SHE'S READY FOR YOU NOW...
I GOTTA TELL YA- READ "GOLDFISH" FROM BEGINNING TO END AND I LOVED IT. DIDN'T LIKE IT, LOVED IT.
YOU KNOW WHAT MY FAVORITE PART WAS? THAT PART IN THE BEGINNING WHERE...

AND HERE I AM GOING FROM MEETING TO MEETING TO MEET PEOPLE WHO FORGET ME THE SECOND I LEAVE THEIR OFFICE.

AND EVEN IF THEY ARE TOTALLY DAZZLED BY ME, THEY REALLY AREN'T IN ANY POSITION TO DO ANYTHING ABOUT IT.

I'M A COMIC BOOK ARTIST. WHAT AM I DOING HERE WITH THESE GUYS?

I DECIDED IT WAS TIME FOR ME TO GO HOME AND DO SOME WORK.

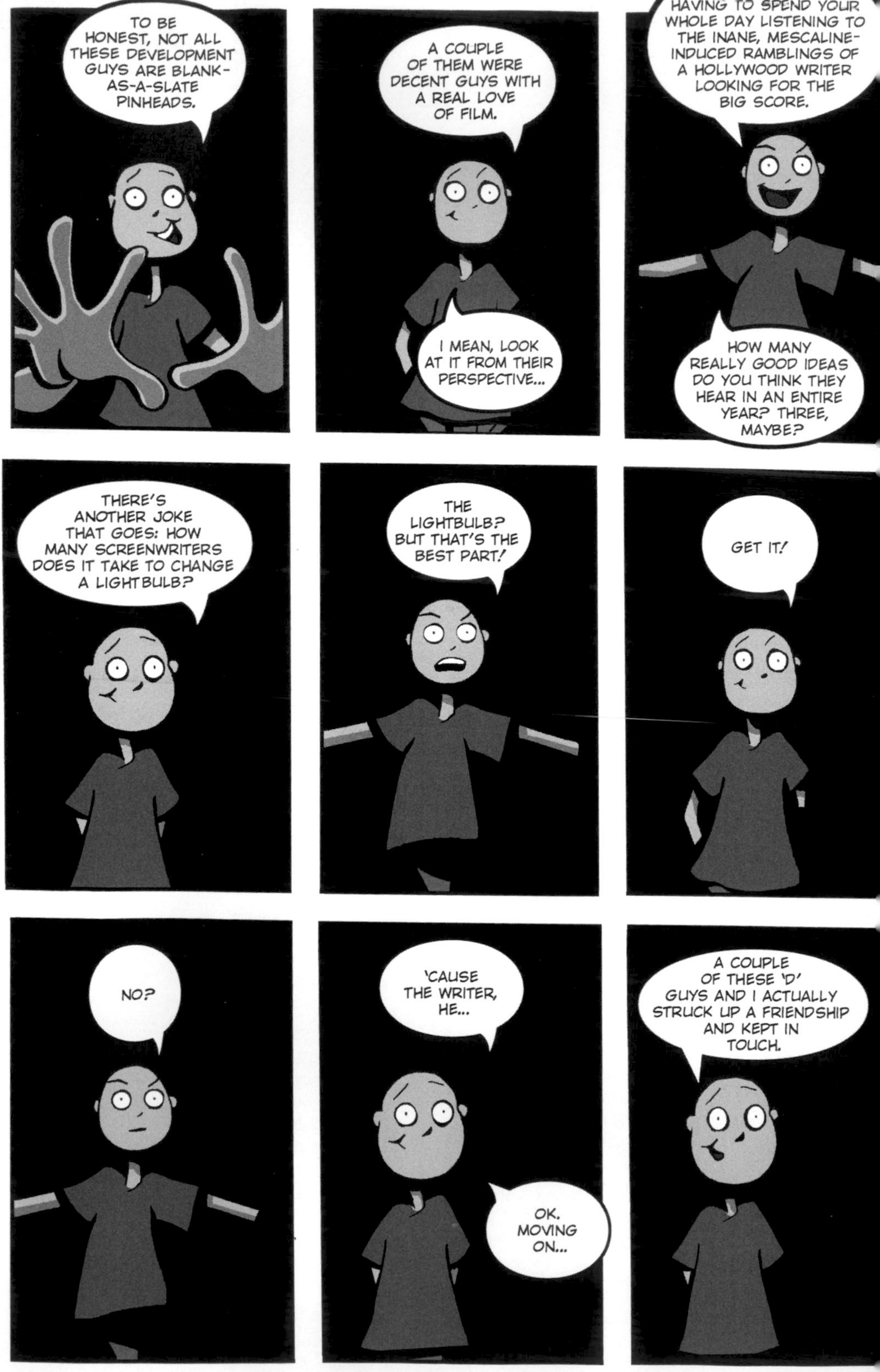

TO BE HONEST, NOT ALL THESE DEVELOPMENT GUYS ARE BLANK-AS-A-SLATE PINHEADS.
A COUPLE OF THEM WERE DECENT GUYS WITH A REAL LOVE OF FILM.
I MEAN, LOOK AT IT FROM THEIR PERSPECTIVE...
IMAGINE HAVING TO SPEND YOUR WHOLE DAY LISTENING TO THE INANE, MESCALINE-INDUCED RAMBLINGS OF A HOLLYWOOD WRITER LOOKING FOR THE BIG SCORE.
HOW MANY REALLY GOOD IDEAS DO YOU THINK THEY HEAR IN AN ENTIRE YEAR? THREE, MAYBE?
THERE'S ANOTHER JOKE THAT GOES: HOW MANY SCREENWRITERS DOES IT TAKE TO CHANGE A LIGHTBULB?
THE LIGHTBULB? BUT THAT'S THE BEST PART!
GET IT!
NO?
'CAUSE THE WRITER, HE...
OK. MOVING ON...
A COUPLE OF THESE 'D' GUYS AND I ACTUALLY STRUCK UP A FRIENDSHIP AND KEPT IN TOUCH.

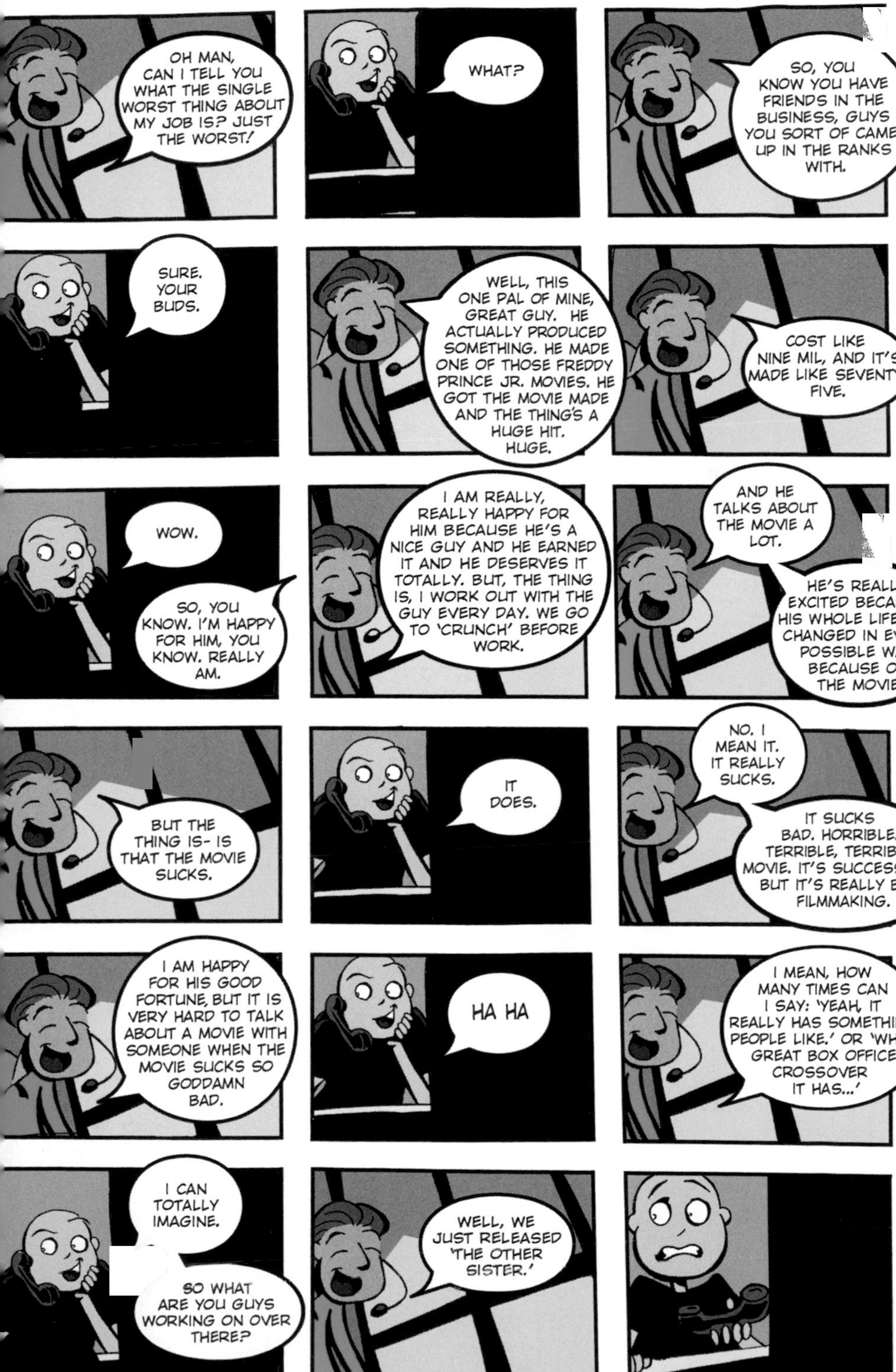

OH MAN, CAN I TELL YOU WHAT THE SINGLE WORST THING ABOUT MY JOB IS? JUST THE WORST!
WHAT?
SO, YOU KNOW YOU HAVE FRIENDS IN THE BUSINESS, GUYS YOU SORT OF CAME UP IN THE RANKS WITH.
SURE. YOUR BUDS.
WELL, THIS ONE PAL OF MINE, GREAT GUY. HE ACTUALLY PRODUCED SOMETHING. HE MADE ONE OF THOSE FREDDY PRINCE JR. MOVIES. HE GOT THE MOVIE MADE AND THE THING'S A HUGE HIT. HUGE.
COST LIKE NINE MIL, AND IT'S MADE LIKE SEVENTY-FIVE.
WOW.
SO, YOU KNOW. I'M HAPPY FOR HIM, YOU KNOW. REALLY AM.
I AM REALLY, REALLY HAPPY FOR HIM BECAUSE HE'S A NICE GUY AND HE EARNED IT AND HE DESERVES IT TOTALLY. BUT, THE THING IS, I WORK OUT WITH THE GUY EVERY DAY. WE GO TO 'CRUNCH' BEFORE WORK.
AND HE TALKS ABOUT THE MOVIE A LOT.
HE'S REALLY EXCITED BECAUSE HIS WHOLE LIFE HAS CHANGED IN EVERY POSSIBLE WAY BECAUSE OF THE MOVIE.
BUT THE THING IS- IS THAT THE MOVIE SUCKS.
IT DOES.
NO. I MEAN IT. IT REALLY SUCKS.
IT SUCKS BAD. HORRIBLE. TERRIBLE, TERRIBLE MOVIE. IT'S SUCCESSFUL- BUT IT'S REALLY BAD FILMMAKING.
I AM HAPPY FOR HIS GOOD FORTUNE, BUT IT IS VERY HARD TO TALK ABOUT A MOVIE WITH SOMEONE WHEN THE MOVIE SUCKS SO GODDAMN BAD.
HA HA
I MEAN, HOW MANY TIMES CAN I SAY: 'YEAH, IT REALLY HAS SOMETHING PEOPLE LIKE.' OR 'WHAT GREAT BOX OFFICE CROSSOVER IT HAS...'
I CAN TOTALLY IMAGINE.
SO WHAT ARE YOU GUYS WORKING ON OVER THERE?
WELL, WE JUST RELEASED 'THE OTHER SISTER.'

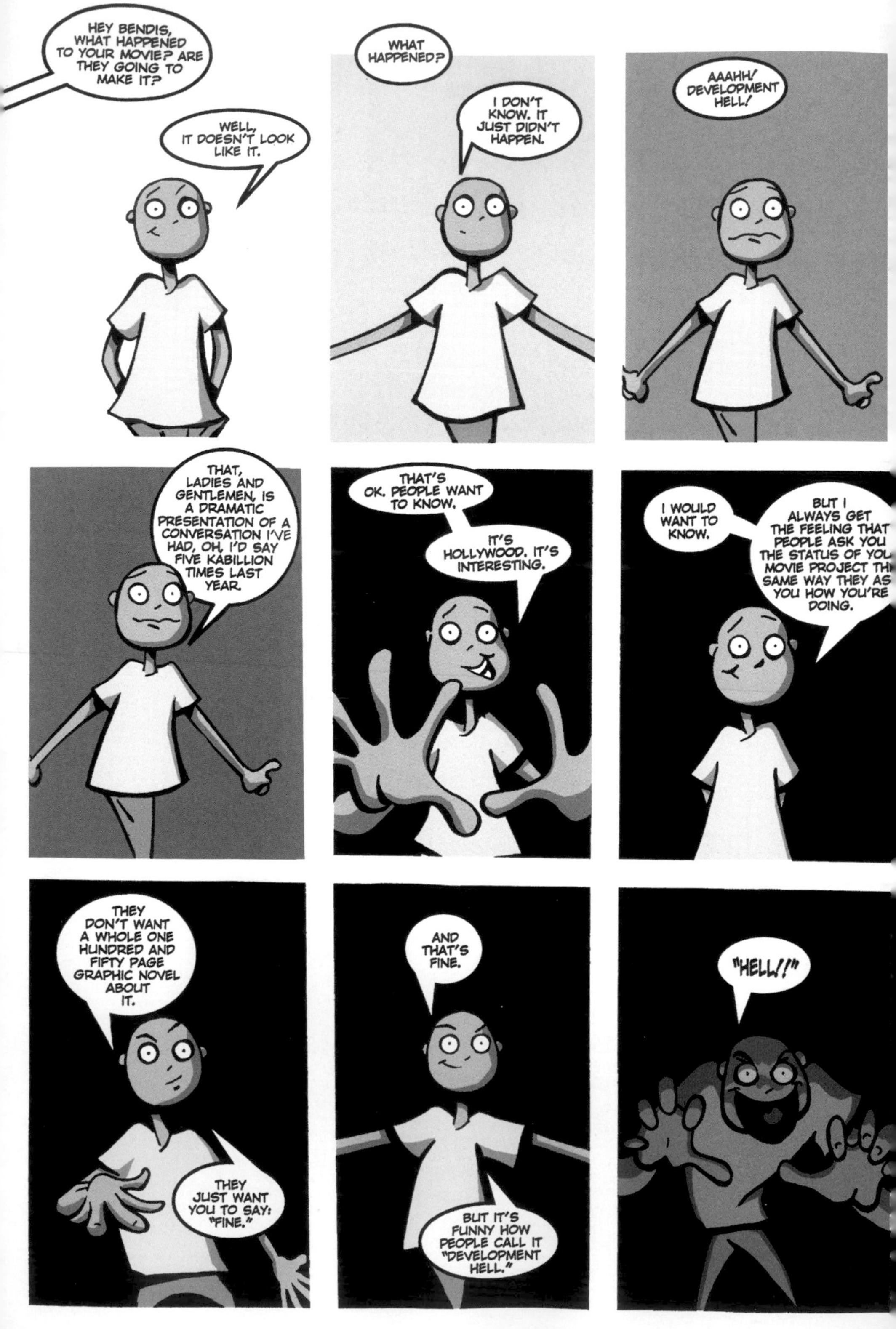

HEY BENDIS, WHAT HAPPENED TO YOUR MOVIE? ARE THEY GOING TO MAKE IT?
WELL, IT DOESN'T LOOK LIKE IT.
WHAT HAPPENED?
I DON'T KNOW. IT JUST DIDN'T HAPPEN.
AAAHH! DEVELOPMENT HELL!
THAT, LADIES AND GENTLEMEN, IS A DRAMATIC PRESENTATION OF A CONVERSATION I'VE HAD, OH, I'D SAY FIVE KABILLION TIMES LAST YEAR.
THAT'S OK. PEOPLE WANT TO KNOW.
IT'S HOLLYWOOD. IT'S INTERESTING.
I WOULD WANT TO KNOW.
BUT I ALWAYS GET THE FEELING THAT PEOPLE ASK YOU THE STATUS OF YOU MOVIE PROJECT TH SAME WAY THEY AS YOU HOW YOU'RE DOING.
THEY DON'T WANT A WHOLE ONE HUNDRED AND FIFTY PAGE GRAPHIC NOVEL ABOUT IT.
THEY JUST WANT YOU TO SAY: "FINE."
AND THAT'S FINE.
BUT IT'S FUNNY HOW PEOPLE CALL IT "DEVELOPMENT HELL."
"HELL!!"

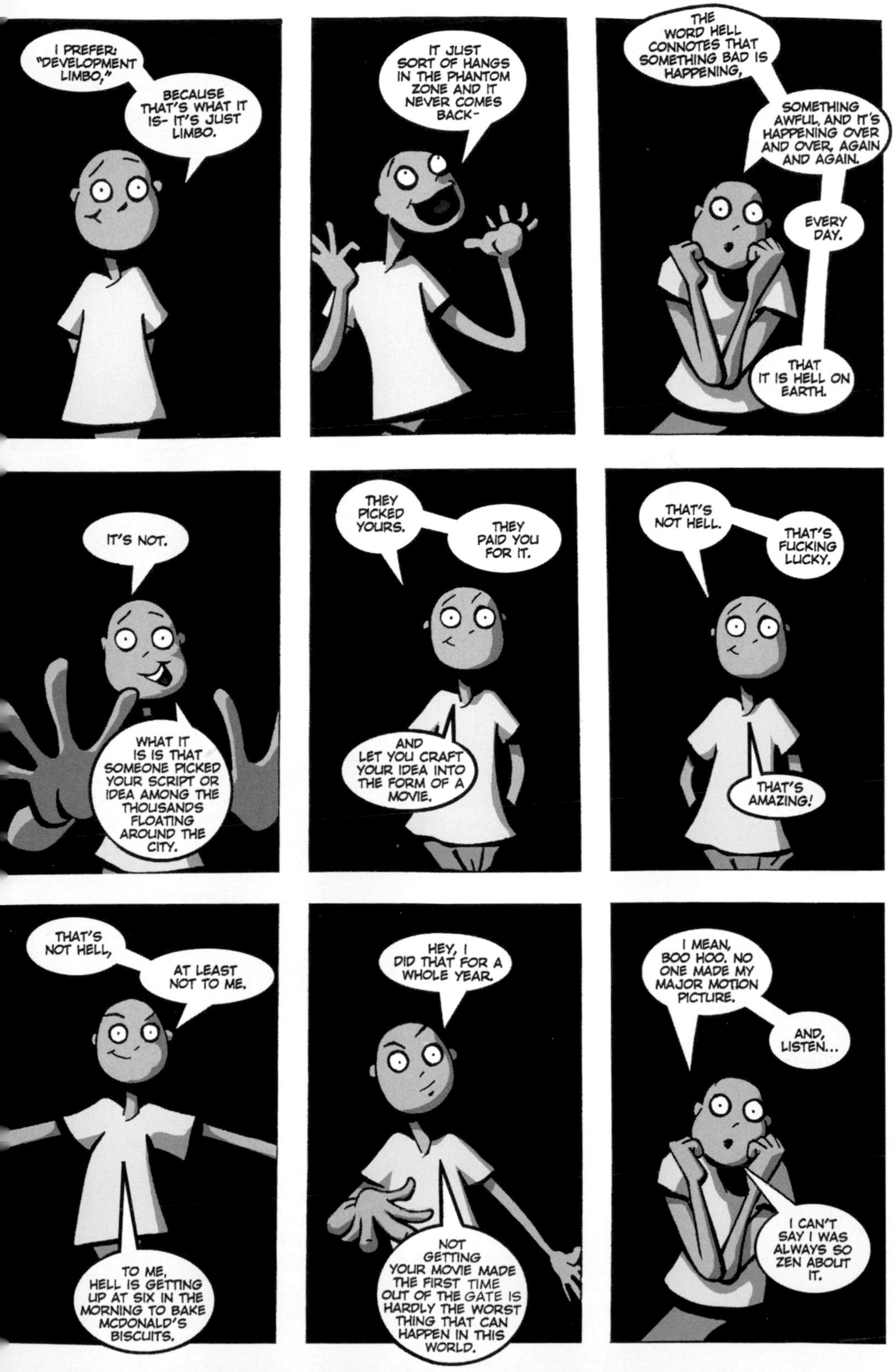
I PREFER: "DEVELOPMENT LIMBO,"
BECAUSE THAT'S WHAT IT IS- IT'S JUST LIMBO.
IT JUST SORT OF HANGS IN THE PHANTOM ZONE AND IT NEVER COMES BACK-
THE WORD HELL CONNOTES THAT SOMETHING BAD IS HAPPENING,
SOMETHING AWFUL, AND IT'S HAPPENING OVER AND OVER, AGAIN AND AGAIN.
EVERY DAY.
THAT IT IS HELL ON EARTH.
IT'S NOT.
WHAT IT IS IS THAT SOMEONE PICKED YOUR SCRIPT OR IDEA AMONG THE THOUSANDS FLOATING AROUND THE CITY.
THEY PICKED YOURS.
THEY PAID YOU FOR IT.
AND LET YOU CRAFT YOUR IDEA INTO THE FORM OF A MOVIE.
THAT'S NOT HELL.
THAT'S FUCKING LUCKY.
THAT'S AMAZING!
THAT'S NOT HELL,
AT LEAST NOT TO ME.
TO ME, HELL IS GETTING UP AT SIX IN THE MORNING TO BAKE MCDONALD'S BISCUITS.
HEY, I DID THAT FOR A WHOLE YEAR.
NOT GETTING YOUR MOVIE MADE THE FIRST TIME OUT OF THE GATE IS HARDLY THE WORST THING THAT CAN HAPPEN IN THIS WORLD.
I MEAN, BOO HOO. NO ONE MADE MY MAJOR MOTION PICTURE.
AND, LISTEN...
I CAN'T SAY I WAS ALWAYS SO ZEN ABOUT IT.

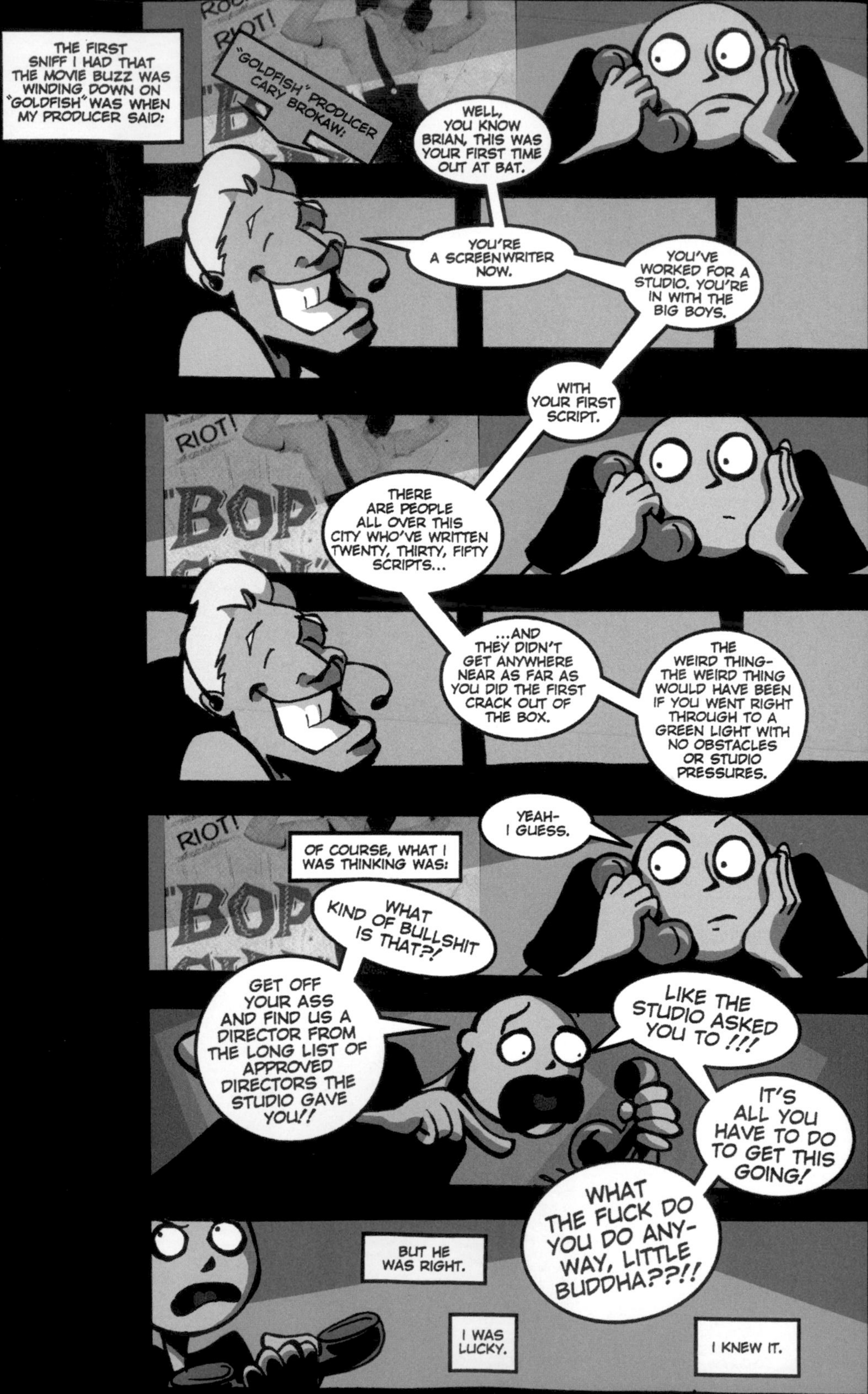
THE FIRST SNIFF I HAD THAT THE MOVIE BUZZ WAS WINDING DOWN ON "GOLDFISH" WAS WHEN MY PRODUCER SAID:
"GOLDFISH" PRODUCER CARY BROKAW:
WELL, YOU KNOW BRIAN, THIS WAS YOUR FIRST TIME OUT AT BAT.
YOU'RE A SCREENWRITER NOW.
YOU'VE WORKED FOR A STUDIO. YOU'RE IN WITH THE BIG BOYS.
WITH YOUR FIRST SCRIPT.
THERE ARE PEOPLE ALL OVER THIS CITY WHO'VE WRITTEN TWENTY, THIRTY, FIFTY SCRIPTS...
...AND THEY DIDN'T GET ANYWHERE NEAR AS FAR AS YOU DID THE FIRST CRACK OUT OF THE BOX.
THE WEIRD THING- THE WEIRD THING WOULD HAVE BEEN IF YOU WENT RIGHT THROUGH TO A GREEN LIGHT WITH NO OBSTACLES OR STUDIO PRESSURES.
YEAH- I GUESS.
OF COURSE, WHAT I WAS THINKING WAS:
WHAT KIND OF BULLSHIT IS THAT?!
GET OFF YOUR ASS AND FIND US A DIRECTOR FROM THE LONG LIST OF APPROVED DIRECTORS THE STUDIO GAVE YOU!!
LIKE THE STUDIO ASKED YOU TO!!!
IT'S ALL YOU HAVE TO DO TO GET THIS GOING!
WHAT THE FUCK DO YOU DO ANY-WAY, LITTLE BUDDHA??!!
BUT HE WAS RIGHT.
I WAS LUCKY.
I KNEW IT.

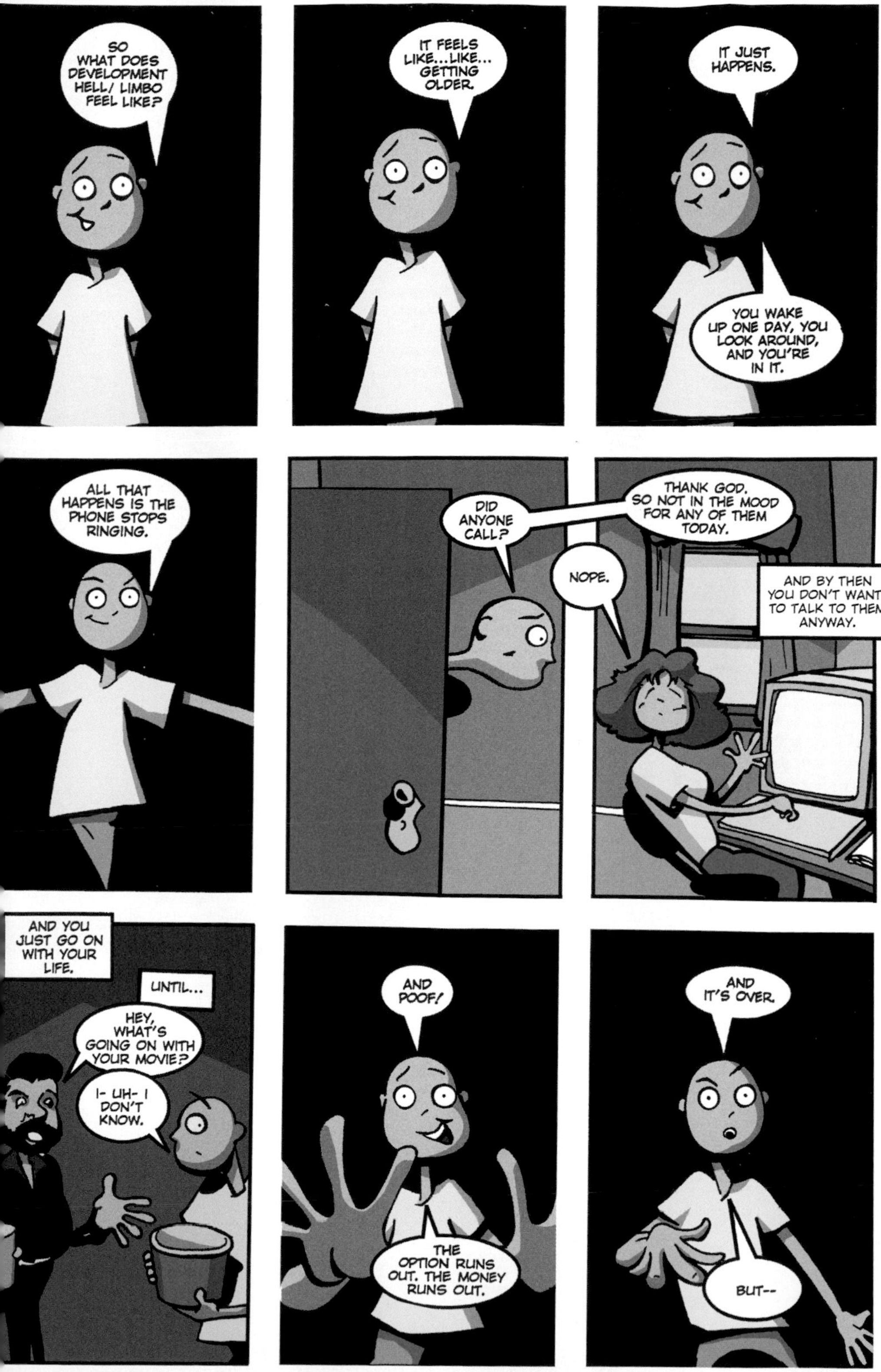
SO WHAT DOES DEVELOPMENT HELL/ LIMBO FEEL LIKE?
IT FEELS LIKE...LIKE... GETTING OLDER.
IT JUST HAPPENS.
YOU WAKE UP ONE DAY, YOU LOOK AROUND, AND YOU'RE IN IT.
ALL THAT HAPPENS IS THE PHONE STOPS RINGING.
DID ANYONE CALL?
NOPE.
THANK GOD. SO NOT IN THE MOOD FOR ANY OF THEM TODAY.
AND BY THEN YOU DON'T WANT TO TALK TO THEM ANYWAY.
AND YOU JUST GO ON WITH YOUR LIFE.
UNTIL...
HEY, WHAT'S GOING ON WITH YOUR MOVIE?
I- UH- I DON'T KNOW.
AND POOF!
THE OPTION RUNS OUT. THE MONEY RUNS OUT.
AND IT'S OVER.
BUT--

WHILE THE CLOCK WAS TICKING ON MY VIRGIN EXPERIENCE IN HOLLYWOOD.

A DAMN GOOD FRIEND OF MINE, MARC ANDREYKO, CAME OVER FOR WHAT WE NOW REFER TO AS "THE PASSOVER SEDER OF DESTINY!"

MY WIFE AND I LIKE TO TAKE THE JEWISH HOLIDAY OF PASSOVER AND INVITE AS MANY GENTILE FRIENDS AS WE CAN TO THE TRADITIONAL DINNER CEREMONY.

MANY ARE THRILLED TO BE INVITED TO THE NEW EXPERIENCE AND EAGERLY ACCEPT...

...ONLY TO FIND OUT THAT US INVITING THEM TO THE FIVE HOUR DINNER CEREMONY OF READING THE HISTORY OF THE JEWS FROM THE SEDER IS OUR VERSION OF A JEWISH PRACTICAL JOKE.

I MEAN, THE JEWS HAD TO SUFFER THROUGH THE DESERT FOR FORTY DAYS AND FORTY NIGHTS...

WE'RE GOING TO MAKE AS MANY OF YOU SUFFER AS WE CAN GET OUR HANDS ON.

HEE HEE.

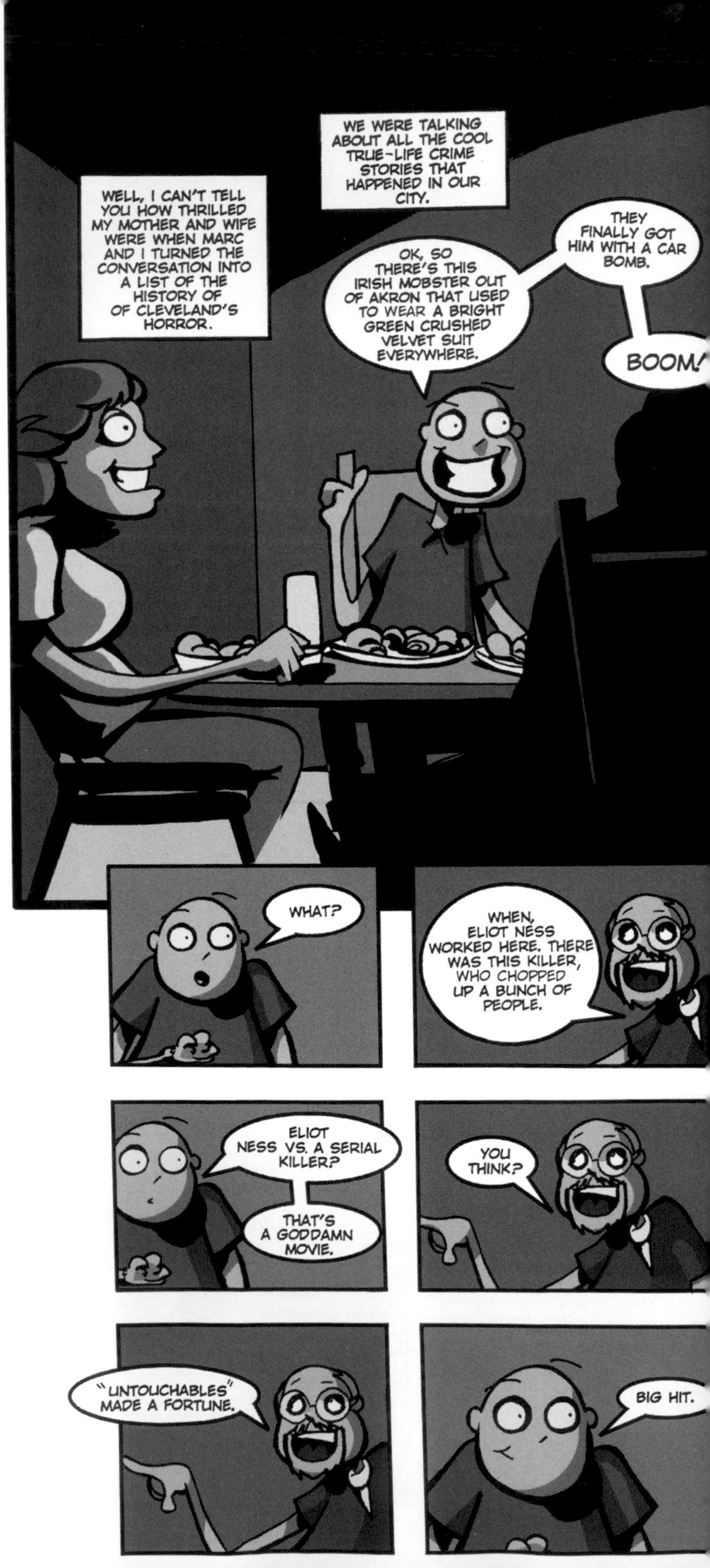

WE WERE TALKING ABOUT ALL THE COOL TRUE-LIFE CRIME STORIES THAT HAPPENED IN OUR CITY.
WELL, I CAN'T TELL YOU HOW THRILLED MY MOTHER AND WIFE WERE WHEN MARC AND I TURNED THE CONVERSATION INTO A LIST OF THE HISTORY OF OF CLEVELAND'S HORROR.
OK, SO THERE'S THIS IRISH MOBSTER OUT OF AKRON THAT USED TO WEAR A BRIGHT GREEN CRUSHED VELVET SUIT EVERYWHERE.
THEY FINALLY GOT HIM WITH A CAR BOMB.
BOOM!
WHAT?
WHEN, ELIOT NESS WORKED HERE. THERE WAS THIS KILLER, WHO CHOPPED UP A BUNCH OF PEOPLE.
ELIOT NESS VS. A SERIAL KILLER?
THAT'S A GODDAMN MOVIE.
YOU THINK?
"UNTOUCHABLES" MADE A FORTUNE.
BIG HIT.

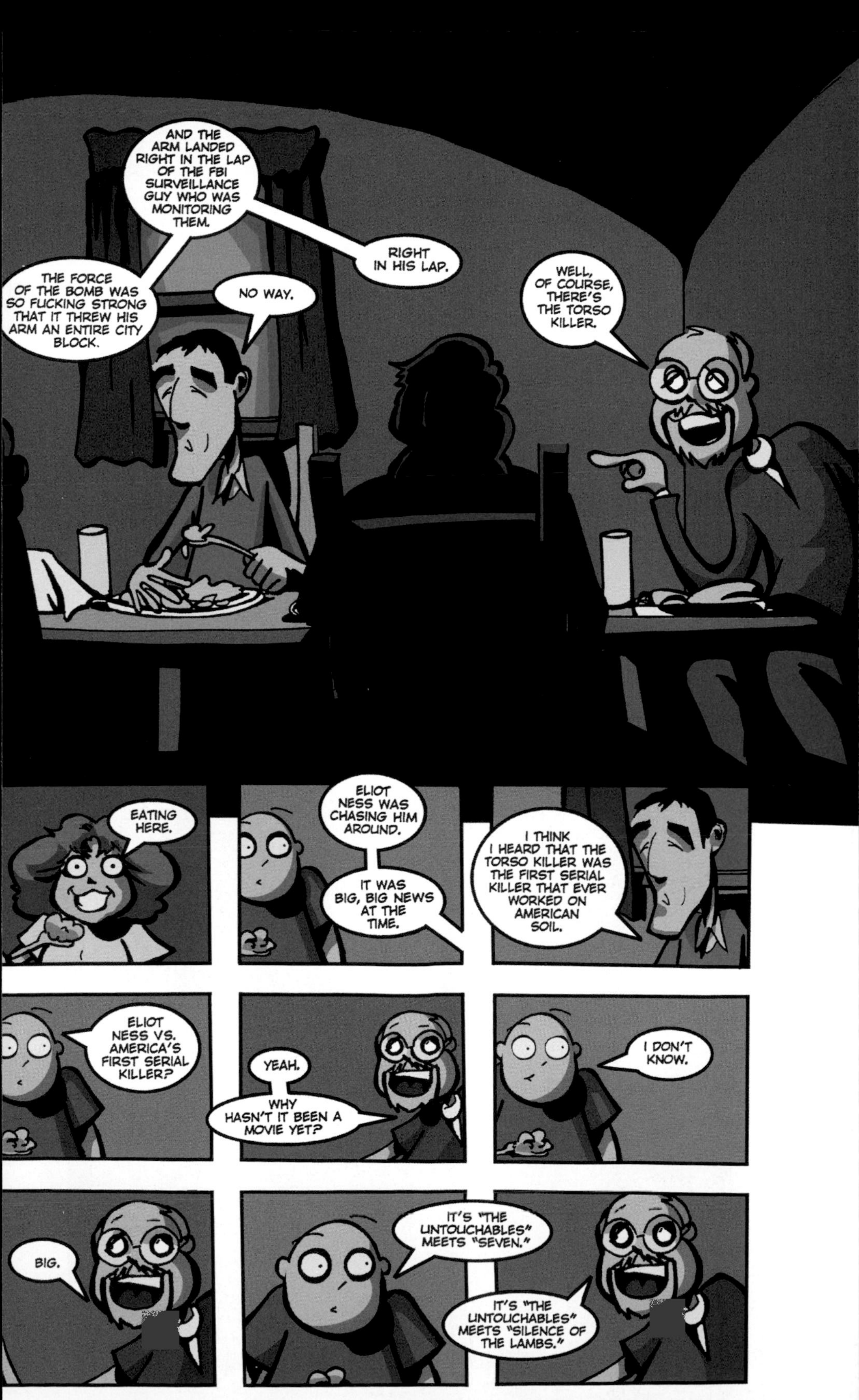
AND THE ARM LANDED RIGHT IN THE LAP OF THE FBI SURVEILLANCE GUY WHO WAS MONITORING THEM.
THE FORCE OF THE BOMB WAS SO FUCKING STRONG THAT IT THREW HIS ARM AN ENTIRE CITY BLOCK.
RIGHT IN HIS LAP.
NO WAY.
WELL, OF COURSE, THERE'S THE TORSO KILLER.
EATING HERE.
ELIOT NESS WAS CHASING HIM AROUND.
IT WAS BIG, BIG NEWS AT THE TIME.
I THINK I HEARD THAT THE TORSO KILLER WAS THE FIRST SERIAL KILLER THAT EVER WORKED ON AMERICAN SOIL.
ELIOT NESS VS. AMERICA'S FIRST SERIAL KILLER?
YEAH.
WHY HASN'T IT BEEN A MOVIE YET?
I DON'T KNOW.
BIG.
IT'S "THE UNTOUCHABLES" MEETS "SEVEN."
IT'S "THE UNTOUCHABLES" MEETS "SILENCE OF THE LAMBS."

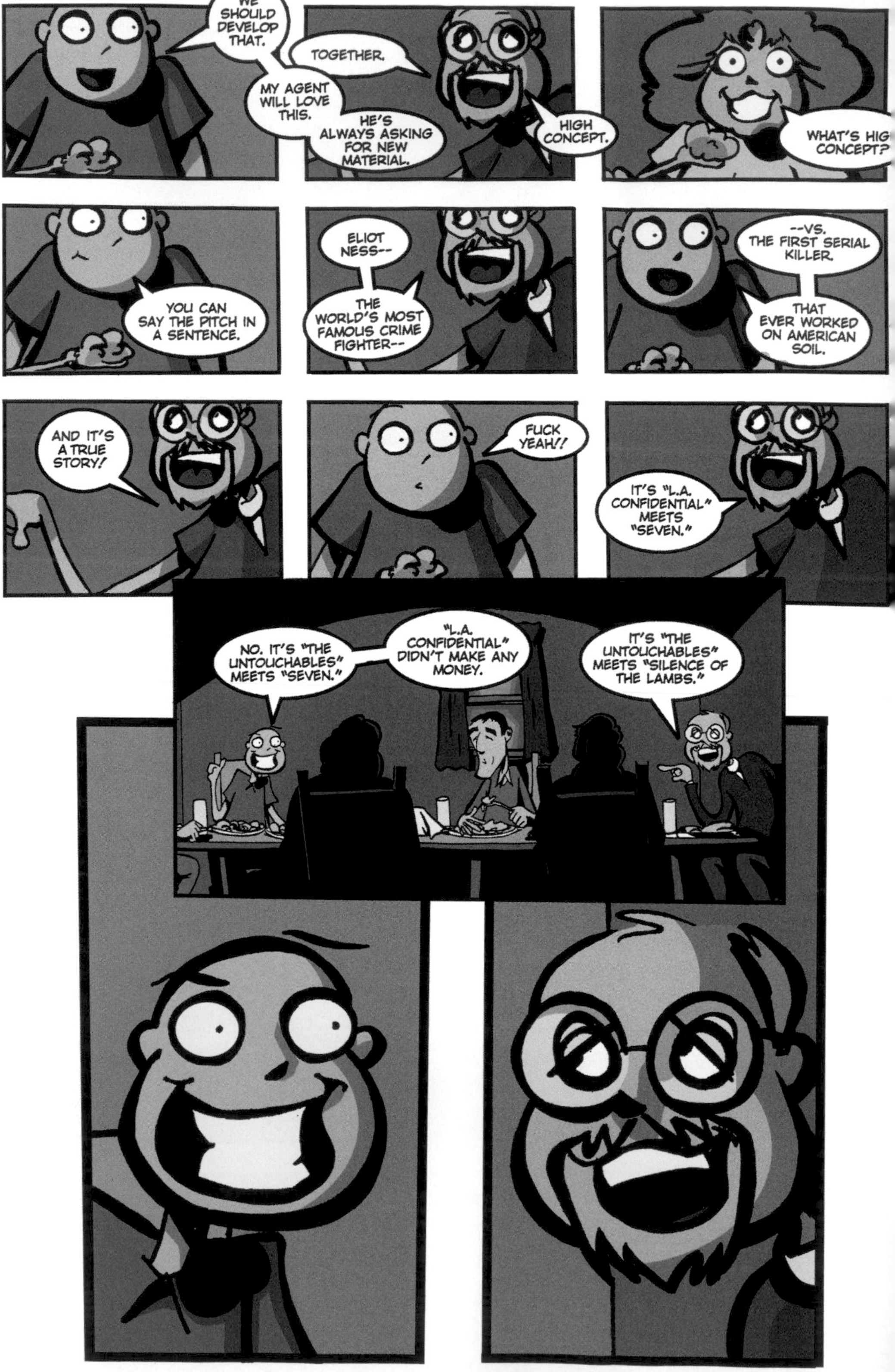
WE SHOULD DEVELOP THAT.
TOGETHER.
MY AGENT WILL LOVE THIS.
HE'S ALWAYS ASKING FOR NEW MATERIAL.
HIGH CONCEPT.
WHAT'S HIG CONCEPT?
YOU CAN SAY THE PITCH IN A SENTENCE.
ELIOT NESS--
THE WORLD'S MOST FAMOUS CRIME FIGHTER--
--VS. THE FIRST SERIAL KILLER.
THAT EVER WORKED ON AMERICAN SOIL.
AND IT'S A TRUE STORY!
FUCK YEAH!!
IT'S "L.A. CONFIDENTIAL" MEETS "SEVEN."
NO. IT'S "THE UNTOUCHABLES" MEETS "SEVEN."
"L.A. CONFIDENTIAL" DIDN'T MAKE ANY MONEY.
IT'S "THE UNTOUCHABLES" MEETS "SILENCE OF THE LAMBS."

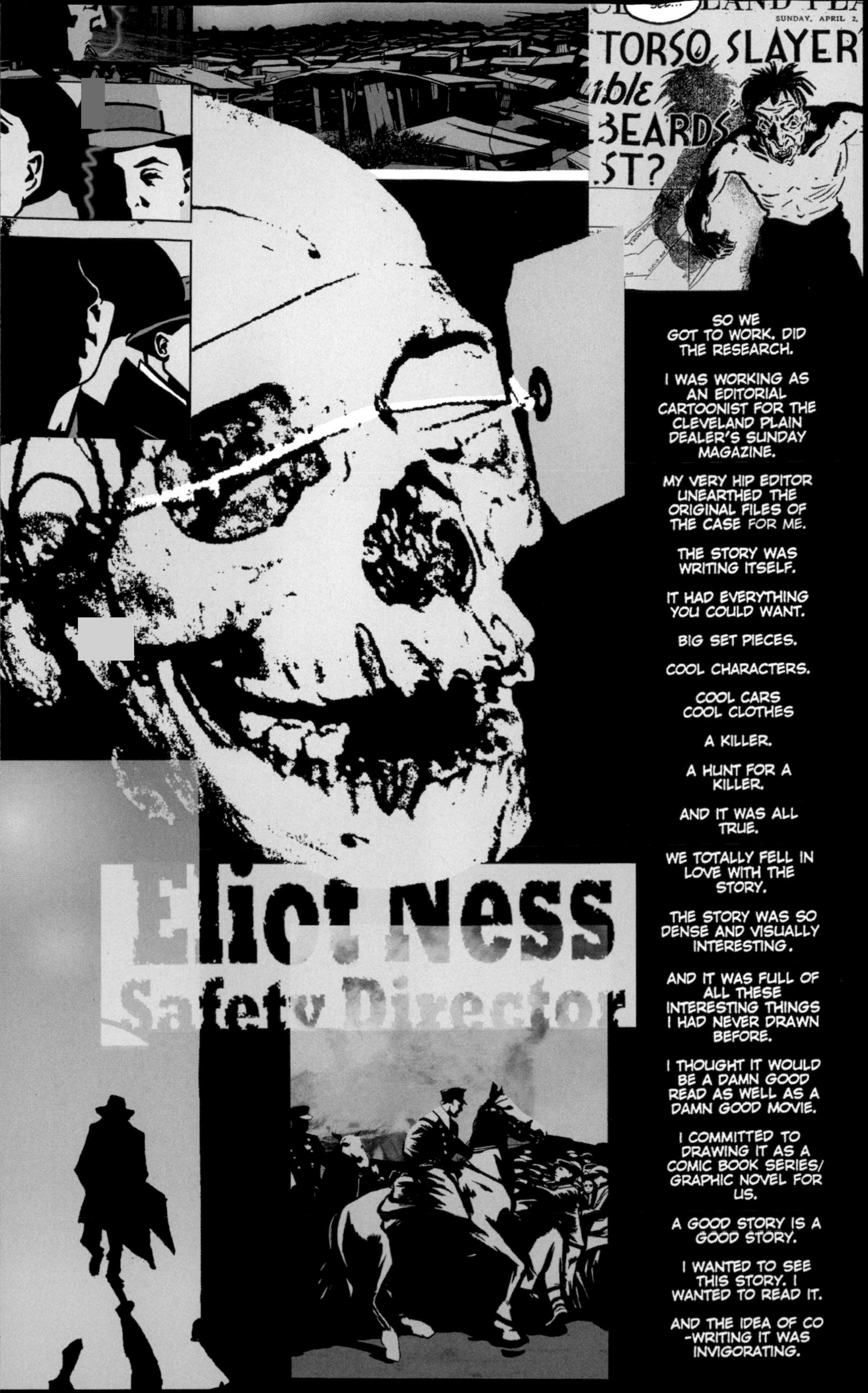
SUNDAY, APRIL 2,
TORSO SLAYER
SO WE GOT TO WORK. DID THE RESEARCH.
I WAS WORKING AS AN EDITORIAL CARTOONIST FOR THE CLEVELAND PLAIN DEALER'S SUNDAY MAGAZINE.
MY VERY HIP EDITOR UNEARTHED THE ORIGINAL FILES OF THE CASE FOR ME.
THE STORY WAS WRITING ITSELF.
IT HAD EVERYTHING YOU COULD WANT.
BIG SET PIECES.
COOL CHARACTERS.
COOL CARS COOL CLOTHES
A KILLER.
A HUNT FOR A KILLER.
AND IT WAS ALL TRUE.
WE TOTALLY FELL IN LOVE WITH THE STORY.
THE STORY WAS SO DENSE AND VISUALLY INTERESTING.
AND IT WAS FULL OF ALL THESE INTERESTING THINGS I HAD NEVER DRAWN BEFORE.
I THOUGHT IT WOULD BE A DAMN GOOD READ AS WELL AS A DAMN GOOD MOVIE.
I COMMITTED TO DRAWING IT AS A COMIC BOOK SERIES/ GRAPHIC NOVEL FOR US.
A GOOD STORY IS A GOOD STORY.
I WANTED TO SEE THIS STORY. I WANTED TO READ IT.
AND THE IDEA OF CO -WRITING IT WAS INVIGORATING.

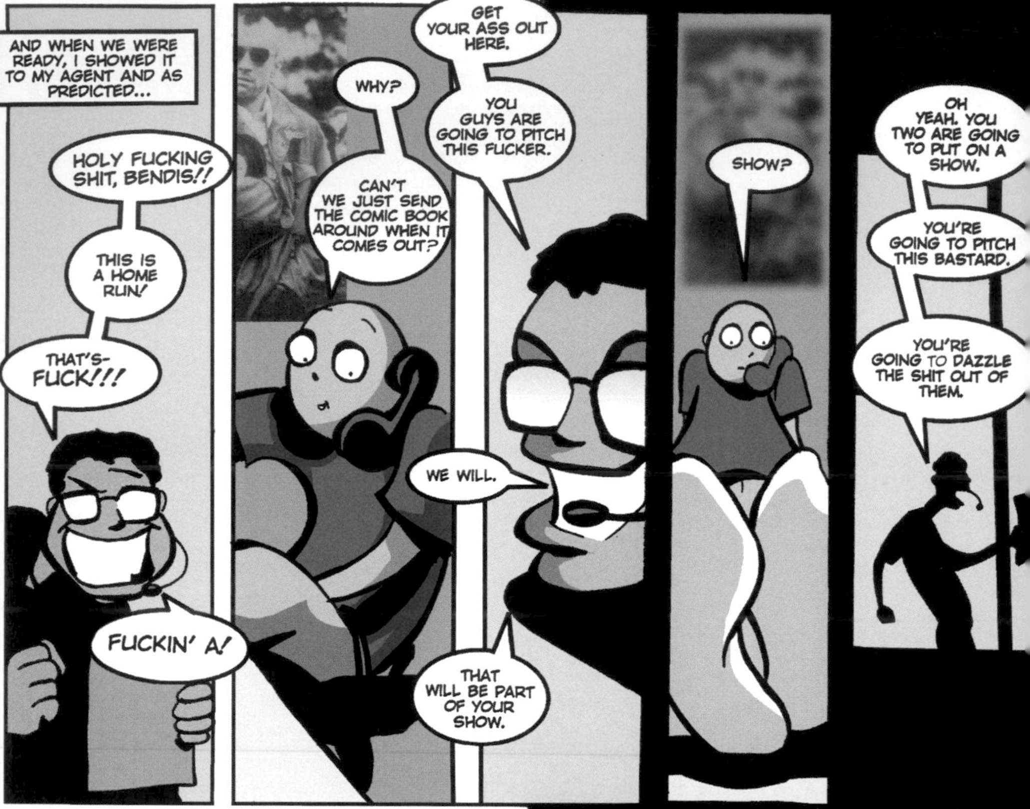
AND WHEN WE WERE READY, I SHOWED IT TO MY AGENT AND AS PREDICTED...
HOLY FUCKING SHIT, BENDIS!!
THIS IS A HOME RUN!
THAT'S- FUCK!!!
FUCKIN' A!
WHY?
CAN'T WE JUST SEND THE COMIC BOOK AROUND WHEN IT COMES OUT?
GET YOUR ASS OUT HERE.
YOU GUYS ARE GOING TO PITCH THIS FUCKER.
WE WILL.
THAT WILL BE PART OF YOUR SHOW.
SHOW?
OH YEAH. YOU TWO ARE GOING TO PUT ON A SHOW.
YOU'RE GOING TO PITCH THIS BASTARD.
YOU'RE GOING TO DAZZLE THE SHIT OUT OF THEM.

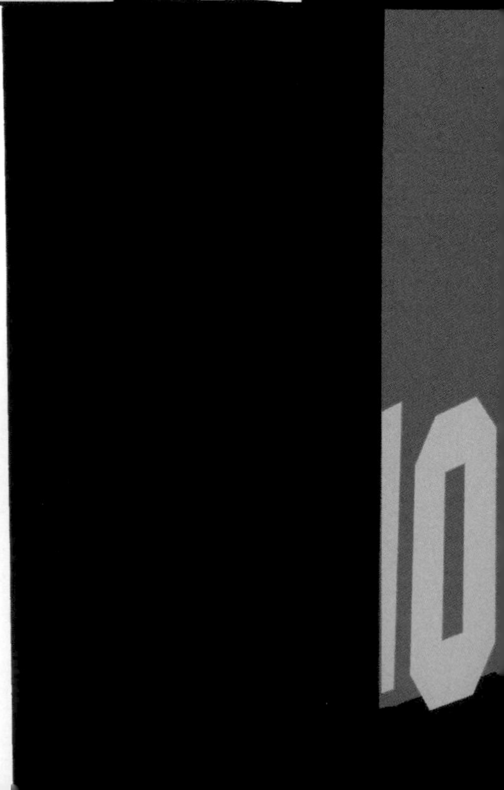

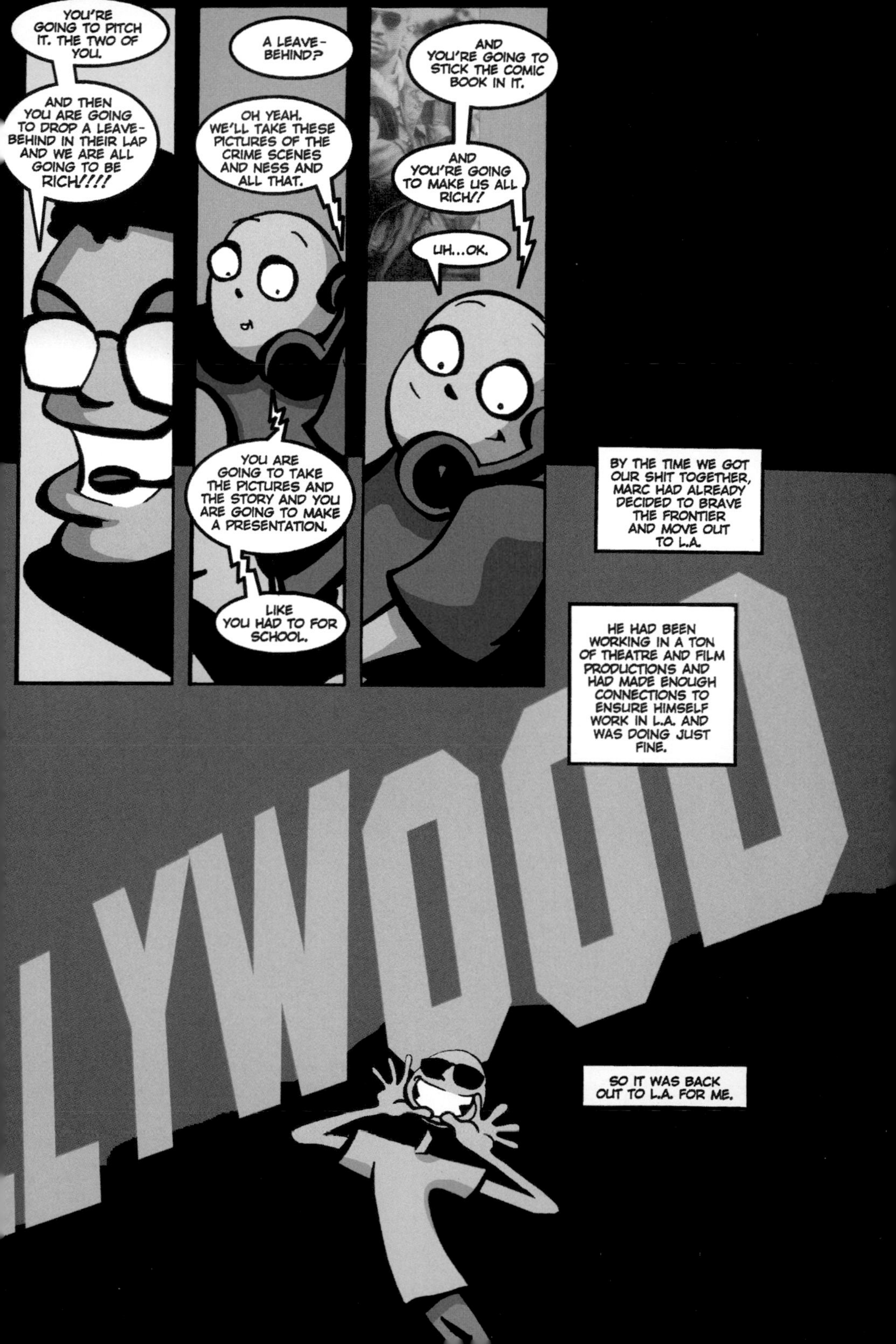

YOU'RE GOING TO PITCH IT. THE TWO OF YOU.
AND THEN YOU ARE GOING TO DROP A LEAVE-BEHIND IN THEIR LAP AND WE ARE ALL GOING TO BE RICH!!!!
A LEAVE-BEHIND?
OH YEAH. WE'LL TAKE THESE PICTURES OF THE CRIME SCENES AND NESS AND ALL THAT.
YOU ARE GOING TO TAKE THE PICTURES AND THE STORY AND YOU ARE GOING TO MAKE A PRESENTATION.
LIKE YOU HAD TO FOR SCHOOL.
AND YOU'RE GOING TO STICK THE COMIC BOOK IN IT.
AND YOU'RE GOING TO MAKE US ALL RICH!!
UH...OK.
BY THE TIME WE GOT OUR SHIT TOGETHER, MARC HAD ALREADY DECIDED TO BRAVE THE FRONTIER AND MOVE OUT TO L.A.
HE HAD BEEN WORKING IN A TON OF THEATRE AND FILM PRODUCTIONS AND HAD MADE ENOUGH CONNECTIONS TO ENSURE HIMSELF WORK IN L.A. AND WAS DOING JUST FINE.
LYWOOD
SO IT WAS BACK OUT TO L.A. FOR ME.

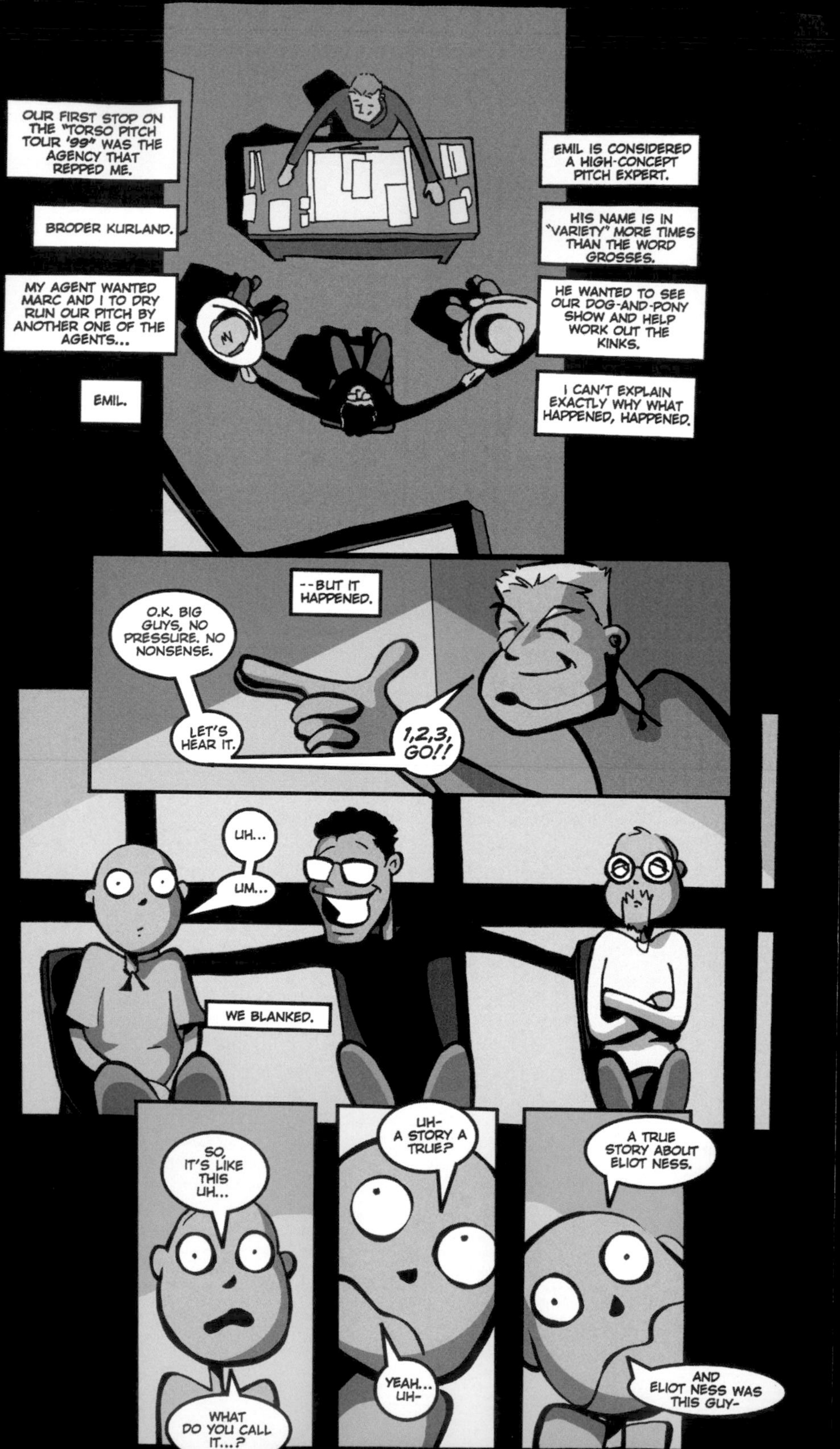
OUR FIRST STOP ON THE "TORSO PITCH TOUR '99" WAS THE AGENCY THAT REPPED ME.
BRODER KURLAND.
MY AGENT WANTED MARC AND I TO DRY RUN OUR PITCH BY ANOTHER ONE OF THE AGENTS...
EMIL.
EMIL IS CONSIDERED A HIGH-CONCEPT PITCH EXPERT.
HIS NAME IS IN "VARIETY" MORE TIMES THAN THE WORD GROSSES.
HE WANTED TO SEE OUR DOG-AND-PONY SHOW AND HELP WORK OUT THE KINKS.
I CAN'T EXPLAIN EXACTLY WHY WHAT HAPPENED, HAPPENED.
--BUT IT HAPPENED.
O.K. BIG GUYS, NO PRESSURE. NO NONSENSE.
LET'S HEAR IT.
1,2,3, GO!!
UH...
UM...
WE BLANKED.
SO, IT'S LIKE THIS UH...
WHAT DO YOU CALL IT...?
UH- A STORY A TRUE?
YEAH... UH-
A TRUE STORY ABOUT ELIOT NESS.
AND ELIOT NESS WAS THIS GUY-

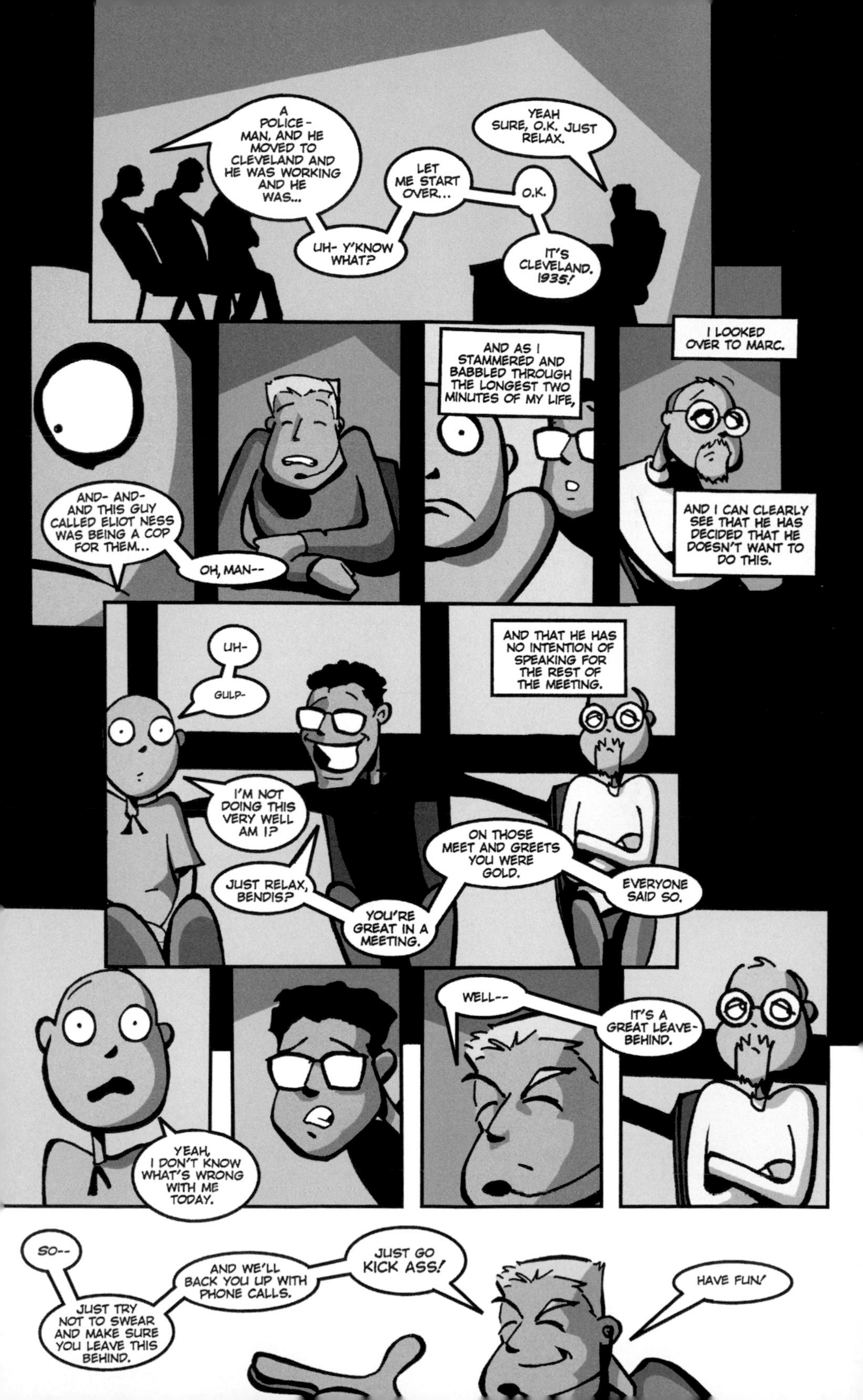
A POLICE-MAN, AND HE MOVED TO CLEVELAND AND HE WAS WORKING AND HE WAS...
UH- Y'KNOW WHAT?
LET ME START OVER...
O.K.
YEAH SURE, O.K. JUST RELAX.
IT'S CLEVELAND. 1935!
AND- AND- AND THIS GUY CALLED ELIOT NESS WAS BEING A COP FOR THEM...
OH, MAN--
AND AS I STAMMERED AND BABBLED THROUGH THE LONGEST TWO MINUTES OF MY LIFE,
I LOOKED OVER TO MARC.
AND I CAN CLEARLY SEE THAT HE HAS DECIDED THAT HE DOESN'T WANT TO DO THIS.
UH-
GULP-
AND THAT HE HAS NO INTENTION OF SPEAKING FOR THE REST OF THE MEETING.
I'M NOT DOING THIS VERY WELL AM I?
JUST RELAX, BENDIS?
YOU'RE GREAT IN A MEETING.
ON THOSE MEET AND GREETS YOU WERE GOLD.
EVERYONE SAID SO.
YEAH, I DON'T KNOW WHAT'S WRONG WITH ME TODAY.
WELL--
IT'S A GREAT LEAVE-BEHIND.
SO--
JUST TRY NOT TO SWEAR AND MAKE SURE YOU LEAVE THIS BEHIND.
AND WE'LL BACK YOU UP WITH PHONE CALLS.
JUST GO KICK ASS!
HAVE FUN!

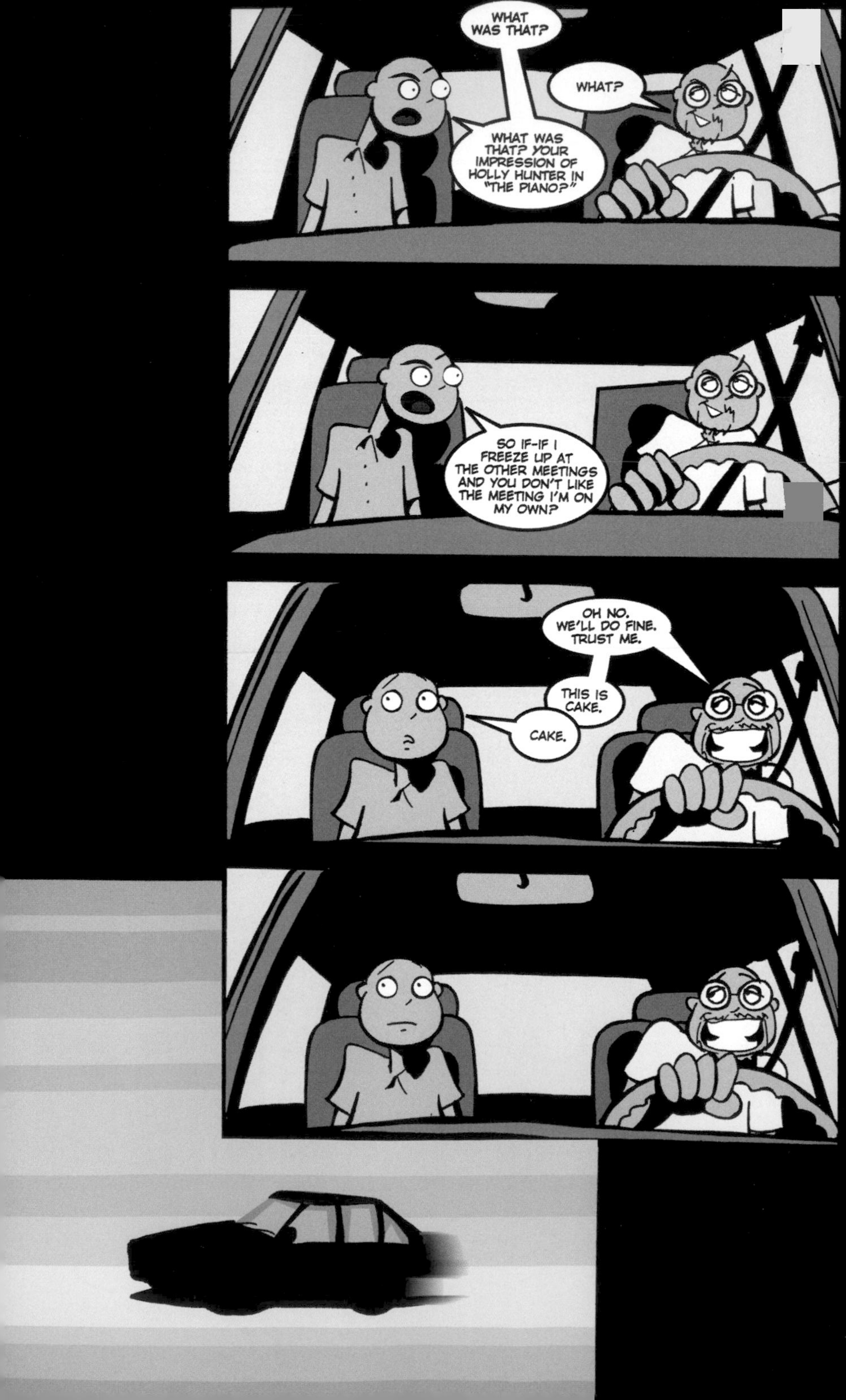
WHAT WAS THAT?
WHAT?
WHAT WAS THAT? YOUR IMPRESSION OF HOLLY HUNTER IN "THE PIANO?"
SO IF-IF I FREEZE UP AT THE OTHER MEETINGS AND YOU DON'T LIKE THE MEETING I'M ON MY OWN?
OH NO. WE'LL DO FINE. TRUST ME.
THIS IS CAKE.
CAKE.

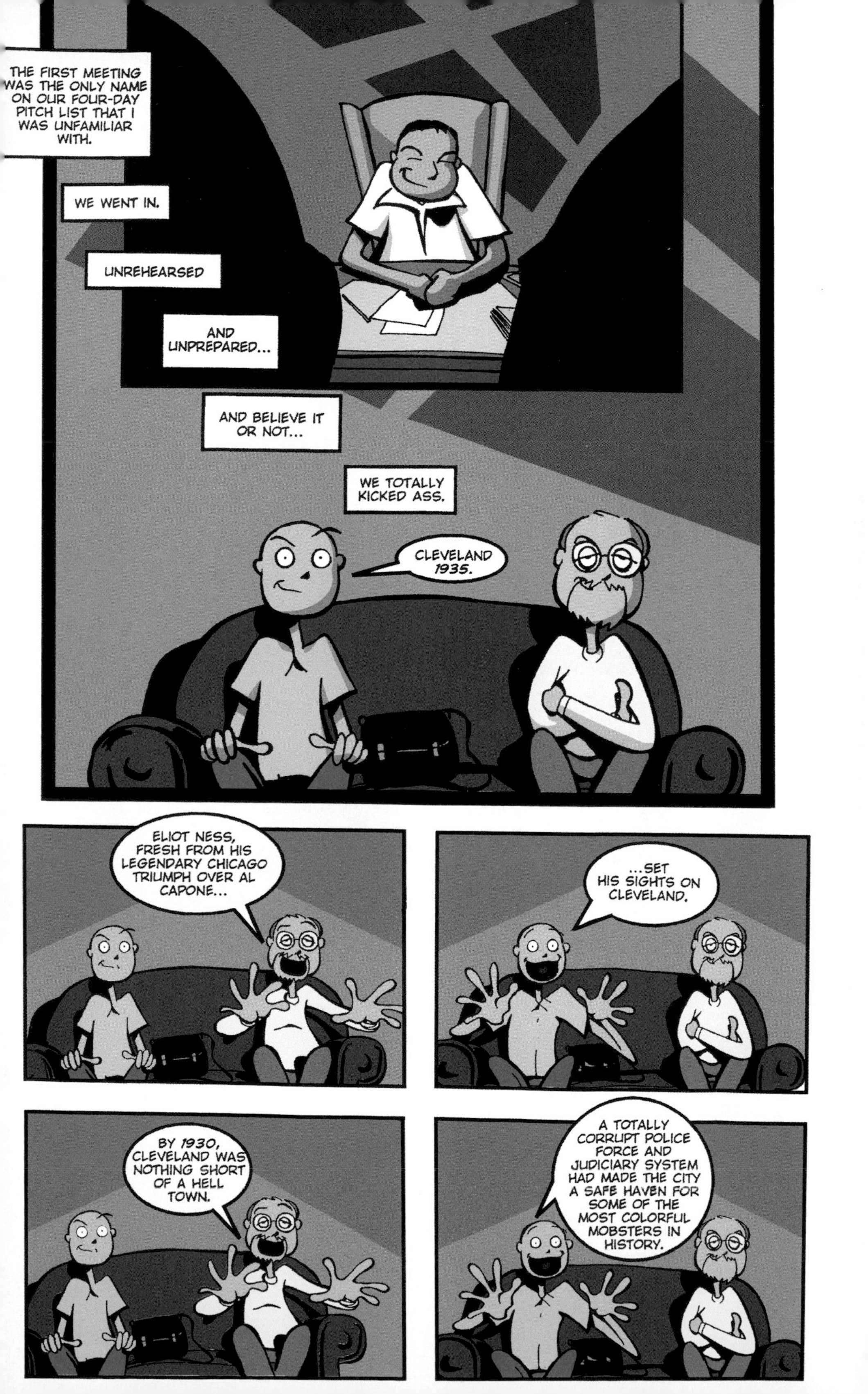
THE FIRST MEETING WAS THE ONLY NAME ON OUR FOUR-DAY PITCH LIST THAT I WAS UNFAMILIAR WITH.
WE WENT IN.
UNREHEARSED
AND UNPREPARED...
AND BELIEVE IT OR NOT...
WE TOTALLY KICKED ASS.
CLEVELAND 1935.
ELIOT NESS, FRESH FROM HIS LEGENDARY CHICAGO TRIUMPH OVER AL CAPONE...
...SET HIS SIGHTS ON CLEVELAND.
BY 1930, CLEVELAND WAS NOTHING SHORT OF A HELL TOWN.
A TOTALLY CORRUPT POLICE FORCE AND JUDICIARY SYSTEM HAD MADE THE CITY A SAFE HAVEN FOR SOME OF THE MOST COLORFUL MOBSTERS IN HISTORY.

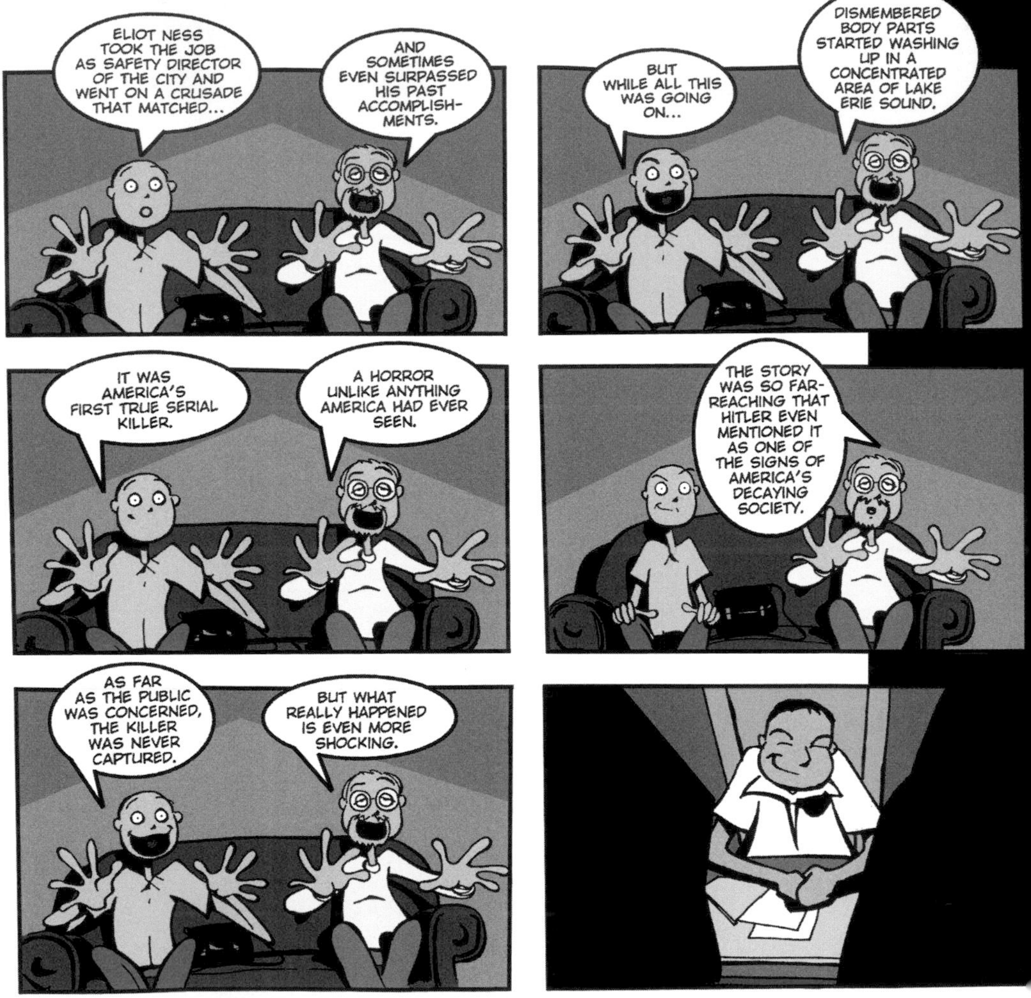
ELIOT NESS TOOK THE JOB AS SAFETY DIRECTOR OF THE CITY AND WENT ON A CRUSADE THAT MATCHED...
AND SOMETIMES EVEN SURPASSED HIS PAST ACCOMPLISH-MENTS.
BUT WHILE ALL THIS WAS GOING ON...
DISMEMBERED BODY PARTS STARTED WASHING UP IN A CONCENTRATED AREA OF LAKE ERIE SOUND.
IT WAS AMERICA'S FIRST TRUE SERIAL KILLER.
A HORROR UNLIKE ANYTHING AMERICA HAD EVER SEEN.
THE STORY WAS SO FAR-REACHING THAT HITLER EVEN MENTIONED IT AS ONE OF THE SIGNS OF AMERICA'S DECAYING SOCIETY.
AS FAR AS THE PUBLIC WAS CONCERNED, THE KILLER WAS NEVER CAPTURED.
BUT WHAT REALLY HAPPENED IS EVEN MORE SHOCKING.

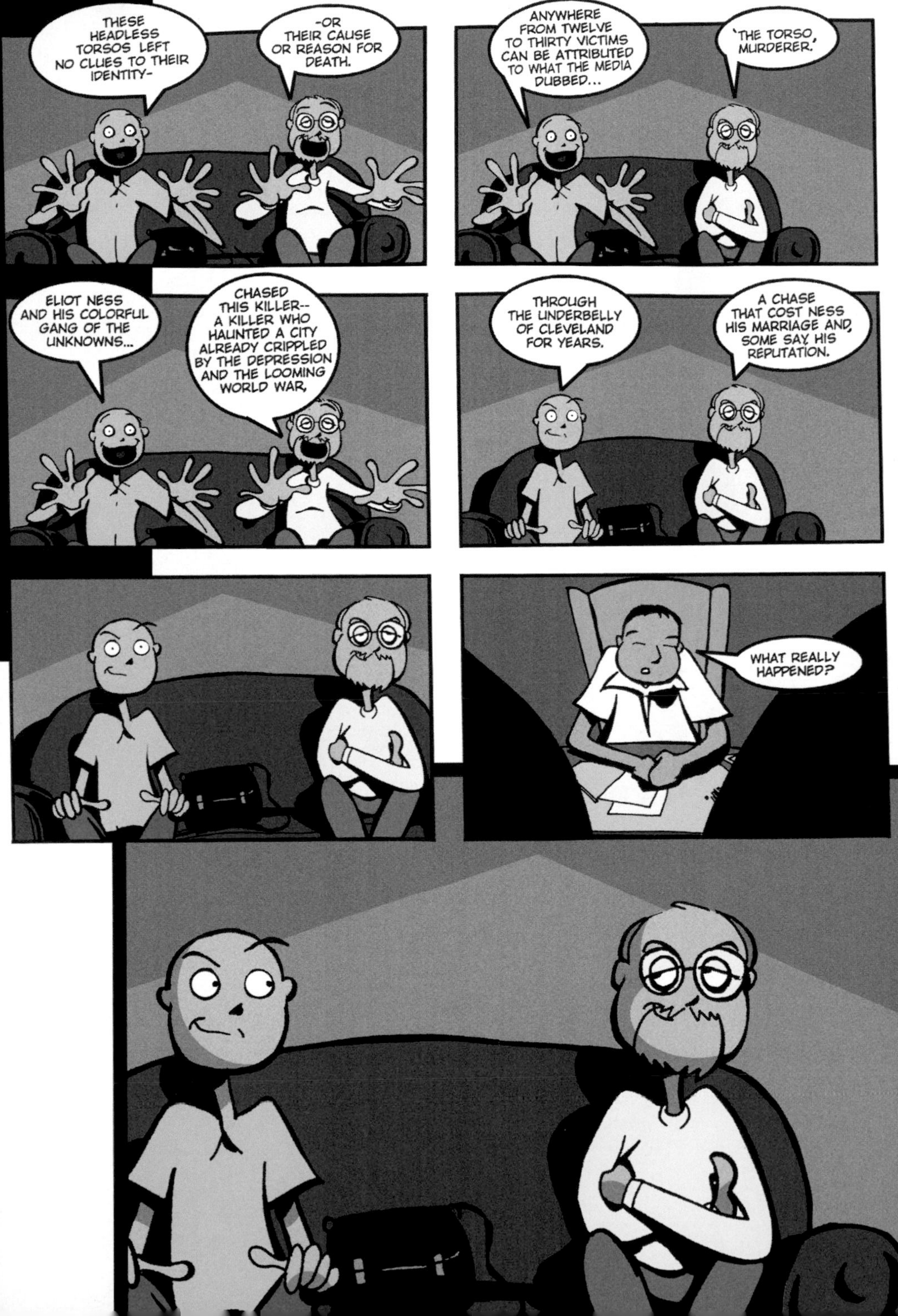

THESE HEADLESS TORSOS LEFT NO CLUES TO THEIR IDENTITY-
-OR THEIR CAUSE OR REASON FOR DEATH.
ANYWHERE FROM TWELVE TO THIRTY VICTIMS CAN BE ATTRIBUTED TO WHAT THE MEDIA DUBBED...
'THE TORSO MURDERER.'
ELIOT NESS AND HIS COLORFUL GANG OF THE UNKNOWNS...
CHASED THIS KILLER-- A KILLER WHO HAUNTED A CITY ALREADY CRIPPLED BY THE DEPRESSION AND THE LOOMING WORLD WAR,
THROUGH THE UNDERBELLY OF CLEVELAND FOR YEARS.
A CHASE THAT COST NESS HIS MARRIAGE AND, SOME SAY, HIS REPUTATION.
WHAT REALLY HAPPENED?

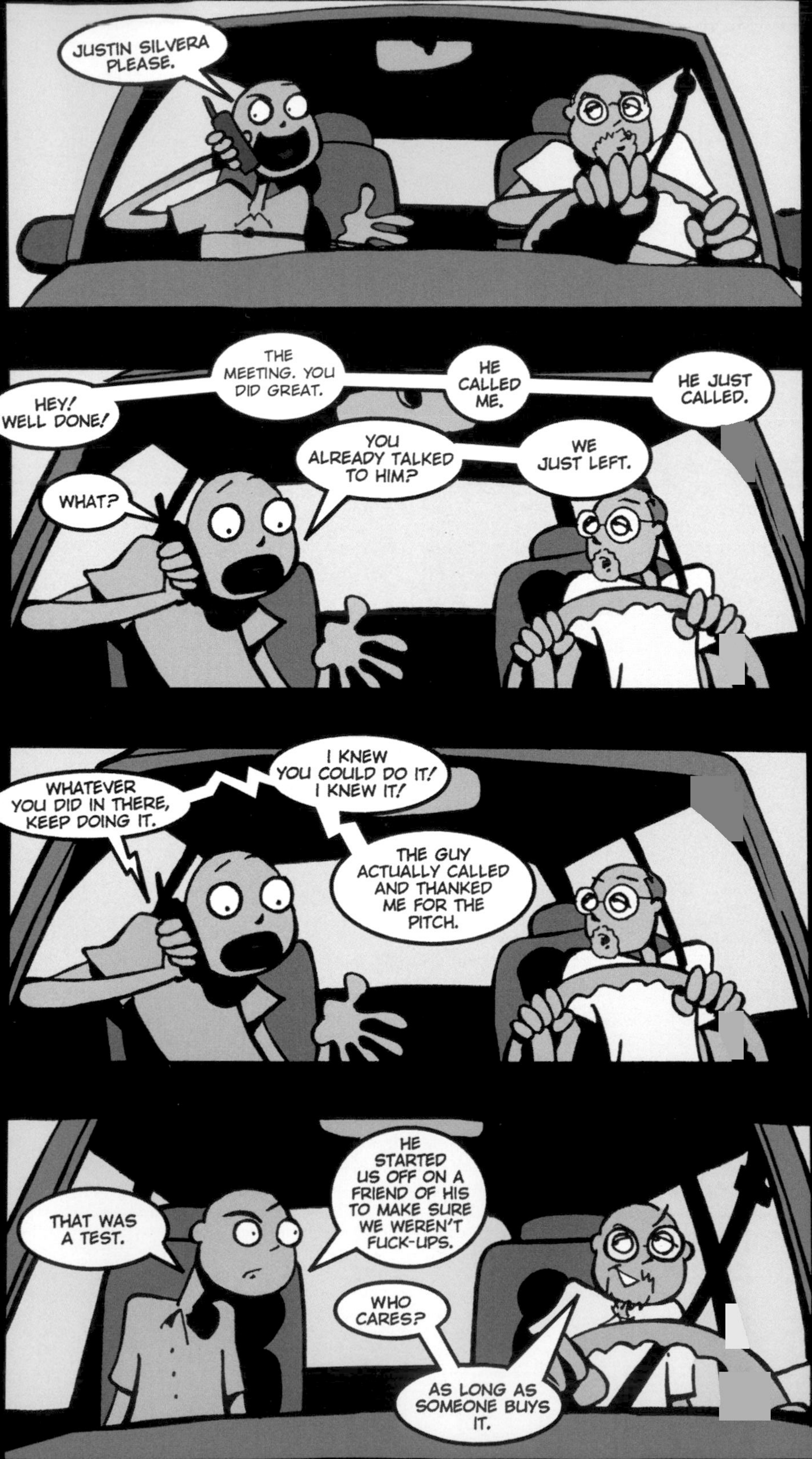
JUSTIN SILVERA PLEASE.
HEY! WELL DONE!
THE MEETING. YOU DID GREAT.
HE CALLED ME.
HE JUST CALLED.
WHAT?
YOU ALREADY TALKED TO HIM?
WE JUST LEFT.
WHATEVER YOU DID IN THERE, KEEP DOING IT.
I KNEW YOU COULD DO IT! I KNEW IT!
THE GUY ACTUALLY CALLED AND THANKED ME FOR THE PITCH.
THAT WAS A TEST.
HE STARTED US OFF ON A FRIEND OF HIS TO MAKE SURE WE WEREN'T FUCK-UPS.
WHO CARES?
AS LONG AS SOMEONE BUYS IT.

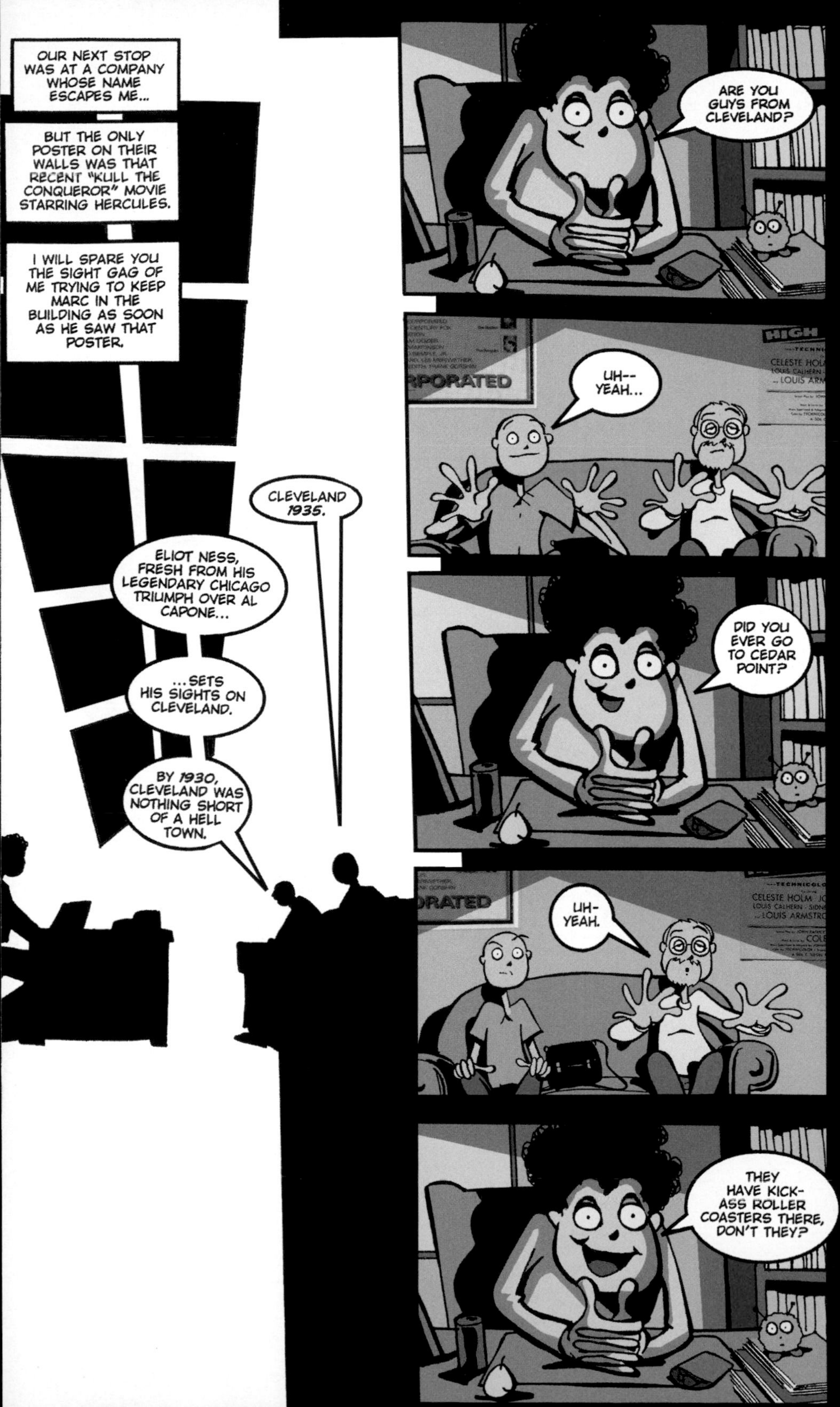
OUR NEXT STOP WAS AT A COMPANY WHOSE NAME ESCAPES ME...
BUT THE ONLY POSTER ON THEIR WALLS WAS THAT RECENT "KULL THE CONQUEROR" MOVIE STARRING HERCULES.
I WILL SPARE YOU THE SIGHT GAG OF ME TRYING TO KEEP MARC IN THE BUILDING AS SOON AS HE SAW THAT POSTER.
ARE YOU GUYS FROM CLEVELAND?
UH-- YEAH...
DID YOU EVER GO TO CEDAR POINT?
UH- YEAH.
THEY HAVE KICK-ASS ROLLER COASTERS THERE, DON'T THEY?
CLEVELAND 1935.
ELIOT NESS, FRESH FROM HIS LEGENDARY CHICAGO TRIUMPH OVER AL CAPONE...
...SETS HIS SIGHTS ON CLEVELAND.
BY 1930, CLEVELAND WAS NOTHING SHORT OF A HELL TOWN.

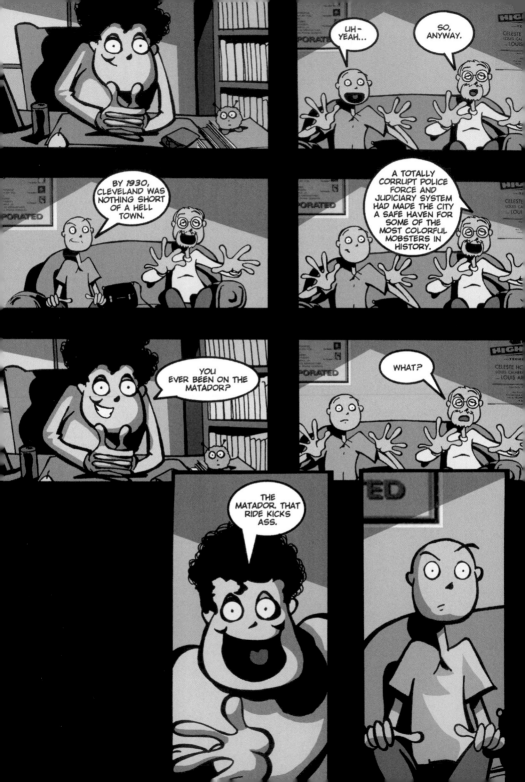

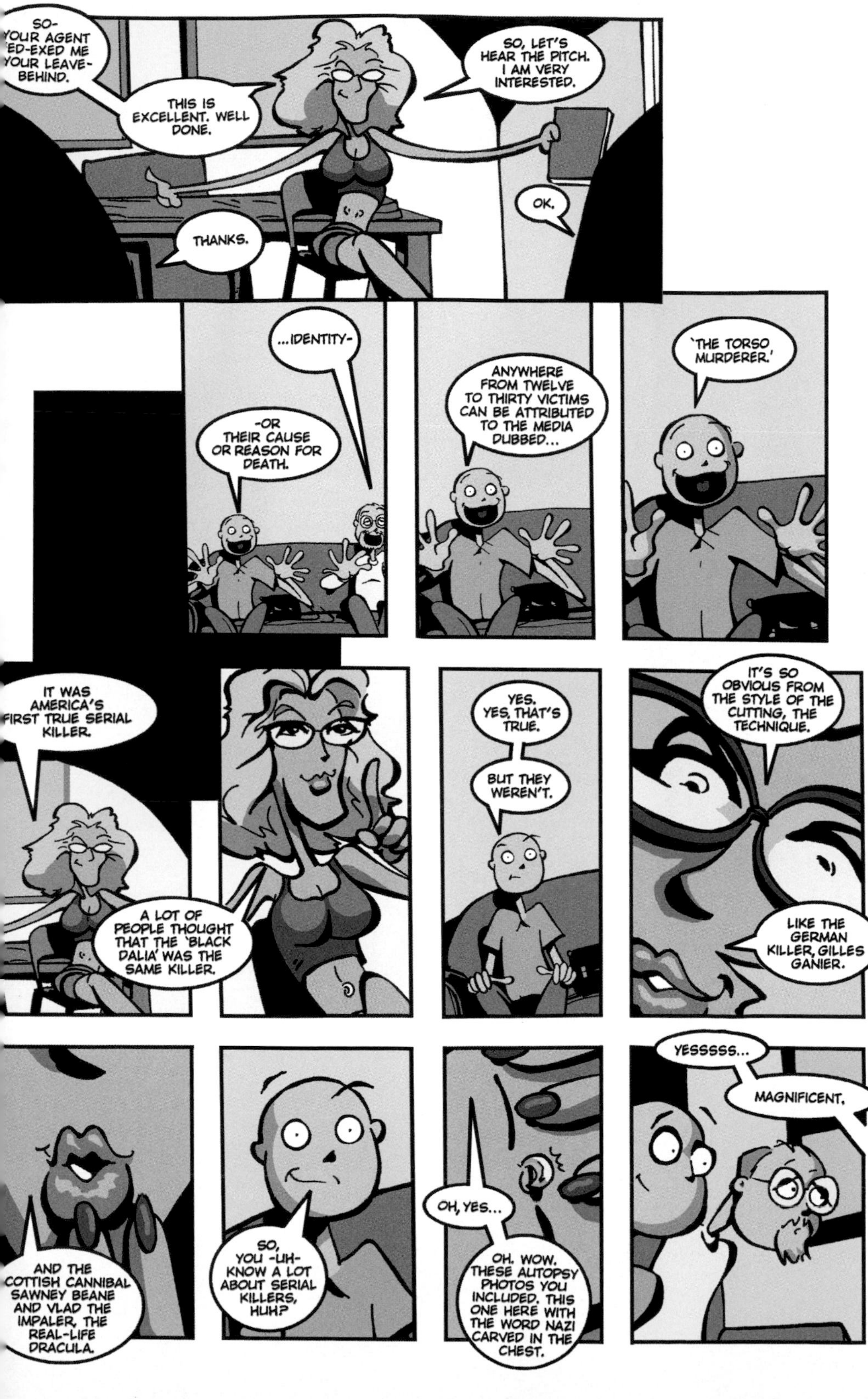
SO-
YOUR AGENT FED-EXED ME YOUR LEAVE-BEHIND.
THIS IS EXCELLENT. WELL DONE.
THANKS.
SO, LET'S HEAR THE PITCH. I AM VERY INTERESTED.
OK.
...IDENTITY-
-OR THEIR CAUSE OR REASON FOR DEATH.
ANYWHERE FROM TWELVE TO THIRTY VICTIMS CAN BE ATTRIBUTED TO THE MEDIA DUBBED...
'THE TORSO MURDERER.'
IT WAS AMERICA'S FIRST TRUE SERIAL KILLER.
A LOT OF PEOPLE THOUGHT THAT THE 'BLACK DALIA' WAS THE SAME KILLER.
YES. YES, THAT'S TRUE.
BUT THEY WEREN'T.
IT'S SO OBVIOUS FROM THE STYLE OF THE CUTTING, THE TECHNIQUE.
LIKE THE GERMAN KILLER, GILLES GANIER.
AND THE SCOTTISH CANNIBAL SAWNEY BEANE AND VLAD THE IMPALER, THE REAL-LIFE DRACULA.
SO, YOU -UH- KNOW A LOT ABOUT SERIAL KILLERS, HUH?
OH, YES...
OH. WOW. THESE AUTOPSY PHOTOS YOU INCLUDED. THIS ONE HERE WITH THE WORD NAZI CARVED IN THE CHEST.
YESSSSS...
MAGNIFICENT.

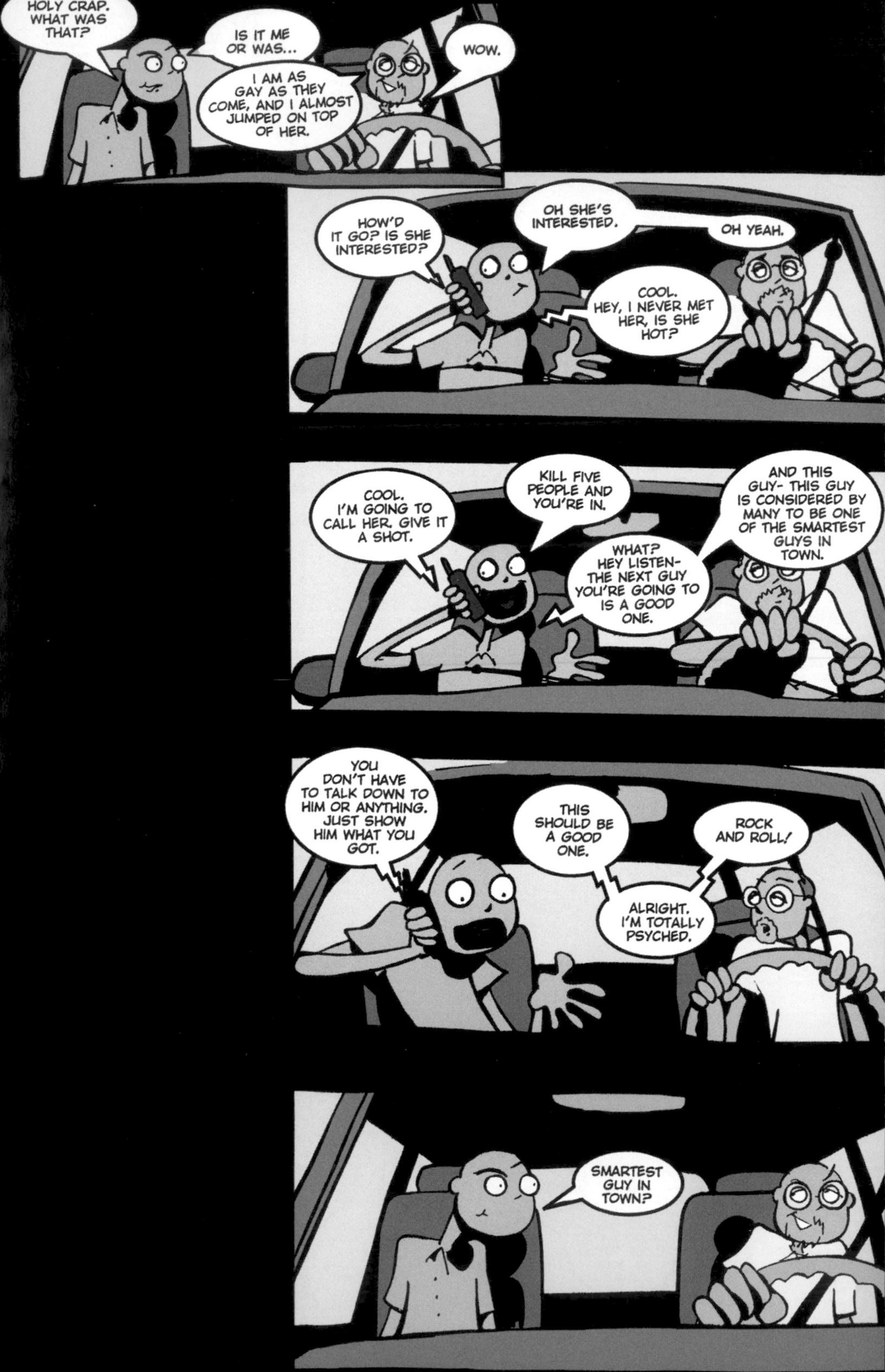
HOLY CRAP. WHAT WAS THAT?
IS IT ME OR WAS...
WOW.
I AM AS GAY AS THEY COME, AND I ALMOST JUMPED ON TOP OF HER.
HOW'D IT GO? IS SHE INTERESTED?
OH SHE'S INTERESTED.
OH YEAH.
COOL. HEY, I NEVER MET HER, IS SHE HOT?
COOL. I'M GOING TO CALL HER. GIVE IT A SHOT.
KILL FIVE PEOPLE AND YOU'RE IN.
AND THIS GUY- THIS GUY IS CONSIDERED BY MANY TO BE ONE OF THE SMARTEST GUYS IN TOWN.
WHAT? HEY LISTEN- THE NEXT GUY YOU'RE GOING TO IS A GOOD ONE.
YOU DON'T HAVE TO TALK DOWN TO HIM OR ANYTHING. JUST SHOW HIM WHAT YOU GOT.
THIS SHOULD BE A GOOD ONE.
ROCK AND ROLL!
ALRIGHT. I'M TOTALLY PSYCHED.
SMARTEST GUY IN TOWN?

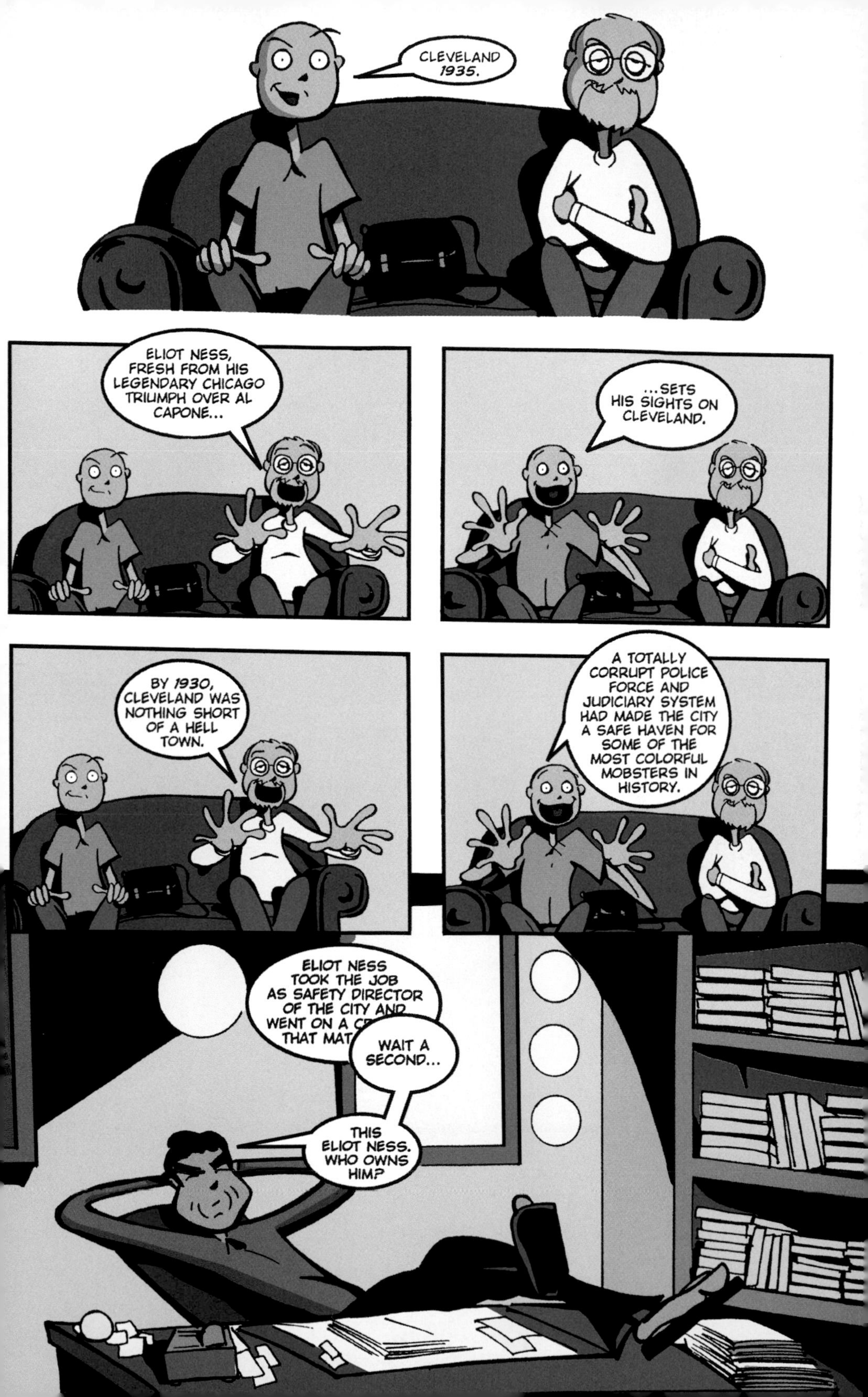
CLEVELAND 1935.
ELIOT NESS, FRESH FROM HIS LEGENDARY CHICAGO TRIUMPH OVER AL CAPONE...
...SETS HIS SIGHTS ON CLEVELAND.
BY 1930, CLEVELAND WAS NOTHING SHORT OF A HELL TOWN.
A TOTALLY CORRUPT POLICE FORCE AND JUDICIARY SYSTEM HAD MADE THE CITY A SAFE HAVEN FOR SOME OF THE MOST COLORFUL MOBSTERS IN HISTORY.
ELIOT NESS TOOK THE JOB AS SAFETY DIRECTOR OF THE CITY AND WENT ON A C
THAT MAT
WAIT A SECOND...
THIS ELIOT NESS. WHO OWNS HIM?

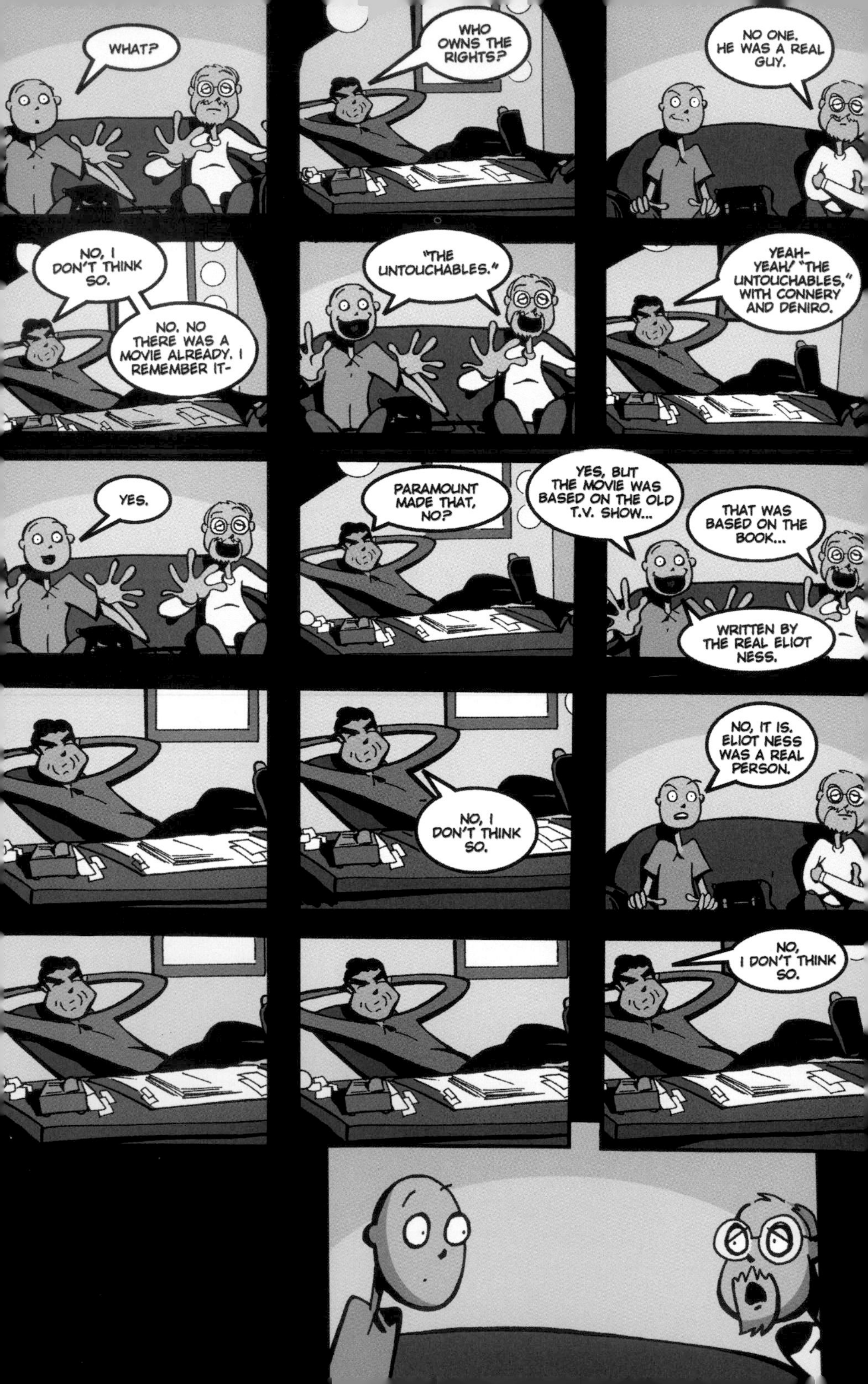
WHAT?
WHO OWNS THE RIGHTS?
NO ONE. HE WAS A REAL GUY.
NO, I DON'T THINK SO.
NO, NO THERE WAS A MOVIE ALREADY. I REMEMBER IT-
"THE UNTOUCHABLES."
YEAH-YEAH! "THE UNTOUCHABLES," WITH CONNERY AND DENIRO.
YES.
PARAMOUNT MADE THAT, NO?
YES, BUT THE MOVIE WAS BASED ON THE OLD T.V. SHOW...
THAT WAS BASED ON THE BOOK...
WRITTEN BY THE REAL ELIOT NESS.
NO, I DON'T THINK SO.
NO, IT IS. ELIOT NESS WAS A REAL PERSON.
NO, I DON'T THINK SO.

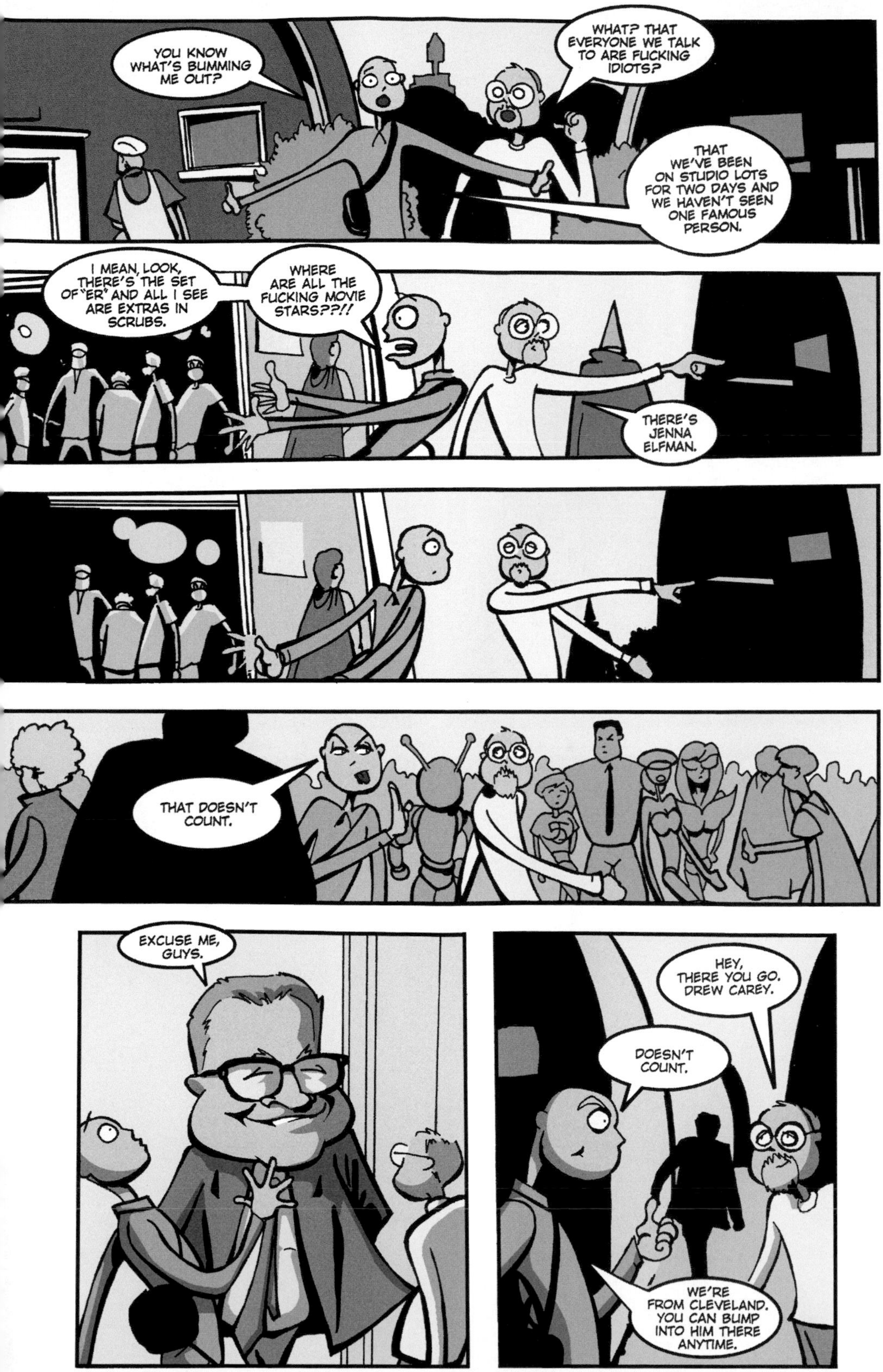
YOU KNOW WHAT'S BUMMING ME OUT?
WHAT? THAT EVERYONE WE TALK TO ARE FUCKING IDIOTS?
THAT WE'VE BEEN ON STUDIO LOTS FOR TWO DAYS AND WE HAVEN'T SEEN ONE FAMOUS PERSON.
I MEAN, LOOK, THERE'S THE SET OF "ER" AND ALL I SEE ARE EXTRAS IN SCRUBS.
WHERE ARE ALL THE FUCKING MOVIE STARS??!!
THERE'S JENNA ELFMAN.
THAT DOESN'T COUNT.
EXCUSE ME, GUYS.
HEY, THERE YOU GO. DREW CAREY.
DOESN'T COUNT.
WE'RE FROM CLEVELAND. YOU CAN BUMP INTO HIM THERE ANYTIME.

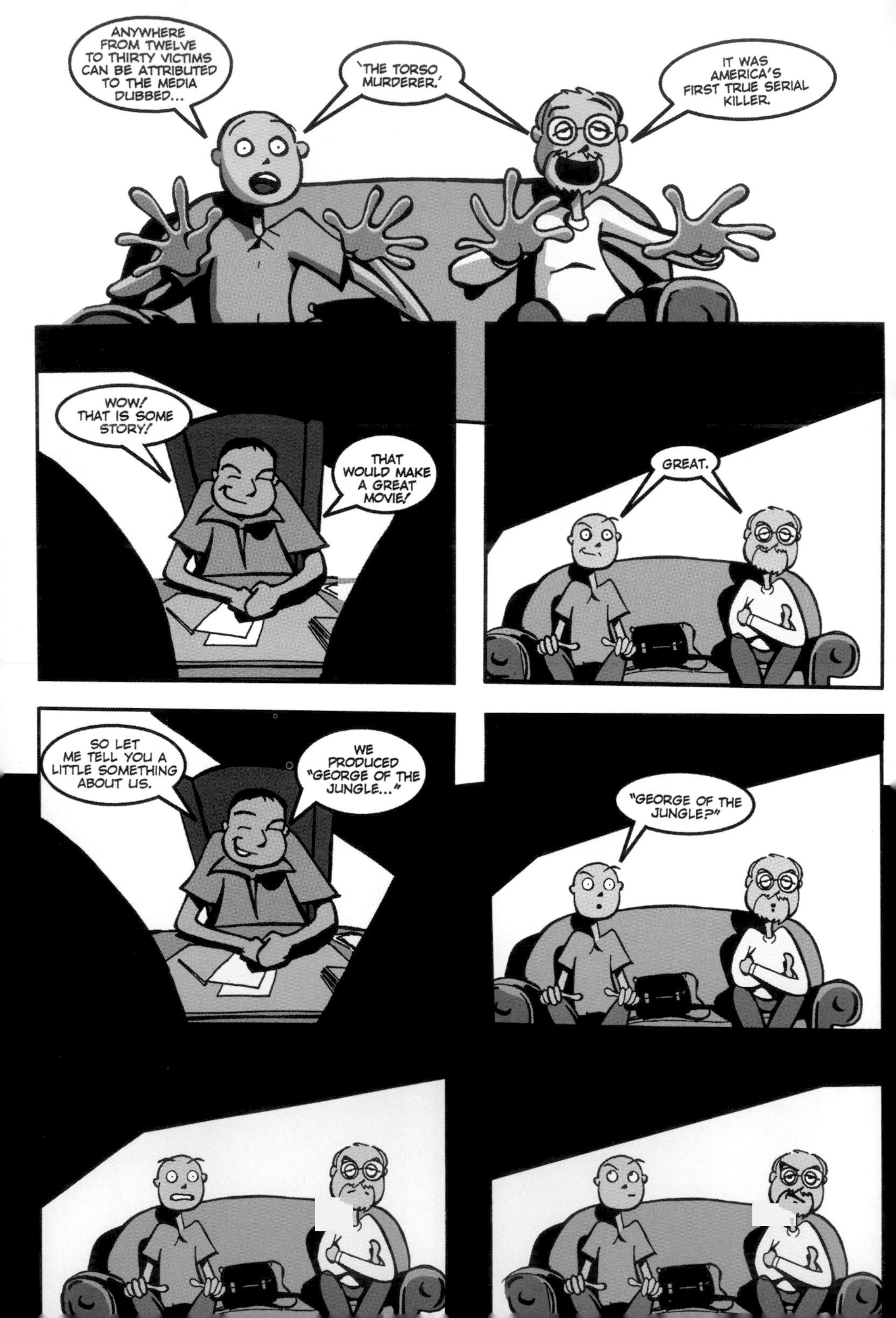
ANYWHERE FROM TWELVE TO THIRTY VICTIMS CAN BE ATTRIBUTED TO THE MEDIA DUBBED...
'THE TORSO MURDERER.'
IT WAS AMERICA'S FIRST TRUE SERIAL KILLER.
WOW! THAT IS SOME STORY!
THAT WOULD MAKE A GREAT MOVIE!
GREAT.
SO LET ME TELL YOU A LITTLE SOMETHING ABOUT US.
WE PRODUCED "GEORGE OF THE JUNGLE..."
"GEORGE OF THE JUNGLE?"

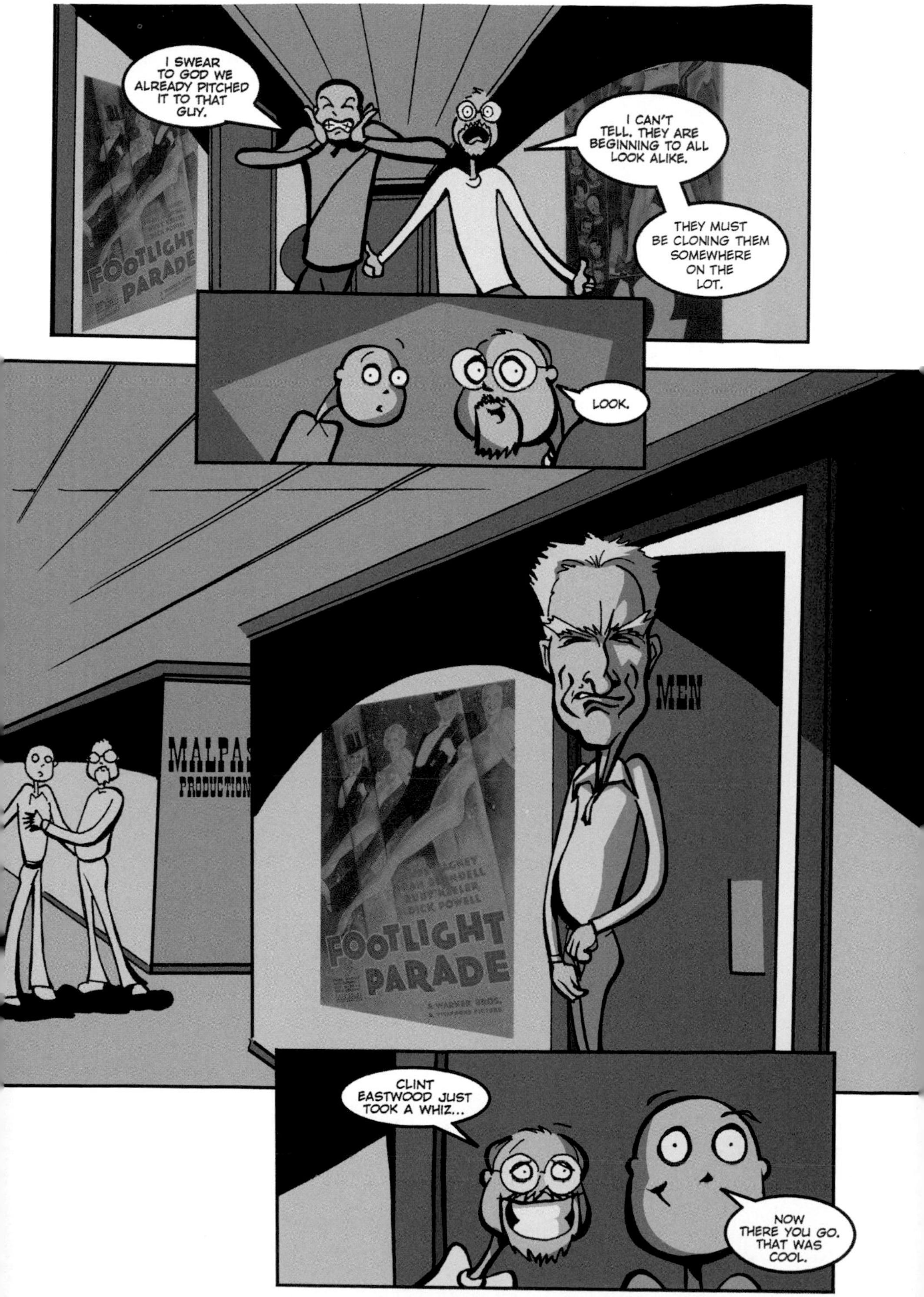
I SWEAR TO GOD WE ALREADY PITCHED IT TO THAT GUY.
I CAN'T TELL. THEY ARE BEGINNING TO ALL LOOK ALIKE.
THEY MUST BE CLONING THEM SOMEWHERE ON THE LOT.
LOOK.
MALPAS PRODUCTION
MEN
FOOTLIGHT PARADE
DICK POWELL
A WARNER BROS.
CLINT EASTWOOD JUST TOOK A WHIZ...
NOW THERE YOU GO. THAT WAS COOL.

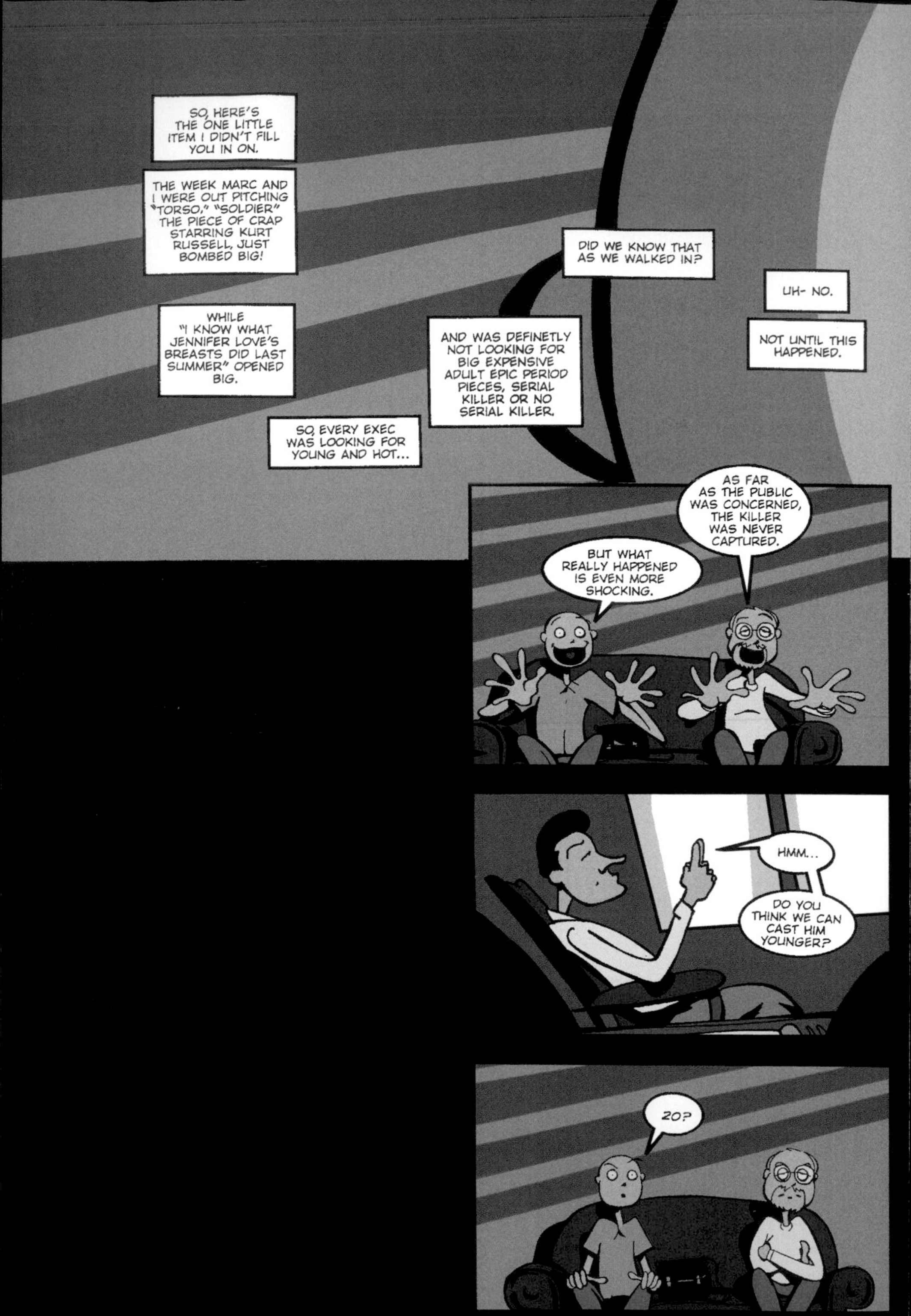
SO, HERE'S THE ONE LITTLE ITEM I DIDN'T FILL YOU IN ON.
THE WEEK MARC AND I WERE OUT PITCHING "TORSO," "SOLDIER" THE PIECE OF CRAP STARRING KURT RUSSELL, JUST BOMBED BIG!
WHILE "I KNOW WHAT JENNIFER LOVE'S BREASTS DID LAST SUMMER" OPENED BIG.
SO, EVERY EXEC WAS LOOKING FOR YOUNG AND HOT...
AND WAS DEFINETLY NOT LOOKING FOR BIG EXPENSIVE ADULT EPIC PERIOD PIECES, SERIAL KILLER OR NO SERIAL KILLER.
DID WE KNOW THAT AS WE WALKED IN?
UH- NO.
NOT UNTIL THIS HAPPENED.
AS FAR AS THE PUBLIC WAS CONCERNED, THE KILLER WAS NEVER CAPTURED.
BUT WHAT REALLY HAPPENED IS EVEN MORE SHOCKING.
HMM...
DO YOU THINK WE CAN CAST HIM YOUNGER?
20?

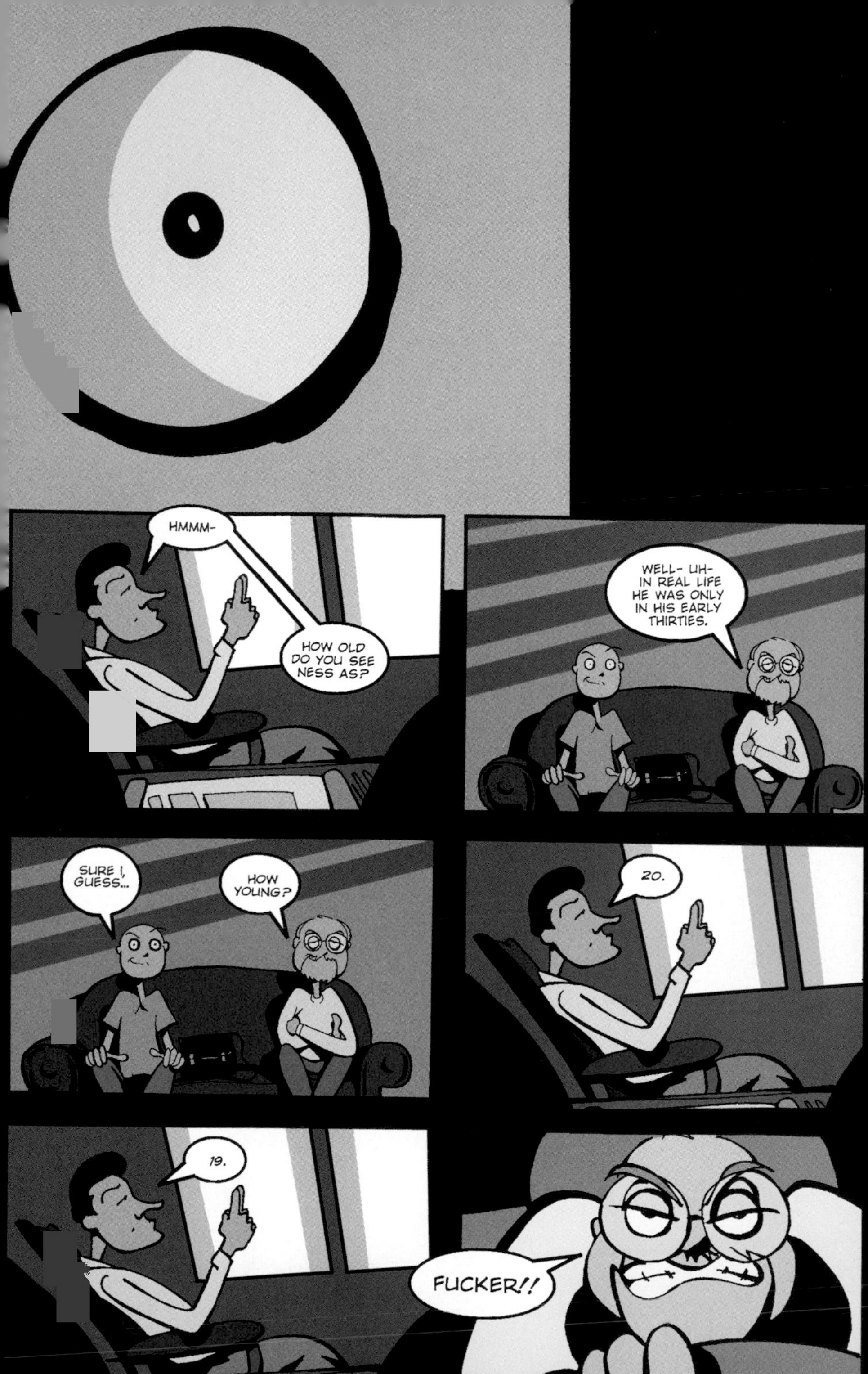
HMMM-
HOW OLD DO YOU SEE NESS AS?
WELL- UH- IN REAL LIFE HE WAS ONLY IN HIS EARLY THIRTIES.
SURE I, GUESS...
HOW YOUNG?
20.
19.
FUCKER!!

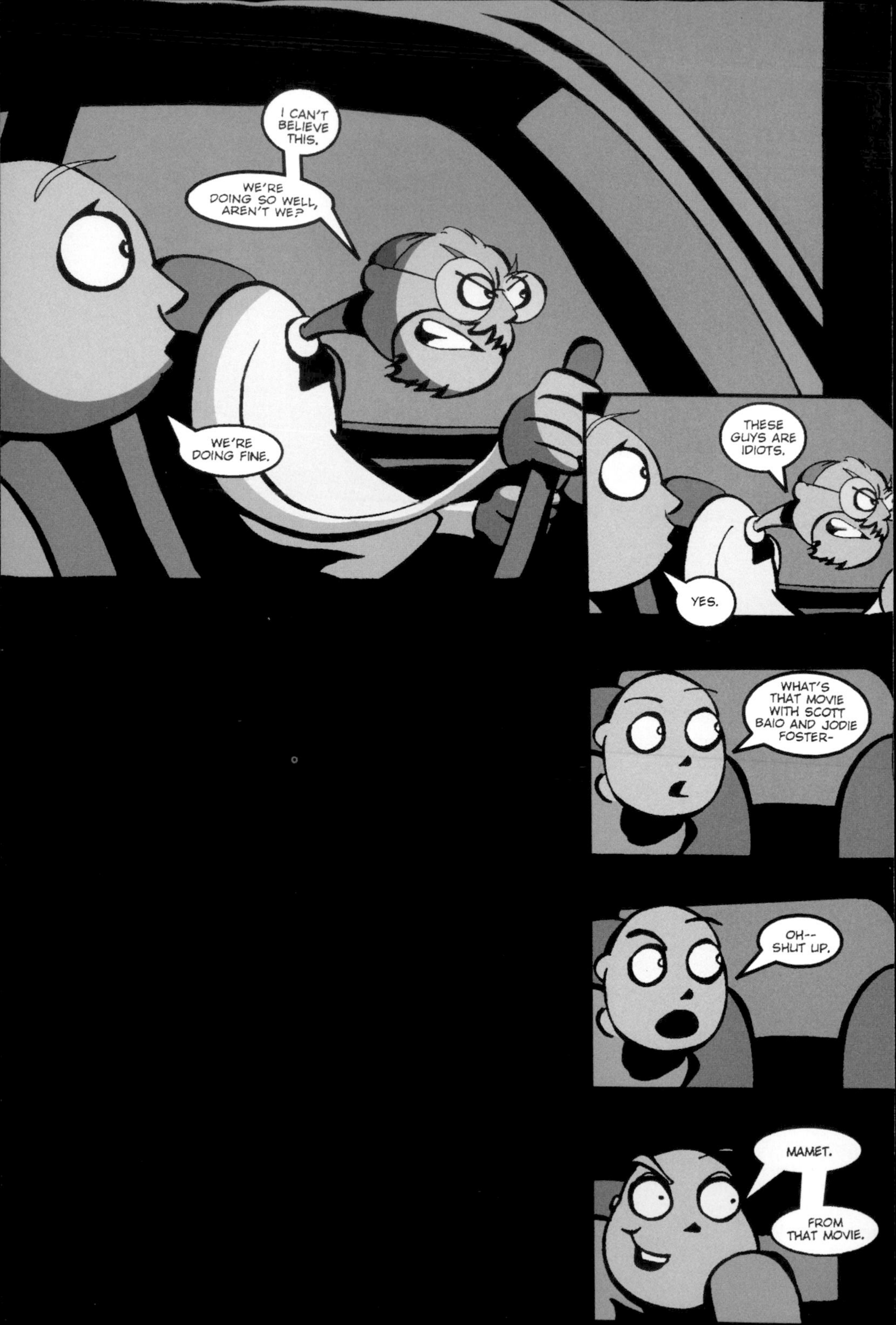
I CAN'T BELIEVE THIS.
WE'RE DOING SO WELL, AREN'T WE?
WE'RE DOING FINE.
THESE GUYS ARE IDIOTS.
YES.
WHAT'S THAT MOVIE WITH SCOTT BAIO AND JODIE FOSTER-
OH-- SHUT UP.
MAMET.
FROM THAT MOVIE.

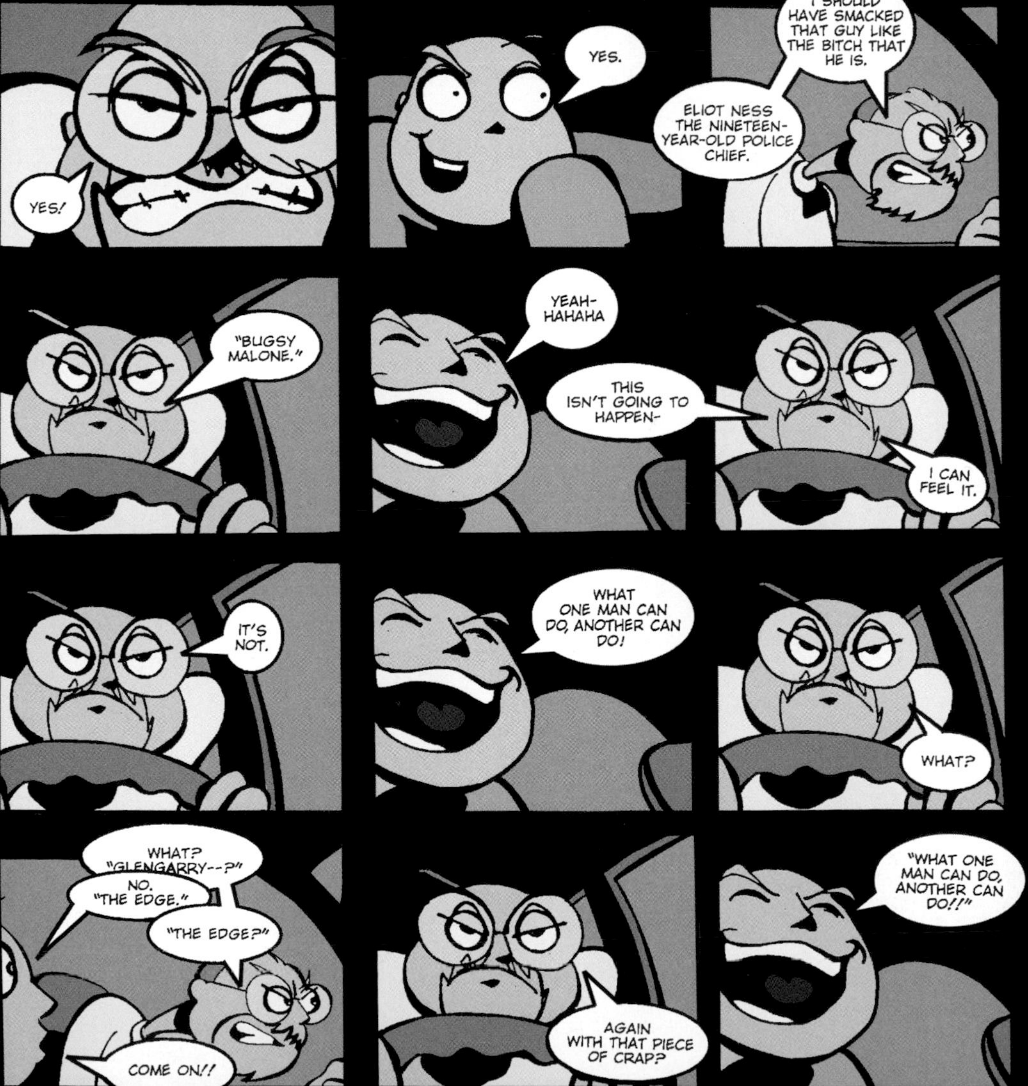
YES!
YES.
ELIOT NESS THE NINETEEN-YEAR-OLD POLICE CHIEF.
I SHOULD HAVE SMACKED THAT GUY LIKE THE BITCH THAT HE IS.
"BUGSY MALONE."
YEAH-HAHAHA
THIS ISN'T GOING TO HAPPEN-
I CAN FEEL IT.
IT'S NOT.
WHAT ONE MAN CAN DO, ANOTHER CAN DO!
WHAT?
WHAT? "GLENGARRY--?"
NO. "THE EDGE."
"THE EDGE?"
COME ON!!
AGAIN WITH THAT PIECE OF CRAP?
"WHAT ONE MAN CAN DO, ANOTHER CAN DO!!"

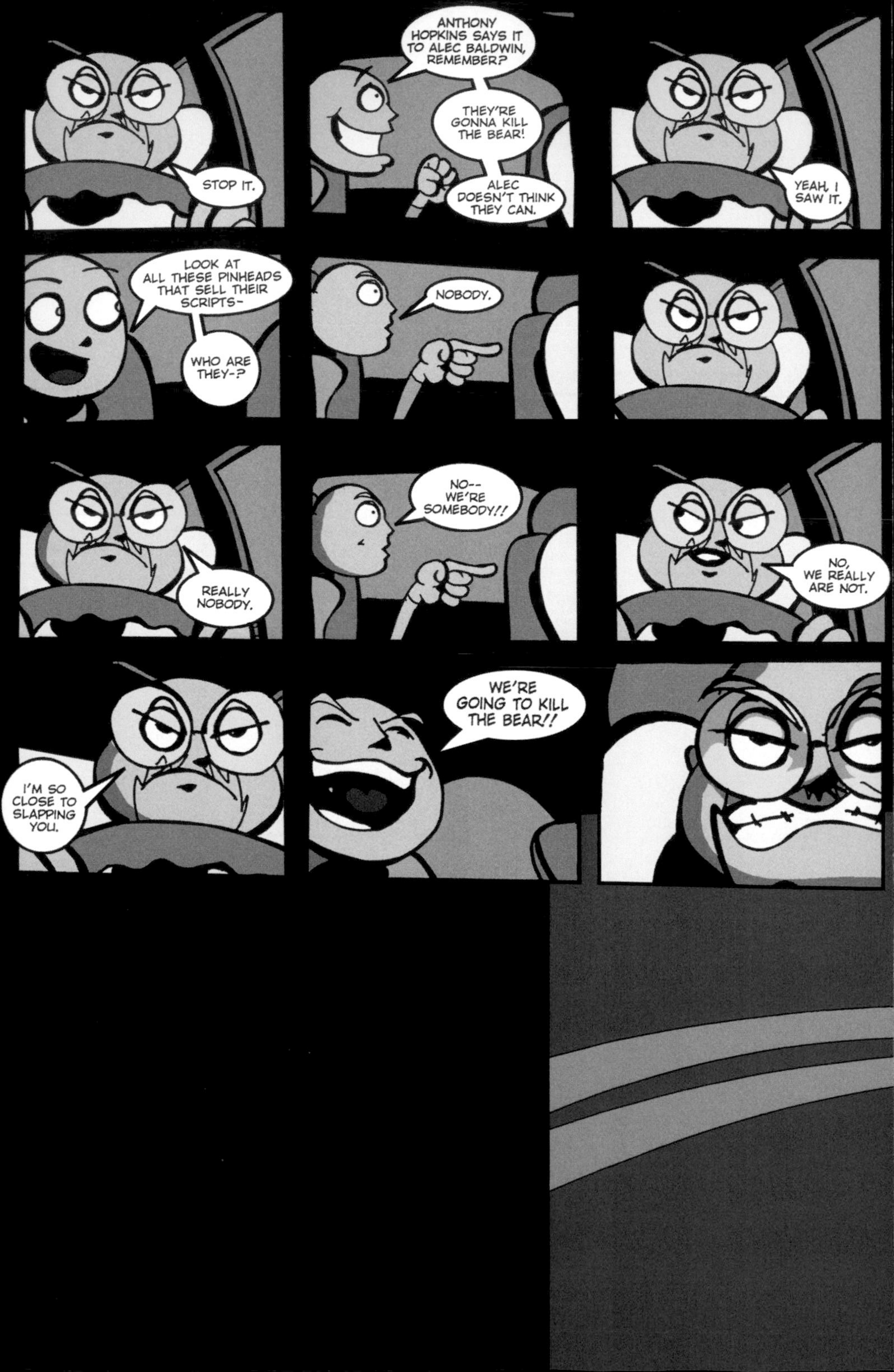
STOP IT.
ANTHONY HOPKINS SAYS IT TO ALEC BALDWIN, REMEMBER?
THEY'RE GONNA KILL THE BEAR!
ALEC DOESN'T THINK THEY CAN.
YEAH, I SAW IT.
LOOK AT ALL THESE PINHEADS THAT SELL THEIR SCRIPTS-
WHO ARE THEY-?
NOBODY.
REALLY NOBODY.
NO-- WE'RE SOMEBODY!!
NO, WE REALLY ARE NOT.
I'M SO CLOSE TO SLAPPING YOU.
WE'RE GOING TO KILL THE BEAR!!

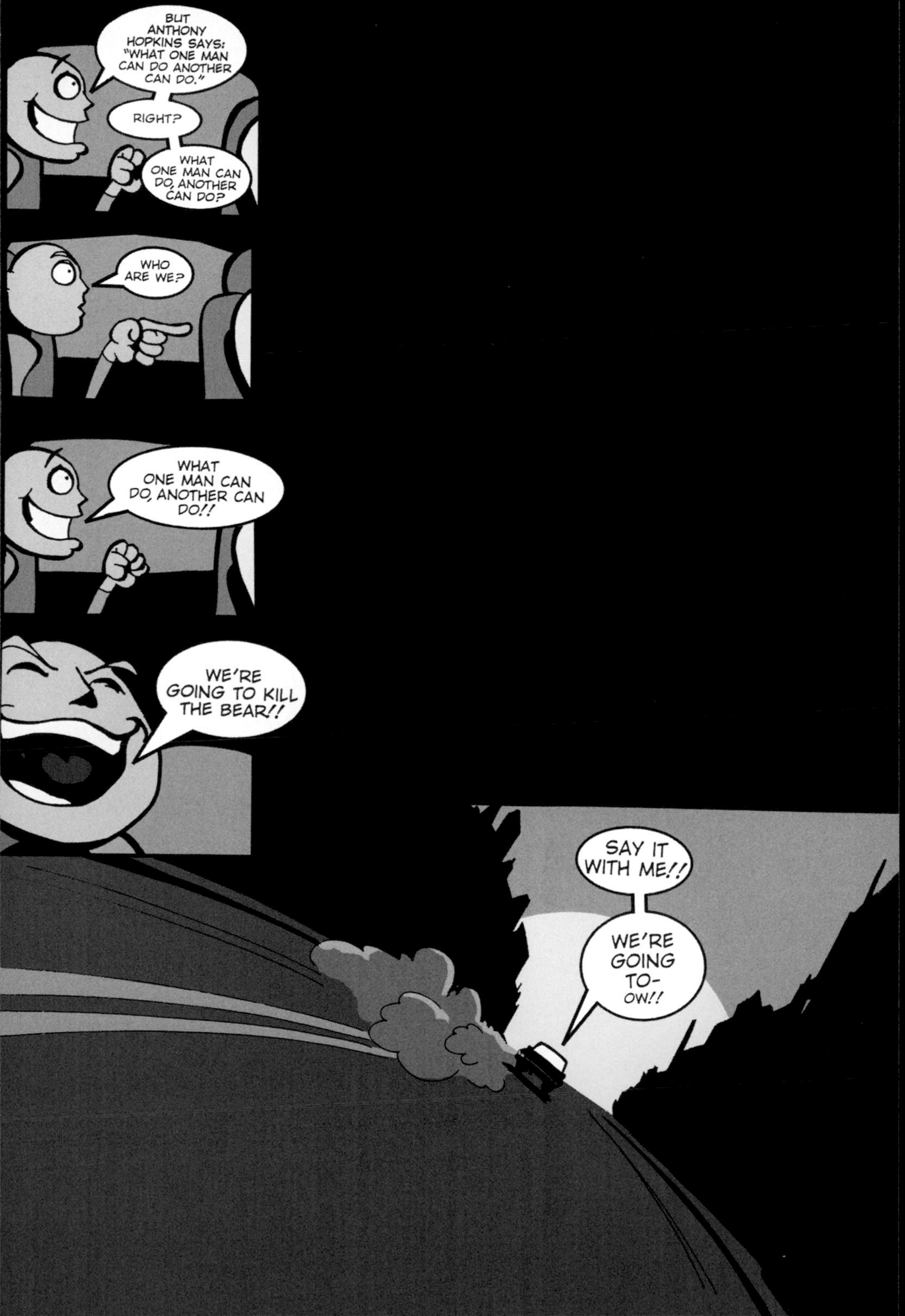
BUT ANTHONY HOPKINS SAYS: "WHAT ONE MAN CAN DO ANOTHER CAN DO."
RIGHT?
WHAT ONE MAN CAN DO, ANOTHER CAN DO?
WHO ARE WE?
WHAT ONE MAN CAN DO, ANOTHER CAN DO!!
WE'RE GOING TO KILL THE BEAR!!
SAY IT WITH ME!!
WE'RE GOING TO-
OW!!

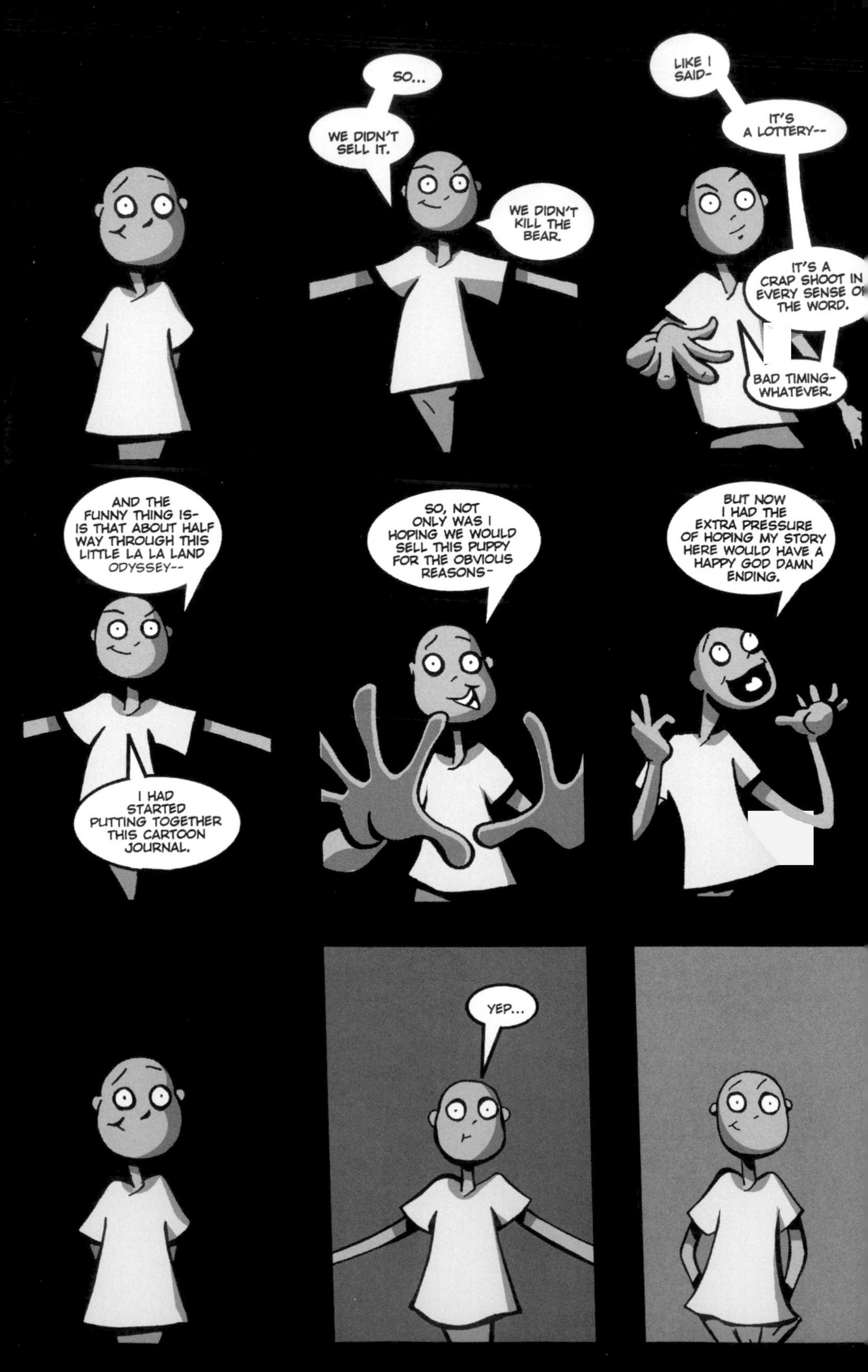
SO...
WE DIDN'T SELL IT.
WE DIDN'T KILL THE BEAR.
LIKE I SAID-
IT'S A LOTTERY--
IT'S A CRAP SHOOT IN EVERY SENSE OF THE WORD.
BAD TIMING- WHATEVER.
AND THE FUNNY THING IS- IS THAT ABOUT HALF WAY THROUGH THIS LITTLE LA LA LAND ODYSSEY--
I HAD STARTED PUTTING TOGETHER THIS CARTOON JOURNAL.
SO, NOT ONLY WAS I HOPING WE WOULD SELL THIS PUPPY FOR THE OBVIOUS REASONS-
BUT NOW I HAD THE EXTRA PRESSURE OF HOPING MY STORY HERE WOULD HAVE A HAPPY GOD DAMN ENDING.
YEP...

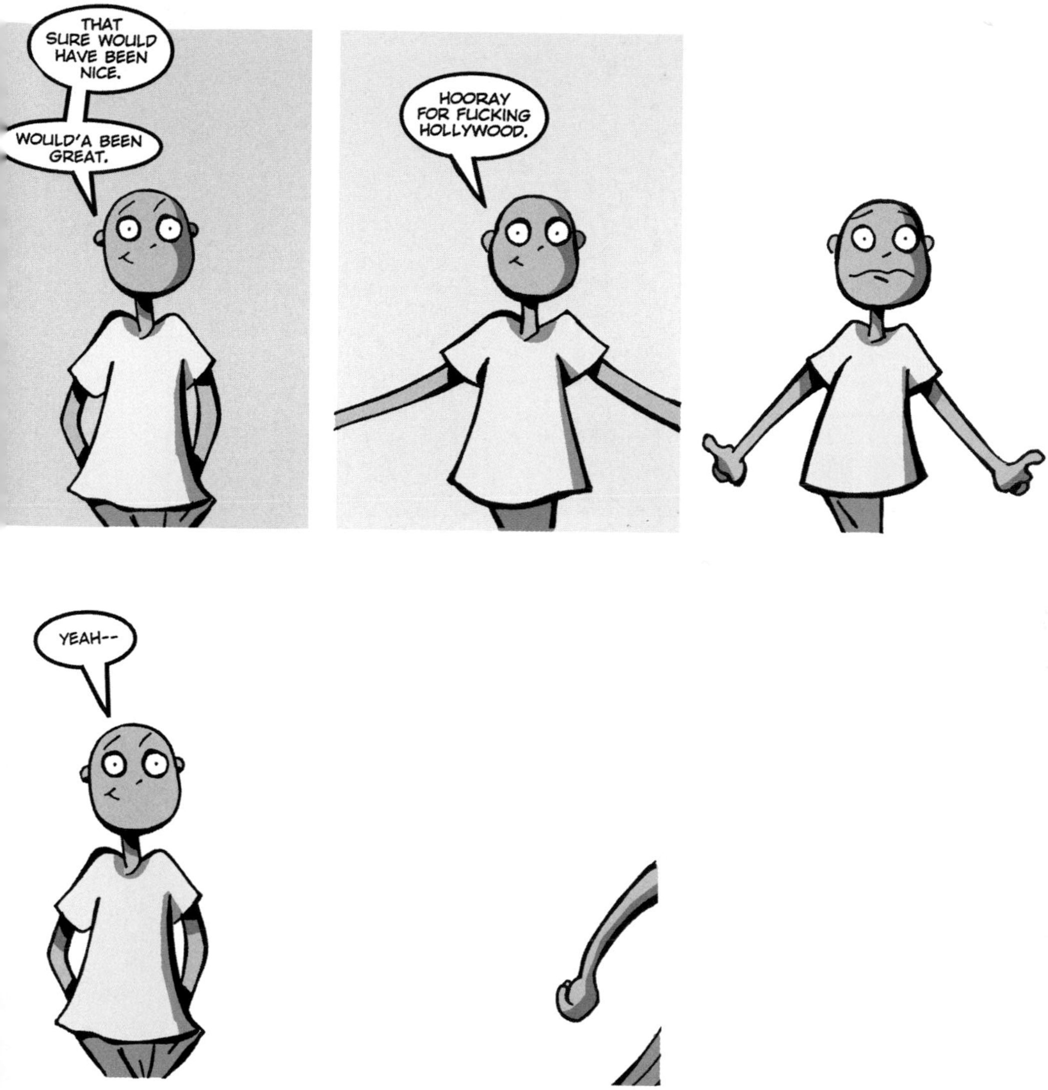
THAT SURE WOULD HAVE BEEN NICE.
WOULD'A BEEN GREAT.
HOORAY FOR FUCKING HOLLYWOOD.
YEAH--

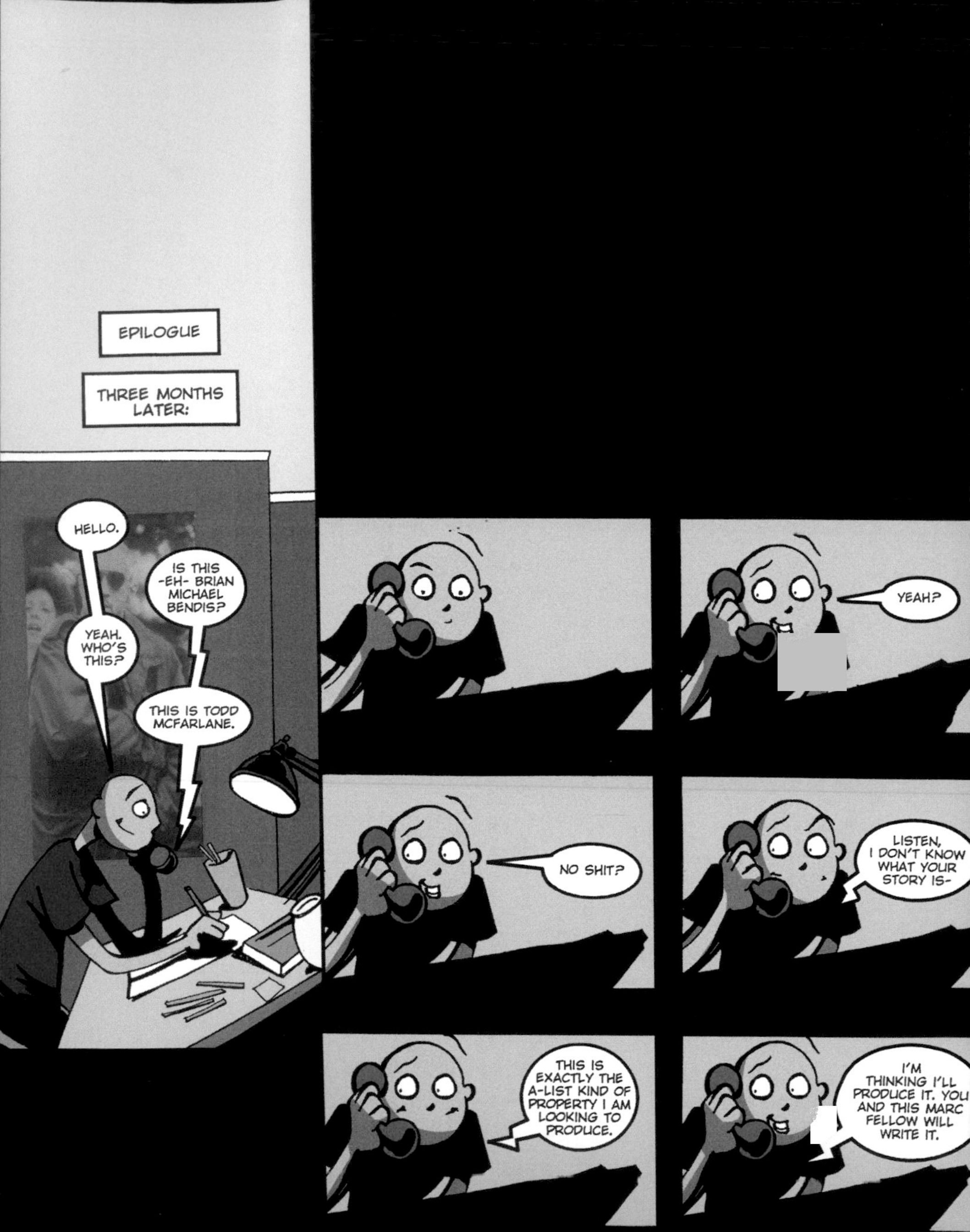
EPILOGUE
THREE MONTHS LATER:
HELLO.
IS THIS -EH- BRIAN MICHAEL BENDIS?
YEAH. WHO'S THIS?
THIS IS TODD MCFARLANE.
YEAH?
NO SHIT?
LISTEN, I DON'T KNOW WHAT YOUR STORY IS-
THIS IS EXACTLY THE A-LIST KIND OF PROPERTY I AM LOOKING TO PRODUCE.
I'M THINKING I'LL PRODUCE IT. YOU AND THIS MARC FELLOW WILL WRITE IT.

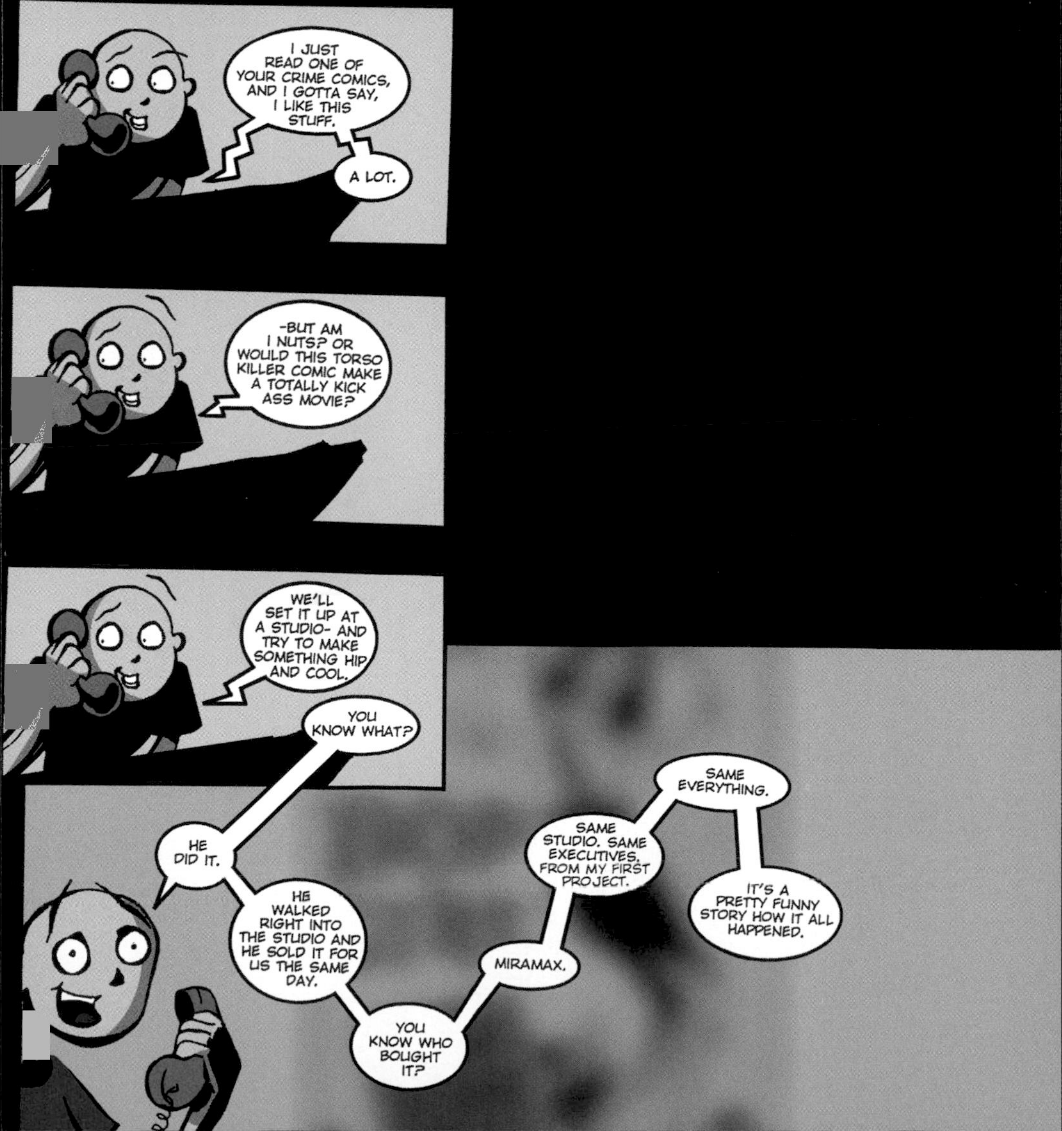
I JUST READ ONE OF YOUR CRIME COMICS, AND I GOTTA SAY, I LIKE THIS STUFF.
A LOT.
-BUT AM I NUTS? OR WOULD THIS TORSO KILLER COMIC MAKE A TOTALLY KICK ASS MOVIE?
WE'LL SET IT UP AT A STUDIO- AND TRY TO MAKE SOMETHING HIP AND COOL.
YOU KNOW WHAT?
HE DID IT.
HE WALKED RIGHT INTO THE STUDIO AND HE SOLD IT FOR US THE SAME DAY.
YOU KNOW WHO BOUGHT IT?
MIRAMAX.
SAME STUDIO. SAME EXECUTIVES. FROM MY FIRST PROJECT.
SAME EVERYTHING.
IT'S A PRETTY FUNNY STORY HOW IT ALL HAPPENED.

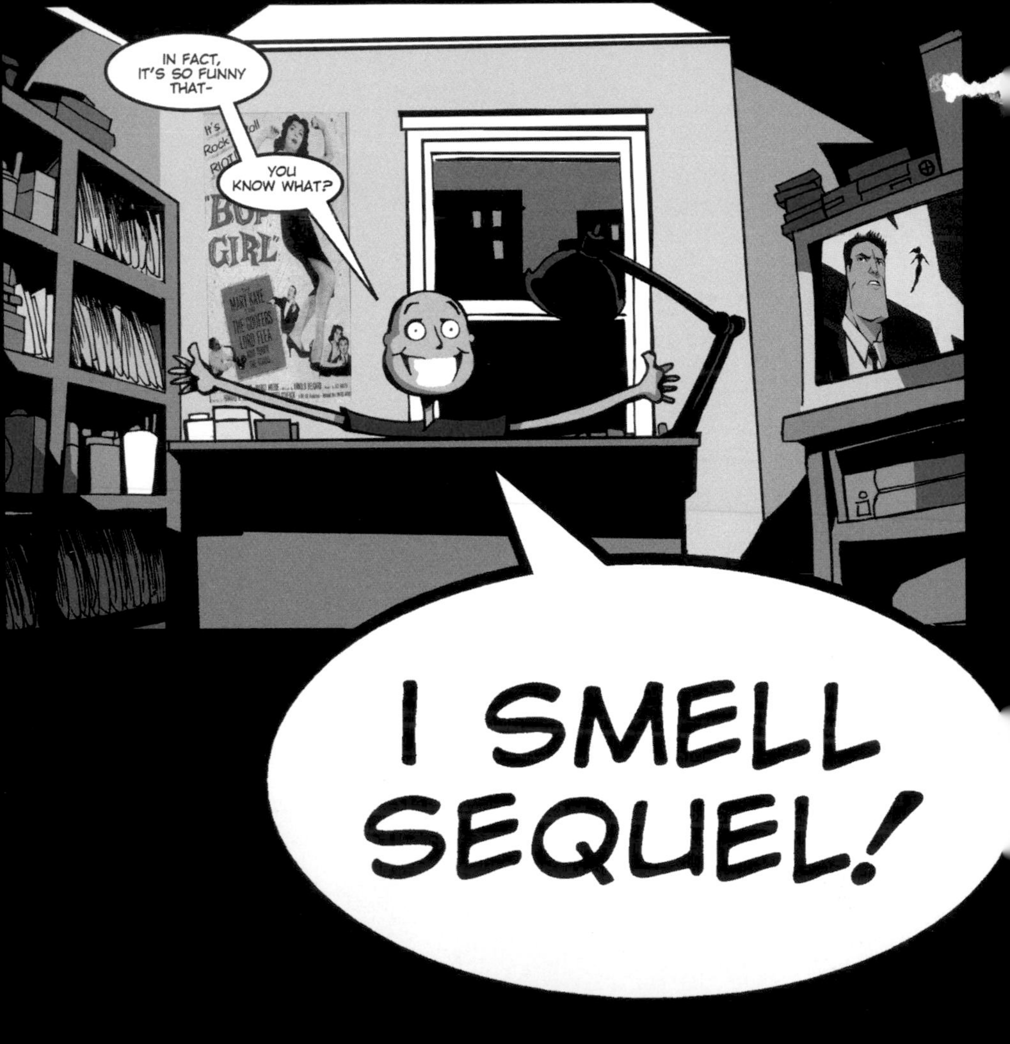
IN FACT, IT'S SO FUNNY THAT-
YOU KNOW WHAT?
I SMELL SEQUEL!

THE END?

EPILOGUE

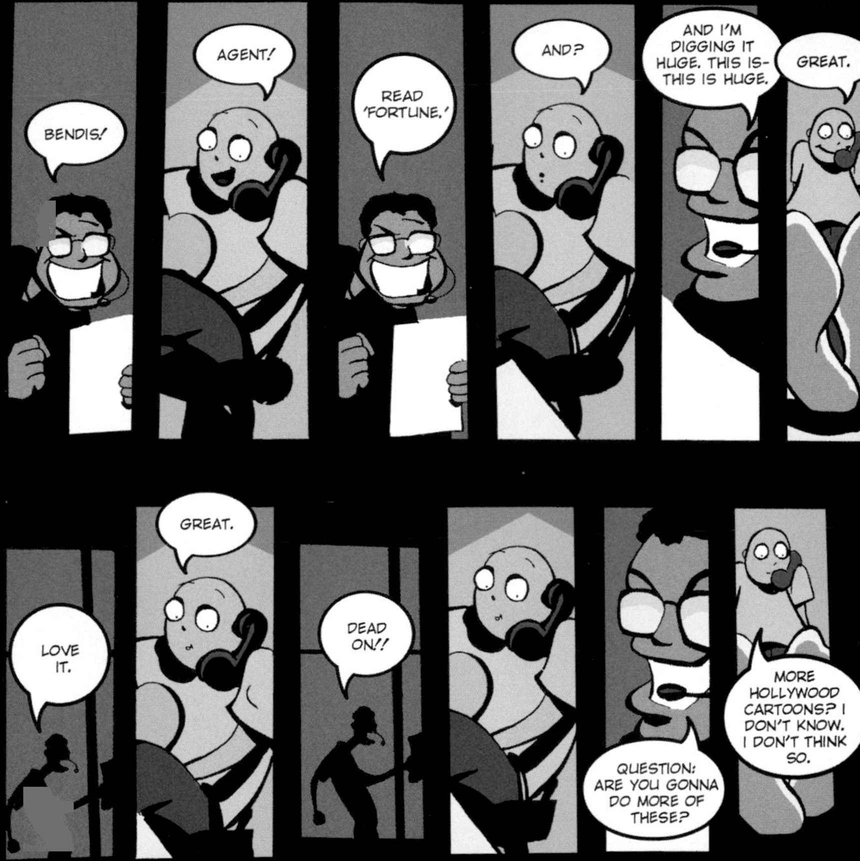
BENDIS!
AGENT!
READ 'FORTUNE.'
AND?
AND I'M DIGGING IT HUGE. THIS IS- THIS IS HUGE.
GREAT.
LOVE IT.
GREAT.
DEAD ON!!
QUESTION: ARE YOU GONNA DO MORE OF THESE?
MORE HOLLYWOOD CARTOONS? I DON'T KNOW. I DON'T THINK SO.

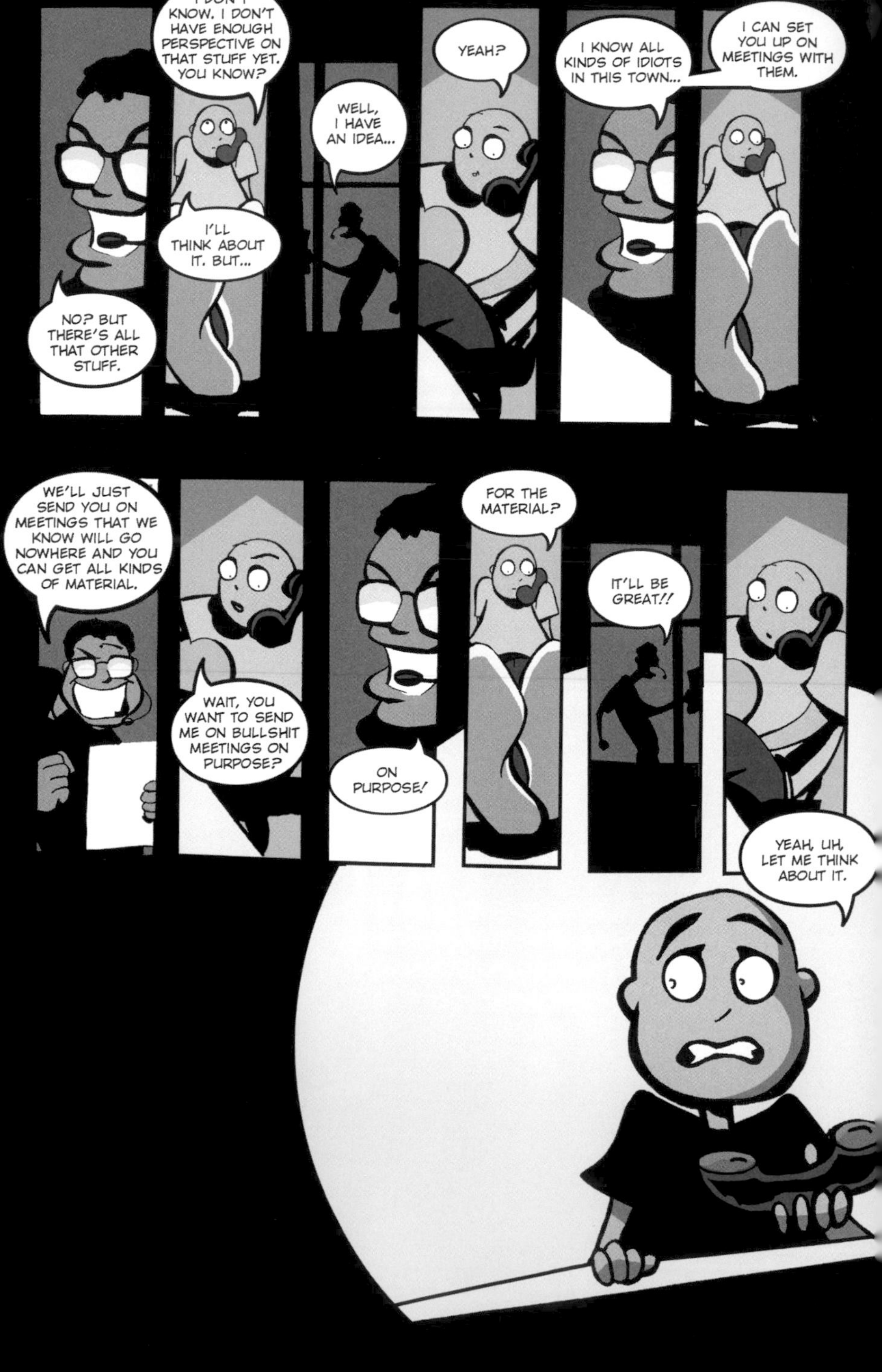
I DON'T KNOW. I DON'T HAVE ENOUGH PERSPECTIVE ON THAT STUFF YET. YOU KNOW?
NO? BUT THERE'S ALL THAT OTHER STUFF.
I'LL THINK ABOUT IT. BUT...
WELL, I HAVE AN IDEA...
YEAH?
I KNOW ALL KINDS OF IDIOTS IN THIS TOWN...
I CAN SET YOU UP ON MEETINGS WITH THEM.
WE'LL JUST SEND YOU ON MEETINGS THAT WE KNOW WILL GO NOWHERE AND YOU CAN GET ALL KINDS OF MATERIAL.
WAIT, YOU WANT TO SEND ME ON BULLSHIT MEETINGS ON PURPOSE?
ON PURPOSE!
FOR THE MATERIAL?
IT'LL BE GREAT!!
YEAH, UH, LET ME THINK ABOUT IT.

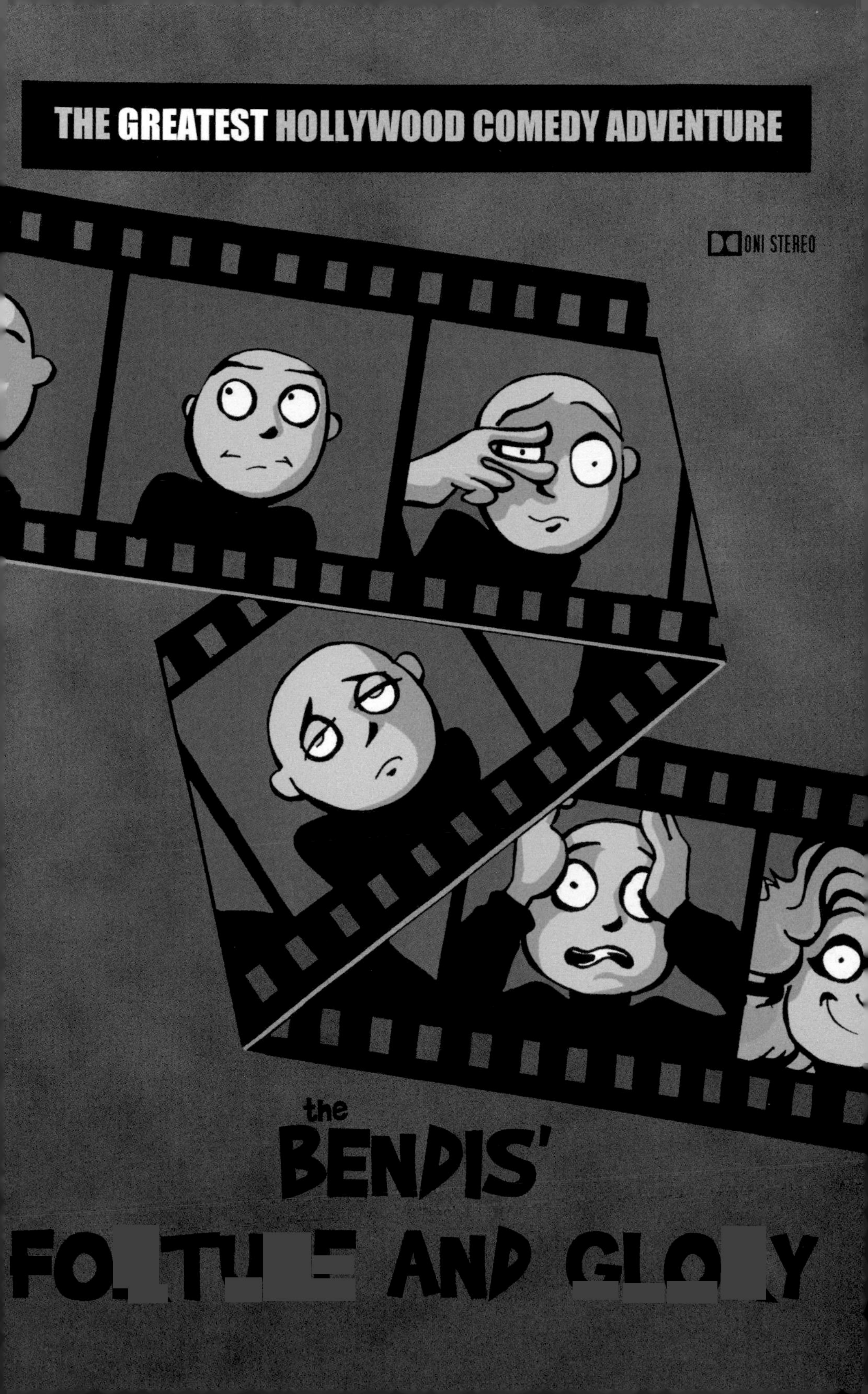
THE GREATEST HOLLYWOOD COMEDY ADVENTURE
ONI STEREO
the BENDIS'
FO[redacted]TU[redacted] AND GLO[redacted]Y

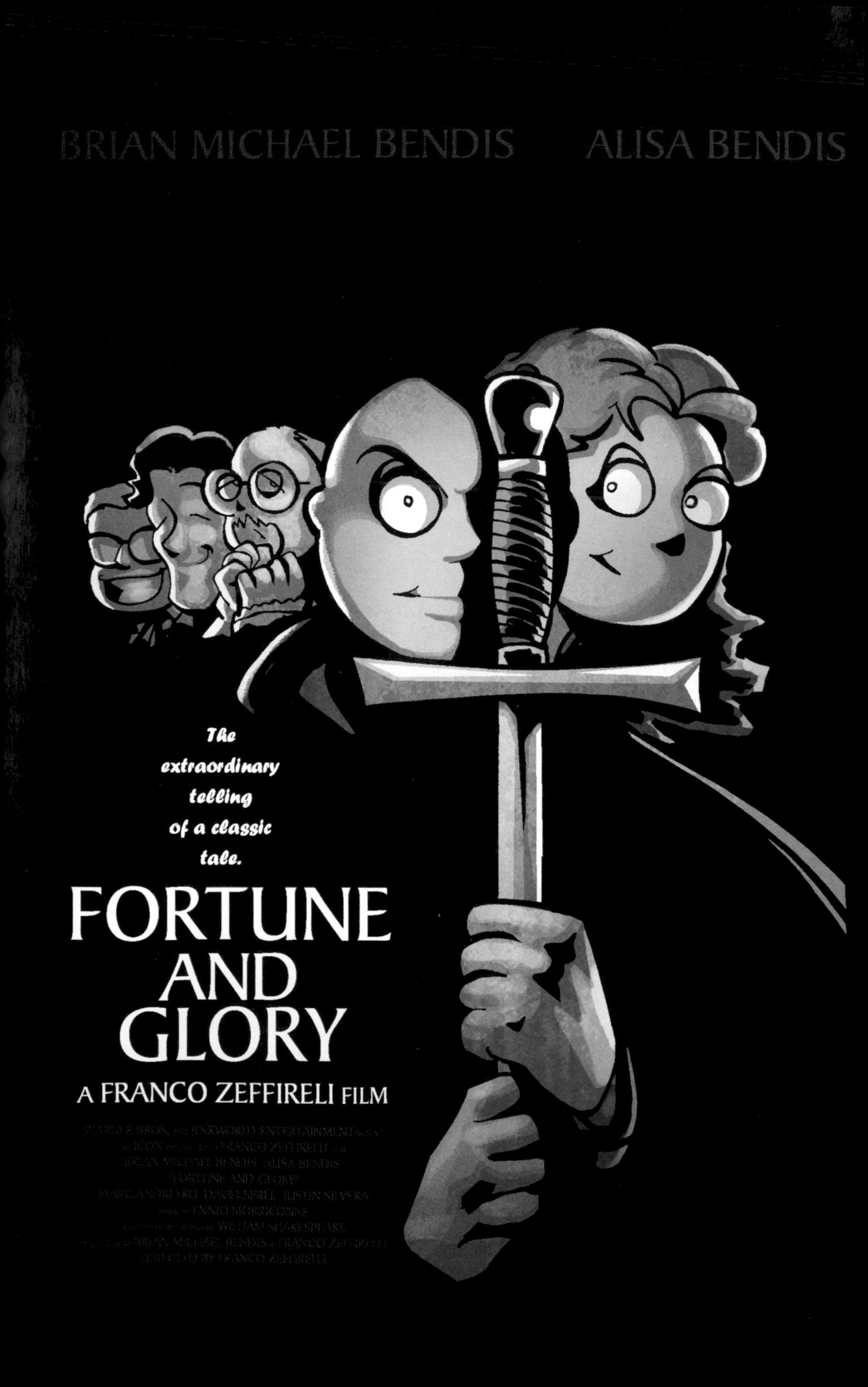
BRIAN MICHAEL BENDIS
ALISA BENDIS
The extraordinary telling of a classic tale.
FORTUNE AND GLORY
A FRANCO ZEFFIRELI FILM

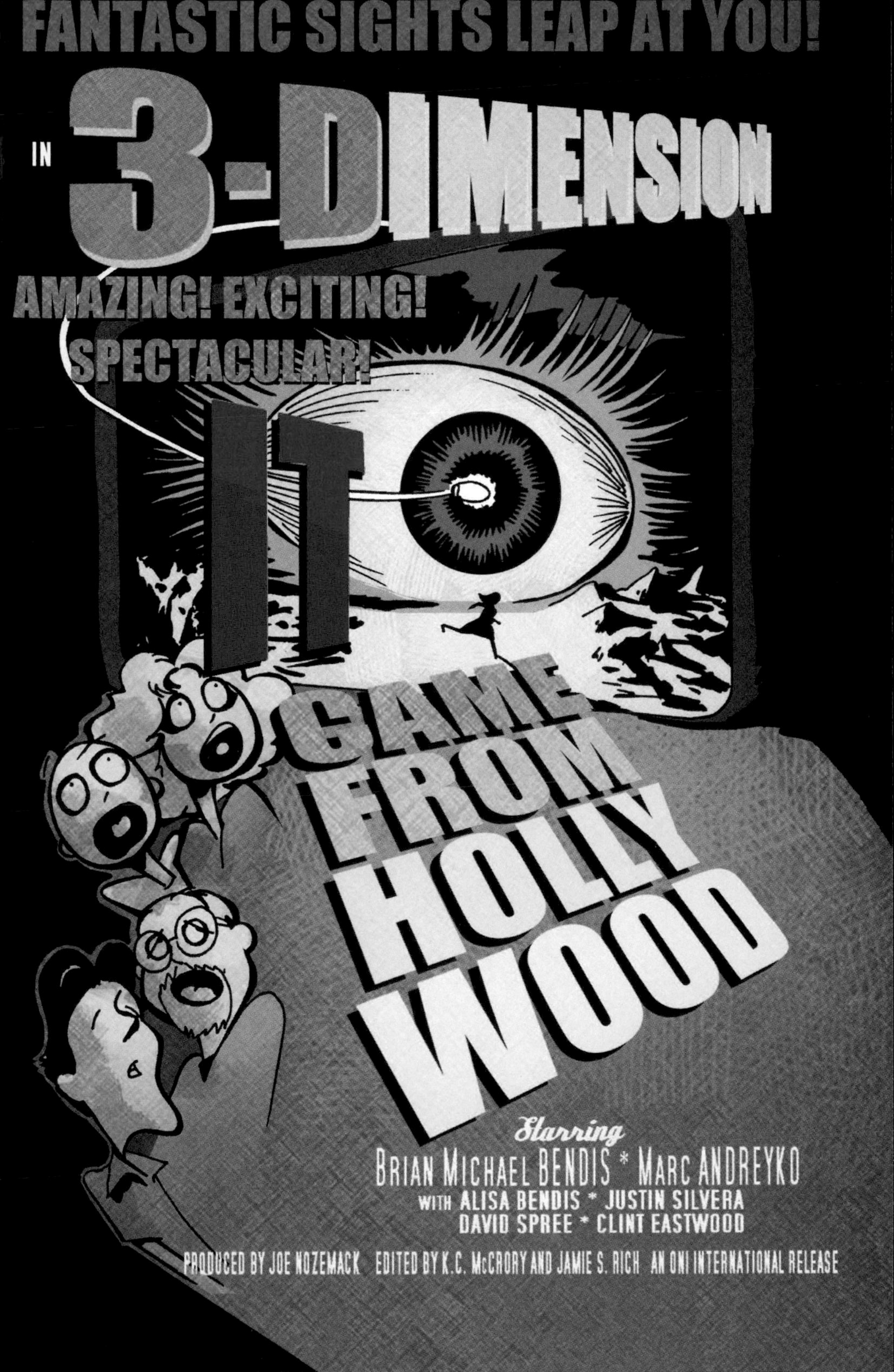

FANTASTIC SIGHTS LEAP AT YOU!
IN 3-DIMENSION
AMAZING! EXCITING!
SPECTACULAR!
IT CAME FROM HOLLYWOOD
Starring
BRIAN MICHAEL BENDIS * MARC ANDREYKO
WITH ALISA BENDIS * JUSTIN SILVERA
DAVID SPREE * CLINT EASTWOOD
PRODUCED BY JOE NOZEMACK EDITED BY K.C. McCRORY AND JAMIE S. RICH AN ONI INTERNATIONAL RELEASE

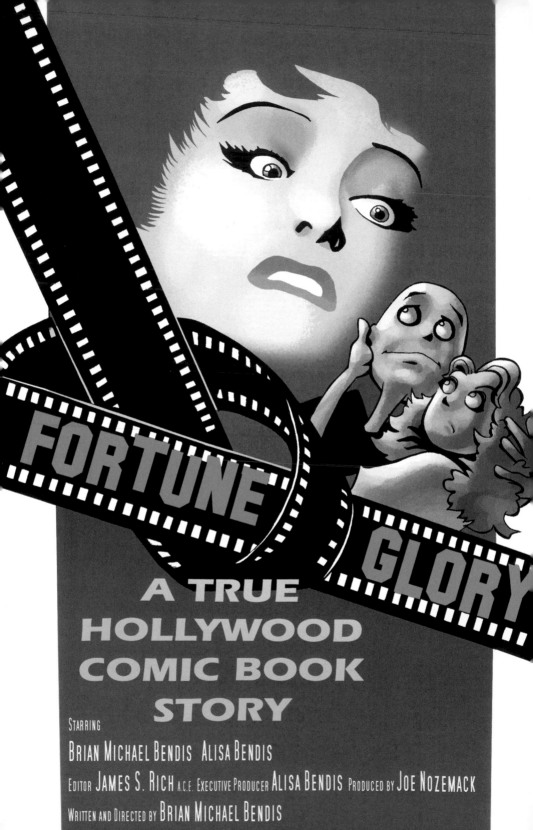

FORTUNE

GLORY

A TRUE HOLLYWOOD COMIC BOOK STORY

Starring

BRIAN MICHAEL BENDIS   ALISA BENDIS

EDITOR JAMES S. RICH A.C.E. EXECUTIVE PRODUCER ALISA BENDIS   PRODUCED BY JOE NOZEMACK

WRITTEN AND DIRECTED BY BRIAN MICHAEL BENDIS

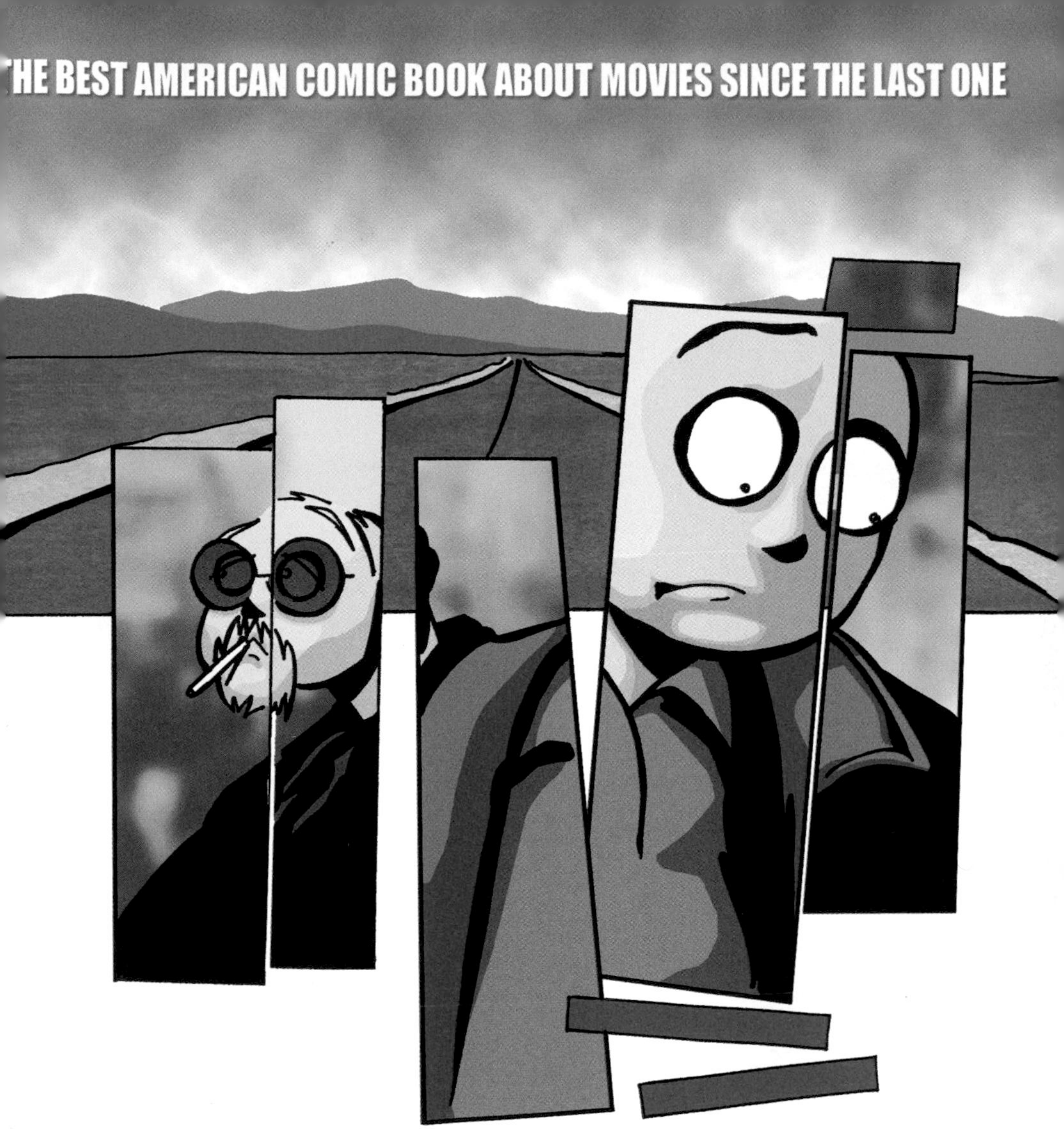
THE BEST AMERICAN COMIC BOOK ABOUT MOVIES SINCE THE LAST ONE

MY OWN PRIVATE FORTUNE AND GLORY

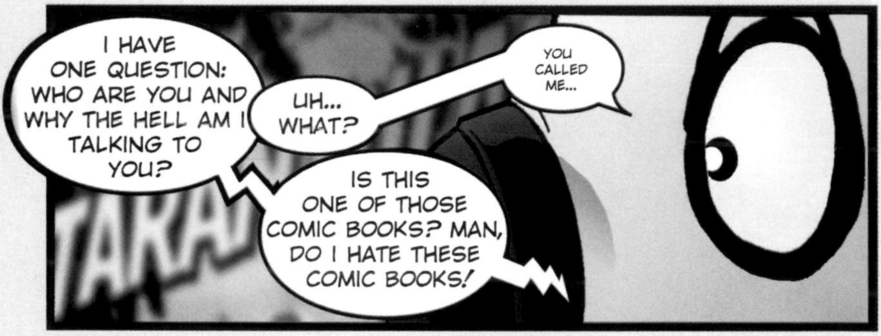
I HAVE ONE QUESTION: WHO ARE YOU AND WHY THE HELL AM I TALKING TO YOU?
UH... WHAT?
YOU CALLED ME...
IS THIS ONE OF THOSE COMIC BOOKS? MAN, DO I HATE THESE COMIC BOOKS!

The cartoons...

The following cartoons are pieces I did for various other publications on or around the time of *Fortune and Glory*'s original publication. They are presented here for the first time in color...thanks to the genius of Matthew Wilson.

HEY KiDS!!! LET'S TAKE A PEAK iNSiDE AN ACTUAL EDiTORiAL MEETiNG FOR A LOCAL FREE NEWSPAPER

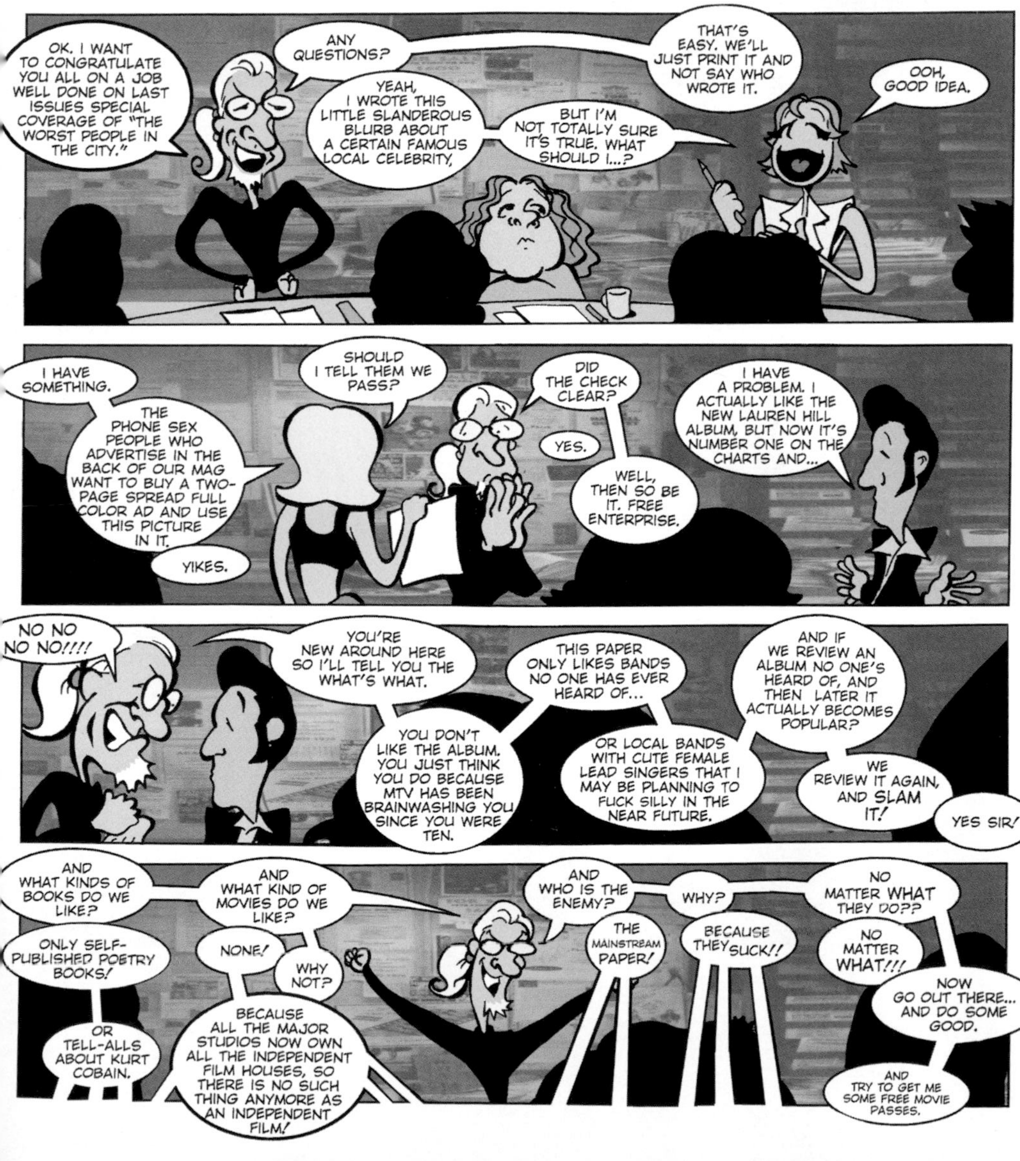

OK. I WANT TO CONGRATULATE YOU ALL ON A JOB WELL DONE ON LAST ISSUES SPECIAL COVERAGE OF "THE WORST PEOPLE IN THE CITY."
ANY QUESTIONS?
YEAH, I WROTE THIS LITTLE SLANDEROUS BLURB ABOUT A CERTAIN FAMOUS LOCAL CELEBRITY,
BUT I'M NOT TOTALLY SURE IT'S TRUE. WHAT SHOULD I...?
THAT'S EASY. WE'LL JUST PRINT IT AND NOT SAY WHO WROTE IT.
OOH, GOOD IDEA.
I HAVE SOMETHING.
THE PHONE SEX PEOPLE WHO ADVERTISE IN THE BACK OF OUR MAG WANT TO BUY A TWO-PAGE SPREAD FULL COLOR AD AND USE THIS PICTURE IN IT.
YIKES.
SHOULD I TELL THEM WE PASS?
DID THE CHECK CLEAR?
YES.
WELL, THEN SO BE IT. FREE ENTERPRISE.
I HAVE A PROBLEM. I ACTUALLY LIKE THE NEW LAUREN HILL ALBUM, BUT NOW IT'S NUMBER ONE ON THE CHARTS AND...
NO NO NO NO!!!!
YOU'RE NEW AROUND HERE SO I'LL TELL YOU THE WHAT'S WHAT.
YOU DON'T LIKE THE ALBUM. YOU JUST THINK YOU DO BECAUSE MTV HAS BEEN BRAINWASHING YOU SINCE YOU WERE TEN.
THIS PAPER ONLY LIKES BANDS NO ONE HAS EVER HEARD OF...
OR LOCAL BANDS WITH CUTE FEMALE LEAD SINGERS THAT I MAY BE PLANNING TO FUCK SILLY IN THE NEAR FUTURE.
AND IF WE REVIEW AN ALBUM NO ONE'S HEARD OF, AND THEN LATER IT ACTUALLY BECOMES POPULAR?
WE REVIEW IT AGAIN, AND SLAM IT!
YES SIR!
AND WHAT KINDS OF BOOKS DO WE LIKE?
ONLY SELF-PUBLISHED POETRY BOOKS!
OR TELL-ALLS ABOUT KURT COBAIN.
AND WHAT KIND OF MOVIES DO WE LIKE?
NONE!
WHY NOT?
BECAUSE ALL THE MAJOR STUDIOS NOW OWN ALL THE INDEPENDENT FILM HOUSES, SO THERE IS NO SUCH THING ANYMORE AS AN INDEPENDENT FILM!
AND WHO IS THE ENEMY?
THE MAINSTREAM PAPER!
WHY?
BECAUSE THEY SUCK!!
NO MATTER WHAT THEY DO??
NO MATTER WHAT!!!
NOW GO OUT THERE... AND DO SOME GOOD.
AND TRY TO GET ME SOME FREE MOVIE PASSES.

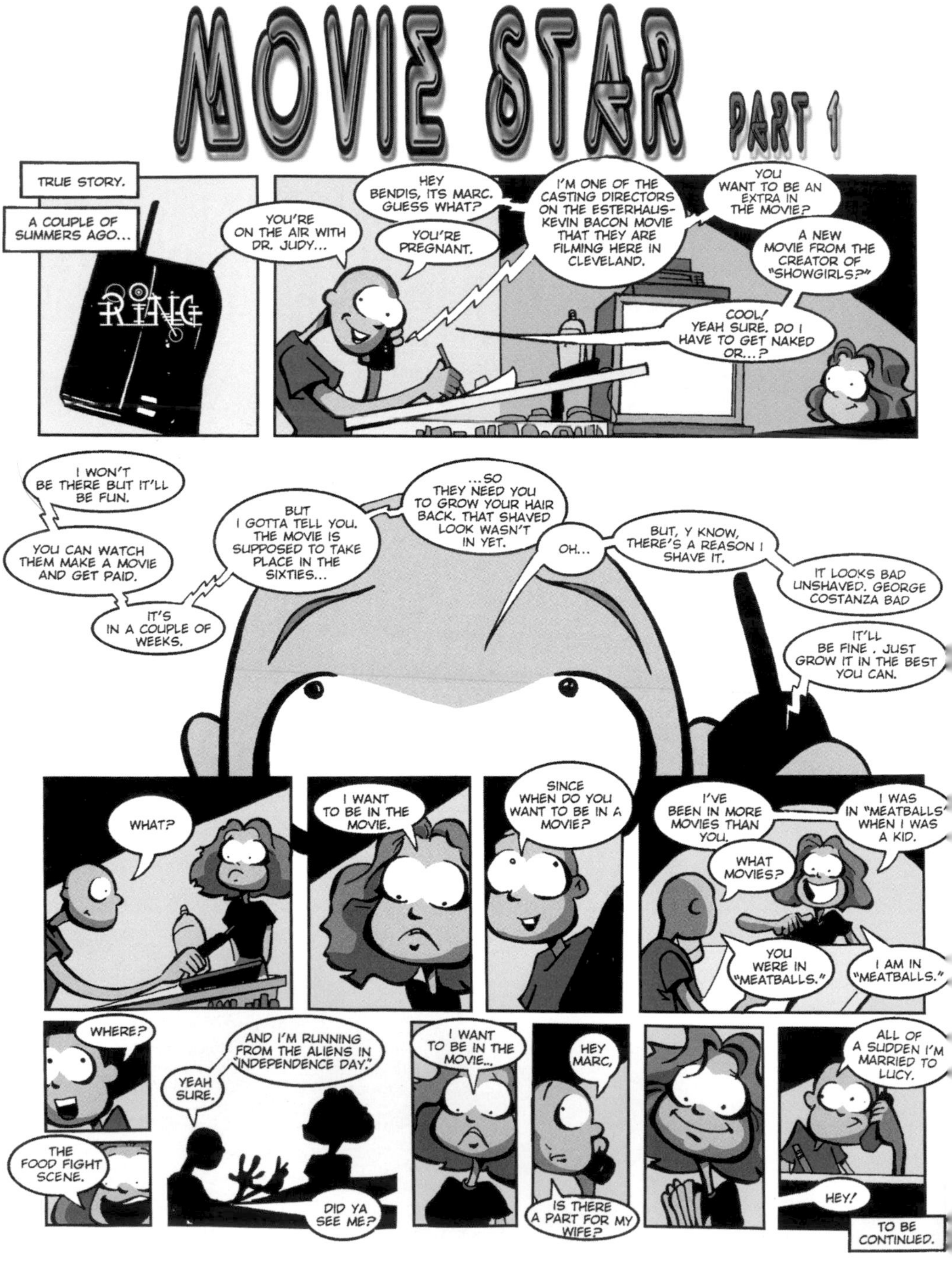
MOVIE STAR PART 1
TRUE STORY.
A COUPLE OF SUMMERS AGO...
RING
YOU'RE ON THE AIR WITH DR. JUDY...
HEY BENDIS, ITS MARC. GUESS WHAT?
YOU'RE PREGNANT.
I'M ONE OF THE CASTING DIRECTORS ON THE ESTERHAUS-KEVIN BACON MOVIE THAT THEY ARE FILMING HERE IN CLEVELAND.
YOU WANT TO BE AN EXTRA IN THE MOVIE?
A NEW MOVIE FROM THE CREATOR OF "SHOWGIRLS?"
COOL! YEAH SURE. DO I HAVE TO GET NAKED OR...?
I WON'T BE THERE BUT IT'LL BE FUN.
YOU CAN WATCH THEM MAKE A MOVIE AND GET PAID.
IT'S IN A COUPLE OF WEEKS.
BUT I GOTTA TELL YOU. THE MOVIE IS SUPPOSED TO TAKE PLACE IN THE SIXTIES...
...SO THEY NEED YOU TO GROW YOUR HAIR BACK. THAT SHAVED LOOK WASN'T IN YET.
OH...
BUT, Y KNOW, THERE'S A REASON I SHAVE IT.
IT LOOKS BAD UNSHAVED. GEORGE COSTANZA BAD
IT'LL BE FINE . JUST GROW IT IN THE BEST YOU CAN.
WHAT?
I WANT TO BE IN THE MOVIE.
SINCE WHEN DO YOU WANT TO BE IN A MOVIE?
I'VE BEEN IN MORE MOVIES THAN YOU.
WHAT MOVIES?
I WAS IN "MEATBALLS" WHEN I WAS A KID.
YOU WERE IN "MEATBALLS."
I AM IN "MEATBALLS."
WHERE?
THE FOOD FIGHT SCENE.
YEAH SURE.
AND I'M RUNNING FROM THE ALIENS IN "INDEPENDENCE DAY."
DID YA SEE ME?
I WANT TO BE IN THE MOVIE...
HEY MARC,
IS THERE A PART FOR MY WIFE?
ALL OF A SUDDEN I'M MARRIED TO LUCY.
HEY!
TO BE CONTINUED.

MOVIE STAR PART 2

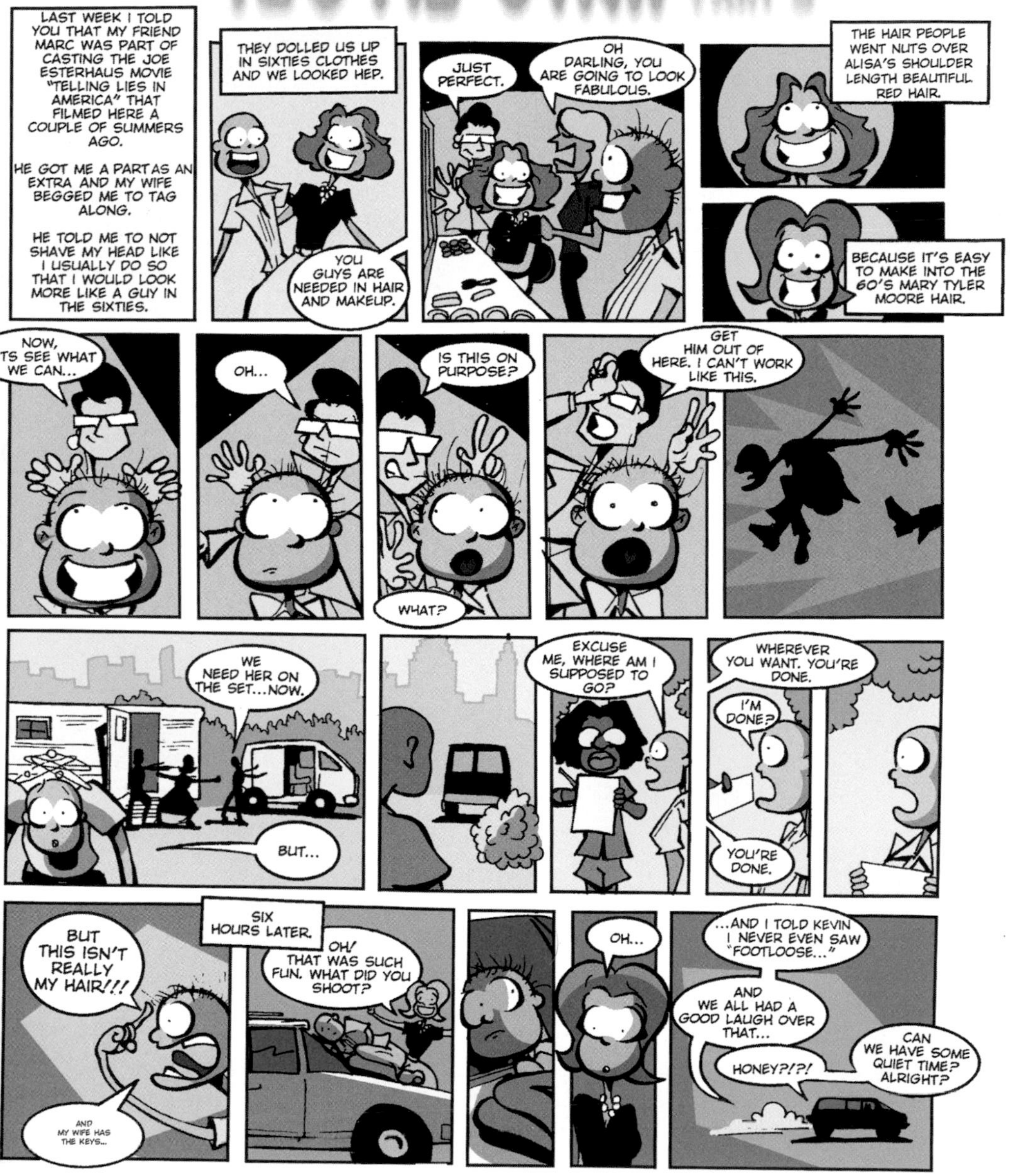

LAST WEEK I TOLD YOU THAT MY FRIEND MARC WAS PART OF CASTING THE JOE ESTERHAUS MOVIE "TELLING LIES IN AMERICA" THAT FILMED HERE A COUPLE OF SUMMERS AGO.
HE GOT ME A PART AS AN EXTRA AND MY WIFE BEGGED ME TO TAG ALONG.
HE TOLD ME TO NOT SHAVE MY HEAD LIKE I USUALLY DO SO THAT I WOULD LOOK MORE LIKE A GUY IN THE SIXTIES.
THEY DOLLED US UP IN SIXTIES CLOTHES AND WE LOOKED HEP.
YOU GUYS ARE NEEDED IN HAIR AND MAKEUP.
JUST PERFECT.
OH DARLING, YOU ARE GOING TO LOOK FABULOUS.
THE HAIR PEOPLE WENT NUTS OVER ALISA'S SHOULDER LENGTH BEAUTIFUL RED HAIR.
BECAUSE IT'S EASY TO MAKE INTO THE 60'S MARY TYLER MOORE HAIR.
NOW, TS SEE WHAT WE CAN...
OH...
IS THIS ON PURPOSE?
WHAT?
GET HIM OUT OF HERE. I CAN'T WORK LIKE THIS.
WE NEED HER ON THE SET...NOW.
BUT...
EXCUSE ME, WHERE AM I SUPPOSED TO GO?
WHEREVER YOU WANT. YOU'RE DONE.
I'M DONE?
YOU'RE DONE.
BUT THIS ISN'T REALLY MY HAIR!!!
AND MY WIFE HAS THE KEYS...
SIX HOURS LATER.
OH! THAT WAS SUCH FUN. WHAT DID YOU SHOOT?
OH...
...AND I TOLD KEVIN I NEVER EVEN SAW "FOOTLOOSE..."
AND WE ALL HAD A GOOD LAUGH OVER THAT...
HONEY?!?!
CAN WE HAVE SOME QUIET TIME? ALRIGHT?

The interviews...

Here are a couple of interviews I did around the time of *Fortune and Glory*'s original release. I picked these interviews as extras because I thought they showed, warts and all, who and what I was back when this book was being produced. And boy was I just completely out of my mind.

In this space, I was originally going to show you some script excerpts but looking over the scripts they aren't that interesting. I was writing something for me to draw. Scripts are only really interesting when you get to compare and contrast the writer's vision to the artist's vision, like we show you often in the *Powers* collections. In this case there was little to no difference between the script and the final page because I knew what I was going to do.

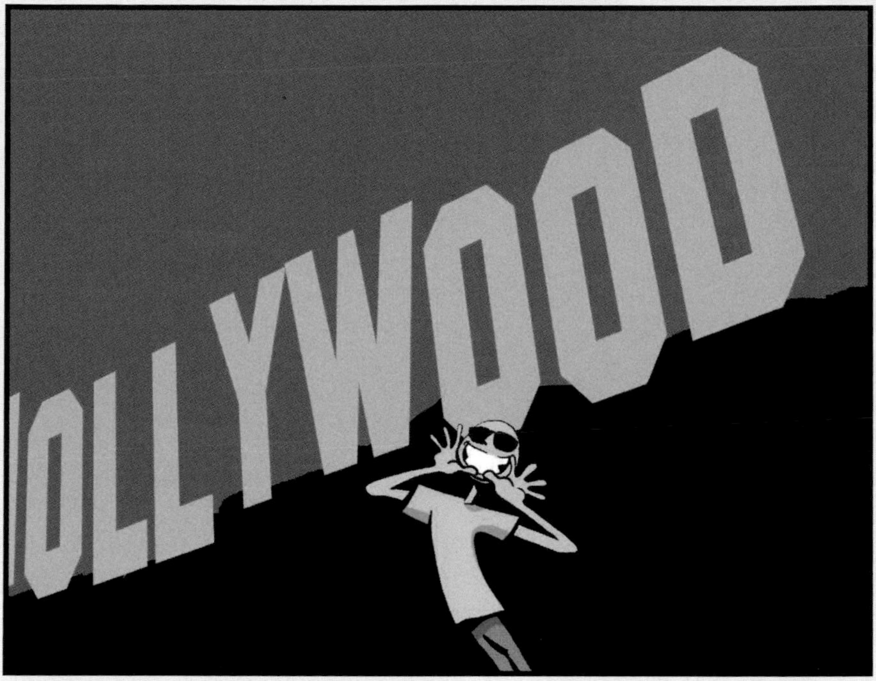
OLLYWOOD

An Interview with Brian Michael Bendis
by Andrew Goletz

After gaining critical fame and a cult following on books like *Fire*, *AKA: Goldfish* and *Jinx*, Brian took his talent to Image Comics where he continued to publish *Jinx* and later began writing *Sam and Twitch*, a *Spawn* spin-off and *Torso*, a mini-series about the infamous torso killer. In the meantime he won an Eisner Award and an even more prestigious Grayhaven Griffin Award. Then, *Fortune and Glory*, a 3-issue auto-biographical series about his mis-adventures in Hollywood became a surprise hit, earning more mainstream praise.

Does the man take a break and a well deserved vacation after this? No. He takes on two more monthly writing assignments: *Hellspawn* (another on-going *Spawn* title) and *Powers*, his first creator-owned full-color book. Add a Batman story, a 3-issue *Daredevil* arc, a top secret Spider-Man project and some more secrets that should be blown by the time you read this and you have Brian Michael Bendis, the hardest working man in comics.

Brian would also like to make it known that *Fire*, *AKA: Goldfish*, *Jinx*, *Torso*, *Fortune and Glory*, *Powers*, *Sam and Twitch* and *Hellspawn* original art and t-shirts are all available through him at Jinxworld. Check it out and stay for the message boards; you'll be hooked like a heroin addict.

AG: *So Brian, when we first did an interview years ago in Gray Haven, you had just taken Jinx to Image and I had gotten the best sales ever on Gray Haven Magazine. Several years later, you're writing 4 monthly books, you're an Eisner winner, a screen writer and you're writing some of the biggest icons in comics while I am just starting over from scratch. What the hell did I do wrong?*

BMB: What? I guess you didn't sell your soul to the devil. Seriously, though. Its very cool that you've decided to give this another shot. I think its a great idea and you need to go with your passions on this and give it a try.

AG: *How does it feel to have such a huge following now? You had the cult fan base with* Jinx *and* Goldfish, *then a more aggressive core group with* Sam *and* Twitch *and* Powers *and now you'll be getting serious fanboy glory with* Batman *and* Daredevil.

BMB: I'd love to tell you that this was part of some grand master plan of mine, but it wasn't. To an outsider, it may seem like this all happened rather quickly, but it didn't. This was a slow and steady process that has gone on for 8 or 9 years. There were never any guarantees that any of this would work. I think it's just that the industry was in such bad shape that if anyone stayed with it long enough, it would be their turn to shine. It's like, great, now it's our turn to be popular.

AG: *So a fair share of luck was involved?*

BMB: Luck and hard work. And a passion to do what I wanted to do. Honestly, *Fortune and Glory* was done just for me. I never expected anyone to like it. If anything, I thought my agent would drop me and I'd be blacklisted from Hollywood after it came out. I never thought that it would get the critical and fan reaction that it did. It was a tremendous surprise. It's the same thing with *Powers.* Mike [Oeming] and I took a huge gamble with this. We never did anything on this level and we wanted to give it a try.

AG: *The love of the work had a lot to do with it, too.*

BMB: I think you need to pick projects that mean something to you. My goal is always to make a story as good as I can make it without second-guessing what an audiences reaction will be. I can't please everyone, but I need to at least be proud of the work that I do and do it to the best of my ability. And I think that's where some of the success came from. People start to seek you out and ask you to work with them instead of the other way around.

AG: *What's the difference for you in writing a character like Batman or Daredevil, with such a rich history and writing* Powers *or even* Sam and Twitch?

BMB: I think it's great to work on something you own yourself because you get to make up all your own rules. With other people's characters, it's different. People do have some expectations, but you need to not only give them what they want, but give them something more. *Sam and Twitch* was more flexible than I thought, though.

AG: *How so?*

BMB: With *Sam and Twitch*, no one expected anything from me. No one really thought it would work, and no one thought anyone would like it. It was an underdog situation from the beginning and I loved it. There really was no editorial imput. Todd didn't come and say to me, "You should do this and you can't do that." My first feedback from him was after the book came out. Todd was like, I'm glad you didn't make them like Abbott and Costello. But the thing is, I knew that was the key to the books success. Not to. I'm just glad it worked and that people have been so receptive to it.

AG: *So the pressure was off?*

BMB: Exactly. And that was the fun part. It was like the situation Frank Miller had on *Daredevil* or Alan Moore on *Swamp Thing*. Those books were shit before they took over and no one expected them to do well, but they turned it around. I mean, I still get some people who were flipping out over small stuff, like Twitch's goatee.

AG: *His goatee?*

BMB: Yeah. Twitch always had this little Hitler mustache and the artists hated drawing that thing, and now he is a leading character and not a secondary, so I made him have a goatee. Then there was this goatee vs. Hitler mustache faction. It's just amazing and it's genuinely cool that everything came together like it has.

AG: *Any plans to draw again?*

BMB: Not this year. Oni and I have a handshake on another series but it's too early to talk about. And I promised Matt Wagner that I'd do something for *Grendel: Black and White*, because well, it's Matt Wagner and Grendel.

AG: *But nothing as involved as* Jinx *or* Torso?

BMB: No. With *Fire*, *Goldfish*, *Jinx* and *Torso*, I was drawing like, thousands of pages for a stretch. Honestly, I think I'm a better writer than artist. I'm not exactly working with chimps for artists. I think I'm fortunate to have people like Mike and Angel and David and Ashley drawing my stories. I think they're the best in the business and it's great to work with them. But I still have a hand in the art.

AG: *What do you mean?*

BMB: I get very visually involved with my scripts. I don't do it to the extent where I don't give them enough room to be creative, but I have very loose story boards that I create for the scripts. Plus, now that I'm not writing, it's fun to tell them to do huge crowd scenes or wide shots and city streets.

AG: *And you're content not to draw for now?*

BMB: Yeah, and I don't think I was that great at it to begin with. That's something I really respect about Todd. People are always asking when he's going to draw *Spawn* or anything else again and he just tells them he doesn't think he wants to compete with the fondness people had for his art six years ago. He could do it if he wanted to and it'd sell a million copies, but he doesn't feel like he's right for it. He's concentrating on running his business properly instead of doing all these little things half-assed.

AG: *You'll be at a lot of conventions this year, with some reluctance?*

BMB: I made a commitment to be at them and people were nice enough to invite me, but after this year, I think I'm going to take it easy on the convention scene for awhile.

AG: *They're known for their horror stories. Any favorites you'd like to share?*

BMB: I don't think I could say anything that would visualize it better than Trekkies. I do have some good memories, though. I mean, it's great to meet the fans and be there to meet new readers and people who love what I'm doing. It's an honor and I love to have a chance to talk to them face to face. And I've met a lot of good friends and people that I now work with at conventions. I mean part of the problem is the fact that I don't feel like they're really trying to market the comics. People like Roger Price do an excellent job of trying to bring some class and dignity to these shows, but in most other cases.

AG: *I love the wall of faux celebrities.*

BMB: I mean, really. And the convention whores. There was a goddamn Hooters booth at one of them. I've got nothing against seeing beautiful, half-naked women, but what business does Hooters or any of these other things have being at a comic show? You're not going to bring your kids to these things (alienating the target audience) and you're not going to bring your girlfriend to them (alienating a new audience). It's ridiculous. I do have a couple favorite memories, though, now that I think about it.

AG: *What are they?*

BMB: One of my favorites was at a Detroit show a few years back. There was a costume contest, which I usually assume are for kids, but this guy showed up on Friday in a *Solar: Man of the Atom* costume. Only, he didn't have the body for Solar. He looked more like Danny DeVito. The costume contest was over on Friday, but he was dressed again on Saturday, looking worse for wear. On the third day, he was an absolute mess; big belly sticking out, black from leaning against comic boxes all day.

AG: *Oh my god.*

AG: *Sigh.*

BMB: And there was the argument some guy had with John Byrne.

AG: *Really? That's a shock.*

BMB: Yeah, right. I didn't hear the whole thing, but it must have been pretty heated, because as this guy walks away, he turns around and screams to John, "And another thing, you don't know Galactus for shit!"

AG: *John tends to get that sort of reaction. He's a pretty outspoken guy.*

BMB: Oh, man. I think some people really go insane from this business, especially if they only concentrate on work-for-hire stuff.

AG: *Do you think the industry is getting better, in general?*

BMB: Yes. I think people are starting to take risks and do something to correct the problems. Basically, it's because the industry was downhill in the first place. No one cared about comics or gave them any respect, so people said "screw it" and started to do more daring stuff. Image is doing it. Marvel is starting to do it more. I think it's important to do books that are accessible to new readers, where you don't have to have read 100 issues of something to follow along. Sci-fi shows don't explain what a spaceship is 20 times. They know that people know what it is. With *Powers*, we try to do that. We know people know what super-heroes are. We didn't need to set that up.

AG: *How was your experience working with Marvel?*

BMB: Marvel Knights is a blast. I tell you, Joe Quesada has a great head on his shoulders. He's a very smart guy and he's the reason those books don't suck. I mean, take Kevin Smith and *Daredevil*. You know Kevin is a huge comic fan, so Joe asks if he wants to write a comic.

AG: *What are your favorite reads now?*

BMB: *Hellblazer* is great. I really get into *Heavy Liquid* and *Transmetropolitan*. *Kabuki*, of course. Scott Morse kicks me in the nuts. And I love the Oni books. I think they're doing a great job both with the books and the way they market them.

AG: *What do you mean?*

BMB: Well instead of pushing all their books at once, they spread them out. This gives each book a chance to get featured and some attention on its own, without competing against another Oni book. I think its a great idea.

AG: *Besides* Powers, Sam and Twitch, *and* Hellspawn, *what else are you working on?*

BMB: I have the Batman story in *Batman Chronicles #21* that comes out this month. Its a six-page short story called "Citizen Wayne." Can you guess what it's about?

AG: *It's too subtle. I don't get it.*

BMB: We have the *Daredevil* arc that I'm writing and David Mack is painting, which is *Daredevil #16, 17* and *18.* That comes out in a couple of months. I'll also be doing a top secret Marvel Knights project with Rob Haynes at the end of this year.

AG: *How about the movie projects? You're doing an animated Jinx movie, right?*

BMB: Yeah. I'm going to be writing it and directing it on some level. I doubt I'll direct the animation, since I have never done it before, but I'm jazzed about the idea. Basically there are all these creators taking their own stuff and putting it on the web. It's full animation too, not just flash. And then we'll probably put it on DVD, but you'll be able to download it for free.

AG: *And* Torso?

BMB: We handed in the script. We'll see what happens. We had a great time writing it, but there's no sure fire way in getting it done. Todd is handling most of it now, so we'll see. I'd love to have it happen.

AG: *Could be another* Fortune and Glory *story?*

BMB: The funny thing is we were talking about that. I mean, everyone has had these crazy stories, but a lot of people never talked about them. After *Fortune and Glory* people were coming up to me and saying, "I went through the same thing and didn't realize how funny it was till I read about it happening to you."

AG: *Everyone can relate to it.*

BMB: We'd like to do an anthology version somewhere down the line, with different creators telling their horror stories. I would be like the Crypt-Keeper, introducing the stories at the beginning of the comic.

AG: *By tomorrow, that rumor will be all over and most people will be reporting it as fact.*

BMB: God, these rumors.

AG: *You're apparently replacing Howard Mackie on the Spider-Man books with Paul Jenkins and you've become group editor as well.*

BMB: That's a new one.

AG: *Do the rumors annoy you?*

BMB: I am curious about them. Sometimes they're so dead-on right, I'm thinking, were you in the fucking meeting with us. I mean there was one story posted about how I was originally going to do *Nick Fury* for Marvel Knights and I don't know how anyone found out about it. I eventually moved to *Daredevil*. But then there was this *Ghost Rider* rumor. I mean this guy must have pulled this thing right out of his ass. There was never any *Ghost Rider* book. I don't even like Ghost Rider. And of course the message boards were lit up the next day with questions about me doing *Ghost Rider*. So it does get a little crazy sometimes, but it fills my huge fucking ego with glee glee glee.

AG: *And it's starting again with Spider-Man.*

BMB: I can't even say anything about that. But it's like, a rumor gets started or leaked and all of a sudden you have people bitching about it before they even know any facts.

AG: *Would you like to plug* Sam and Twitch, Hellspawn, Powers, Daredevil *or* Jinxworld.com *one more time?*

BMB: Sure. Go to Jinxword. It's the best message board on the web. The fans are great and it's a lot of fun. And we've added a lot of new stuff. There's new *Powers* art and some merchandise.

AG: *What's your favorite shirt?*

BMB: I like the Jinx shirt. My wife designed it, and I think it's the coolest looking shirt. Were actually thinking of doing a full color shirt soon, too. It doesn't even look comic-booky. You could wear it in public.

Well there you have it.

Copyright©2000 GrayHaven Magazine and contributors.

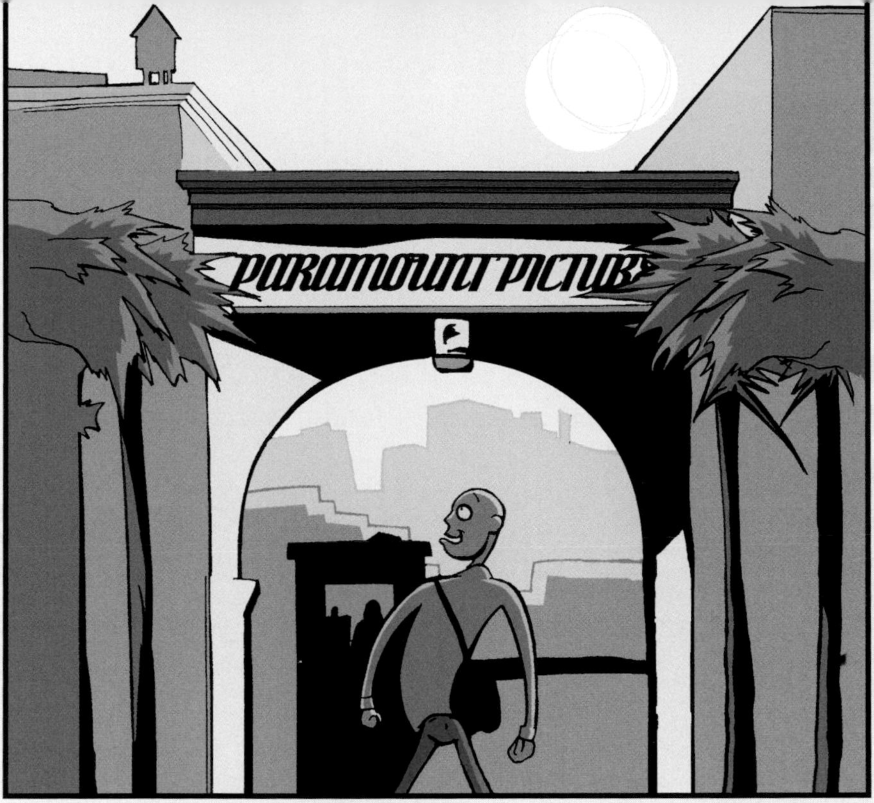
PARAMOUNT PICTURE

In Search of Fortune and Glory
Brian Bendis

by Lee Atchison

Brian Michael Bendis is about as dark and gloomy as your typical Labrador Retriever. And yet, the tales that spring from his mind are some of the finest examples of crime noir that the comics industry has ever seen. At once accessible and literate, Bendis' works wrap their readers up in imaginary worlds of dark alleyways and shady criminals. But recently, Bendis entered an even darker land — Hollywood. Oni Press is currently publishing the comic that resulted from that episode, and in order to find out more, Tart Lee Atchison tailed Bendis and managed to get the low down.

Sequential Tart: *First of all, congratulations on winning an Eisner last year. There were a lot of great creators in that category. How do you feel about the award?*

Brian Bendis: Well, it was a true geek moment and a real surprise. I did not expect to win. I truly did not.

The thing is that I grew up not far from P. Craig Russell's house and got to visit from time to time. And he has Eisners all over the place. Tons of them. Laying in piles in the corner, using them as coasters, and one props up the leg of his drawing table.

So my measly one doesn't seem like all that. (grin)

ST: *Now, for those readers not intimately familiar with you (yet), what can you tell us about Bendis the creator?*

BB: I am surprisingly, almost hypnotically, handsome. I have no formal dance training. And I was secretary of agriculture from 1983-86.

ST: *Right. And while we're at it, what about Bendis the man?*

BB: See previous, but the opposite.

ST: *What inspires you to continue to do comics?*

BB: I love comics. I do. I love them. I like the staples and the paper and everything. I like that the industry is in free fall and no one cares. It's great.

But mostly, comics is a truly megalomaniacal way to tell a story and that suits me perfectly.

ST: *I understand that* Fortune and Glory *has garnered quite a bit of attention, specifically from* Entertainment Weekly. *What can you tell us about it?*

BB: Like many independent comics creators, once I made a name for myself Hollywood came calling. In this brand new comic book miniseries, *Fortune and Glory*, I give a hilarious yet shockingly honest portrayal of my fascinating personal Hollywood experiences, filled with a fantastically eccentric cast of characters and anecdotes so outrageous they have to be true. Plus real life cameo appearances by Clint Eastwood, Uma Thurman, Drew Carey and many others. It's printed at digest size: 6" x 9".

I hope that doesn't sound like I cut and pasted my solicitation copy.

ST: *Uh, no — not at all. What was it, then, that inspired you to write a "Hollywood tell-all" like* Fortune and Glory*?*

BB: Honestly, I had, in lieu of success, accumulated exactly 150 pages of great anecdotes from my adventures in Hollywood. And I am a storyteller by trade, so when you find yourself with a story worth telling — you tell.

Did I know that it would be so well received? No. This comic was just for me to blow off some steam really. I wish I were smart enough to know that it would be appealing to people like this.

ST: *How did it come to be involved with Oni Press?*

BB: Joe and I had traded comics and emails over the years. When I had finished developing *Fortune and Glory* in the privacy of my own home, I thought that it sounded to me that it would do better at Oni than at my usual home, Image Central. This is solely from a marketing perspective. I told Joe about it, and he agreed.

ST: *What do you think of Oni Press? How have they handled your endeavors compared to other publishers that you've worked with?*

BB: Well, I could do without the punching and slapping. I don't know what that is all about.

Of course, I am joking. Only Jamie Rich slaps people. But other than that the company is as savvy and friendly and as well organized as they appear. Which is very nice.

I am spoiled with my relationship with Image so I crossed my fingers and hoped for a repeat. I am happy to say that I now have two safe homes to publish. I love the Oni guys. They have done everything for me they said they would, and that is all I ask of anyone.

ST: *You're very well known for your own projects* Goldfish *and its sequel,* Jinx. *Each has a very crime noir feel to it. And later, your work on* Torso *deals with the same genre. Have you always been attracted to this?*

BB: Well, the attraction to write it is the same attraction as it is to read it. Film noir is realism escapism. It is a story that takes place in a world that is very similar to the one we live in. And people would like to think that if they lived in that kind of world, they would be tough talking and savvy.

Most people aren't of course; they're ninnies. So that's the appeal. You get to not be a ninny for a while.

ST: *You've mentioned researching bounty hunters and other elements that have found their way into your comic book. Do you think that research is an important tool? And how do you go about researching the criminal element?*

BB: You know, that's funny, 'cause in the world of actual real book writing, it's par for the course. You know what I mean? Rarely do you see someone writing anything that they haven't researched. We were very lucky because in the instance of this *Torso* series, the facts of the case were better than anything we would have thought up.

I ride with cops often. I seek out people in the professions that I want to use and I pick their brain. All people have great stories to tell and no outlet to tell them. People love to share and more times than not they have material 50 times better than anything you would make up.

Recently I delved into the real worlds of witchcraft and paganism for a storyline in *Sam and Twitch*. I am using real witches and warlocks as research. It is my attempt to counteract the horrible misuse of witches in comics.

ST: *Cop ride alongs? That sounds fascinating, and certainly explains the sense of realism. What's it like? Anything like* Cops*? Or maybe like the Cops episode of* X-Files*?*

BB: Didn't see that. I don't watch Chris Carter programming in protest to the horrible shit he tried to pull on Jim Hudnall [with Harsh Realm]. But riding with cops is a surreal experience. It is exactly what you think and different in ways you couldn't believe. Many cop anecdotes you see in my books are from ride alongs. Imagine cruising in a patrol car at the normal speed, they get the call, and BAM! you are going 110 mph down a city street.

ST: *Anyone who's seen your artistic work realizes right off the bat that it's unique. How did your art style develop?*

BB: Slowly... painfully... I really don't feel that I have the authority to speak on such matters.

ST: *Your artistic work is rather experimental. The use of photographs as background images to enhance the panels finds its way into your books every so often. What can you tell us about this method? The pros and the cons?*

BB: Sting said that rock and roll is a bastard art form. What he meant is that it is a hybrid art form. When rock and roll regurgitates on itself, it fails, but when it looks outside itself and brings in country, jazz, opera, etc., it thrives.

It's the same thing with comics. Comics aren't art or writing. They're not painting or line art. They're not poetry or screenwriting. They're all these things and more. All mixed in together to create the bastard art form of comics. But when comics regurgitate on themselves, they fail, too.

The only thing amazing about comics is how easily they get into a rut. Someone discovers Photoshop, and then all the comics look alike. Someone discovers mando format, and then they all look alike.

We need to push and pull at the form, but NOT at the sacrifice of the story.

ST: *You mention comics regurgitating on themselves. What role do you think this has in the current state of the comics industry? And better yet, just how do you think it can be changed?*

BB: Well, it can only be changed by sheer force of will by artists and writers. It's totally up to them. And comics do regurgitate from generation to generation. And the generations are getting closer together.

There are artists now that look like the equivalent of the wacky clone of Michael Keaton in *Multiplicity*. If you keep Xeroxing a Xerox it starts to just look bizarre.

ST: *Light seems to play a very important role in your comics, giving your scenes a sense of the dramatic. In fact, as they're done in black and white, the element of chiaroscuro seems to have far more importance than, say, composition with your artwork. How do you view light as an artistic device?*

BB: Well, it's the rules of film noir again. Don't be afraid of the blacks; be afraid of the white. Black and white is a beautiful, harsh abstraction of the world. It really speaks to me. I know it does, because I still get chills when I see images like this.

The shadows can be an emotional expression unto themselves. At least, they are to me.

Black and white is a warts and all view of comic art. There's nowhere to hide. It's all there.

Many feel black and white is incomplete or some such thing. Black and white is beautiful and immediate. David Lynch said it is an immediate abstract way to see the world.

ST: *By contrast, the figures themselves are often done as simply as possible. Details are stripped, leaving only minimal indicators to impart atmosphere and emotion. What drew you to this method? Do you find it comes naturally to you? What sort of benefits do you think this style brings to your artwork?*

BB: Less is more. It always is. In life and in art.

I learned the hard way that anything that isn't enhancing the momentum or mood of the story is unnecessary. Get rid of it. Over-rendering can do, and usually does, nothing but hide the fact that the story isn't working.

We work in a medium that has so many ticks and whistles to it. You know? Littlest chimes and bells to hide the fact that the story sucks or the concept has holes in it.

ST: *What are some of the bells and whistles that you think the medium has immersed itself in? Does anything in particular jump out at you?*

BB: Well, all comics are colored the same now. All Photoshop gradations without any thought to whether the artist's style suits it. John Byrne and [George] Pérez's art looks terrible colored the same way you color Jim Lee's. Ugh!

And also, full-color doesn't mean all-color. There's a lot of over-coloring going on.

ST: *Okay, enough art questions. Back to Jinx. A leading woman, who's smart, pretty but not a floozy, strong but not written as if she were a man in drag, and working in a, well, "non-traditional" profession. How did she come about? What inspired you to follow a female archetype (that of the young woman warrior) that isn't typically used in comics? And is she based either in looks or personality on anyone in particular?*

BB: Thanks for saying that. It shouldn't be such a big deal for a lead female character to be written as a real person. Only in comics is this such a phenomenon. And that's all I did. I tried to write her as true as possible.

Jinx is based on a real woman — a statuesque, hard, smart woman that hunts people for a living. This is a really bizarre way to choose to make a living, especially if you are a woman and especially if you are smart.

I was fascinated by the dichotomy of this life, and she was a perfect vehicle for me.

And you asked, "What inspired you to follow a female archetype (that of the young woman warrior) that is not typically used in comics?" Commercial suicide...

ST: *Do you have plans to return to her in a new series at any point? Okay, I admit, this is a selfish question. I'm a big fan of* Jinx.

BB: Well, then, I finally have good news. Starting with issue 16, Jinx guest stars in *Sam and Twitch*, the cop drama I write for McFarlane, for four whole issues. They are already written and I really enjoyed writing them.

She is a perfect catalyst for those two. We delve into the bounty hunter world, from the POV of the cops, which is the only POV I wasn't able to get across in the *Jinx* novel.

And I am glad you dig her. I do as well.

But as for a sequel, I am a big believer that a lot of good comics overstay their welcome. Almost all do. I would rather look to the future and new products and projects and new challenges, than take the chance of putting out something sucky and take away the nice feeling that most people have for the story as it is.

The thing is that I actually know every single thing that happens to Jinx and Goldfish throughout their entire lives. I know them so intimately. But I feel we have seen the things we need to see of these characters.

ST: *And finally, what future plans do you have? Anything new coming out that our readers should rush to find?*

BB: Oh yeah.

The last *Fortune and Glory* comes out April 9.

Powers, my new full-color crime comic with Mike Oeming, debuts in April. If you liked Jinx, wait till you get a load of Deena Pilgrim. She kicks ass. I adore this character and this book.

My run of *Daredevil* with fully painted art by David Mack supposedly debuts in July.

My new horror comic for McFarlane, *Hellspawn*, with fully painted art by the insanely talented Ashley Wood debuts in August. And we are really throwing things up against the wall in this book. We are shooting very high.

And my monthly run on *Sam and Twitch* continues every month.

And I had a nice chat with Joe Nozemack today actually, and I can tell you that I will be returning to the Oni line up in December with:

Drumroll...

The untitled Bendis project for December 2000.

And as always, all the info on my books, including a Flash trailer for *Powers* and a cool message board can be found at www.jinxworld.com.

AFTERWORD

So, uh…

What you just read was just fucking painful to write. Painful. For numerous reasons. And while I wrote it around ten years ago all those wounds are still pretty open — probably because I keep picking at the scabs.

Hope you enjoyed my pain, y'all.

I don't have an accent, I don't know why I just y'alled.

But that is why I wrote this book in the first place. I was desperate to turn all the time wasted in Hollywood into something useful. Something worth something. In my day job, if you can call it that. I sit. I write. I draw (sometimes). And if I want it to see the light of day, it does. I'm just not used to doing something for nothing. I know I am spoiled. But I don't know how to do that. Waste time. I hate wasting time. I like to fill my day. I like to produce. I like to *do*.

So when I get stuck in a meeting with someone and I realize it's not even a real meeting, or not a meeting that is going to go anywhere… That I'm just another slot filled in some dude's call sheet so he can look busy to his boss and peers — my heart sinks. It's just not how I want to spend my day. So I wrote this not because I thought it would find an audience. I wrote it just so I could make the useless into something useful.

I really didn't think this was for anyone but me. I really didn't. I thought this book, or tantrum *at best*, would be a snarky little side thing I did that maybe a couple of movie nerds, like myself, would find morbidly interesting. I did not see the avalanche of letters and commiseration coming my way. I mean, it has poured all over me for the entire last decade. It has been an avalanche. From the out-of-work screenwriter, to the never-worked screenwriter to the low level exec all the way to some actual honest-to-god studio bosses, I have heard the cries of: "Oh my god, me too." That stunned me. The book got read, understood, and I didn't get tossed out of the world media on my ass.

See, my manager and dear friend David Engel (and he is still both) was worried that I was creating a "Fuck you, Hollywood!! Go fuck yourself in your rotted-ass corpse!!" letter to the industry and pretty much slamming the door on any and all chances of getting anything done in Hollywood ever. And maybe I was. I don't know. But I think, subconsciously, I was writing a: "Go fuck yourself people who are going to waste my time" letter. Because I did want those people to fuck off. Right? Who wouldn't? And maybe those kind of people out there would be a little worried I would write about them they'd steer clear. It was fair warning, I thought. You meet with me at your own peril. And for the most part I think it worked. For a while there the meetings were not the usual riffraff. They were definitely of a higher caliber. And I could tell people were on their toes.

Almost every meeting I had after this book was published had someone in the room who read *Fortune* or knew someone who warned them about *Fortune* and they'd say: "Ha ha, you're not going to write about me now are you? Hee-hee." And I'd think: "Don't say anything stupid or lie to my face and I won't write about you." And then there was the one producer who was absolutely trying to say or do something that would get him in print. He absolutely was. He eventually told me. I'm not even going to tell you who because I'm not going to give him the satisfaction, but I do remember thinking: "Oh, my god! Someone would purposely want to look like an idiot??" And that's how I invented reality television.

But I know why you are reading this. You want to know what happened next. Did I ever get anything made? Well, no.

Wait, that's not true. I did get a *Spider-Man* cartoon pilot made. MTV made a Spidey cartoon a few years ago and I was exec producing it until someone at MTV called a meeting to ask "Why does it have to be a spider?" So I stopped coming to those meetings. And the show went away.

I hooked up with a big movie star in Charleze Theron and sold *Jinx*; that was fun. David Fincher and Matt Damon signed on to make *Torso*. The movie was green-lit, and then it wasn't. No one will tell us why. Actually I know why, but if I say why someone will probably sue me. It was a big old mess. As of this writing it probably still is. Too bad. Fincher was cool and he was going to shoot it in black and white.

All of that would make an interesting sequel — no doubt. And that doesn't even include stories I haven't ever told anyone. Like how I was the writer of the Spider-Man Broadway musical for five days. Or the Marvel video game I was hired to write but was fired from when someone somewhere decided the *Infinity Gauntlet* reminded them of Paris Hilton. What? Yeah, you heard me. Or the network who read this very book and toyed with their own idea of turning my family life into the next *Simpsons* only to decide my family was not anything anyone could relate to. Uh huh.

Yes, all of these wacky anecdotes would make awesome stories for a *Fortune and Glory* sequel. And one day they will. I have been writing as I go all these years, but I am still waiting for that one different thing. To show you something different than what you saw here. Maybe the *Powers* TV show at FX will be getting green-lit, or maybe *Torso* will happen. Who knows? Maybe *Jinx*. Maybe *Fire*. Maybe some of the new stuff I got cooking.

The point is that's why I love the comics!! Every screenwriter I heard from, all who had horror stories that made mine look like an episode of *Pee Wee's Playhouse*, didn't have the outlet I had. To vent. To express. I can make comics. And no coked-up, dead-eyed, Hollywood fucktard can take that away from me. Too much? Sorry it's late night here and I'm punchy.

The point is that I am working on the sequel to this book. Many of you have asked. And I am. And it will be full of awesome. But I will know when it is time. And I am sure just like *Chinatown 2*, *Godfather 3* and *Another Stakeout*…the wait will be worth it.

Before I go I want to thank all my friends who generously and bravely appeared in this book. I want to thank David Engel for pussying out the first time and not letting me use his real name ENGEL!! But now that the book was well received and successful he told me it was ok to go back in and put his name in. Like I'm going to go back into all the files and reletter it just for that. No. And yes, he asked me to name him after Spreewell. Big dweeb!!

I want to thank my heroine Jennifer Grünwald for putting this book together. She has put all my books together now for years and if you think working with a disorganized basket case like me is easy, well, it kind of is. I make up for my disorganization by being impossible to get a hold of.

I also want to thank our colorist Matthew Wilson, who I discovered after everyone else I know discovered him. It was a scary proposition to color a book that was not meant to be colored. It had the potential to be very *Star Wars* redo Lucas-y of me. It had to be right. And I've been considering it forever but I was waiting for just that right flavor. And when I saw Matt's work I knew he was it. He did such a good job on this book that Marvel has scooped him up and put him on some awesome gigs. Let that be a lesson to you up-and-comers. No job is too small, no art is too shitty. Kick ass, you get gigs.

And I really want to thank you guys who may have been duped…I mean…*kind* enough to double-dip into this puppy and who have been talking up the book and supporting it all these years. You are the reason this book is still in print and the reason I get to continue to go to Hollywood and take meetings and gigs that go nowhere. So, uh, fuck you very much.

BENDIS!

Portland, 2010

(sweet jesus, I'm still alive)

THANKS AND WHERE ARE THEY NOW?

First, a huge salute to the very brave, very generous and very, very multi-talented Mr. Marc Andreyko. Part of this is his story as well and I thank him for his good humor in my portrayal of him.

Marc went on to do all kinds of things. But the highlight so far for me and tons of others was creating the fantastic *Manhunter* for DC comics. He has books coming out from IDW and Dark Horse as we speak.

The same goes ten-fold for my smart and beautiful wife Alisa, whose love, support and belief in me never fails. It takes a special kind of cool chick to be open to a little comic-book ribbing. Man, did I marry well.

Alisa and I are still awesomely married. We moved to Portland not long after this book was first published. We have two amazing children, Olivia and Sabrina, who will one day read this book and wonder if daddy ever had hair. Alisa runs Jinxworld, our company, and has been lovingly referred to by Marvel publisher Dan Buckley as VP of Marvel Portland.

David Spree is actually my manager David Engel, partner of the awesome managing firm Circle of Confusion. He has seen his career take off since our meager beginnings, and no one deserves it more. He is a good friend and my producing partner on everything I do.

The lovely and talented K.C. McCrory who is my much, much, much needed copy editor. You are a wonderful friend and excellent masseuse for whose contributions all my fans thank you. And Jen Grünwald who has been putting my collections together for years and who I think is an amazing editor and one of the real unsung heroes of all that is good in comics and the world. And I'm not just saying this because I know she is editing this and I might get her to uncharacteristically tear up in her cubicle.

As for me, I've had a hell of run working for Marvel Comics. But 10 to 1 says you probably knew that if you bought this book. As far as Hollywood, you can Google me and see versions of all the high and lows, dreams and nightmares that have been my relationships with tinsel land ever since this book came out.

I wrote the pilot to the animated CGI *Spider-Man* show for MTV. A show that should probably have never made it to air even though the animation is kind of amazing.

I wrote a screenplay adaptation of my graphic novel *Jinx* for Charleze Theron after she won her Oscar. I wrote a pilot adaptation of the comic book *Alias* for Fox.

We sold *Powers* to Sony where it struggled as a feature only to thrive as a TV project for Sony and FX. It might even be green-lit by the time you read this. Or not.

The story you film nerds may have read the most about regarding me was what happened to *Torso* as a film project. It was to be directed by the amazing David Fincher, it was to star Matt Damon, it was green-lit... and then the plug was pulled. What happened? I have no damn idea. Why its struggles made it to the pages of EW and other places was as fascinating to me as anything that has happened out there.

Right now I'm writing an adaptation of my earliest graphic novel *FIRE* for Zach Efron and Universal Studios. I'm on the Marvel Studios creative committee. That means I've consulted on *Iron Man*, *Iron Man 2*, *Captain America*, *Thor* and *Avengers*. I get to meet and study at the feet of all these amazing writers and directors and Marvel pays me for the privilege. You know that little bit with Nick Fury at the end of *Iron Man*? I wrote it. Still the coolest thing my kid thinks I have ever done.

The struggle continues. If you would define struggle as being paid money to write cool things and meet interesting people.

I also would like to thank David Mack, Joe Quesada, James Hudnall, Greg Horn, Jared Bendis, Marc Ricketts, Michael Hahn, James Valentino, Joe Nozemack, Anthony Bozzi, Michael Avon Oeming, and my mom. To be honest, most of these people really didn't do anything worth mentioning, but they'll give me shit if they don't see their names in the book.

If I forgot to thank you and you think you deserve it, it's just that I feel our relationship is so special that I didn't want to cheapen it by publicly acknowledging it.